This modern text is designed to prepare you for your future professional career. While theories, ideas, techniques, and data are dynamic, the information contained in this volume will provide you a quick and useful reference as well as a guide for future learning for many years to come. Your familiarity with the contents of this book will make it an important volume in your professional library.

EX LIBRIS

ORGANIZATIONAL BEHAVIOR
An Applied Psychological Approach

ORGANIZATIONAL BEHAVIOR
An Applied Psychological Approach

By

Dennis W. Organ
Indiana University

and

W. Clay Hamner
Duke University

Revised Edition • 1982

BUSINESS PUBLICATIONS, INC.
Plano, Texas   75075

ISBN 0-256-02431-6

Library of Congress Catalog Card No. 81–70931

Printed in the United States of America

1 2 3 4 5 6 7 8 9 0 D 9 8 7 6 5 4 3 2

Preface

With this revised edition, we have sought to refine and update a framework that may serve as a set of premises for managing behavior in organizations. Like its predecessor, we hope this volume will provide a basis for informed judgment by current and prospective managers in organizations. Again, we start from a fundamentally "micro" level of analysis and therefore have leaned upon psychology as the underlying discipline from which to borrow concepts and methods for studying individual and group behavior in organizations. However, we have been much more concerned with a balanced and mature treatment of organizational behavior as a discipline in its own right. And, since organizational behavior has its roots in a variety of disciplines, we have not labored under any misguided motive of disciplinary purity or consistency.

This edition reflects a number of changes, inspired in many instances by feedback from users of the first edition. In other cases, we have worked from our own interpretation of the trends gathering momentum in the continuing evolution of organizational behavior as an area of inquiry. We now offer three chapters, compared to a single chapter in the previous version, concerned with the organization itself as a behaving entity subject to analysis. A chapter discusses the internal structure of organizations, and another chapter treats the issue of the organization as affected by its external environment. A concluding chapter addresses the problem of organizational change and development, and in so doing attempts to pull together some of the more fundamental object lessons treated separately in preceding chapters.

In the first edition, Chapter 1 offered little more than the usual ritualistic opening remarks. In this version, Chapter 1 is more substantive in character. Some readers will doubtless also judge it to be rather controversial in tone. The intent is to provide a preview of some of the issues that confront managers and professionals in their careers in organizations and to note the relevance of specific topics in the book for those issues.

The two chapters in the earlier version which reported on applied programs for enhancing the quality of work life have been condensed into one chapter with a more unified theme concerning work motivation.

The chapter on conflict has been deleted. We concluded that it was more useful to discuss specific forms of conflict as the issue arises in different contexts and at different levels of analysis.

A number of short cases now appear in the book at the ends of certain chapters. We hope that the cases will prove instructive in the task of bringing to bear the conceptual material upon the more recurring concerns of managers in organizations.

Stylistically, we have attempted to maintain more consistency across the various chapters and resort, to an extent of which we are capable, to less complex forms of sentence and paragraph structure. We have also tried to prune unnecessary citations within the narrative.

We view this volume as an appropriate text, either at the introductory level (e.g., for courses such as "Managing Behavior in Organizations") of undergraduate and master's programs, or for adoption in a more advanced, elective course (e.g., "Organizational Psychology," "Behavioral Sciences in Management"). Obviously, the purpose for which the book is used has implications for which chapters would be included or omitted (for example, at the introductory level, the instructor might choose to skip the chapter on research methods) and what type of companion texts or readings to accompany this volume.

The structure, content, and style of this edition reflect the many constructive comments generously offered by a number of colleagues. David Cherrington, who reviewed the entire manuscript, stood guard against overblown prose, lapses of discontinuity, and needless jargon; he also offered valuable advice on substance. Jim Wall, who also reviewed the whole manuscript, had excellent suggestions for the organization of content and points of emphasis and elaboration. Edward Morrison extended sound advice concerning changes that would improve this edition over its predecessor. Tom Mawhinney, during the course of numerous stimulating conversations, planted the seeds of ideas that bore fruit in the treatment of certain themes and perspectives. Quite a few useful suggestions flowed from first edition users who graciously responded to requests for feedback from the publisher and field staff. Edgar Williams, Paul Champagne, and W. D. Heier generously gave permission for us to include their cases, and for this

Contents

ganizations. Subsystem Environments. Organization Boundaries. Boundary Roles. The Turbulent Environment. The Evolution of New Structural Forms.

1

Organizational
Behavior:
An Overview

What is organizational behavior?

What hath OB wrought?

Whither goeth OB?

Views of OB: Student and practitioner

WHAT IS ORGANIZATIONAL BEHAVIOR?

To know what organizational behavior (OB) is all about, it might help to mention some things that OB is *not*. It is not personnel management. Personnel management is a specific function or job responsibility charged with the administration of such activities as employee compensation and other benefits, training, labor relations, recruiting, and manpower planning. People who perform such functions may certainly benefit (as do others) from studying OB, but the knowledge and expertise that personnel officers require go well beyond that—for example, intelligent personnel management often requires knowledge about the law (especially as it pertains to hiring and labor practices), economics, and statistics. The point is that OB does not exist solely or even primarily for those who aspire to careers in personnel and industrial relations.

OB is not management. Again, OB represents a tool or resource of sorts for managers, but management ("getting things done through people," or simply "getting things done") entails more than OB. To manage is to plan, coordinate, procure, analyze, concepualize, and a great many other activities that usually involve people, but they also touch upon dimensions usually beyond the pale of OB. Furthermore, one does not need a job title that includes the term *manager* or *administrator* to find relevance in OB. OB has something to offer for professionals, staff experts, salespeople, and other organizational officials not formally charged with supervisory responsibility.

Nor is OB just "the human side of management," any more than finance is simply the "money side of management" or accounting the "numbers side of management." OB is a field of study unto itself, and one does not have to be a manager to appreciate it or to benefit from it.

What, then, is OB? In the most straightforward way that we can define it, stripping down to essentials, *OB is the application of concepts, theories, methods of inquiry, and empirical generalizations from the behavioral sciences to the observation of behavioral phenomena in organizations.* Now, let us examine some of the key terms in this definition.

Concepts, Theories. OB is not just a list of truisms or a catalog of facts. It is, above all, a *framework* or *structure* for thinking about behavior and organizing bits of knowledge. Some of the concepts— the building blocks of this structure—are familiar to the layman; many are not. The test of their power, in any case, is their ability to "tie things together," to give coherence and meaning to an otherwise disorganized, jumbled array of sense data and opinions, to enable one to see relationships and go beyond the unique event in the here and now. The concepts and theories of OB give us the "big picture" or "bird's-eye view" for seeing patterns and order in behavior.

Methods of Inquiry. OB is more than just a storehouse of accumulated facts and opinion. It provides a means of adding to that storehouse, of testing opinions, of modifying facts as we go. The game is never over, the ledgers are never closed. OB is, in part, a continual process of learning. Some of these methods of learning, once again, are already familiar to you; some are not. As we will see in the next chapter, all of the available methods have their respective shortcomings; so what we "learn" is never with 100 percent confidence or etched in stone.

Empirical Generalization. We prefer this ungainly phrase to the simple word *facts*. *Fact* implies a bit of knowledge that is fixed and certain. There are facts in OB, but ultimately, of much more interest to us all are the tentative conclusions, or statements of relationship, which extend the scope of a number of facts. It is a fact that, in XYZ corporation, most of the people who quit last year previously reported less job satisfaction than those who stayed. Similar observations in other organizations, of varying types and at varying times, would lead us to the empirical generalization that job dissatisfaction is related to turnover. We can never know for sure that this will be true in every instance, but it is both useful and not unreasonable to assume such a relationship in the absence of contradictory information. In short, empirical generalizations represent a small trade-off of certainty or confidence for greater scope and breadth than contained in a fact. Fortunately, there are enough empirical data from OB and the supporting behavioral sciences to provide us with a useful set of empirical generalizations; and with ongoing research using various methods of inquiry, we are optimistic that further such empirical generalizations will continue to emerge.

Behavioral Science. In organizations, people learn how to do things, form impressions of others, influence one another, develop ties to groups, make decisions, are motivated to act in certain ways, and experience stress. People also do these things at home, with friends, and in the pursuit of hobbies. Thus, human behavior in organizations should have many similarities to behavior in other settings, and we would expect to find much of value in the behavioral sciences for understanding behavior in organizations.

Table 1–1 shows several disciplines from the behavioral sciences and how they contribute to OB. Each of these disciplines addresses a significant, fundamental dimension of human behavior. Furthermore, each discipline is wedded to the scientific method of using theory and empirical observation to study behavior. In each of these disciplines there is an accumulated fund of knowledge from which to draw for understanding behavior in organized settings. OB seeks to capitalize upon this fund of knowledge, at least as a broad foundation on which to build. Work groups, for example, are not the same thing as friendship groups, but if we understand the determinants of status in friend-

Table 1–1
Related Disciplines Contributing to Organizational Behavior

Discipline	Relevant Topics
Experimental psychology	Learning; motivation; perception; effects of physical environment on psychomotor performance; stress
Social psychology	Group dynamics; attitudes and attitude change; impression formation; personality; leadership
Clinical psychology	Human adjustment; emotional stress; abnormal behavior; human development throughout the life cycle
Sociology	Socialization processes; social satisfaction; status systems; effects of major social institutions such as family, community, religion, organization structure
Political science	Interest groups; conflict; power, bargaining; coalitions, strategic planning; control
Anthropology	Comparative organizational structures; their functions in varying cultures; cultural influences on organizations; adaptation of organization to environment
Economics	Human resource planning; labor market changes; productivity analysis; cost/benefit analysis

ship groups, that gives us a basis for exploring patterns of influence in work groups.

There is a very fine line between what we normally call *organizations* and the many other social contexts which actually are characterized by some degree of organization. Thus, behavior in organizations is not radically different from behavior in most other settings. Hitting a baseball is different from hitting a tennis ball, but the fundamental principles are much the same. OB assumes that certain fundamental principles underly behavior in any context and readily turns to those disciplines that have long studied such principles.

Behavioral Phenomena in Organizations. While behavior in organizations is, as we have stated, not discontinuous with behavior in other contexts, there are reasons for viewing the formal organization as a rather special kind of environment. To begin with, organizations place more *constraints* on behavior than other settings. Official authority, job duties, and explicit expectations take away some of the natural variability and spontaneity manifested in behavior in the home or on the playground. Formal organizations, in a sense, are unnatural; they represent the culmination of developments in society which constrain the individual in the interests of the larger culture. People do not naturally constrain themselves; one must learn and adapt to this fact, and this process of learning and adapting to external constraints is in itself both intellectually interesting and pragmatically important.

Second, organizations have ongoing purposes and goals to an extent not usually found in unorganized settings. To be sure, the real goals of organizations are not always what they are stated to be. Nonetheless, business corporations do have to make a profit (sooner or later), which in turn means they have to produce goods or services with reasonably efficient use of resources; hospitals have to treat the sick; schools must educate. In short, organizations must have a rationale, an overriding reason for existence. That rationale, whatever its form or nature, becomes the point of departure for *evaluating* the behavior that occurs in the organizational environment. For this reason, those of us who study OB—whether we be managers, students, or behavioral scientists—will never demonstrate cool objectivity toward the behavior we observe in organizations. We will naturally and inevitably seek to evaluate that behavior: Does it hinder or promote the effectiveness of the unit in reaching its goal? Will it improve the organization's functioning with respect to certain criteria? Will it help to achieve some ends but not others? In sum, OB is "results oriented." Of course, we must exercise caution against prematurely prescribing with respect to such matters as leadership styles, job design, or methods of group problem solving. The fact remains that we study those issues in the hope of ultimately coming up with some conclusions about how to make organizations more effective.

This ultimate concern for knowledge that will make organizations more effective does not in itself provide a sharp, absolute distinction between OB and its sister sciences. Scholars in the fields of psychology, sociology, and political science also aspire to provide a contribution towards better social policies and conditions of life; and those who study OB frequently manifest a concern for basic science, for knowledge as its own reward. But qualitatively there is a difference between OB and the others in that OB has more immediate concern with designing, administering, and changing organizations.

Two criteria ultimately provide the bases for evaluating phenomena in organizations. One of these is *performance,* the effectiveness of the organization in attaining the ends or purposes which bring it into existence. Performance, of course, is far from being a simple criterion. Almost always it is complex in nature. For a private corporation performance may represent some weighted combination of return on stockholder investment, growth in sales, rate of introduction of new products, and efficiency in use of resources. Maximizing the attainment of any one of these goals typically means a trade-off on the others. Some performance criteria—such as net contributions to the larger culture—may be so subjective as to preclude their operational use as a basis of evaluation. Researchers in OB, in order to retain a footing on objectivity, generally avoid the issue of evaluation in terms of *total* performance by dealing empirically with one measurable facet of performance at a time. Supervisory styles may be compared in terms of their relationship with a measure of productivity or product quality (such as percent rejects); differing methods of organizing research and development activities are compared with respect to number of patents secured; personality traits of purchasing officers may be tested as to how well they predict cost savings in procurement of supplies. Weighting and combining various indices as a basis for policy requires a value judgment, which must be made by a manager, executive, or public administrator, or sometimes by the public through directly or indirectly expressed wishes. The point is that we can scarcely escape using some criterion of assessing various behaviors in organizations.

The other criterion used by OB to assess organizational practices is *member welfare*. Empirically this often takes the form of some measure of *satisfaction*, especially when the members are full-time employees. Other aspects of fulfillment include personal safety, psychological growth, physical and emotional health, and self-esteem. The phrase *quality of work life*, much in use today, captures the essence of what we mean by member fulfillment.

Figure 1–1 elaborates upon these two criteria which underly the evaluative judgments by OB.

We hasten to underscore the point that performance and member welfare are indeed *separate* criteria and that favorable judgments of organizations concerning either criterion do not automatically imply favorable views on the other. One company with which the authors are familiar had a long history of recording a high return on investment for stockholders (largely represented by a single family) and an

Figure 1–1
Criterion Values in the Study of Organizational Behavior

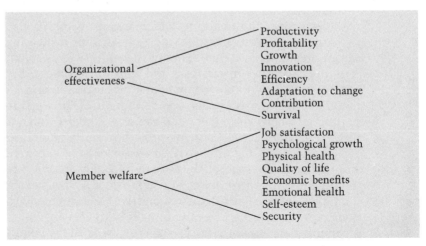

industry reputation for making a good product at a fair price, even though most members of its labor force did not feel they were treated equitably. Conversely, we are aware of organizations in which professional employees are well paid, supervised with respect and consideration, and given abundant opportunities for personal growth and development—yet, by most accounts, these same organizations somehow do not render the amount or quality of services that would justify the resources allocated to them.

As OB continues to develop as a field of study, we hope to bring about theories and applications which will enable us to improve both the effectiveness of organizational performance and the benefits of organizational life for participants. In the meantime, we have to accept the fact that performance and member welfare stand more or less as independent criterion values, sometimes correlated with each other but with no guarantee that improving either one will improve the other.

OB as a Community of Interests

OB also represents a community of interests. This community includes OB teachers and researchers (such as those employed by schools of business and public administration), teachers and researchers in supporting disciplines, consultants, and managers.

A significant event in the evolution of this community occurred in 1959. That year marked the publication of the Gordon-Howell report, so named for the two economists commissioned by the Ford Foundation to evaluate programs of business education in institutions of higher learning. Gordon and Howell concluded that business school curricula in too many instances lacked solid intellectual content. They urged business schools to include exposure to more basic disciplines such as economics, mathematics, and the behavioral sciences. Very soon, psychologists and sociologists with special interests in applying their expertise to organizational behavior found their way into schools of administration. Gradually they developed their own graduate programs of study in OB, formed associations with like-minded colleagues, founded journals to communicate their theories and findings, and collaborated with both behavioral scientists and managers to study such issues as job motivation and leadership.

Managers, by and large, welcomed such developments. Although a few of them were skeptical that the behavioral sciences could ever add much to the tough-minded analysis of organizational problems, most managers had been conditioned since the 1930s to incorporate the behavioral dimension into their thinking. This awareness resulted from the influence of the celebrated Hawthorne experiments, conducted by Western Electric in the 1920s and early 1930s and reported in the book *Management and the Worker* (1938) by Roethlisberger and Dickson. Those experiments—originally intended to study the effects of a number of factors on worker fatigue—began at a time when prevailing theories of organizations emphasized mainly the cold logic of the formal structure of organizations. Results of some of the early experiments, however, could not be accounted for by such logic. The investigators realized the need to recognize a "logic of sentiments," different from the logic of facts. Subsequently, a large-scale program, in which thousands of workers were interviewed, and an in-depth observation of a work group in action over several months confirmed the importance of such "sentiments." There existed an informal organization—with its own power, leadership, status system, criteria, and codes of behavior—not found in the organization chart. Indeed, the informal organization shaped the organization's functioning in such a manner that it confounded the accepted "rational" and "scientific" principles of organization. The dissemination of these findings introduced into management thinking the concepts of job satisfaction, group cohesion, group norms, participative supervision, and resistance to change, and these were seen to be just as important as the earlier notions of authority, efficiency, unity of command, and line-staff distinction.

The direction of influence in the OB community runs both ways. Those who teach OB stay in touch with the basic disciplines' developments in the study of motivation, attitudes, personality, influence, groups, social values, and the like. They ponder the implications of these developments for job design, job satisfaction, selection and placement, supervision, use of committees to solve problems and make decisions, and how the organization adapts to the larger social environment. Useful findings are communicated in the scholarly journals, in "softer" publications available to practitioners, and in classes for degree-pursuing students and management development. Consultants, many of them trained in graduate OB programs, frequently serve as linking pins from OB scholars to executives, especially for in-house developmental programs and the analysis of site-specific problems.

But, as is characteristic of the history of science, the direction of influence often runs also from interest in a practical problem back to basic research. A good example of this is the study of the "risky-shift." A graduate student in industrial management (Stoner, 1961) produced evidence that groups make riskier decisions than the average individual acting alone (or, more precisely, individuals tended to revise their initial preferences in decision making toward a greater risk after group deliberation). For about a decade, social psychology pursued the explanation of this mystery, and the eventual result was a vastly altered conception of the influence groups have on individuals.

WHAT HATH OB WROUGHT?

The OB community, whether we date it from the 1959 Gordon-Howell report or the earlier Hawthorne studies, is still in its infancy compared to many other sciences. It would be unfair and unrealistic to expect the same order of accomplishments that have occurred in medicine, physics, or biology. OB has scarcely had the time to develop the same structure and coherence that characterize other fields. Nonetheless, it is not too early to inventory our progress.

On a *theoretical* level, we have made considerable strides toward the development of our own conceptual language. We began by accepting the everyday concepts of the layman and the practicing manager. We soon realized that these concepts posed limitations for a scientific study of behavior in organizations. All too often, such concepts proved to be loaded with bias, as, for example, in popular thinking about the relative merits of autocratic and democratic leadership styles. Frequently, commonly used terms (e.g., *morale*) were conceived at such a level of ambiguity or multiple meanings that statements concerning them could not even be tested. In other cases, concepts took so narrow a focus around very specific contexts that it was difficult to interrelate knowledge about those contexts to others, and vice versa. Gradually, OB theorists and researchers have begun to think in terms of their own constructs, defined for their own purposes, and linking behavioral phenomena in organizations to broader knowledge about human behavior generated by other disciplines.

OB has found numerous instances in which "facts" long seen as "obvious" were neither obvious nor facts. While not rejecting wholesale the proverbs and philosophies of generations of administrators, OB has begun the systematic process of cataloguing the qualifications and complexities we must attach to what had seemed to be straightforward, simple common sense.

As Cummings (1978) has pointed out, OB has also generated an array of technologies, or practical techniques, which have become increasingly evident in use by organizations. Some of these techniques existed in crude and varying forms long before OB was "born," but OB research has in many cases vastly increased their power, validity, and precision. Among these management tools can be numbered the job attitude survey, techniques of performance appraisal, formats for group decision making, and methods fo designing employee training and development programs.

WHITHER GOETH OB?

The years ahead will doubtless see OB progressing along some of the same paths already taken in the past few decades. Technologies of the sort described above will be fine-tuned. Conceptual language will undergo further refinements as theories of broader, more unifying character evolve from empirical work. Some of the apparent contradictions will dissolve in the light of new perspectives either generated within OB or reflected from sister disciplines.

We may also expect that OB will will be influenced by changes in values of the society, nation, and world around us. In the years ahead, it will probably become apparent that some of our current postures in OB have been biased by values in ways to which we are now blind. For example, OB of the 1960s and 1970s witnessed a considerable emphasis on worker satisfaction and individual fulfillment, perhaps because it was assumed that economic growth and material affluence could be guaranteed. The 1980s and 1990s could see this orientation toward job satisfaction eclipsed by an urgent concern for productivity, now that we have become sensitive to a globe of shrinking resources. Such a change would surely affect the way we think about systems of rewards in organizations, leadership, and organization structure. No social science, no matter how much it prides itself on objectivity, can escape the spirit of the times. "History makes fools out of wise men."

But the future manager, to fully appreciate changing trends in ideas and values, must first appreciate the legacy of the immediate past and the present. In the pages ahead, we have attempted to provide the reader an up-to-date account, a scoreboard reading, of behavior in organizations as OB now interprets it. The continuing intellectual growth and professional development of the administrator follow from a solid grounding in a set of conceptual and empirical frameworks. These frameworks are not substitutes for common sense; they are complements to it. They do not take the place of judgment; they lead to informed judgment.

VIEWS OF OB: STUDENT AND PRACTITIONER

One of the authors recently participated, along with several teachers from other schools of business, in a panel discussion on teaching organizational behavior. One of the discussants described a survey which his school regularly conducts among students in the graduate program of business administration. The survey asked students to evaluate the various courses they had taken in terms of the *importance* of those courses for their professional careers. The survey, year after year, revealed that students placed OB at or near the *bottom* of the list, well below such courses as accounting, finance, marketing, operations research, and others.

We suspect that similar findings would result from such surveys at many schools of business and administration. Note that we do *not* say that students find OB to have no *interest* for them. The point, rather, is that often they do not view it as *important* to them for their careers; they do not see it, by and large, as having the same priority as the courses in the "functional" areas of the curriculum.

Why do students react this way? Why do they see OB as perhaps "nice but not very significant"? We suspect, from hearing a few oblique comments here and there, that several plausible explanations can account for the reaction.

1. *For most students, the criterion of the importance of a course is the extent to which it helps them get a good job offer.* In other words, for students, as for most of us, concern for short-run objectives takes priority over the vague, shadowy consideration of the long run. They simply do not see how knowledge of OB will help them with job placement. And they are probably right. We doubt if many students land jobs because they have a sophisticated, rigorous conception of behavior in organizations. Sure, you have to come across in interviews and correspondence with recruiters as a reasonably sane, mature, perceptive sort of person. But most people could satisfy that requirement without the formal study of OB; and anyone who falls seriously short of such a profile, who cannot behave in a minimally acceptable fashion of politeness, probably would not find a remedy in these pages.

2. *Many students believe that understanding behavior in organizations is mostly a matter of common sense.* "Behavioral sciences either tell you what is already obvious or try to mask their sterility with esoteric jargon." For example, we note in the pages ahead (Chapters 3, 7) that people tend to do those things for which they are rewarded. Profound? Hardly. We observe (Chapter 15) that leaders who are described as being considerate and supportive tend to have the most satisfied subordinates. Surprising? Most people would have suspected as much. So to some extent, clearly, the students are correct: many of the observations of the "man in the street," many of the popular conceptions of behavioral phenomena in and outside of organizations, do survive the tests of more rigorous study. People do learn about behavior from their own experience (or "naturalistic observations," Chapter 2); they learn also from the communicated wisdom of parents, coaches, managers, novelists, essayists, and others. Human behavior in organizations has a pretty long history to it, and many astute people have had the occasion to comment on it. No one begins the study of OB with a "blank slate," as one might with accounting or calculus.

3. *Students view OB concepts and principles as too vague and abstract to have practical utility on the job.* It seems that one can't really "apply" much of OB in the direct, clear-cut fashion that you can with capital budgeting techniques, production and inventory control methods, and cash-flow analysis. Here again, we sympathize with this point of view. OB does not lend itself to the straightforward,

unambiguous, precise solution to a structured problem. One cannot identify precisely when emotional stress (Chapter 10) improves job performance, as opposed to when it impairs performance; one cannot describe unerringly the nature of someone's personality (Chapter 9) or, even if one could, know for sure whether that type of personality matches the requirements posed by a certain job; one cannot state with exactitude where the boundaries of a group (Chapter 12) begin and end. Every job situation has its own important idiosyncratic features, so how do general concepts really help?

4. *Students see OB as helpful, if at all, to the "general manager," a role with which they do not identify.* OB deals, essentially, with "handling people" or "getting along with people," getting them to do things, maintaining their morale, influencing their behavior. That's OK for the general manager, but the truth of the matter is that most students do not aspire to be managers. John B. Miner of the Georgia State University has spent many years trying to measure the "motivation to manage" among students; his data suggest that this motive has declined over the last decade or more (Miner, 1976). Rather, students identify with an area of specialized expertise, such as market research, portfolio planning, cost accounting, or systems analysis. Practicing their craft, it seems, has nothing to do with management. They expect to exert their influence (Chapter 14) by sharing their expertise, not by cajoling or psychoanalyzing (as a *manager* would have to do). With expertise, supposedly you're on the solid ground of fact and logic in decision making, not in the bogland of emotions, motives, attitudes (Chapter 6), and sentiments.

5. *Students assume that if they do become managers, they will use authority as the most efficient means of influence.* Organization boils down to who has the final authority over someone else. That authority is explicitly accepted by people, when all is said and done. Generally, people acquiesce to legitimate authority, perhaps after voicing some initial resistance; but sooner or later, they have to come around to accepting your decision or run the risk of adverse consequences.

As we have at times implied, these reactions by students are not altogether unreasonable. We do not reject or condemn these views as inspired by ignorance or insubordination, nor do we as instructors feel despair over a futile task. We regard such views as the reflections of a particular perspective in place and time. For there is evidence that this perspective changes over the years as place and time vary.

The same school which conducts the survey among students concerning the importance of different courses repeats the survey periodically among their graduates after they have launched their professional careers. The findings of the repeated surveys show OB gradually moving up the scale of importance. Among alumni with several years of full-time experience in organizations, OB ranks near the top.

Furthermore, when business school graduates resume or update their training—for example, in executive development programs on college campuses, at weekend seminars, and with in-house programs provided by corporations—frequently their first preferences are OB-related topics: models of job motivation, group decision making, styles of leadership and supervision, managing stress, career planning, to name just a few.

This turnabout in reaction to OB does not always occur, of course, but it occurs often enough to make us wonder why it does. We submit that it evolves from a change in perspective. The professional who has spent several years, full-time, in one or more organizations, experiencing varying degrees of success and failure, begins to think about human behavior in organizations in a different way. We offer the statements below as possible explanations for the change in reaction to OB.

1. *The criterion of importance is no longer getting a good job, but getting things done in the job, and that means dependence on other people.* Edgar Schein (1978) reports that a persistent theme in interviews with alumni of the Sloan School of Management (MIT) concerned the "reality shock" of recognizing the extent of their dependence on others. Even the nonmanagers among the alumni expressed frustration over "having to check with everyone all the time": "people are a nuisance"; "you have to work with people you can't control"; "dependence on other people makes things move too slowly" (Schein, 1978, pp. 94–95). Schein concluded that many of them did not want to accept this condition at an emotional level, but sooner or later they were compelled to accept it; and when they finally came to terms with it, they accepted with it the need for a mental framework of problem solving that had some behavioral overtones.

2. *The working professional discovers from experience that some behavioral phenomena defy conventional wisdom or common sense.* Common sense would have you believe that satisfied employees should be productive; yet that does not always seem to be the case. Common sense argues that, if you want to reduce conflict between groups, you plan occasions to bring them together; yet such meetings sometimes intensify conflict. Common sense says that people will do what is clearly in their best interest; yet often they seem willing to "cut off their nose to spite their face." And need we trot out the ancient (but pertinent) argument that common sense often contradicts itself ("absence makes the heart grow fonder" versus "out of sight,

14

Figure 1–2

Working professionals and managers usually express considerable interest in studying organizational behavior for personal and career development. Seminars in OB-related topics (such as group decision making, *above*) constitute a sizable portion of most executive development programs.

out of mind,"; "birds of a feather flock together" versus "opposites attract")? To be sure, a perceptive professional will refine his or her own thinking as a function of experience, but what they seem to reach for, and report that they actually do obtain from OB, is a "conceptual map" to sort out and interrelate the isolated insights their experience has provided.

3. *The working professional learns that there are many forms of application of concepts, and that "cranking out a solution" is not the only form of application.* Other forms of application involve using concepts to formulate questions and define problems; the examination of one's assumptions undergirding an observation or conclusion; the sensitivity to what is or isn't important in a situation. These types of application are deeper, more indirect, and broader than plugging numbers into an equation. Furthermore, they are actually the most important applications, not only of the behavioral sciences, but of other disciplines as well. For example, the importance of the economic concept *price elasticity of demand* is not that any manager will someday compute it; rather, it sensitizes the marketing executive to some of the subtle relationships between price, sales, and total revenue. It is precisely in constituting such a backdrop of assumption,

categories of thought, and interpretative observation that one applies knowledge about behavior.

4. *Working professionals find that technical expertise is not enough.* The expert discovers that making use of that expertise in a large organization involves more than just hanging up a shingle and waiting for business to roll in. Those who adopt this passive approach soon realize that they can apply their crafts only to rather insignificant tasks. To use expertise in a way that really counts is to become involved in more important projects, and that usually means developing relationships with a host of professional and administrative personnel from other departments. To do this requires more than expertise, because expertise brandished in the wrong way can threaten people, arousing ego-defensive attitudes (Chapter 6). The expert has to develop a political sense for "what will fly," for the sore spots and sensitivities that even the most competent people have. Schein (1978) heard a recent graduate lament, "I thought I could sell people with logic and was amazed at the hidden agendas people have, irrational objectives; really bright people will come up with stupid objectives" (pp. 94–96).

5. *Working professionals realize how fragile authority can be as a basis of influence.* Even with direct subordinates, authority provides little more than a symbolic background. Also, it seems to work most effectively when resorted to only rarely, or when soft-pedaled. With the increasing emphasis on the "worker's bill of rights," more and more constraints are placed on what a manager can order people to do or not do, there are more avenues of appeal open to the subordinate, and when these are not available, the resentful employee can turn to any number of time-honored techniques for demonstrating covert resistance. Furthermore, the working professional, in order to generate genuine success, has to influence a great many people—superiors, clients, colleagues, personnel who provide supporting services—over whom he or she does not have authority.

Whatever the reasons, it appears that some measure of full-time professional work experience leads to a different perspective on the value and importance of a systematic, conceptual approach to behavior in organizations. The point of the discussion is not to exalt OB above any other parts of an educational program, but to place it in the larger context of training and preparation for a lifetime career and a program of continuing self-education. It is from this perspective that accrediting bodies specify required courses in OB for degree-granting institutions in schools of business and public administration. While the authors hope to arouse the interest of the reader in OB for its own intrinsic appeal, we couple this aim with the obligation to provide the foundations for long-run professional development.

QUESTIONS FOR DISCUSSION

1. Talk informally to one or more senior officials of a large organization (one with more than 50 full-time employees). Try to elicit the officials' views of what the major problems are in an organization. How many of these are technical in nature? How many are primarily behavioral in nature?

2. A person may pursue an activity—such as photography, woodworking, cooking—either as a leisure-time hobby or in the employ of an organization. Will the same variables or factors influence behavior in that activity in both cases? Explain?

3. Explain why staff people without managerial responsibilities in organizations might benefit from studying organizational behavior.

CASE

Frank Parson, the administrative director of the MBA program at Midwest State University, heaved a sigh of relief as he finished the last of his paperwork. The opening week of the school year, with its heavy schedule of student counseling, orientation, and registration, was nearing its end, and aside from the usual quota of minor gripes and unforeseen communication lapses, all had gone well.

Just as he was tidying up his desk before leaving, he heard a knock on his open door as a student stepped inside. Introducing himself as Roy Burton, he said he had a bit of a problem. Parson noted that it was quite late and all of the other staff had already left, but he said, "Sure, what can I help you with?"

"It's this BA501 (Behavior in Organizations) requirement for MBAs," he began. "I really don't see why I should have to take it."

"Well," Parson countered with a tolerant grin, "that course is a standard requirement, not just here but at almost all other schools. Managers need some exposure to this area, you know. I can tell you, just from the kind of work I do around here, that a lot of time gets devoted to smoothing over the people-type problems that come up."

"That's just the point," Burton said. "I can see how a manager might find some of those courses applicable. But you see, I'm concentrating my course work as much as possible in finance. I'm not interested in personnel or general management. I have some very definite career goals. I want to get a position right after graduation either with one of the large consulting firms or one of the Chicago-based banks. So I need to gear up with as much expertise as I can in financial analysis, portfolio planning, and quantitative methods. Besides, I had three undergraduate courses in psychology, and I think my two years of experience as a foundry foreman show I know how to get along with people."

Parson could see already that this was going to be a tough case to deal with. As he loosened his tie, he wondered what he could say to convince Burton why he should take BA501.

Questions

What considerations should Parson discuss with Burton? What factors should Parson weigh in describing whether to exempt Burton from the course requirement?

REFERENCES

Cummings, L. L.   Toward organizational behavior. *Academy of Management Review*, 1978, 3, 90–98.

Miner, J. B.   Presidential address to Midwest Academy of Management meetings, Clayton, Mo., 1976.

Roethlisberger, F. J., & Dickson, W. J.   *Management and the worker.* New York: Wiley Science Editions, 1964.

Schein, E. H.   *Career dynamics: Matching individual and organizational needs.* Reading, Mass.: Addison-Wesley, 1978.

Stoner, J. A. F.   *A comparison of individual and group decisions including risk.* Unpublished master's thesis, School of Industrial Management, MIT, 1961.

2

Theory and Research in Organizational Behavior

What is the nature of theory in organizational behavior?

What are the functions of theory?

How do we evaluate theories?

What are the different methods used to study behavior in organizations? What are their advantages and disadvantages?

We noted in Chapter 1 that working professionals show a decided preference for OB-related topics when they resume their studies in seminars, training programs, or advanced degree programs. Their work experience has already given them numerous insights into behavior in organizations, but what they seek is a *framework* for sorting out such insights in a coherent, systematic way. When they feel such a framework jelling, they derive a deep sense of satisfaction at being able to look back on some episode and see connections among certain conditions, personalities, and events. In a sense, they "know" what they already knew, but now they have a feeling for how it "all fit together."

One of the aims of this chapter is to demonstrate how theory helps us piece together frameworks that facilitate this dimension of "knowing." As we shall see, theory construction in OB is really just an extension of some fundamental thought processes that we use all the time. It is important, however, to know how to evaluate theories; some are better than others. The student who understands the functions of theory and knows how to evaluate theories develops a keener understanding of behavioral science knowledge.

Theories are related to data and observations in a circular fashion: theories develop from existing data and theories suggest what new data to collect. There are a number of methods for observing behavior in organizations, some of which you have already used. All of these methods have their place in extending and deepening our knowledge about OB. Each of them also has certain weaknesses. It behooves the student and practicing professional to assess the validity of any statements about behavior by examining the methods of observation which led to those statements. Think for a moment about any conclusion you have recently drawn from your experience: that a certain type of fuel makes your car run better, that eating more of a certain food makes you feel more energetic, that wearing certain apparel made you more attractive to the opposite sex, and so forth. Seldom would your thinking about the matter really stop at that point. You would ask, Why? and relate your observations to some underlying principles (for example, the black sweater perhaps made you more attractive because dark-colored clothing has a "slenderizing" effect in the perception of an observer). You would also be likely to feel less than 100 percent sure of your conclusions (maybe it isn't the bran flakes that have produced a higher energy level but the sunnier weather that began about the time you changed your breakfast habits). In sum, the marks of mature thinking include not only knowledge, but pondering the implications of that knowledge while simultaneously appraising the tentative, uncertain character of that knowledge. So it is with knowledge about behavior in organizations.

THEORY

The impatience of students and management practitioners with behavioral science theory is legendary. The student's ultimate put-down of a disliked course or reading assignment is, "It's too theoretical"; the practitioner's response to a conceptually based argument is "That's fine in theory, but it doesn't work in practice." To the action-oriented seeker of knowledge about organizational psychology, theory is something with a capital *T* that stands totally apart from life and experience.

This attitude toward theory probably stems from misunderstanding of what theory is and what a theory attempts to do. Moreover, it reflects an unawareness of students and practitioners that they themselves are active users of theory.

A *theory* is a set of statements about how certain concepts or constructs are interrelated. The statements are implicitly or explicitly based on certain assumptions or premises, and the statements permit the logical deduction of propositions, hypotheses, or hunches which predict the occurrence of events or explain why certain events have already occurred. Neither esoteric jargon nor mathematical symbols are essential to a theory, although it will be shown later why specialized language often figures importantly in theories used by scientists.

Percepts, Concepts, and Constructs

In order to understand how theory construction extends the natural processes of thinking, it is helpful to examine the distinctions among *percept, concept,* and *construct*. A *percept* is a single bit of sensation; it represents a unique, nonrepeatable event. You see a red stoplight at Fourth Street and Main at 5:33 P.M. on January 18, 1980; you taste a morsel of turkey drumstick at 1:45 P.M. on Thanksgiving Day; you see your friend Joe Dokes light up a Kent Golden Light after class this morning. All of these are percepts: raw sense data. They are the stuff of human experience. Each day brings forth millions of new percepts—most of them similar to previously experienced percepts, but each one unique in at least some microscopic way.

Since each percept is unique, and since we experience millions of them each day, we seldom really *attend* to them in terms of their uniqueness. Such a task would immediately overwhelm our neural capacities. Nor could we respond to each percept in a different way. Instead, we instinctively group percepts together in terms of categories of thought.

A *concept,* then, really is the smallest unit of our thought materials. A concept is a category of thought, or a category for grouping sense data together "as if they were all the same." All percepts involving the stoplight at Fourth and Main become a category of thought, although a relatively narrow one. All stoplights, regardless of location, becomes a broader concept. The important thing to note here is that a concept is an abstraction, a category of thought. Conceptualizing is obviously a very powerful process. It enables us to *simplify* experiences by glossing over microscopic distinctions that are not important; it *facilitates memory* because we can use a smaller number of labels; and it enables us to *generalize* from experience with some members of a category to others. Sometimes we group smaller categories into larger ones (e.g., stoplights and stop signs may be grouped together); sometimes we break categories down into smaller ones in order to highlight an important distinction (long stoplights from short stoplights, blinking ones from nonblinking ones), moving across various levels of *abstraction* as suits our purpose, and scanning or cutting across categories for new combinations.

In theory building, we essentially continue this process, except that in doing so we relate categories of thought to one another. We use informal theories when we think of certain *classes* of behavior (as defined by a category, such as "driving fast") in a *class* of environmental conditions ("slick roads"), resulting in a *class* of outcomes ("loss of control of the vehicle's motion").

More-formal theories extend this process, with an important distinction: the categories of thought become *constructs*. A construct is a concept intended purely for theoretical use. We use concepts in our informal theory building and thinking; we use constructs in formal theories in science. Typically, the construct will be more abstract than everyday concepts and is likely to cut across various preexisting categories of thought. The value of specific constructs depends on how useful they are in constructing a good theory, just as the value of everyday concepts depends on how much they assist us in everyday affairs. In theories of OB, constructs will in fact often be quite similar to already familiar concepts, even frequently having the same label, although perhaps defined somewhat differently or more explicitly.

We use a number of rules for grouping things together to form categories. Sometimes we group things on the basis of similar physical appearance, sometimes on the basis of proximity, sometimes on the basis of common purpose. In forming constructs for theories, we are less likely to use observable physical characteristics as a basis of grouping and more likely to use *function, effect,* or *patterns of covariation* as defining characteristics. Fleishman (1973), for example, used the construct "consideration" to refer to all forms of supervisory behavior that promote two-way communication between the superior and subordinates. "Reinforcers (Chapter 3) designate any consequences of behavior that have the effect of making those behaviors more likely to occur. "Need for achievement" as a construct in motivation and personality theory (Chapter 9) denotes a characteristic mix of behaviors that tend to cluster together within and among persons.

Informal versus Formal Theories

Consider the following example. A supervisor oversees the work of several subordinates who have varying abilities, work at a number of different tasks of varying levels of difficulty, and perform at varying levels of quantity and quality. The supervisor, drawing upon observations of these workers as well as other experiences, concludes that individual performance is best when the task level is neither too far below nor too far above the abilities of the worker. If the task is too easy, the worker soon becomes bored and blasé about the job; if the task is too difficult, the worker becomes tense, anxious, or inhibited. The supervisor, whether consciously or unwittingly, has formulated a theory. The components of the theory are task difficulty, worker abilities, emotional states of the individual worker, and performance. The theory contains the statements that: (1) when a task is easy relative to the worker's ability, the emotional state of boredom results; (2) when a task is very difficult relative to the worker's ability, anxiety results; (3) both boredom and anxiety impair performance. A number of predictions about specific cases could be drawn from these statements. If several bright people are working on a humdrum task, it won't be long before they begin to indulge in a lot of horseplay—because when people get bored, they seek out stimulation to eliminate the boredom. Or you would predict that if changes have to be made in jobs which make the jobs more difficult, and if people are presently performing those jobs at an optimal level, the changes will have to be made gradually so that worker abilities can adapt.

Consider, now, a more *formal* theory about *task scope* and employee performance. For example, a theory formulated by Schwab and Cummings (1976) draws upon the larger body of *expectancy theory of motivation*. The core notion of the theory is that the motivational force upon a person to perform an act depends upon the *valence* (attractiveness or reward value) of the outcomes of the act and the *expectancy* (or subjective, privately believed probability) that those outcomes will occur. For a worker of a given level of competence, there is an ideal task scope which will maximize the product of valence × expectancy. As the task scope falls below the ideal, then the valence of successful performance declines; that is, the successful performance which results from the person's acts doesn't mean much to him or her, doesn't generate any feeling of pride, accomplishment, or achievement. As the task scope exceeds the ideal, the valence of successful performance increases. For example, a high jumper gets more satisfaction clearing a bar at seven feet than one at four feet. However, the expectancy that the person's actions will result in successful performance begins to decrease. The high jumper would feel good about successfully clearing a bar at eight feet, but no one on record has ever done this; so you won't motivate many high jumpers by putting the bar that high. Since jumping ability varies, there are many people you wouldn't motivate to jump by placing the bar at seven feet, six feet, or less. The position of the bar will maximize the motivation of different jumpers at different heights.

Space does not permit a discussion sufficient to do the Schwab and Cummings theory justice, but we hope that the reader can see how the theory addresses phenomena similar to those of interest to the hypothetical supervisor described above. The supervisor's theory is just as much a theory as that formulated by Cummings and Schwab: both contain concepts (though labeled somewhat differently) and statements about how those concepts are interrelated.

If managers and other action-oriented people use behavioral theories, then why their discomfort with theories in behavioral science? The reasons have to do, not with the intrinsic nature of theory, but rather with certain qualitative differences between theory-in-use or "informal theory" and the reconstructed theory or "formal theory" used by behavioral scientists. First of all, the concepts and the components of informal theory are usually couched at a *low level of abstraction*, close to the level of actual physical or biological entities. The behavioral scientist, on the other hand, typically works with constructs at a more abstract level. In the Schwab and Cummings theory, for example, "task scope" represents a construct sufficiently abstract to cover not only the dimension of difficulty, but also complexity and the degree of ambiguity versus clarity in task operations. Second, and related to the first difference, informal theory usually addresses a very specific, sometimes unique, problem or set of problems, whereas formal theory in behavioral science encompasses a greater range of related problems. The manager theorizes about how performance is determined on a particular job; the behavioral scientist theorizes about performance in general or on a relatively broad category of jobs which share certain definitive properties. Third, the manager uses ordinary, everyday language or labels in theory construction, whereas the behavioral scientist often prefers new terms with special meanings. Finally, the manager tends to be less explicit about the assumptions on which a theory rests, whereas the behavioral scientist insists on specifying unambiguously the premises underlying a theory and the conditions within which the theory is appropriate.

Perhaps it would be helpful, then, to explain why the behavioral scientist uses abstract, general concepts with exotic or awkward labels. Behavioral science uses abstractions so that knowledge accumulated about some aspects of behavior can be applied to superficially unrelated behavioral phenomena. Consider, for example, the case of a worker who works harder and faster than the other workers in the group believe to be appropriate. To the social psychologist, this is not merely an instance of "rate-busting"—it represents the case of a *deviant* who violates a *group norm.* Thus, it is conceptually similar to the Democratic congressman who votes in line with the policy of a Republican president; to the dissenter in a discussion group which seeks consensual unanimity; to the bank loan officer who defies orthodox colleagues by sporting mod apparel; or to the commissioned officer who fraternizes easily with enlisted personnel. Moreover, research conducted by social psychologists with discussion groups supplies a fund of knowledge about how the group will react to the deviant. For example, Schachter (1951) found that if the group is not very cohesive, if the norm being violated is of marginal relevance to the group's objectives, or if the deviant occupies special status because of other contributions to group goals, the group probably won't react strongly. But if the norm is highly relevant to group values or purposes and the group is cohesive, the group will try to bring the dissident in line: first by cajolery or gentle persuasion, and if that doesn't work, then by threat and intimidation. If the latter fail, the group psychologically "amputates" the deviant from the bonds of group belongingness. (See Harold Leavitt, 1978, chapter 21 "Independence and conformity: The problem of truth in the face of pressure.")

This fund of knowledge is applicable to the case of the rate-buster only by way of the connecting concepts "deviant," "group norm," "group cohesion," and "status" (the concepts are further discussed in Chapters 12 and 13 of this volume). Without those concepts, the relevance of observations of a discussion group would not be apparent. Abstract concepts, then, serve to integrate diverse phenomena so that knowledge in one sphere is useful in other spheres. We might add that only by theories which employ concepts at a considerable level of abstraction can research findings ever be applied to the "real world." Abstract concepts are the linking pins between scientific data and practical affairs.

The reader might agree at this point, but reply, The English language of everyday life is rich with concepts; why not use the language of everyday life so that we can more easily understand what a theory is saying, rather than use such unfamiliar terms as *valence, task scope, alienation, reinforcement, cohesion,* and *initiating structure?* One reason for using specialized terms is that the more familiar concept labels have different shades of meaning in the minds of different people; by inventing a new term with a given definition, the behavioral scientist avoids the misinterpretations which would otherwise occur in scholarly discourse. A more important reason, however, is that everyday concepts often carry value-charged connotations which get in the way of detached, logical analysis. To talk about democratic as opposed to autocratic leadership is to invite preexisting prejudices or emotions into the arena of inquiry. Phrasing the issue in terms of directive versus participative supervision is less likely to trigger preconceived biases and more likely to facilitate a patient, open-minded exploration of the effects of different styles of management.

What Functions Does Theory Serve?

One of the functions served by theory has already been implied by the foregoing discussion. Theory helps *organize* our knowledge into a pattern whereby facts, data, and observed regularities are interconnected in such a way that they take on a new meaning not evident when viewed in isolation. Theory brings to light similarities in seemingly dissimilar phenomena.

Second, a theory is a useful means of *summarizing* in symbolic form a diverse body of knowledge. As Shaw and Costanzo (1970) state, a theory "permits us to handle large amounts of empirical data with relatively few propositions" (p. 9). Theory, then, functions as a wieldly shorthand method of stating what we have learned or believe about a class of phenomena; it relieves us of the tedium of having to attend to a cumulative record of raw observations.

Third, theory *points the way to continued research*, or the pursuit of new facts. Theory prompts us to ask new questions about the phenomenon we are studying, questions that might not otherwise have occurred to us. Indeed, a good theory may raise more questions than it answers. Furthermore, theory helps us distinguish between trivial questions and important questions. Theories do not end with the data or experiences which gave birth to them; they go beyond such data to suggest tentative inferences or predictions about what new data or experiences will look like. Without a theory, we would not know what to study, or if we did, just how to study it.

The organizing, summarizing, and guiding functions are as important in informal theories as in formal theories. The problem-solving manager stores his or her accumulated observations in an organized and symbolic form. The tentative conclusions drawn from his or her experiences then suggest new solutions to old problems or new problems to be attacked in the never-ending quest for organizational improvement. The effective manager operates in a conceptual world of assumptions, logic, and tentative conclusions about relationships among variables, and the design of activities to test the truth-value or usefulness of those conclusions.

Alfred P. Sloan, Jr., in his autobiographical *My Years with General*

Motors, states that "every enterprise needs a concept of its industry." Sloan's ensuing account makes clear that he was very much a theorist—and self-consciously so—about the automobile industry. Furthermore, he attributed much of General Motors's success to the exercise of theory construction. Theory, then, is not something that the action-oriented individual need view as alien, artificial, or barren.

Former National Security Advisor to the President and Secretary of State Henry Kissinger also recognized the importance of theory. As Kissinger put it:

> Yet in foreign policy there is no escaping the need for an integrating conceptual framework. . . . A conceptual framework—which "links" events—is an essential tool [Kissinger, 1979, p. 130].

What Are the Criteria for Evaluating a Theory?

Abraham Kaplan, in his book *The Conduct of Inquiry* (1964), discusses a number of criteria by which the scientific community assesses the worth of a theory. The *norm of correspondence* is the most obvious one: How well does the theory fit the facts? How closely do predictions drawn from the theory match up with actual events? The layman tends to think of this as the sole and ultimate acid test of a theory. But suppose that several theories all explain the data equally well. How do we decide which is best?

The *norm of coherence* enters into consideration here. A theory should be internally consistent and straightforward in its logic. It should not depend on its author for drawing out the connections between its component statements; the connections should not be so loose or imprecise that totally opposite conclusions could be drawn from the theory. According to the *principle of parsimony,* a theory should contain no more concepts or assumptions than are necessary to account for the data. A simple theory is preferable to a complex theory unless the added complexity can account for additional findings not explained by the simple theory. A new theory must also fit with the larger body of preexisting theories in the field, assuming that there is good reason to think that these theories have validity. For example, a theory of leadership which assumes that subordinate satisfaction is a direct cause of performance does violence to fairly well-established theories about how attitudes and performance are related; such a leadership theory, then, no matter how well it fits the facts of a study or one's informal observations, would not get high marks.

The *norm of pragmatism* refers not, as the label might imply, to the practical applications of a theory in everyday affairs, but rather to how a theory furthers the activities of scientists. This relates quite closely to the guidance function of theories. How much new research is suggested by the theory? What new puzzles or questions does the theory bring to light? To test well on the norm of pragmatism, a theory must at the very least be testable; it must be capable of being put to a test in which only certain results, and not just any conceivable results, could support the theory. A theory so flexible that it could account for results of any kind is by definition untestable and thus does not guide us in seeking new knowledge. Some theories are appealing because they have the ring of plausibility; they seem to sum up much of what we have felt or observed with an eloquent, convincing tone. Some theories appeal to us because they implicitly support our deeply ingrained views about human nature and its limitations or potentialities. Some theories simply have certain esthetic attractions because of the imagery or models they convey. Even in the supposedly "hard" sciences, like physics and astronomy, it has been suggested that scientists' choices of competing theories are determined in part by the perceived "beauty" of a particular theory. Maslow's need hierarchy theory (Chapter 7) continues to occupy a special niche among motivation theorists largely because of its intuitive appeal, even though it is not very well supported empirically and may not even be testable in its original form.

LIFE CYCLE OF THEORY

In every field of study, theories come and go; they are born and eventually die. This causes some discomfort on the part of students, as if the time and effort taken to understand a theory would be wasted if the theory were later discarded. But even as a theory falls by the wayside, it passes something along to the theories which succeed it.

A theory at any time serves as a *provisional* statement, couched in conceptual language, of how various phenomena in nature or behavior are interrelated. A theory is, if you will, a *perspective* on the state of knowledge as it then exists, coupled with some speculations about what additional knowledge may come to light. As new knowledge develops, the theory undergoes revision—its constructs may be redefined, special conditions may be noted in which it does not seem to hold, qualifying statements are added, exceptional cases not accounted for by the theory are compiled. As these developments occur, the theory becomes cumbersome, less appealing esthetically, and less satisfying intellectually. Eventually a new theory emerges which shows how seeming contradictions and exceptional cases fall neatly into place. The new theory preserves the contribution provided by the old and passes it along, yet also provides a perspective which dissolves the nagging riddles.

Robert B. Zajonc (1960), noting the special cases unexplained by current theories of attitude change, drew an analogy from the ancient theory that "nature abhors a vacuum." Centuries ago, that theory seemed to account simply and adequately for an array of physical phenomena, such as the action of pumps and suction. But pumps were known not to be capable of drawing water to a height of over 34 feet. Thus, the theory was modified: "Nature abhors a vacuum up to 34 feet." Even the amended theory, however, could not handle the subsequent finding that mercury could be drawn into a vacuum only up to 30 inches. Torricelli formulated a different theory: The pressure of air acting on the surface of a liquid forces it to rise into a pressureless vacuum—the height reached by the liquid determined by the weight of the liquid and the weight of the atmosphere at the surface of the earth.

Note that the newer theory could not have been possible without the old one. It was, as Zajonc notes, precisely the effect of the "nature abhors a vacuum" principle that exceptions to it were noted and had to be accounted for. A few discrepant facts did not kill the older theory: the theory stayed in use and served its role until a rival theory came along which could do all the old one did, plus a little bit more. The new theory did not nullify the old one, nor did it mean that the old one had been a waste; the new was an organic outgrowth of the old. Note, too, that even today one could effectively apply the "outmoded" idea that "nature abhors a vacuum" in many instances.

You may be sure that some of the theories you read about in the pages ahead will in time become historical curiosities. This will not mean you have studied them in vain. To the extent that they now serve well the essential ends of any theory, their contributions will have been well preserved by new theoretical developments.

TESTING AND APPLYING THEORIES

We test and apply our theories by descending from the region of abstract concepts or constructs to the more earthly realm of observable events. There are various methods of doing this, as we shall see, but in one sense they all do the same thing: they make use of *operational definitions* of the constructs in order to see if the relationships theorized to exist between the concepts are reflected in a sample of observed events. An operational definition of a construct is not the construct itself, but a concrete means of illustrating the construct.

Suppose we theorize that the more formalized or bureaucratized an organization becomes, the less innovative it becomes. Conceptually, in other words, we suppose formalization and innovativeness to be interrelated. For the moment, never mind the logic or rationale for why we believe it. We cannot test the usefulness of the theory until we provide some means of defining these concepts in concrete, observable terms. We might choose, as an operational definition of formalization, the number of distinct administrative units an organization has; we might illustrate the concept of innovativeness by the number of new products marketed by an organization in the last three years. Both of these measures are arbitrary, in a sense; they do not capture the full meaning of what we have in mind by "formalization" and "innovativeness," but they give us a start. Suppose we find that, of several organizations in a particular industry (e.g., petrochemicals), those organizations with fewer administrative units actually do show a larger number of new products marketed in the previous three years. Have we *proved* our theory? No, we have marshaled a bit of evidence *supportive* of our theory, *consistent* with our theory. Our theory would have limited usefulness if it were restricted to these findings alone. We would have more confidence in our theory if it were supported when different kinds of operational definitions were used. For example, we could probe further and define formalization in terms of the number of levels of authority between the president or chief executive officer and the bottom-level operating employees; we might define innovativeness by asking industry experts to rate the organizations on a scale from 1 (not at all innovative) to 10 (extremely innovative). If those companies with fewer levels of authority were rated as the more innovative, we would have yet more support for the theory.

Of course, our theory may have actually sprung from the very observation that companies with fewer administrative units, or fewer levels of authority, had brought forth more new products or had the reputation in the industry of being more innovative. In that case, we would have leaped from the specific to the more general, or more abstract. Theory is stimulated by empirical observation, and theory stimulates further empirical observations, some of which will eventually force changes in the theory or stimulate a new and better theory as the life cycle of a theory develops. The more useful and powerful theories tend to be the ones consistent with observed relationships between various means of operationally defining the constructs of the theory (see Figure 2–1).

Theories, then, do not exist apart from data of some kind. Both formal and informal theories are inspired, tested, applied, modified, and ultimately abandoned as a consequence of using methods of research.

METHODS OF RESEARCH

A method of research is any means by which we observe or learn about a phenomenon. Several different types of research methods are used to learn about behavior in organizations. All of these methods

Figure 2–1
Relationship between Theory and Research

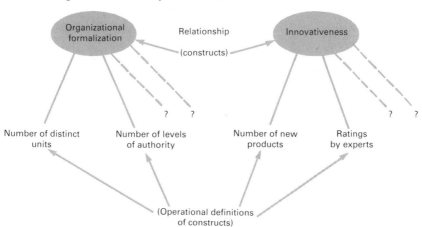

play important roles in our learning. Each method also has its distinctive limitations. The user of knowledge about organizational behavior must be able to qualify that knowledge on the basis of the limitations posed by the method(s) used to produce it.

Naturalistic Observation

The most primitive method of research in organizational behavior is represented by the impressions we draw from simply witnessing the events around us in organizations and living in the stream of organizational experience. All of us have spent a considerable amount of time in organizations of various kinds, be they educational, voluntary, or commercial. We have some notion about how organizational size, organizational reward systems, and styles of leadership have affected our own behavior. We have also observed how certain characteristics of individual or group behavior seem to correlate or covary with changes or differences in organization characteristics. To the extent that we have voiced these impressions, we may have discovered that others agree with us. Each of us, then, has a private fund of knowledge about behavior in organization. Furthermore, this knowledge has been supplemented by the accounts of others who have offered their observations in the form of conversations, speeches, popular magazine articles, autobiographies (for example, Sloan's *My Year at General Motors*), even fiction (as in *Executive Suite* and other business novels written by Cameron Hawley, who drew from his own experience as an executive).

A more systematic form of naturalistic observation is represented by the *case study*. In using this method, one or more researchers enter an organization—sometimes as participants, otherwise as consultants or guests—solely for the purpose of observing what goes on. Usually the researchers have some particular focus already planned for their observations. For example, Alvin Gouldner entered a gypsum plant with the intent of finding out what would happen when a new plant manager was sent in from corporate headquarters in order to tighten up bureaucratic rules and procedures (his observations are recorded in the book *Patterns of Industrial Bureaucracy*). Melville Dalton, a sociologist, became an employee on the payrolls of an industrial organization in order to examine the politics of management (his impressions formed the basis of his book *Men Who Manage*). In conducting the case study, researchers often keep diaries or journals of their daily experiences and usually supplement their own perceptions by examining company records, documents, archieves, memos, and selected interviews with personnel.

The attractiveness of naturalistic observation as a method of research results mainly from the fact that it is a method which confronts its subject head-on; it deals with behavior in the raw, with the "real world." The data are rich with human drama and existence. Accounts of such studies are easy for readers to identify with; at their best, such studies enthrall and spark the imagination of the reader as well as any journalistic medium is capable of doing. Furthermore, the sensitive observer may glimpse subtle insights not obtainable from more rigorous methods, such as the laboratory experiment.

Table 2–1
Naturalistic Observation as a Method of Learning about Organizational Behavior

Forms:	Personal experience; biographical statements; journalistic accounts; clinical case study.
Advantages:	Contextual richness; source of personal insights; generation of hypotheses; raw material for theory construction.
Disadvantages:	Selective observation and recall; biased focus toward the dramatic; difficult to separate the unique from the more generalizable; not subject to quantitative analysis.

The shortcomings of naturalistic observation, however, are numerous and quite serious.[1] First of all, the "original data" are actually soon

---

[1]The shortcomings discussed refer to the case study as a method of formal science. This is not to deny the obvious advantages of the case study as a method of instruction, learning, and discussion.

and irretrievably lost, transformed, mangled because of the limited information-processing capabilities of human beings. When we read, say, Sloan's account of his experiences at General Motors, we are not privy to the events as they actually occured. We are totally dependent upon Sloan's subjective frame of reference as it affected both his perceptions and his memories of events. We do not know what things he chose *not* to attend to; we do not know what part of his account represents inferential leaps of faith concerning things he did not directly experience or observe; we do not know the extent to which, or the manner in which, filtering has occurred, as it must inevitably occur in the transmission of information; we do not know whether other observers would have drawn the same conclusions.

It is precisely because naturalistic observation is so rich, colorful, and pulsating that knowledge based on it must be hedged about with qualifications and cautions. Psychological research has shown that human beings have a very limited short-term storage capacity for processing information. Our perceptions are therefore highly selective, and under conditions not optimal for observing—for example, when the stimulus field is rapidly changing, as would be the case with real-life experience in organizations—the perceiver instinctively uses economizing but error-prone shortcuts to overcome the limitations of channel capacity (the perceptual process is discussed at greater length in Chapter 5). Experiments demonstrate that in naturalistic observation people make woefully inaccurate estimates of the degree of correlation among events; typically, their subjects deluded themselves into thinking that they saw systematic causál relationships where in fact such relationships did not exist. Rainmakers, politicians, bookies, and fortune-tellers exploit this weakness in naturalistic observation.

Still another shortcoming of informal observation or case studies is that they tend to have a biased focus on dramatic, unusual, or otherwise newsworthy phenomena (Weick, 1969). Mergers, strikes, changes in leadership, reorganizations, and the like are frequently the occasions for starting case studies. It is far from obvious that such "exciting" events provide the best material for learning about organizational behavior. As Karl Weick (1965) notes, much of organizational behavior is routine, bland, and uninspiring; indeed, routinization is the goal if not the foundation of organization. Yet we still have much to learn about such routine phenomena as why most people exhibit reliable role behavior in the absence of overt pressures to do so.

Another problem with case studies is untangling the unique properties of the host organization or its participants from more generalizable relationships. Suppose that a case study of a beer-bottling plant in a small town finds that the introduction of automated processes is followed by a wildcat strike. Does this tell us something about a lawful relationship between technological change and aggressive behavior? Or do the causes of the strike stem from factors woven into the history of the community, the ambitions of a labor leader, or the fact that the duck-hunting season had just begun? To what extent could we generalize from this organization to a steel mill, an insurance office, or the local grocery store?

Finally, naturalistic observation of human behavior defies quantification. Statistics are not the be-all and end-all of any science, but comparative judgments of some sort are essential, and quantification through measurement renders such judgments much more reliable and communicable. Case studies seldom give us much to work with in estimating the *strength* of relationships among variables or in gauging the *relative contribution of different factors to an end result.*

These shortcomings make naturalistic observation more useful in the exploratory rather than the advanced stages of studying a phenomenon. Case studies provide a crude sketch of the terrain we plan to embark upon; more rigorous, sophisticated methods are essential for producing a workable map. Naturalistic observation can be a fruitful source of hypothesis creation, and at times it provides a corrective for the mistake of studying only trivial issues rigorously, but by itself it is a very insecure foundation for a body of knowledge about organizational behavior.

Field Survey Research

An alternative to naturalistic observation in organizations is the design of systematic surveys of the opinions, perceptions, attitudes, or self-reported behavior of participants in organizations. Whereas naturalistic observation relies almost totally on the perceptions of the researcher, survey research taps the perceptions of others, at least as they are reported and described by others. Whereas the naturalistic observer might conclude, from watching workers perform a repetitive task, that they are bored with or "alienated" from their jobs, survey research would solicit the workers' own feelings about their work. The workers might, in fact, express considerable satisfaction with their jobs (and possibly even rejoice in their freedom from the paperwork and statistical computations of a behavioral science researcher).

One form of survey research is the *person-to-person interview.* The researcher sits down with a subject and asks questions, to which the subject responds. The interview may be *unstructured* in format, in which case the questions would be open-ended and the interviewer would selectively probe in greater depth, depending on how the respondent answered. If the interview were *structured,* the questions would all be formulated in advance so that the respondent could answer by choosing among a few response alternatives, such as "yes" or "no," "agree" or "disagree," and the same questions would be used over and over again with subsequent interviewees.

Alfred Kinsey, for example, used the interview as his basic method of researching the sexual behavior of males and females (Kinsey, Pomeroy, & Martin, 1949). David Granick interviewed Soviet and European managers in order to assess the cross-cultural similarities and differences in the role of the executive (Granick, 1961). People in different types of organizations can be interviewed to see whether they have correspondingly different experiences in their work, different levels of stress, different types of problems, and so on. People can be interviewed about the leadership style of their superiors and about whether or not their work attitudes are related to such differences in their superiors.

The chief advantage of the interview is that it offers observations independent of, and supplementary to, those of the researcher. There are problems, however, with the interview as a method of research. First of all, the person being interviewed might feel a bit awed or threatened by the presence of the interviewer. The subject might refrain from offering opinions or information which could place him or her in an embarrassing or vulnerable position. Only if the interviewer has a knack for putting subjects completely at ease and winning their confidence can he or she reliably elicit candid responses; Kinsey apparently had this knack, even with very unusual subject populations, such as prison inmates (Christenson, 1971). Second, the interviewer can unwittingly shape a certain pattern to the subjects' verbal responses merely by characteristic nods, grimaces, or other nonverbal cues (the phenomenon of *shaping* is discussed in the next chapter). Again, considerable skill and training in interviewing are necessary to avoid such biases. Finally, interviews are very expensive in terms of the researcher's time. For all these reasons, most contemporary research in organizational behavior utilizes the direct interview primarily in the initial, preliminary phases of a more elaborate project using other methods.

The questionnaire represents a more efficient means of survey research which avoids some of the pitfalls of the interview. Questionnaires, like interviews, may be unstructured or highly structured in format; increasingly, researchers attempt to use the more structured versions. Typically the researcher either mails a large number of questionnaires to potential subjects or distributes questionnaires to an assembled group. Under such conditions, the anonymity of the respondent can be guaranteed and a vast amount of data in the form of written responses can be collected and machine processed.

One reason for the increased use of questionnaires in survey research is the recent development of a number of standardized instruments for measuring subjects' perceptions of relevant organizational attributes. Psychologists have designed scales to measure job satisfaction, supervisor's style, beliefs about the kinds of rewards related to performance, and so on. Scales are scored by weighting the extremity of the answer in a given direction (for example, 5 for "strongly disagree" versus 1 for "strongly agree," or 4 for "frequently" versus 2 for "occasionally") and summing across all items in the scale. The average scores of different groups can then be compared (for example, the mean job satisfaction score for males versus females). Or scores on one scale can be compared with scores on another scale to see whether they are statistically related: Do higher scores by respondents on a scale measuring job satisfaction tend to go along with higher scores on a scale measuring leader considerateness and vice versa? In short, the use of standardized scales in questionnaires facilitates quantification.

Despite the advantages of the written questionnaire over the interview, the former nevertheless has its own problems. Its use presumes that respondents are both able and willing to describe their feelings or perceptions by circling a number or checking a blank space. Test-

Figure 2–2

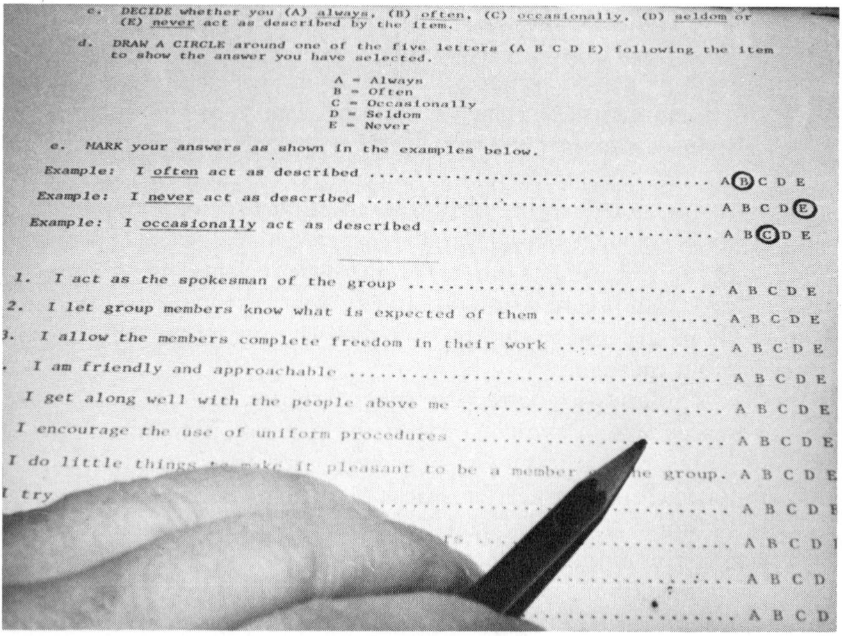

The structured questionnaire has played a major role as a method for collecting data in organizational behavior. Like other methods of research, the questionnaire has certain advantages as well as disadvantages for learning about behavior in organizations.

ing conditions that assure anonymity make this assumption somewhat plausible, but even then there is the problem that respondents
might sometimes consciously or unwittingly slant their responses in
a direction which is more consistent with how they would *like to see
themselves* than with their actual behavior. Consider, for example,
self-report studies of how people rank the various outcomes of their
jobs (see, for example, Opsahl & Dunnette, 1966). People often do not
rank money as the most important job consideration; to do so would
apparently be to view themselves as materialistic. Yet, as Opsahl and
Dunnette note, people apparently behave as if money were quite important: professors move to institutions that pay them more; super-
star athletes play out their contract options if they don't get the salary they want; and movie stars go to court to recover commissions
on the distribution of their films. One has to take into account, then,
the complicating factor of *social desirability in response set* in interpreting the results of questionnaire studies.

Another problem with questionnaires is that people tend to structure their answers to different scales in a manner which they perceive
to be consistent and logical, even if doing so inaccurately portrays life
situations which in fact are not always consistent and logical. One
finding from questionnaire studies of supervisory styles is that people
who describe their boss as autocratic report lower job satisfaction
than do those who view their boss as democratic or participative. It
would be tempting to conclude from this that type of supervisory
style is a determinant of subordinate satisfaction. But an alternative
explanation could simply be that dissatisfied workers describe everything else in their work environment in such a way as to make it
seem consistent with their dissatisfaction. This would be especially
likely when they are describing something which is very subjective
and open to differences in interpretation, as would be true with leadership style or "organizational climate." It would be less of a problem
when respondents are asked for reasonably straightforward, more objective, or emotionally neutral information, such as their hours of
work, the frequency with which they have job-related interaction

Table 2–2
**Field Survey Research as a Method of Learning about Organizational
Behavior**

Forms:	Face-to-face interviews; questionnaires.
Advantages:	Enables reseracher to assess others' subjective frames of reference; allows a degree of quantitative analysis; formats can be standardized across studies.
Disadvantages:	Possible spurious relationships due to various forms of bias or distortion by subjects in responding.

with persons outside their departments, their degree of dependence on others for their own job performance, or the number of formal performance appraisals they have had in the past two years.

Correlational Field Studies Using Objective Indices

All of the methods of research we have discussed so far are essentially *correlational* in nature. This means that they are methods which attempt to ascertain the extent to which two or more variables correlate or covary as we find them in nature. To say that job satisfaction correlates with job tenure is to say that the more satisfied people tend to be the ones with longer experience on the job and that the less satisfied people tend to be those with less tenure on the job. Analogously, we would be stating that those people who have been on the job longer tend to report a higher level of work satisfaction than do the shorttimers. Note that we are not saying that either one causes the other—that staying on the job longer makes a person more satisfied, or that satisfaction makes a worker stay around longer— only that satisfaction and tenure vary in a similar fashion.

The correlation coefficient is a statistical estimate of the degree of linear relationship between two variables—a device for expressing the degree to which two things vary together. The correlation coefficient can range from −1.00 (meaning that two variables vary in a completely opposite pattern, or that as one increases the other always decreases and vice versa) through 0.00 (meaning that the two variables are totally unrelated, the variation in either one telling us nothing about the variation in the other) to 1.00 (meaning that the two variables change in the same direction in perfect agreement, that an increase or decrease in either is accompanied by the same relative increase or decrease in the other). Usually correlation coefficients between different variables in organizational behavior are well below 1.00 in absolute value. This is simply a reflection of these two facts: (1) that our measurement devices themselves yield a substantial amount of error; and (2) that any important aspect of human behavior—such as the level of individual job satisfaction or the group performance level—usually has a large number of causes, no one of which can fully predict or account for all of the variation in the variable we are trying to explain.

The *statistical significance* of a correlation coefficient is simply a statement about how unlikely it is that a given correlation coefficient could have been obtained by chance alone if the two variables were in fact totally unrelated. For example, the statement that a correlation of .40 between worker's age and performance is "significant at the level of .01" means that there was only 1 chance in 100 that we could have obtained such a coefficient if in fact there were no relationship at all between age and performance on that type of job. However, the statistical significance depends not only on the size of the coefficient, but also on the size of the sample studied. A coefficient of .20 in a sample of 1,000 workers is more significant in a statistical sense—less likely to be due to chance—than one of .50 in a sample of 16 workers. The latter coefficient, however, is significant at the .05 level (there is only 1 chance in 20 that it would have occurred randomly in the absence of some relationship), which has traditionally been the level of significance considered acceptable in scientific study for a relationship to be inferred. Moreover, when the .50 coefficient is squared (.50 × .50), this tells us that .25, or 25 percent, of the variance in either age or performance can be predicted by variance in the other. A coefficient of .20, on the other hand, regardless of its level of statistical significance, means that only 4 percent of either variable can be accounted for by the other.

We should emphasize that a study which is correlational in design does not necessarily have to compute or report a correlation coefficient. It is correlational if it shows by tables, bars, graphs, or charts how two or more variables covary.

A correlational field study using objective indices measures at least one variable by means other than self-reports. One objective index is either correlated with another or with responses to questionnaire items. Such variables as absence rate, number of subordinates supervised by a manager, number of patents obtained by a research division, frequency of grievances processed by a bargaining unit, and attrition rate are examples of objective indices. They are "hard data" in the sense that measurements of such variables are unlikely to be distorted by subjective perceptions or emotions, although the measurements may be subject to other kinds of errors (for example, sloppiness in record keeping). Even appraisals of subordinates' performance by superiors, although subjective in nature, may be considered an objective index in a study if they were obtained *independently* of other variables in the study, such as subordinates' descriptions of the supervisors' leadership style. In that case, the performance rating would have been obtained from a source different from that of the subordinates' reported perceptions, and thus any correlation between the two would probably not have arisen because of response set tendencies of either superior or subordinate in the direction of social desirability or consistency (provided, of course, that subordinates were not aware of how they had been appraised and that superiors were not privy to subordinates' descriptions of their leadership style).

Consider, for example, a study of supervisory styles reporting the results shown in Table 2–3. The study, which took place in the home office of a large insurance company, assessed the styles of the supervisors by means of questionnaires distributed to workers in various

Table 2–3
Correlation between Style of Supervisor and Productivity of Supervisor's Section

	Job-Centered Supervisors	Employee-Centered Supervisors
High-Producing Sections	1	6
Low-Producing Sections	7	3

Source: Adapted from P. Hersey and K. H. Blanchard, *Management of Organizational Behavior* (Englewood Cliffs, N.J.: Prentice-Hall, 1969), p. 70.

sections of the company headquarters. From subjects' responses to questions concerning the typical behavior of their bosses, the researchers could classify the styles of the supervisors as predominantly employee-centered (a greater concern with the welfare of the employees) or job-centered (a dominant concern with getting the work out). The researchers obtained measures of productivity by consulting company records of the volume of paperwork processed by the different groups. As the findings show, employee-centered supervisors obviously tended to have more productive work units. Conclusion: The employee-centered style of supervision causes a higher level of group productivity than does the job-centered style. But is this the only tenable explanation for the results? No, because all correlational studies have in common the limitation that they cannot show what is cause and what is effect, and that is their major shortcoming.

Anytime we have a correlation between two variables, say, A and B, it could be that A caused B or that B caused A. In the study described above, it seems logical to think that supervisory style caused the level of productivity. But it could very well be that the level of group productivity caused the supervisor to act in a certain way. The leader of a good group does not have to be critical, punitive, or concerned about production; he or she has the luxury of attending primarily to personal relationships and promoting a comfortable work climate. The unfortunate soul who inherits a group of incompetent or foot-dragging workers does not have that luxury and must set about improving the level of work. Thus, the productivity of the section could have been the cause and supervisory style a consequence or effect due to that cause.

Yet another explanation for the correlation between two variables is that they each may have been caused by some other unknown or unmeasured variable, C. A study conducted some years ago found a strikingly high correlation between consumption of a certain soft drink and the incidence of polio (before polio vaccines were available). This was not because the drink made people more susceptible to polio, nor was it because polio made you like the taste of the pop. Both variables were caused by climate. Polio occurred more often in the summer months and in the warmer regions, and of course people drink more liquids in hot weather.

In order to infer that a correlation between A and B is due to A causing B, we have to be able to manipulate A at our discretion, holding other possible causes of B constant, and then see whether B changes as we manipulate A. In correlational studies, controlled manipulation has not occurred; instead, we have recorded observations of things "changing as they will."

Despite the absence of manipulation, correlational field studies may sometimes shed some light on causal relationships if they incorporate a *longitudinal* dimension. A longitudinal study requires that we collect data on the variables of interest over a period of time long enough for those variables to undergo some changes. Suppose, for example, that we are interested in the relationship between job performance and emotional stress. We find that, as of a given date, the better performers report fewer problems with emotional stress than less-effective performers. We have found a relationship, but it is not clear whether stress causes poor performance, whether poor performance itself creates stress, or whether something else (conceivably poor diet or marital problems) coincidentally affects both performance and stress. But suppose we could keep tabs on the people in our study, long enough for some people to experience some changes in both degree of stress experienced and quality of performance. If *earlier* changes in stress levels matched *subsequent* changes in performance, we have some basis for inferring that stress is the cause, performance level the effect; if earlier declines (improvements) in performance were correlated with later increases (decreases) in stress levels, it would appear that stress is the *effect* of poor performance rather than its cause. If we observed neither of these patterns, it is quite likely that some other variable accounted for their initial correlation.

Longitudinal studies have been reported with increasing frequency in organizational behavior recently. Also, a variety of statistical tools suited to their analysis has come to light. Many of the causal inferences drawn from previous correlational studies have been reinvestigated using the longitudinal design. At this point it appears that more and more researchers are adding this touch to their field studies and that it could soon become the dominant investigative tool in our discipline.

There remain some technical problems in the analysis of longitudinal data, problems which we cannot appropriately address here. Basically these problems pertain to the researcher's ability to rule our spurious relationships. Even correlations between *changes* in variables can be influenced by unknown factors. Thus, even the longitudinal design is not a perfect substitute for direct manipulation of variables in the attempt to draw causal inferences.

Table 2–4
Correlational Field Studies Using Objective Indices as a Method of Learning about Organizational Behavior

Forms:	Use of archival data; records; measures obtained from instruments developed by researcher; any of these as supplement to self-report measures.
Advantages:	Reduces likelihood of spurious relationships caused by obtaining all data from self reports.
Disadvantages:	Difficult to infer cause-effect relationships.

Field Experiments

In a field experiment, we change an organizational variable in one setting and observe the consequent changes as compared to the changes occurring in a similar setting where that variable was not altered, or as compared to the changes in a similar setting where the change was made in the opposite direction or to a different extent. For example, Morse and Reimer (1956) decentralized the level of decision making in some sections of a company by letting employees make more work-related decisions. In other sections of the company, they centralized decision making by restricting the number of work-related decisions an employee could make. In both situations the type of employee and the type of job were otherwise similar. At the end of 18 months, Morse and Reimer compared the two groups in terms of productivity. Both groups increased productivity over previous levels, but the increase was slightly greater in the centralized sections. Note that if the change had been made *only* in the decentralized sections, the increased productivity would have suggested that the decentralization of decision making was the cause of the increase. However, with the comparison (centralized) sections also showing an increase in productivity, we know that decentralization per se was not the causative factor.

In another field experiment, Muczyk (1976) conducted a study on the effects of a management-by-objectives (MBO) program on organizational performance. The site of the study was a multibranch bank, in 13 branches of which the MBO program was introduced. A comparable number of other branches—matched by market areas, types and volumes of business, and personnel profiles similar to those in the experimental groups—served as controls, or baselines against which to assess the effects of the MBO program. Although the branches using the MBO program did show positive changes in a number of banking performance criteria 6 months and 12 months later, performance had increased by comparable levels in the control branches. In the absence of the control group, the performance improvements might have been erroneously attributed to the MBO program rather than, for example, to changes in the national or state economic climates.

In the field experiment, then, the essential features include not only the ability to change or manipulate something, but also the ability to control other relevant variables, either by using a comparison group or by holding all other factors constant. The latter is virtually impossible in a live organization, so comparison groups are usually necessary.

True field experiments are somewhat rare in the study of organizational behavior. In order to conduct them, researchers need permission to make the necessary changes and to take the steps essential for proper controls. Organizational officials are understandably reluctant to permit such changes if they regard the changes as risks to the reliability of normal operations. Those who do permit the changes may be so unusual—in either their philosophy or their tolerance for such risks—that the results obtained could not be safely generalized as applicable to other settings.

A particularly troublesome issue in field experiments concerns the time dimension. It may take months or years for the full effects of a change in an organizational variable to be felt (for example, Muczyk had reason to believe that the MBO program was just beginning to have an impact when his study was concluded). Yet the longer the experiment, the greater the opportunity for noncomparabilities between experimental and control groups to develop. In the Morse and Reimer field experiment, for example, one group (the centralized sections) experienced a higher rate of turnover in personnel than did the other. This left a smaller group with the same amount of work to do, resulting in a higher rate of production per employee work hour.

When organizational experiments provide the researcher with reasonable control over important variables they form perhaps the ideal research method by combining rigor and realism. There is reason to believe that an increasing number of organization leaders welcome the chance to assess rigorously the effects of new programs; if so, the study of organizational behavior will profit from a richer data base.

Table 2–5
Field Experiments as a Method of Learning about Organizational Behavior

Forms:	Experimenter-induced change in one or more organizational units, with appropriate comparisons possible; natural experiments in which changes that occur in one or more units are not matched by comparable units.
Advantages:	Naturalistic environment; permits some degree of causal inference.
Disadvantages:	Occasions that permit such studies are not as frequent as desired and may not be representative; difficult to allow time for changes to take full effect while still controlling for other factors.

Laboratory Experiments

Undoubtedly the most misunderstood and least appreciated method of research in organizational behavior is the laboratory experiment. Since much of the knowledge base described in this volume rests on data generated by laboratory experiments, it is important that the reader comprehend the logic and rationale for studying and observing behavior in the laboratory.

The term *laboratory* denotes nothing more than a setting which makes observation easier. A laboratory does not have to be on a college campus or in a psychology department, nor does it require the presence of exotic, futuristic apparatus. A unused classroom, a vacant office, or a materials storeroom could constitute a laboratory. Nothing more awesome than tables, chairs, pencils, and paper need be used. As Weick (1965) points out, all you need for a laboratory is a setting, some subjects, and a task (that is, something for the subjects to do). With these minimal requirements satisfied, the experimenter can proceed to study a virtually unlimited range of behavioral phenomena, including many that characterize the organizational environment.

The purpose of the laboratory setting is, first of all, to screen out the presence of distractions which are not of immediate interest but which inevitably get in the way when one is trying to observe organizational behavior in the raw state. Suppose, for example, that you were interested in the effects of feedback on performance. You want to find out how the timeliness of feedback, the accuracy of feedback, or positive versus negative feedback affect people's work. You could probably spend a few hours or days in a real, live organization watching how people perform when they get no feedback, when it is delayed, when it is erroneous, and so on. But if you honestly appraised the limits of your knowledge thus gained, you would be forced to hedge any conclusions drawn with numerous doubts and qualifications. For example, the kind of supervisor who gives quick feedback is likely to be different in a variety of ways from the kind who delays giving feedback to subordinates; he or she may also be more considerate, a better planner, or simply more knowledgeable, and these differences obscure our observation of the effect of feedback per se. You would probably also find that positive feedback is given more quickly than negative feedback. If so, is any difference in the effect on worker performance due to the difference in timing or to the difference in positivity versus negativity? Suppose that the people who get positive feedback are simply better friends of the boss as well as better workers, or that the people who get faster feedback tend to be the ones who work on certain jobs? There is no way of unscrambling the separate effects of all these varying factors from the feedback itself.

The laboratory filters out those details which, though interesting in their own right, are irrelevant to the question of theoretical interest. In so doing, the reader is likely to argue, the laboratory makes the situation "unrealistic" or "artificial." That is precisely the purpose in taking the issue into the laboratory: to see the phenomenon for what it actually is, not as we ordinarily find it camouflaged in the natural elements. In the laboratory, the only reality that counts is the reality of the variable we are looking at, and it is just as real there as it is anywhere else.

Second, in the laboratory the researcher can exert more control over the structure of events. The experimenter makes things happen at his or her own convenience or dictates. The experimenter can also vary combinations of factors. For example, subjects can be given either positive or negative feedback, and the speed with which feedback is given after performance can also be varied. Thus, the experimenter can observe the separate as well as the additive or interacting effects of both timing and the positivity or negativity of feedback on subsequent performance. In the "real world" we would not be likely to find proportionate representation of all four combinations, or we might have to wait an inordinately long time for a particular combination— say, quick negative feedback—to occur. Furthermore, the nature of the task, the time of day, and the personality or the manner of the feedback presenter can be kept constant across all of these combinations so that those factors can be excluded as alternative explanations of the results. If the difficulty of the task happens to be of interest, however, that too can be systematically varied in all possible combinations of easy-difficult task, quick-delayed feedback, and positive-negative feedback. The point is that the researcher can arrange at his or her own discretion the combinations of factors judged relevant, and either exclude or hold constant any irrelevant variables.

Third, the researcher knows and can state in unambiguous terms the conditions under which results were obtained. A certain task was used, subjects were drawn from a specified population of known attributes, certain instructions were given, and so on. These statements are part and parcel of experimental findings, for they serve as a baseline from which to assess the generalizability of the findings. Laboratory experiments thus engender a healthy caution in interpreting the limits of our knowledge. Unfortunately, this virtue is often mistaken by the general public as a vice. The layman's typical response to a set of laboratory findings is "Yes, but you can't generalize from that set of conditions to the situation in my factory." True enough, in one sense, but neither can the results of a field study at the launderette, welfare agency, or power plant; more important, in the latter settings we are hard pressed to specify precisely the conditions under which the results were obtained. In the strict sense, we cannot generalize the data obtained in a steel mill to situations in textile mills, or vice versa, any more than we can generalize from the lab to either. Only theory can bridge the gap, and it can do so only to the extent that idiosyncratic features of any setting are known and can be interpreted within a theoretical overview.

It is theory, after all—in the sense that we have defined it earlier in this chapter—that directs experimentation, telling us what is important to vary, what should be excluded, what to hold constant. A number of defining characteristics of organizations can be conceptualized in abstract terms so that they can then be simulated in the lab. For example, if hierarchy is one of the intrinsic attributes of organizations, then a group of seven subjects can be organized into a chief, two lieutenants, and four bottom-line workers. Reward systems, indirect communication, stress, or the interdependence of workers upon one another can all be simulated in the lab if theory suggests that these earmarks of organization are integral to the phenomenon of interest. It is the theory which determines what to include in the lab, not the realism of everyday life.

Some critics argue that in laboratory experiments the subjects are not sufficiently "involved" in what happens. There are, in fact, ways of increasing subject involvement (the interested reader may consult Weick, 1965, for a discussion of involvement-enhancing techniques), but we should remember that much of everyday life is also characterized by passive involvement. The frequent dependence upon college freshmen and sophomores is also cited as a shortcoming of lab studies, but once again only theory can guide us as to whether such subjects are so radically different from others in the general population on the relevant attributes that different subjects should be studied, and if that be the case, then there is no reason why laboratory experiments cannot use supervisors, sales personnel, or night watchmen as subjects.

One limitation of laboratory experiments stems from *professional ethics.* Responsible investigators are prohibited, both by conscience and professional guidelines, from subjecting persons to any conditions which might run the risk of physical or emotional injury. In real organizations, participants are occasionally cheated, humiliated, driven to nervous collapse, or otherwise unmercifully exploited. While a few psychologists have been accused of somewhat amoral conduct in the pursuit of science, all psychologists recognize that there are bounds beyond which they dare not tread in the treatment of subjects. Thus, the seamier side of organizational life, including such occurrences as brutal political infighting, lies beyond the pale of experimental methods.

A second problem often encountered in the use of the laboratory experiment concerns the *reactivity* of the method. When we say that a measurement device is reactive, we mean that the attempt to use it to measure something automatically alters the state of that which we would measure; for example, when you apply a tire pressure gauge to the valve stem, you release air, thus changing the pressure to a level other than that recorded on the gauge. Laboratory experiments are often reactive because the subjects, being human, wonder what the experimenter's hypothesis is and try to adjust their behavior accordingly—to "help" the experimenter prove something, to behave in a light which makes the subjects look "good," or sometimes to obstinately act in a manner exactly opposite of the way they think the experimenter would predict. Experimenters, aware of this potential reactivity, then may exert extreme efforts to disguise the true purpose of the experiment, and sometimes the entire enterprise is a theater of the absurd in which experimenter and subject try to outsmart each other. The reactiviy problem is a threat to the internal validity of findings from some experimental studies, but by no means all; the degree of threat depends upon the particular behavioral phenomenon under scrutiny, the craftsmanship of the experimenter, and the amount of experience the subject has had in previous experiments.

Table 2–6
Laboratory Experiments as a Method of Learning about Organizational Behavior

Forms:	Simulation of organizational variables.
Advantages:	Control; elimination of confounding factors; permits causal inference.
Disadvantages:	Reactivity of subjects; limitations posed by ethics; for some purposes, artificiality of environment; seldon suited to studying long-term effect.

Strategies for Learning about Behavior in Organizations: Concluding Note

In practice, methods of research in organizational behavior seldom fit neatly into any one single class of the methods we have described. Any given study may actually germinate in the solitude of a researcher's reflection on past experiences in organizations, the insights that occur during a casual conversation, or a hunch that comes from reading the newspaper or magazine accounts of current local or national events. The researcher may or may not have a theory to work with at this point—perhaps there is only a vague sense of some forces that are interrelated. The person then becomes a bit more sensitive to future happenings that seem to be drawn like a conceptual magnet to earlier ponderings. Eventually the researcher develops a more clear-cut sense of what these ponderings are all about, and curiosity leads to an exploratory study. This may consist of a series of semistructured interviews with some officials in an organization. The next step may be the distribution of questionnaires to a sample of employees and tabulation of results. All the while, the researcher's thinking becomes a bit more codified. A more grandiose study is designed with more rigorous measures and a longitudinal dimension. Results are published and, if the results are of interest to others, similar studies with some variations in methods, research site, and instruments take place. Eventually every method that we have described comes into service.

The optimal strategy of research, then, is one that combines various methods. Because of the limitations characteristic of each method, we remain skeptical about any findings produced by one method alone. When different methods produce similar findings, we have a lot more confidence in the validity of the results. For example, naturalistic observation, field studies, and laboratory experiments all suggest that a *specific, quantitative goal* has more effect on performance than a *general* ("do your best") goal. On the other hand, while correlational field studies seem to show that certain leadership styles affect performance, laboratory experiments do not seem to confirm this effect. So we have to live with a degree of uncertainty about this relationship.

The reader may readily join in the use of optimal strategies of learning about organizational behavior. Learn from your experience, and learn what you can from others' experience. You may not conduct your own opinion surveys or controlled experiments, but you have access to results of such studies: use such results as a check on your own conclusions. If the results agree, you may justifiably have a great deal of confidence in your knowledge. If the results disagree, by no means should you immediately scrap your accumulated observations, nor should you close your mind to what others have found in field studies or laboratry experiments. The latter may be suspect because of the inherent limitations in them as methods of research; the same qualification should apply to the conclusions drawn from your own less-rigorous methods. Adopt a flexible, tentative view of your knowledge in such a case; see if the discrepancy has any effect on how you see and interpret future experience and revise your previous conclusions. That is what learning is all about.

SUMMARY

A theory is a set of statements describing the relationships among conceptual variables. Both behavioral scientists and administrators are active users of theory; the characteristic differences between their respective theories have to do with level of abstraction, the breadth of the behavioral phenomena under study, and specialization of terminology. Theory serves the functions of organizing and summarizing existing knowledge and guiding the search for new knowledge. Theories are evaluated on the bases of conformity to empirical observations, internal consistency, parsimony, congruence with other well-established theories, utility in directing the search for new knowledge, and intuitive or aesthetic appeal. No theory ever occupies a permanent place in our knowledge; all theories are transient to varying degrees, surviving only until newer and better theories replace them, carrying forward the contributions of their predecessors.

In the study of organizational behavior, a variety of methods of research contributes to the acquisition of knowledge from theory development and theory testing. These methods include—in order of increasing rigor—naturalistic observation, field surveys, correlational field studies using objective indices, field experiments, and laboratory experiments. All of these methods have their unique advantages and disadvantages, with the result that findings from studies using any single method must be qualified to take methodological imperfections into account. Our confidence in the validity of an assertion about organizational behavior is greatest when it is supported by inquiries using a host of different methods.

CONCEPTS TO REMEMBER

percept

concept

construct

norm of correspondence

norm of coherence

principle of parsimony

norm of pragmatism

operational definition

naturalistic observation

case study

field survey research

social desirability in response set

correlational field studies

longitudinal field study

statistical significance

field experiment

laboratory experiment

reactivity

QUESTIONS FOR DISCUSSION

1. "Theory" is sometimes contrasted with "fact." To what extent is this a valid distinction? To what extent is it an oversimplification?

2. In mystery novels and crime movies, a detective is said to have a theory concerning "who done it." Is this a correct use of the term *theory*? Why or why not?

3. What properties of a theory about some organizationally relevant phenomenon (for example, worker motivation) would be likely to determine its acceptability to practicing managers?

4. What does it mean to say that a "theory has been proved"? Is such a statement misleading? If so, how could it be best restated?

5. Suppose that you have a theory which says that "people are more effectively motivated by love than by fear or hate." What would be the qualifications essential to any conclusions drawn from a study of this theory using (a) naturalistic observation? (b) interviews or questionnaires? (c) field experiments? (d) laboratory experiments?

6. What is a more "rigorous" method of research not necessarily a better one simply because of its rigor?

CASE

Max Ritter again leafed through the tables and charts which summarized the data from the company's opinion survey. Max, as assistant director of personnel and employee relations, felt a sense of personal identification with the survey. He had long been critical of the way his department made seat-of-the-pants decisions about employee programs. One of the convictions he carried away with his MBA degree was that corporations, and especially personnel departments, need to be a lot more systematic in the collection of data as a basis for formulating employee policies. More or less as a result of his persistent urging, the company had agreed to a comprehensive employee opinion audit, designed and conducted by two of Max's former professors from Midstate University's School of Business Administration.

As he got up from his desk to walk to the office of his boss, Jack Kelvin (head of the department), Max placed markers in the two sections that he especially wanted to show Jack. One of the sections concerned comparisons of job satisfaction by different age groups, with the most satisfied groups in the 35–40- (a mean of 5.7 on a 7-point scale) and 41–50- (mean of 5.9) year-old groups. The least satisfied were those in their 20s (mean of 5.2)

"Jack, could you take a look at some of these analyses? I think they're pretty revealing about some of the things we do here," said Max as he handed Jack the report.

Jack looked over the figures for a few minutes, sat back in his chair, and reached for his pipe.

"Well, maybe. What exactly do you have in mind, Max?"

"Actually, the overall emphasis of our programs—pay, promotions, benefits, you name it. They all seem to be slanted toward seniority and tenure more than anything else. We do a good job for the older, maybe more experienced people, but I think we slight our younger employees. An you know very well that we've lost several of our good younger prospects in the last few months."

Jack—whom Max respected as an experienced personnel man, who had no formal training in personnel but wound up there after several years in sales—puffed on his freshly lit pipe for a few minutes before answering.

"Well, sure we've lost some of the younger ones. But I don't recall them leaving with any real grievances. Either they had opportunities they couldn't pass up, or they felt they weren't cut out for this kind of business. You're always going to have more turnover among younger people. That's pretty much in the nature of things." Jack reached to point an index finger at the chart on the open page. "Anyway, is there really all that much difference in a 5.2 and a 5.7? Both of those figures look pretty good to me."

Max reached over the corner of the desk to thumb back a few pages. "Look, it's the consistency of the difference that really tells the story. Not just overall attitudes, but feelings about supervision, working conditions, vacation policy, even the work itself. What it all seems to add up to is that we reward loyalty and experience more than we do qualifications, ability, and quality and quantity of work."

Jack leaned back and crossed his arms. "Well, I think loyalty's worth something, but aside from that I think you're making too much of some of these things. Maybe there's something in what you're saying, I just don't hear too much around here about any discontent among younger employees. They seem to produce as well as the others, so they can't be too upset."

Questions

Assess the appropriateness of Max's conclusions and Jack's counterarguments. Should Max press further for changes in personnel policies? Why or why not? Suppose the consultants were asked to comment on what to do as a follow-up on the survey findings—what do you think their recommendations would probably be? In general, what can organizational officials do when different methods of observation suggest conflicting courses of action?

REFERENCES

Christenson, C. V. *Kinsey: A biography.* Bloomington: Indiana University Press, 1971.

Cummings, L. L. & Scott, W. E. Jr., (Eds.). *Readings in organizational behavior and human performance.* Homewood, Ill.: Irwin-Dorsey, 1969.

Dalton, M. *Men who manage.* New York: John Wiley & Sons, 1959.

Fleishman, E. A. Twenty years of consideration and structure. In E. A. Fleishman & J. G. Hunt (Eds.), *Current developments in the study of leadership.* Carbondale: Southern Illinois University Press, 1973.

Gouldner, A. W. *Patterns of industrial bureaucracy.* Glencoe, Ill.: Free Press, 1954.

Granick, D. *The red executive.* New York: Anchor Books, Doubleday, 1961.

Hersey, P., & Blanchard, K. H. *Management of organizational behavior.* Englewood cliffs, N.J.: Prentice-Hall, 1969.

Jenkins, H. M., & Ward, W. C. Judgment of contingency between responses and outcomes. *Psychological Monographs: General and Applied,* 1965, 79(1, Whole No. 594).

Kaplan, A *The conduct of inquiry.* San Francisco: Chandler, 1964.

Kinsey, A. C., Pomeroy, W. B., & Martin, C. E. *Sexual behavior in the human male.* Philadelphia: Suanders, 1949.

Kissinger, H. *The White House years.* Boston: Little, Brown, 1979.

Leavitt, H. J. *Managerial psychology* (4th ed.). Chicago: University of Chicago Press, 1978.

Morse, N., & Reimer, E. The experimental change of a major organizational variable. *Journal of Abnormal and Social Psychology,* 1956, 52, 120–129.

Muczyk, J. P. A controlled field experiment measuring the impact of MBO on performance data. Unpublished paper, Cleveland State University, 1976.

Opsahl, R. L., & Dunnette, M. D.   The role of financial compensation in industrial motivation. *Psychological Bulletin,* 1966, *66*(2), 94–118.

Schachter, S.   Deviation, rejection, and communication. *Journal of Abnormal and Social Psychology,* 1951, *46,* 190–207.

Schwab, D. P., & Cummings, L. L.   A theoretical analysis of the impact of task scope on employee performance. *Academy of Management Review,* 1976, *1*(2), 36–46.

Shaw, M. E., & Costanzo, P. R.   *Theories of social psychology.* New York: McGraw-Hill, 1970.

Sloan, A. P., Jr.   *My years with General Motors.* New York: MacFadden Books, Doubleday, 1965.

Weick, K. E.   Laboratory experimentation with organizations. In J. G. March (Ed.), *Handbook of organizations.* Chicago: Rand McNally, 1965.

Weick, K. E.   *The social psychology of organizing.* Reading, Mass.: Addison-Wesley, 1969.

Zajonc, R. B.   The concepts of balance, congruity, and dissonance. *Public Opinion Quarterly,* 1960, *24,* 280–296.

3

Management and the Learning Process:

Using Reinforcement to Shape Behavior

How is behavior acquired, strengthened, maintained, and changed?

How can managers design effective environments for strengthening desired behavior in organizations?

Traditionally management has been defined as the process of getting things done through other people. The succinctness of this definition is misleading in that, though it is easy to say *what* a manager does, it is difficult to describe the determinants of behavior—that is, to tell *how* the behavior of the manager influences the behavior of the employee in such a way that the latter willingly accomplishes the desired task. Human behavior in organizational settings has always been a phenomenon of interest and concern. However, only in recent years have social scientists made a concerted effort to describe the principles of reinforcement and their implications for the theory and practice of management. Traditional management methods reinforce employee behavior, but in a less systematic way, and generally without the benefit of well-developed theory.

Organizational leaders must resort to environmental changes as a means of influencing behavior. Reinforcement principles are the most useful method in this regard because they indicate to leaders how they might proceed in designing or modifying the work environment in order to effect specific changes in behavior. A reinforcement approach to management does not consist of a "bag of tricks" to be applied indiscriminately for the purpose of coercing unwilling people. Unfortunately, many people who think of reinforcement think of manipulation and punitive control over employees. Much more knowledge of the positive aspects of conditioning as applied to worker performance is available today, which should dispel these false notions.

The purpose of this chapter is to describe the determinants of behavior from the standpoint of reinforcement theory, and to describe how the management of the *contingencies of reinforcement* in organizational settings is a vital key to being a successful manager. We hope that this effort will enable the manager to understand how his or her behavior affects the behavior of subordinates and to see that, in most cases, the failure or success of the worker is in part a direct function of the manager's own behavior. Since a large portion of the manager's time is spent in the process of modifying behavior patterns and shaping them so that they will be more goal oriented, it is only natural to begin this chapter by describing the processes and principles that govern behavior.

LEARNING AS A PREREQUISITE FOR BEHAVIOR

Learning is such a common phenomenon that we tend to overlook its occurrence. Nevertheless, a major premise of reinforcement theory

Note: Portions of the material presented in this chapter were first published by the junior author in H. L. Tosi and W. C. Hamner, *Organizational Behavior and Management,* St. Clair Press, 1974. Reprinted here by permission of the publisher.

is that all behavior is learned. For example, a worker's skill, a supervisor's attitude, and a secretary's manners are all learned.

There seems to be general agreement among social scientists that learning can be defined as *a relatively permanent change in behavior potentiality that results from reinforced practice or experience.* Note that this definition states that there is change in behavior *potentiality* and not necessarily in behavior itself. The reason for this distinction rests on the fact that we can observe other people respond to their environment, see the consequences which accrue to them, and be vicariously conditioned. For example, a boy can watch his older sister burn her hand on a hot stove and learn that pain is the result of touching a hot stove. This definition therefore allows us to account for "no-trial" learning. Bandura (1969) describes this as imitative learning and says that while behavior can be *acquired* by observing, reading, or other vicarious methods, *"performance* of observationally learned responses will depend to a great extent upon the nature of the reinforcing consequences to the model or to the observer" (p. 128).

Luthans (1973, p. 362) says that we need to consider the following points when we define the learning process:

1. Learning involves a change, though not necessarily an improvement, in behavior. Learning generally has the connotation of improved performance, but under this definition bad habits, prejudices, stereotypes, and work restrictions are learned.
2. The change in behavior must be relatively permanent in order to be considered learning. This qualification rules out behavioral changes resulting from fatigue or temporary adaptations as learning.
3. Some form of practice or experience is necessary for learning to occur.
4. Finally it should be stressed that practice or experience must be reinforced in order for learning to occur. If reinforcement does not accompany the practice or experience, the behavior will eventually disappear.

From this discussion, we can conclude that learning is the acquisition of knowledge and that performance is the translation of knowledge into practice. The primary effect of reinforcement is to strengthen and intensify certain aspects of ensuing behavior. Behavior that has developed an intricate, complex pattern can be understood and accounted for only in terms of the history of the reinforcement of that behavior. Reinforcement generates a reproducible behavior process in time. A response occurs and is followed by a reinforcer, and further responses occur. When a response is reinforced it subsequently occurs more frequently than before it was reinforced. Reinforcement may be assumed to have a characteristic and reproducible

effect on a particular behavior, and usually it will enhance and intensify that behavior (Skinner, 1953).

TWO BASIC LEARNING PROCESSES

Before discussing in any detail exactly how the *general laws* or
principles of reinforcement can be used to predict and influence behavior, we must differentiate between two types of behavior. One
type is known as *voluntary* or *operant* behavior, and the other is
known as *reflex* or *respondent* behavior. Respondent behavior takes
in all responses of human beings that are *elicited* by special stimulus
changes in the environment. For example, when a person turns a light
on in a dark room (stimulus change), the pupils of his eyes contract
(respondent behavior).

Operant behavior includes an even greater amount of human activity. It takes in all the responses of a person that may at some time be
said to have an effect upon or to do something to the person's outside
world. Operant behavior *operates* on this world either directly or indirectly. For example, when a person presses the up button at the
elevator entrance to "call" the elevator, he or she is operating on the
environment.

The process of learning or acquiring reflex behavior is different
from the process of learning or acquiring voluntary behavior. The two
basic and distinct learning processes are known as classical conditioning and operant conditioning. It is from studying these two learning
processes that much of our knowledge of individual behavior has
emerged.

Classical Conditioning

Classical conditioning (sometimes called *respondent conditioning*)
is a process in which a reflex or emotional response comes under the
control of a new stimulus. This happens when the new stimulus is
associated with, or immediately precedes, the stimulus which already
elicits the reflex.

This form of learning was first studied by the Russian physiologist
Ivan Pavlov (1902). Pavlov originally was interested in research on
digestive processes, which he studied experimentally with laboratory
animals such as dogs. He knew, of course, that when food was placed
in an animal's mouth, certian digestive responses such as salivation
were triggered. He also had noticed, as undoubtedly had many dog
owners, that dogs even began to salivate at the sight of the food, or at
the recognition of a person bringing a container which characteristically contained the food. Pavlov reasoned that the sight of the food or
the container, because such stimuli immediately preceded the con-

tact of the food in the mouth, acquired some sort of neural connection with the response of salivating. He reasoned further that, if this neural connection were due solely to the temporal association of these events, then any stimulus—if suitably paired with the food—ought to have the potential for evoking the salivation response. His subsequent studies strongly supported this notion. When the food was preceded several times by a ringing bell, eventually the bell alone, even without the food, produced a salivation response (though not as strong a response, as measured by the volume of saliva produced). This conditioned response would weaken if the food were not occasionally reintroduced, or if the tone of the bell differed considerably from that originally paired with the food. But even if the conditioned response of salivating to the bell were extinguished, it could be quickly restablished by pairing it again with the food.

The process of classical or respondent conditioning may be diagrammed as:

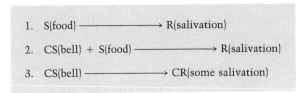

First, some *stimulus* (S) already evokes a reflex or involuntary *response* (R). Second, this stimulus is characteristically associated with or preceded by some new stimulus for some period of time. At some point, the new or *conditioned stimulus* (CS) evokes a *conditioned response* (CR) which is similar to, or some portion of, the original response.

This process occurs among human beings, too. For example, if a bright flashlight shines directly into your eyes, the pupils contract in a reflexive fashion. If someone consistently sounded a buzzer immediately before the light came on, and did this a number of times, soon the buzzer alone would cause some degree of pupillary contraction.

For our purposes, however, the major relevance of classical conditioning lies in its ability to account for certain emotional responses. An emotional response, like a reflex, is involuntary. Often, of course, emotional responses are covert and subtle, although they can be detected with appropriately sensitive instruments. Also, these emotional responses can represent the core component around which attitudes and attitude systems develop, with corresponding systems of beliefs.

Consider, for example, your emotional responses toward certain people. Of course, often you like someone because he or she directly benefits you in some way; his or her behavior actually causes desired events to occur. Conversely, you may dislike or fear someone whose behavior produces harm or discomfort. But if you think about it, you can identify people you like *because their presence was associated with some event(s) that made you feel good.* If you were having coffee with someone when the phone rang and a university official informed you that you had won a $5,000 scholarship, chances are you would feel an enhanced warmth toward your coffee-sipping companion. Your friend, of course, had nothing to do with your attaining the scholarship, but your emotional response to the blessed event "spread" to the other salient objects and persons associated with the context of the event.

You can now easily understand why some people in organizations become objects of fear or dislike. They do not actually cause or produce the events that make us angry or unhappy, but their presence—because of their job duties—is associated typically and closely with such events, in both time and place. The officials whose duty it is to inform us that we have overrun our budgets, that we have to go back and do something over, that we have a rush job to attend to, and so on, do not win popularity contests.

Much of the content of media advertising represents implicitly an attempt to exploit this process. The coffee distributor tries to juxtapose his brand with the warm coziness of a cabin and crackling fireplace in the Rockies; the orange juice promoter tries to stamp in your memory an association between the juice and sunshine.

You will note that classical conditioning is essentially a passive form of learning. The organism does not really "do" anything; things happen and certain involuntary processes operate. In some sense, it is a "gut" form of learning. Because of it, we form likes, fears, and dislikes that sometimes hardly seem rational but which nonetheless can be persistent and powerful influences. We shall explore these implications further in Chapter 6 when we discuss attitudes.

Operant Conditioning

Classical conditioning affects behavior that is largely under the control of the autonomic nervous system and is reflexive. *Operant conditioning,* on the other hand, pertains to voluntary responses. Operant conditioning, also called *instrumental conditioning,* occurs as we experience the consequences of our behavior.

The process of operant conditioning, in its simplest form, may be illustrated as below:

$$S^D \longrightarrow R \longrightarrow S^R$$

First, we have the S^D. This simply represents the stimulus situation in which the organism finds itself. It can be defined by the time, the place, the salient objects or people in the place, even a condition of the organism itself, or all of these things taken together. The S^D does not, however, trigger an involuntary response, as the stimulus did in classical conditioning; it simply provides an occasion, or type of occasion, in which the organism may respond.

The R is the response of the organism. As we have noted above, this usually implies a voluntary response—i.e., a response under the control of the skeletal-muscular system. The R may be a very simple one or a very extended, complex sample of behavior.

The S^R stands for the consequence(s) that follow the behavior. If the consequence has the effect of making that behavior more likely to occur in the future in that type of situation, we call it a *reinforcer* or *reinforcing stimulus* (which is what the S^R actually stands for). Ordinarily we call such stimuli *rewards*, since we infer that the reinforcing stimulus must be something the organism wanted, such as food, attention, or money. But whether the consequence would ordinarily be called a reward or not, it is *technically a reinforcer only if it has the effect of increasing the likelihood of the response in that stimulus setting.* A consequence is an aversive stimulus (S^{av}) if it has the effect of reducing the probability of a response in a given setting.

Human beings find at an early age that no one single response is invariably reinforced. A response that is reinforced in some contexts will go unreinforced (or even punished) in other situations. As I sit here in my study, I look out at the mailbox in front of my home. I put a stamped letter there early this morning and raised the red metal flag. As long as that red flag remains up, I know the mailman has not come, and if I walk out to look for the incoming mail, my behavior will go unreinforced. Only when I see the metal flag lowered is there any chance that my walking out there will be rewarded by a magazine or letter from a friend. The lowered red flag, then, acts as a disciminative stimulus (S^D): it defines the occasion on which a response is more likely to be reinforced. This is why we used the notation S^D to designate the stimulus situation. Operant behavior comes under the control of stimulus cues that signal the relative probability that a given response will be reinforced.

The interrelationships among the (1) *stimulus* setting, (2) *response* or performance, and (3) consequences or *reinforcements* are known as the *contingencies of reinforcement.* Skinner (1969) says, "The class of responses upon which a reinforcer is *contingent* is called an operant, to suggest the action on the environment followed by reinforcements" (p. 7). Operant conditioning presupposes that human beings explore their environment and act upon it. This behavior, randomly emitted at first, can be constructed as an operant by making a reinforcement contingent on a response. Any stimulus present when an operant is reinforced acquires control in the sense that the rate of response for that individual will be higher when it is present. "Such a stimulus does not act as a *goad*; it does not elicit the response [as was the case in the classical conditioning of reflex behavior] in the sense of forcing it to occur. It is simply an essential aspect of the occasion upon which response is made and reinforced" (Skinner, 1969, p. 7).

Therefore, an adequate formulation of the interaction between an individual and his or her environment must always specify three things: (1) the occasion upon which a response occurs, (2) the response itself, and (3) the reinforcing consequences. Skinner holds that the consequences determine the likelihood that a given operant will be performed in the future. Thus, in order to change behavior, the consequences of the behavior must be changed—that is, the contingencies (the ways in which the consequences are related to the behavior) must be rearranged. For Skinner, the behavior generated by a given set of contingencies can be accounted for without appealing to hypothetical inner states (for example, awareness or expectancies). "If a conspicuous stimulus does not have an effect, it is not because the organism has not attended to it or because some central gatekeeper has screened it out, but because the stimulus plays no important role in the prevailing contingencies" (Skinner, 1969, p. 8).

ARRANGEMENT OF THE CONTINGENCIES OF REINFORCEMENT

In order to *understand* and *interpret* behavior, we must look at the interrelationship among the components of the contingencies of behavior. If one expects to influence behavior, he or she must also be able to manipulate the consequences of the behavior. Haire (1964) reports the importance of being able to manipulate the consequences when he says:

> Indeed, whether he is conscious of it or not, the superior is bound to be constantly shaping the behavior of his subordinates by the way in which he utilizes the rewards that are at his disposal, and he will inevitably modify the behavior patterns of his work group thereby. For this reason, it is important to see as clearly as possible what is going on, so that the changes can be planned and chosen in advance, rather than simply accepted after the fact.

After appropriate reinforcers that have sufficient incentive value to maintain stable responsiveness have been chosen, the contingencies between specific performances and reinforcing stimuli must be arranged. Employers intuitively use rewards in their attempts to modify and influence behavior, but their efforts often produce limited results

because the rewards are used improperly, inconsistently, or ineffi-
ciently. In many instances considerable rewards are bestowed upon
workers, but these rewards are not made conditional or contingent on
the behavior the manager wishes to promote. Also, "long delays often
intervene between the occurrence of the desired behavior and its intended consequences; special privileges, activities, and rewards are
generally furnished according to fixed time schedules rather than performance requirements; and in many cases, positive reinforcers are
inadvertently made contingent upon the wrong type of behavior"
(Bandura, 1969, pp. 229–230).

One of the primary reasons that managers fail to "motivate" workers to perform in the desired manner is a lack of understanding of the
power of the contingencies of reinforcement over the employee and
of the manager's role in arranging those contingencies. The laws or
principles for arranging the contingencies are not hard to understand,
and if students of behavior grasp them firmly, these laws are powerful
tools which can be used to increase supervisory effectiveness.

As stated previously, operant conditioning is the process by which
behavior is modified by manipulation of the contingencies of the behavior. To understand how this works, we will first look at various
types (arrangements) of contingencies, and then at various *schedules*
of the contingencies available. There are four basic ways of arranging
the contingencies available to the manager—*positive reinforcement,
avoidance learning, extinction,* and *punishment.* The differences
among these types of contingencies depend on the consequence
which results from the behavioral act. Positive reinforcement and
avoidance learning are methods of strengthening *desired* behavior,
and extinction and punishment are methods of weakening *undesired*
behavior.

Positive Reinforcement

"A positive reinforcer is a stimulus which, when added to a situation, strengthens the probability of an operant response" (Skinner,
1953, p. 73). The reason it strengthens the response is explained by
Thorndike's (1911) Law of Effect. This law simply states that behavior which appears to lead to a positive consequence tends to be repeated, whereas behavior which appears to lead to a negative consequence tends not to be repeated. A positive consequence is often
called a reward and is described as pleasant.

Reinforcers, either positive or negative, are classified as either (1)
unconditioned or primary reinforcers or (2) conditioned or secondary
reinforcers. Primary reinforcers, such as food, water, and sex, are of
biological importance since they are innately rewarding and have effects which are independent of past experiences. Secondary reinfor-

cers, such as job advancement, praise, recognition, and money, derive their effects from a consistent pairing with other reinforcers (that is, they are conditioned). Secondary reinforcement, therefore, depends on the individual and his or her past reinforcement history. What is rewarding to one person may not be rewarding to another. Managers should look for a reward system which has maximal reinforcing consequences to the group he or she is supervising. (See Question 1 at the end of this chapter for an example of how individual differences affect perceptions of rewards.)

Behavior theorists also find it useful to think of positive reinforcers as *noncontrived* or *contrived.* Noncontrived reinforcers are the naturally occurring reinforcers that follow certain behaviors. For example, if you competently play a guitar by the correct use of chords and strumming techniques, the esthetically pleasing sounds which emanate represent noncontrived reinforcement for your actions. The correct sounds are the naturally produced consequences of what you did with your fingers and hands. The sight of a neat bedroom, office, or workplace reinforces in a noncontrived fashion that behaviors that led up to that product—making the bed, arranging books and correspondence in the appropriate patterns, hanging your clothes, sweeping up debris.

Contrived reinforcers are those which do not follow behavior in the naturally occurring scheme of things but are introduced by other agents—such as parents, teachers, friends, superiors—to strengthen certain behaviors which otherwise might not be reinforced. Pay, for example, acts as a contrived reinforcer for any behavior on which it is contingent. We know of no activity which, in the natural order of things, produces money as its logical result. Other tokens, such as gold stars or bonus points, similarly act as contrived reinforcers.

The distinction between a contrived and noncontrived reinforcer can become rather arbitrary. Suppose you perform a task in a very competent fashion and others observing you express their admiration, respect, or encouragement. Is their applause a contrived or noncontrived reinforcement? You could argue that it is contrived if they were consciously trying to induce you to continue to perform as you have done. But you could also insist that in the social world, the positive reactions of other people to a task competently performed are "natural." Thus, the contrived-noncontrived distinction may depend not so much on the specific reactions of others but the intent (or lack thereof). More generally, we may view reinforcers on a continuum, some being obviously contrived, some clearly natural or noncontrived, others somewhat natural but with varying degrees of contrivance.

Many organizational psychologists see some advantage in classifying reinforcers (or rewards) as *intrinsic* or *extrinsic.* The distinction between the two bears some resemblance to that between contrived and noncontrived reinforcers, although the correspondence is only a rough one. Intrinsic reinforcers refer to the covert, internal psychological states, or feelings, that are pleasurably experienced following some response. An example might be the feeling of pride or ego satisfaction derived from the competent execution of some skill. Another illustration would be the reassurance in your own mind that you have "done your duty" following the completion of a set of chores. Some would say that intrinsic rewards represent instances in which the "individual reinforces himself or herself"—that is, the reinforcement comes under the control of the person.

(We should note that a strict operant viewpoint is cautious about assigning a significant role to such mental states. This is not to deny that they exist or to say that people don't consider them important but rather reflects the concern that we may slip into the habit of viewing such states as *causes* instead of effects of the behavior—effects that are coincidental with other effects that can be observed.)

Extrinsic rewards, on the other hand, come from "the outside," rather than inside the person. In practice, this usually means rewards directly or indirectly mediated by other people. Thus, when others use money, praise, tangible gifts, or favors to reward us, they use extrinsic rewards to influence our behavior.

ARE NONCONTRIVED/INTRINSIC REINFORCERS "SUPERIOR" TO CONTRIVED/EXTRINSIC REINFORCERS?

In education as well as in work organizations, one frequently hears the argument that teachers, supervisors, even parents, should generally avoid the use of "artificial" rewards. Students should study because of the intrinsic value and enrichment of what they learn and not for grades or stars; people should pursue activities for their own sake and not to receive the approval of others; employees should work productively because of their natural involvement in the task and not in order to receive bonus pay or fringe benefits. Intrinsic rewards are felt to be "better"—either more effective or more consistent with the values of individual freedom and growth.

Intrinsic rewards are not necessarily more effective than extrinsic rewards, *if* the criterion of effectiveness is measured strength and rate of response and if other aspects of reinforcement (such as timing and scheduling) are held constant. Whether intrinsic rewards are more compatible with humanistic values is an ideological issue we shall not pursue here. But beyond these considerations there is a strong case to be made for the role of extrinsic and/or contrived reinforcers.

Consider again the example of playing a musical instrument. When you first pick it up you will get little or no intrinsic reward. You will simply not have the ability to produce any noncontrived reinforcement from the attempt to play it. In the absence of some artificial (i.e., contrived) reinforcement, the instrument loses its appeal altogether. Your behavior is extinguished. But if a parent rewards you for conscientious practice, and a teacher congratulates you for correct placement of the fingers and hitting individual notes, this will sustain your practice. Soon enough, hearing the simple musical arrangements produced by your own fingers augments the contrived rewards dispensed by others. With continued practice, eventually the delicacy and intricacy of the music you can produce will make contrived reinforcers unnecessary. The point is that artificial incentives often are needed in the early stages of acquiring a skill until the behavior is competent to generate its own rewards.

Another reason for contrived reinforcers derives from the initial *costs* of certain desired behaviors. The noncontrived reinforcement from making your bed, for example, may not be enough to overcome the costs in time and effort of doing it. But if someone else—your mother or roommate—rewards you (verbally or by granting certain privileges), the combination of the contrived and noncontrived reinforcement may sustain your bed-making routine. If this continues, you may well become efficient enough at making the bed so that it takes only a fraction of the original time and effort. At this point, the appearance of neatness alone may suffice to maintain this behavior.

Finally, we should note that consequences which *immediately* follow behavior generally exert more influence on that behavior than consequences farther removed in time. This is especially the case when a response sequence is being learned or acquired. With many constructive behaviors, the noncontrived reinforcements—the naturally occurring benefits of the behavior—are not realized immediately or may occur only very infrequently. Coaches try to instill in young baseball players the habit of running hard to first base even on infield pop-ups and routine ground balls. But the naturally occurring benefits of doing this—reaching first base on infield errors—may not occur soon enough or often enough to strengthen the habits of hustling. Thus, like anyone who seeks to promote constructive habits in others, coaches have to use extrinsic reinforcers (typically verbal or symbolic) to strengthen the behavior. Once the habit acquires reasonable strength, the individual often learns to use covert self-reinforcement to "bridge the gap" between the behavior and the noncontrived reinforcement.

Managerial Use of Positive Reinforcement

The *first step* in the successful application of reinforcement procedures is to select reinforcers that are sufficiently powerful and durable to maintain and strengthen the behavior. We will defer until Chapter 8 a discussion of how to select reinforcers. Suffice it to say here that managers are clearly capable of observing what consequences tend to strengthen behavior. Just to cite an example, timely feedback in almost any form, especially when positive and precise, has a potential that is seldom fully realized in work settings. Various kinds of commodities or consumables—such as coffee, soft drinks, or candy—can be used, as well as tokens (such as Green Stamps) that can later be exchanged for privileges or merchandise. These are very "unnatural," but they may be useful at the outset. The most conspicuous reinforcer in work organizations is, of course, pay.

The *second step* is to design the contingencies in such a way that the reinforcing events are made contingent upon the desired behavior. This is the rule of reinforcement which is most often violated. Rewards must result from performance, and the greater the degree of performance by an employee, the greater should be the reward. Money as a reinforcer will be discussed later, but it should be noted that money is not the only reward available. As a matter of fact, for unionized employees the supervisor has virtually no way to tie money to performance. Nevertheless, other forms of rewards, such as recognition, promotion, and job assignments, can be made contingent on good performance. Unless a manager is willing to discriminate among employees on the basis of their level of performance, the effectiveness of his or her power over the employee is nil.

The arrangement of positive reinforcement contingencies can be pictured as follows:

$$\text{Stimulus} \rightarrow \text{Desired response} \rightarrow \text{Positive consequences}$$
$$(S^D \rightarrow R \rightarrow S^R)$$

The stimulus is the work environment which leads to a response (some level of performance). If this response leads to positive consequences, then the probability of the responses being emitted again increases. Now, if the response is undesired, then the supervisor is conditioning or teaching the employee that undesired behavior will lead to a desired reward. It is therefore important that the reward administered be equal to the performance input of the employee. Homans (1961) labels this the Rule of Distributive Justice and states that this reciprocal norm applies in both formal (work) and informal (friendship) relationships. In other words, the employee *exchanges* his or her services for the rewards of the organization. In order to maintain desired performance, it is important that the manager design the reward system so that the level of reward administered is proportionately contingent on the level of performance emitted.

The *third step* is to design the contingencies in such a way that a reliable procedure for eliciting or inducing the desired response patterns is established. If the desired response patterns rarely occur, there will be few opportunities to influence the desired behavior through contingent management. If the behavior that a manager wishes to strengthen is already present, and occurs with some frequency, then contingent applications of incentives can, from the outset, increase and maintain the desired performance patterns at a high level. However, if the criterion for reinforcement is initially set too high, most, if not all, of the person's responses will go unrewarded, so that his or her efforts are gradually extinguished.

The nature of the learning process is such that the new response patterns can be easily established. The principle of operant conditioning says that an operant followed by a positive reinforcement is more likely to occur under *similar* conditions in the future. Through the process of *generalization*, the more nearly alike the new situation or stimulus is to the original one, the more likely is the old behavior to be emitted in the new environment. For example, if you contract with some electricians to rewire your house, they are able to accomplish the task because they bring with them enough old behavioral patterns that can be generalized to this unfamiliar but similar stimulus setting (the house). They have learned through past reinforcement history that, when in a new environment, one way to speed up the correct behavior needed to get rewarded is to generalize from similar settings with which they have had experience. Perhaps one reason an employer wants a person with work experience is that there is a greater probability that such a person will emit the correct behavior, and thus the job of managing the person is simplified.

Just as generalization is the ability to react to similarities in the environment, *discrimination* is the ability to react to differences in a new environmental setting. Usually when an employee moves from one environment (a job, a city, an office) to another, he or she finds that only certain dimensions of the stimulus conditions change. Although not all of the responses of the employee in this new setting will be correct, by skilled use of the procedures of reinforcement, we can bring about the more precise type of stimulus control called discrimination. When we purchase a new car, we do not have to relearn how to drive a car (generalizable stimulus). Instead we only need to learn the differences between the new car and the old car so that we can respond to those differences in order to get reinforced. This procedure is called *discrimination training*.

The development of effective discriminative repertoires is important for dealing with many different people on interpersonal bases. Effective training techniques will allow the supervisor to develop the necessary discriminative repertoires in new employees.

Using the principles of generalization and discrimination in a well-designed training program allows the manager to accomplish the third goal of eliciting or inducing the desired response patterns. Training is a method of *shaping* desired behavior so that it can be conditioned to come under the control of the reinforcement stimuli. Shaping behavior is necessary when the response to be learned is not currently in the individual's repertoire and when it is a fairly complex behavior. In shaping, we teach a desired response by reinforcing the series of successive steps which lead to the final response. This method is essentially the one your teacher or parents used when they first taught you to drive. You were first taught how to adjust the seat and mirror, fasten the seat belt, turn on the lights and windshield wipers, and then how to start the engine. When you successfully completed each stage you were positively reinforced by some comment. You were then allowed to practice driving on back roads and in empty lots. By focusing on one aspect at a time, and reinforcing proper responses, your teacher was able to shape your driving behavior until you reached the final stage of being able to drive. After your behavior was shaped, driving other cars or driving in new territories was accomplished successfully by the processes of generalization and discrimination. This same process is used with a management trainee who is rotated from department to department for a period of time until he or she has "learned the ropes." After managerial behavior has been minimally shaped, the trainee is transferred to a managerial position where, using the principles of generalization and discrimination, he or she is able to adjust to the contingencies of the work environment.

Avoidance Learning

The second type of contingency arrangement available to the manager is called escape learning or avoidance learning. Like positive reinforcement, this is a method of strengthening desired behavior. A contingency arrangement in which an individual's performance can terminate an already aversive stimulus is called *escape learning.* When an individual's behavior can prevent the onset of a stimulus, the procedure is called *avoidance learning.* In both cases, the result is the development and maintenance of the desired operant behavior.

An example of this kind of control can easily be found in a work environment. Punctuality of employees is often maintained by avoidance learning. The aversive stimulus is criticism by the shop steward or the office manager for being late. In order to avoid criticism the employees make a special effort to come to work on time. Examples of escape behavior can also be found in industry. An employee's home life is so aversive that she leaves for work early in order to escape. A supervisor begins criticizing a worker for "goofing off." The worker starts working to *escape* the criticism of the supervisor and continues working in order to avoid the employer's criticism.

The arrangement of an escape reinforcement contingency can be diagrammed as follows:

$$\text{Aversive stimulus} \rightarrow \text{Desired response} \rightarrow \text{Removal of noxious stimulus}$$
$$(S^{av} \rightarrow R \nrightarrow S^{av})$$

The distinction between strengthening behavior by means of positive reinforcement techniques and by means of avoidance learning techniques should be noted carefully. In one case the individual works hard to gain the consequences from the environment which result from good work, and in the other case the individual works hard to avoid the aversive aspects of the environment itself. In both cases the same behavior is strengthened.

Extinction

While positive reinforcement and avoidance learning techniques can be used by managers to strengthen desired behavior, extinction and punishment techniques are methods available to managers for reducing undesired behavior. When positive reinforcement for a learned or previously conditioned response is withheld, individuals will continue to exhibit that behavior for an extended period of time. Under repeated nonreinforcement, the behavior decreases and eventually disappears. This decline in response rate as a result of nonrewarded repetition of a task is called *extinction*.

The diagram of the extinction process can be shown as follows:

1. Stimulus $\rightarrow$ Response $\rightarrow$ Positive consequences
   $(S^D \rightarrow R \rightarrow S^R$

2. Stimulus $\rightarrow$ Response $\rightarrow$ Withholding of positive consequences
   $(S^D \rightarrow R \nrightarrow S^R)$

3. Stimulus $\rightarrow$ Withholding of response
   $(S^D \nrightarrow R)$

The behavior was previously reinforced because *(a)* it was desired or *(b)* poor reinforcement practices were used. To extinguish this behavior in a naturally recurring situation, response paterns sustained by positive reinforcement (stage 1) are frequently eliminated (stage 3) by discontinuing the rewards (stage 2) that ordinarily produce the behavior. This method, when combined with a positive reinforcement method, is the procedure of behavior modification recommended by Skinner (1953). It leads to the least negative side effects, and when the two methods are used together, the employee can get the rewards he or she desires, and the organization can eliminate the undesired behavior.

Punishment

A second method of reducing the frequency of undesired behavior is punishment. Because of the complexity and controversy surrounding punishment, we have devoted an entire chapter (Chapter 4) to this topic.

RULES FOR USING OPERANT CONDITIONING TECHNIQUES

Several rules concerning the arrangement of the contingencies of reinforcement should be discussed. Although these rules have "commonsense" appeal, the research findings indicate that the rules are often violated by managers when they design their control systems.

Rule 1. Don't reward all people the same. In other words, differentiate employees' rewards on the basis of performance as compared to some defined objective or standard. We know that people compare their performance to their peers' performance to determine how well they are doing and that they compare their rewards to the rewards of their peers in order to determine how to evaluate their rewards. Although some managers seem to think that the fairest system of compensation is one in which everyone in the same job classification gets the same pay, employees want differentiation so that they know their importance to the organization. It can be argued that managers who reward all people the same are encouraging only average performance at best. The behavior of high-performance workers is being extinguished (ignored), whereas the behavior of average-performance and poor-performance workers is being strengthened by positive reinforcement.

Rule 2. Be sure to tell a person what he or she can do to get reinforced. By making clear the contingencies of reinforcement to the worker, a manager may actually increase the freedom of the individual worker. Employees who have a standard against which to measure their job will have a built-in feedback system which allows them to make judgments about their own work. The awarding of the reinforcement in an organization in which the worker's goal is specified will be associated with the performance of the worker and not based on the biases of the supervisor. The assumption is that the supervisor rates the employee accurately and that he or she then reinforces the employee on the basis of the employee's ratings. If the supervisor fails to rate accurately or to administer rewards based on performance, then the stated goals for the worker will lose stimulus control, and the worker will be forced to search for the "true" contingencies—that is, for the behavior to perform in order to get rewarded (for example, ingratiation, loyalty, a positive attitude).

Rule 3. Be sure to tell a person what he or she is doing wrong. As a general rule, very few people find the act of failing rewarding. One behavioral assumption, therefore, is that a worker wants to be rewarded in a positive manner. A supervisor should never use extinction or punishment as the sole method for modifying behavior, but used judiciously in conjunction with other techniques designed to promote more effective response options (Rule 2), these methods can hasten the change process. If the supervisor fails to specify why a reward is being withheld, the employee may associate the action with past undesired behavior instead of the undesired behavior that the supervisor is trying to extinguish. Thus the supervisor may extinguish good performance while having no affect on the undesired behavior.

Used in combination, Rules 2 and 3 should allow the manager to control behavior in the best interests of the organization. At the same time, these rules should give the employee the clarity needed to see that outcomes are controlled by his or her own behavior and not the behavior of the supervisor.

Rule 4. Make the consequences equal to the behavior. In other words, be fair. Don't cheat the worker out of his or her just rewards. If he or she is a good worker, say so. Many supervisors find it very difficult to praise an employee. Others find it very difficult to counsel an employee about what is being done wrong. A manager who fails to use these reinforcement tools is actually reducing supervisory effectiveness. When a worker is overrewarded he or she may feel guilty, and based on the principles of reinforcement, the worker's current level of performance is being conditioned. If this performance level is less than that of others who get the same reward, the worker has no reason to increase output. A worker who is underrewarded becomes angry with the system. Desirable behavior is being extinguished, and the company may be forcing the good, underrewarded employee to seek employment elsewhere while encouraging the poor, overrewarded employee to stay.

SCHEDULES OF POSITIVE REINFORCEMENT

The effectiveness of reinforcement varies as a function of the schedule of its administration. A *reinforcement schedule* is a more or less formal specification of the occurrence of a reinforcer in relation to the behavioral sequence to be conditioned, and the effectiveness of a reinforcer depends as much upon its scheduling as upon any of its other features (magnitude, quality, degree of association with the behavioral act, degree of deprivation, or satiation).

There are many conceivable arrangements of a positive reinforcement schedule which managers can use to reward their workers. Two basic types of schedules which have the most promise for motivating workers are *continuous* and *partial reinforcement* schedules.

Continuous Reinforcement Schedule

Under this schedule, every time the correct response is emitted by the worker it is followed by a reinforcer. With this schedule, the desired behavior increases very rapidly, but when the reinforcer is removed, performance decreases rapidly (extinction). For this reason the schedule is not recommended for use by the manager over a long period of time. It is also impossible for a manager to continuously reward the employee for emitting desired behavior. Therefore, a manager should generally consider using one or more of the partial reinforcement schedules when administering either financial or nonfinancial rewards.

Partial Reinforcement Schedules

Partial reinforcement, in which reinforcement does not occur after every correct operant, leads to slower learning but stronger retention of a response than does total or continuous reinforcement. "In other words, *learning is more permanent when we reward correct behavior only part of the time*" (Bass & Vaughan, 1966, p. 20). This factor is extremely relevant to the observed strong resistance to changes in attitudes, values, norms, and the like.

Ferster and Skinner (1957) have described four basic types of partial reinforcement schedules for operant learning situations. These schedules, shown in Table 3–1, are:

1. *Fixed interval schedule.* Under this schedule, when the desired response occurs, a reinforcer is administered only after the passage of a specified period of time since the previous reinforcement. Thus a worker paid on a weekly basis would receive a full paycheck every Friday, assuming that the worker were performing minimally acceptable behavior. This method offers the least motivation for hard work among employees.

The kind of behavior often observed with fixed interval schedules is a pause after reinforcement and than an increase in the rate of responding until a high rate of performance occurs just as the interval is about to end. Suppose that the plant manager visits the shipping

Table 3–1
Operant Conditioning Summary

Reinforcement Contingencies		Effect on Behavior	
		When Applied to the Individual	*When Removed from the Individual*
Arrangement	*Schedule*		
	Continuous reinforcement	Fastest method to establish a new behavior	Fastest method to extinguish a new behavior
	Partial reinforcement	Slowest method to establish a new behavior	Slowest method to extinguish a new behavior
	Variable partial reinforcement	More consistent response frequencies	Slower extinction rate
	Fixed partial reinforcement	Less consistent response frequencies	Faster extinction rate
Positive reinforcement		Increased frequency over preconditioning level	Return to preconditioning level
Avoidance reinforcement			
Punishment Extinction		Decreased frequency over preconditioning level	Return to preconditioning level

Source: Adapted from O. Behling, C. Schriesheim, and J. Tolliver, "Present Theories and New Directions in Theories of Work Effort," Journal Supplement Abstract Service of the American Psychological Corporation, 1976, by permission of authors.

department each day at approximately 10 A.M. This fixed schedule of supervisory recognition will probably cause performance to be at its highest just prior to the plant manager's visit, and performance will probably steadily decline thereafter and not rise to a peak again until the next morning's visit.

2. *Variable interval schedule.* Under this schedule, reinforcement is administered at some variable interval of time around some average. This schedule is not recommended for use with a pay plan, but it is an ideal method to use for administering praise, promotions, and supervisory visits. Since the reinforcers are dispensed unpredictably, variable interval schedules generate higher rates of response and more stable and consistent performance than do fixed interval schedules.

Suppose that our plant manager visits the shipping department on an *average* of once a day but at randomly selected time intervals (for example, twice on Monday, once on Tuesday, not at all on Wednesday, or Thursday, and twice on Friday, all of his visits occurring at different times during the day). As you would expect, performance will be higher and will fluctuate less than under the fixed interval schedule.

3.   *Fixed ratio schedule.* Here a reward is delivered only when a fixed number of desired responses take place. This is essentially the piecework schedule for pay. The response level here is significantly higher than that obtained under any of the interval (or time-based) schedules.

4.   *Variable ratio schedule.* Under this schedule, a reward is delivered only after a number of desired responses, with the number of desired responses changing around an average from the occurrence of one reinforcer to the next. Thus a person working on a 15 to 1 variable ratio schedule might receive reinforcement after 10 responses, then 20 responses, then 15 responses, and so on, for an average of 1 reinforcer per 15 responses. Gambling is an example of a variable ratio reward schedule. Research evidence reveals that of all the available variations in scheduling procedures, this is the most powerful in sustaining behavior. Gamblers at a blackjack table are a classic example. In industry, it would be impossible to use this as the only plan for scheduling reinforcement. Aldis (1961) gives an example of how the variable ratio method could be used to supplement other monetary reward schedules.

> . . . Take the annual Christmas bonus as an example. In many instances, this "surprise" gift has become nothing more than a ritualized annual salary supplement which everybody expects. Therefore, its incentive-building value is largely lost. Now suppose that the total bonus were distributed at irregular intervals throughout the year and in small sums dependent upon the amount of work done. Wouldn't the workers find their urge to work increased? (p. 63)

An important point to remember is that to be effective a schedule should always include the specification of a contingency between the behavior desired and the occurrence of a reinforcer. In many cases it will be necessary to use each of the various schedules for administering rewards—for example, base pay on a fixed interval schedule, promotions and raises on a variable interval schedule, recognition of above-average performance with a piece-rate plan (fixed ratio schedule), and supplementary bonuses on a variable ratio schedule. The effects on worker performance of the various types of reinforcement schedules and the various methods of arranging reinforcement contingencies are shown in Figure 3–1.

The necessity for arranging appropriate reinforcement contingencies is dramatically illustrated by several studies in which rewards were shifted from a response-contingent (ratio) basis to a time-contin-

Figure 3–1
The Effects of Various Schedules of Reinforcement on Performance

1. Fixed interval schedule of reinforcement

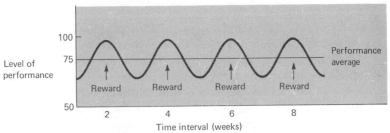

Note: Performance average lower than for a variable interval schedule and fluctuation in performance higher than under variable interval schedule.

2. Variable interval schedule of reinforcement

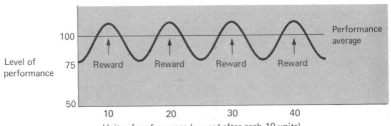

3. Fixed ratio schedule of reinforcement

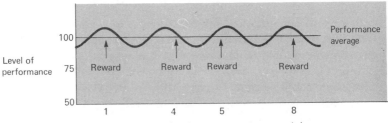

Note: Performance average lower and fluctuation greater than variable ratio schedule but superior to interval schedule.

4. Variable ratio schedule of reinforcement

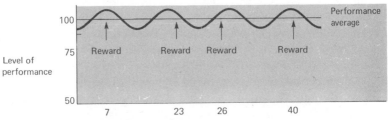

gent (interval) basis. During the period in which rewards were made conditional upon occurrence of the desired behavior, the appropriate response patterns were exhibited at a consistently high level. When the same rewards were based on time and independent of the worker's behavior, there was a marked drop in the desired behavior. The reinstatement of the performance-contingent reward schedule promptly restored the high level of responsiveness. Similar declines in performance were obtained when workers were provided rewards in advance without performance requirements.

Source: © King Features Syndicate Inc. 1976.

The Law of Relative Effect

The Law of Effect, as we have noted, states that a behavior followed by positive (or reinforcing) consequences tends to be repeated. However, every behavior occurs in some *context* in which other behaviors are possible. In some contexts, a behavior that is rewarded *may not* increase in frequency if competing behaviors are reinforced at a greater rate. Where different behaviors compete with each other, the *relative* rate of reinforcement determines which behaviors will occur with greater frequency.

The Law of Relative Effect (also known as the *Correlation-Based Law of Effect* and as the *Matching Law*) is an extension of Thorndike's originally formulated Law of Effect. In order to see how this newer principle extends the scope and power of the older one, let us use as an illustration a college student, Beth, who spends her freshman and sophomore years at a small, all-girl school in a rural area of the state 90 miles from the nearest large city. The school has no intercollegiate sports program, no rock band concerts, and very few social events other than those of an informal nature. As a freshman and later as a sophomore, Beth takes mostly those courses that are required of all students. Some of these Beth enjoys; most of them she finds somewhat dull. She studies an average of about four hours per day outside of class.

For her junior and senior years, Beth transfers to the coeducational state university to pursue her major field of study (journalism). The university (with over 20,000 students at the undergraduate and graduate levels, compared with 800 at the previous school) is located in a city with a population of over 100,000; it has a big-time sports program, frequent concerts, a variety of structured student activities, and numerous visits by national figures in politics and the arts. Beth has more interest in her journalism courses than in the calculus, history, psychology, and so forth that she took at the previous school; obviously, then, her study behavior is reinforced at a greater rate than before. Yet now she studies less, not more. Why? Clearly, because *competing behaviors are reinforced at an even greater rate of increase.*

According to the Law of Relative Effect (Brown and Herrnstein, 1975), it is the *relative* or *comparative* rate of reinforcement for a response that determines its strength or frequency. Beth received little reinforcement from the study of her required courses, but there were few alternative behaviors that offered a greater rate of reinforcement. At the large university, she received a fairly high level of reinforcement for studying the journalism courses she was more interested in—but this contingency competed with even higher reinforcement rates for other activities. The logic of the Law of Relative Effect leads to the following conclusion: The percentage of time and effort you devote to an activity will be determined by the percentage of your *total* reinforcement (available from all available responses) which is provided by that activity.

Consider some of the implications of this principle. As a culture becomes more affluent and large proportions of the labor force can afford to buy sailboats, motorcycles, elaborate stereo equipment, and other leisure-time paraphernalia, nonwork activities are reinforced at an increasing rate. Working behavior is likely to become less frequent—not because jobs provide any less reinforcement in themselves than before (they may even provide greater reinforcement), but because the relative rate of reinforcement for work is less. Result: With greater material wealth producing more reinforcement for nonwork, jobs have to become ever more reinforcing (perhaps due to greater interest level) in order to maintain the levels of effort and productivity which led to that affluence in the first place.

In order to understand another implication of the Law of Relative Effect, imagine a job in which a person has to perform several different functions. One of these functions occurs at a frequency that is judged by organization officials to be less than desired. So, officials design a program in which this activity is reinforced in a special way, such as by supervisory recognition or quantitative feedback on a conspicuously placed poster. We would expect to see that activity become more frequent. But remember, now the *other* functions are being reinforced at a lower *relative* rate. They may very well decrease in frequency as a result. Some such decrease may not represent a cause for alarm, if they are not critical or if they were previously well above acceptable levels of occurrence. The point is that we never increase the rate of any one specific class of behavior in isolation from other behaviors in that context. Any change, increase or decrease, in the rate of reinforcement for one behavior affects not only that behavior but others as well. In other words:

> . . . a response rises in rate *either* when its reward increases *or* when the reward for other concurrent responses decreases. Inversely, a response declines *either* when its reward decreases *or* when other available responses gain reward . . . each separate form of behavior is controlled by all the rewards and punishments operating at a given time [Brown & Herrstein, 1975, p. 84].

MANAGEMENT AND THE DISSEMINATION OF KNOWLEDGE

Previously we defined *learning* as the acquisition of knowledge (by the process of operant conditioning), and performance as the translation of knowledge into behavior (depending on the consequences). It can be argued, therefore, that what managers do is disseminate knowledge to those they manage in order to gain the desired level of performance. The question that remains to be answered is, What is knowledge?—that is, What information should one disseminate in order to control behavior?

There are two types of knowledge, according to Skinner (1969). *Private knowledge* is knowledge established through experience with the contingencies of reinforcement. Skinner says, "The world which establishes contingencies of reinforcement of the sort studied in an operant analysis is presumably 'what knowledge is about.' A person comes to know that world and how to behave in it in the sense that he acquires behavior which satisfies the contingencies it maintains" (p. 156). The behavior which results from private knowledge is called *contingency-shaped behavior.* This is the knowledge which one must possess in order to perform correctly and be rewarded. Such knowledge does not assume any awareness on the part of the person but is based entirely on the person's past reinforcement history. A person can "know how" to play golf, for example, as indicated by a series of low scores—but it is an entirely different thing to be able to tell others how to play golf. A machine operator may be an excellent employee but make a poor supervisor. One reason may be that, while he possesses private knowledge about his job, he is unable to verbalize the contingencies to other people.

Public knowledge, then, is the ability to derive rules from the contingencies in the form of injunctions or descriptions which specify occasions, responses, and consequences (Skinner, 1969, p. 160). The behavior which results from public knowledge is called *rule-governed behavior.*

The possession of public knowledge is important to the manager because the employee looks to the manager for information about what behavior is required, how to perform the desired behavior, and what the consequences of the desired behavior will be. Before a manager can give correct answers to these questions, he or she must personally understand the true contingencies, since a manager's business is not doing but telling others how to do. He or she must be able to analyze the contingencies of reinforcement found in the organization and "to formulate rules or laws which make it unnecessary to be exposed to them in order to behave appropriately" (Skinner, 1969, p. 166).

After living in a large city for a long time, a person is able to go from point A to point B with little trouble. The person's knowledge of how to get around in the city was shaped by previous experience with the environment. This behavior is an example of contingency-shaped behavior. Strangers who arrive in the same city and desire to go from point A to point B, will also have little trouble. They will look at a map of the city and will follow the path specified by the map. This behavior is an example of rule-governed behavior. Whether or not a person will continue to follow the map (rule) in the future is dependent on the consequences of following the map in the past. If the rule specified the correct contingencies, the person will probably continue to use the map, but if the map was found to be in error, then he or she will probably look to other sources of information (for example, asking someone with private knowledge).

The same sort of thing happens in industry. If a manager is correct in the specification of the rules—that is, the new worker follows the rules and receives a reward—then the worker will probably follow the other rules specified by the manager. If the manager specifies incorrect rules, then the worker may look to peers or to other sources of information (for example, the union steward) for the specification of rules which describe behavior that will be rewarded.

There are two kinds of rules that the manager can specify to the employee. A command, or *mand,* is a rule that specifies behavior and consequences of the behavior, where the consequences are arranged by the person giving the command. The specified or implied consequences for failure to act are usually aversive in nature, and the judgment of the correctness of the behavior is made by the person giving the command. A supervisor who tells the worker to be on time for work is giving the worker a command. The implied consequence is that if the employee fails to report on time, the supervisor will take action.

Advice and warnings, called *tacts,* involve rules which specify the reinforcements contingent on prior stimulation from rules, or laws. They specify the same contingencies which would directly shape behavior (private knowledge). The specification of a tact speeds up the conditioning process. If a secretary tells the boss to take an umbrella when going to lunch, the secretary is tacting. The secretary has no control over the consequences (getting wet) of the behavior (not carrying the umbrella). Those are determined by the environment itself (the weather). Skinner (1969) says:

> *Go west, young man* is an example of advice (tacting) when the behavior it specifies will be reinforced by certain consequences which do not result from action taken by the advisor. We tend to follow advice because previous behavior in response to similar verbal stimuli has been reinforced. *Go west, young man* is a command when some consequences of the specified action are arranged by the commander—say, the aversive consequences arranged by an official charged with relocating the inhabitants of a region. When maxims, rules, and laws are advice, the governed behavior is reinforced by consequences which might have shaped the same behavior directly in the absence of the maxims, rules, and laws. When they are commands, they are effective only because special reinforcements have been made contingent upon them. (Skinner, 1969, p. 148)

Although a manager must possess public knowledge as well as private knowledge in order to accomplish the task of "getting things done through other people," in keeping with a plea for positive reinforcement and unbiased reward systems, tacting is the method of rule specification recommended. Skinner (1969) argues that by specifying the contingencies in such a way that the consequences are positive in nature and that failure to respond is met with the withholding of a reward rather than with aversive stimuli, "the 'mand' may be replaced by a 'tact' describing conditions under which specific behavior on the part of the listener will be reinforced" (p. 158). Instead of saying "Give me that report," say "I need the report." "The craftsman begins by ordering his apprentice to behave in a given way but he may later achieve the same effect simply by describing the relation between what the apprentice does and the consequences" (Skinner, 1969, p. 158). Thus, the technique managers use to direct the employee can make a lot of difference in the acceptance of the rule by the employee. A mand operates from an avoidance learning base, while a tact operates from a positive reinforcement base. A tact is more impersonal and gives the employee freedom in that it does not "enjoin anyone to behave in a given way, it simply describes the contingen-

Figure 3–2

Operant concepts and principles form the basis for effective methods of training new employees in the use of complex equipment.

cies under which certain kinds of behavior will have certain kinds of consequences" (Skinner, 1969, p. 158).

The Relevance of Operant Principles

Psychologists have for many years now maintained a spirited debate among themselves over the issue of whether operant principles account for *all* forms of learning and instrumental behavior. The generally accepted view is that much *covert* or *latent* learning does occur without reinforcement, even if *overt* demonstration of the learning in observable behavior depends somewhat on the amount and scheduling of reinforcement.

Operant principles have found application in training programs in work organizations. The technique of shaping, in particular, is useful for teaching new employees complex skills and response sequences.

Operant concepts have also served as the basis for large-scale, formal programs of job motivation (described in greater detail in Chapter

8). Here the aim is, not so much toward learning new behavior, but toward strengthening reponses which for one reason or another do not occur with the desired frequency in a given setting.

Finally, many managers informally (even intuitively) use these principles on an ad hoc, day-to-day basis. They try to ensure that good performance in any fashion, whether it be heroic or mundane, is never taken for granted. They use the limits of their power and abilities to see that constructive job behavior gets rewarded on a timely basis. At the very least, they make it personally known to employees periodically that they appreciate constructive acts. They do not take the view that people "ought" to do things whether rewarded or not, nor do they reward noncontingently. They see that desired behavior is reinforced.

SUMMARY

Behavior is acquired and maintained through two forms of learnings: classical (respondent) conditioning, in which reflexes and emotional responses are brought under the control of different stimuli; and operant (instrumental) conditioning, in which voluntary responses are shaped by their consequences. The importance of classical conditioning in organizational behavior lies in its relevance to attitude formation. Operant conditioning has received the greater emphasis in this chapter because of its importance in the acquisition and maintenance of skills, work habits, and levels of performance.

The core concepts of an operant analysis are the discriminative stimulus, the response, and the reinforcer. Interrelationships among these comprise the contingencies of reinforcement. Positive reinforcers act to strengthen the behavior: they may be primary or secondary, contrived or noncontrived, extrinsic or intrinsic. Positive reinforcement may occur on various types of schedules, which have characteristic effects on the level of responding and resistance to extinction once reinforcement ceases. The Law of Relative Effect accounts for the distribution of behavior when competing responses are reinforced. Contingencies of reinforcement may be learned through direct exposure to them but may also be learned as rules when described as tacts or mands.

CONCEPTS TO REMEMBER

classical conditioning	shaping
operant conditioning	avoidance learning
reinforcer	extinction
discriminative stimulus	reinforcement schedule
contingencies of reinforcement	Law of Relative Effect
noncontrived reinforcer	contingency-shaped behavior
contrived reinforcer	rule-governed behavior
intrinsic reinforcer	mand
extrinsic reinforcer	tact
generalization	covert learning
discrimination	

QUESTIONS FOR DISCUSSION

1. In a recent project, bonuses were given to workers who planted pine seedlings for a wood-products company. Most of the planters were older women from rural southeastern areas, with strong religious backgrounds. In one group, workers were offered, in addition to base pay, a $2 bonus contingent upon planting each bag of seedlings. A second group was told they would get base pay plus a $4 bonus contingent upon planting each bag *and* correctly guessing the outcome of a coin toss. In a third group the contigency for a bonus was planting a bag of seedlings and correctly guessing *two* coin tosses. A fourth crew, geographically separated from the others, received only hourly base wages.
   a. What were the various schedules of reinforcement in operation?
   b. What would you predict the results to be?
2. Identify some habit that is characteristic of your daily behavior (it doesn't matter whether you regard it as a "good" or "bad" habit).
   a. What reinforcement now maintains that habit?
   b. How often does the reinforcement occur?
   c. Did a different form of reinforcement affect it in the past?
   d. What discriminative stimuli exert control over this behavior?
3. In operant terms, explain what we mean when we say someone "has credibility." How do the concepts of discrimination and generalization apply here?

4. We have all experienced reinforcement contingencies that "don't work"—either for ourselves or for others. Identify the major reasons for such faulty contingencies.

CASE

Steve Gibson, third-shift shipping department foreman at the Rapids Valley pulp and paper mill, knew what would happen at 7 A.M. when he touched base with his first-shift replacement. He would get the usual static about "forcing the first shift to play catch-up" with the day's shipment. Try as he might, Steve never could seem to get caught up before the end of the shift.

He had a hunch about where the bottleneck lay. One of his men, Leon Pope, had the job of pushing huge rolls of finished paper off the elevator, turning them, rolling them to the weighing station, recording the weight on the side of the roll, and pushing the rolls out to the loading dock, where they were stacked in freight cars. Pope seemed to keep busy but never could stay ahead of the elevator. As the night went on, the rolls backed up on the floor above because there was no room on the floor below for unloading the paper. If Steve reassigned one or two men to help Leon, then they just got further behind somewhere else. Steven couldn't understand it, because Leon's job required only one man on the first and second shifts, which had to handle even larger volumes of shipping.

During the 3 A.M. lunch break, after the usual chatter about sex and sports had subsided, Steve had an idea. In a casual, half-joking fashion, he nudged Leon and asked, "What would it take for you to keep ahead of the elevator, Leon?"

"I don't know. I'm doing what I can," replied Leon.

"What if—every time you got a shipment weighed before the next elevator load—I let you take a few minutes to go down to the canteen? You know, get a cup of coffee, smoke, read the paper, or whatever. Think it would make a difference?"

Leon, without looking directly at Steve, just shrugged in a noncommittal manner. "Oh, maybe."

"What do you say we try it and see?" Steve suggested. Again, Leon just sucked his teeth and shrugged vacantly.

Nonetheless, a couple of hours later, Steve noticed that Leon was pushing the final roll from the last elevator load out to the dock. The next elevator load hadn't arrived yet. Steve walked up to Leon and said, "Hey, I think you deserve a breather. Want to step down to the canteen? I don't think the next load will be down for a few minutes yet."

Leon just nodded without apparent enthusiasm, but he did amble off in the direction of the canteen.

Steven continued to work this "bargain" with Leon, and over the next couple of weeks he found that Leon usually was caught up when the first shift took over.

One night around 4:30 A.M. Steve's boss, Ray Hudson, came through to check on some shipment figures. Ray suddenly looked up and asked, "Say, where's Leon?"

Steve answered, "Oh, he got caught up and I let him go down to the canteen. He'll be back in a minute. I use that as an incentive to help him stay head of the elevator."

Hudson responded, "You mean you give him a break every time he gets caught up?"

"Sure, why not?"

"Well, we can't do that. That kind of thing just can't go on. If he's caught up, give him a broom and let him sweep up. Tell him he's supposed to keep busy. If he can stay caught up for a break, he can do it without the break. He's paid to do the job right and keep up."

Later that night, Steve explained the situation to Leon.

Questions

What do you predict will happen now that Leon doesn't get his break? Compare the respective managerial philosophies of Steve and his boss, Ray. What could Steve do to maintain the progress he has made, yet keep himself on the good side of Hudson?

REFERENCES

Aldis, O.   Of pigeons and men. *Harvard Business Review*, July-August 1961, pp. 59–63.

Bandura, A.   *Principles of behavior modification*. New York: Holt, Rinehart & Winston, 1969.

Bass, B. M., & Vaughan, J. A.   *Training in industry: The management of learning*. Belmont, Calif.: Wadsworth, 1966.

Behling, O., Schriescheim, C., & Tolliver, J.   Present theories and new directions in theories of work effort. Journal Supplement Abstract Service of the American Psychological Corporation, 1976.

Brown, R., & Herrnstein, R. J.   *Psychology*. Boston: Little, Brown, 1975.

Costello, T. W., & Zalkind, A. A.   *Psychology in administration*. Englewood Cliffs, N.J.: Prentice-Hall, 1963.

Ferster, C. B., & Skinner, B. F.   *Schedules of reinforcement*. New York: Appleton-Century-Crofts, 1957.

Haire, M.   *Psychology in management* (2nd ed.). New York: McGraw-Hill, 1964.

Homans, G. C. *Social behavior: Its elementary forms*. New York: Harcourt, Brace Jovanovich, 1961.

Luthans, F. *Organizational behavior.* New York: McGraw-Hill, 1973.

Michael, J., & Meyerson, L. A behavioral approach to counseling and guidance. *Harvard Educational Review,* 1962, *32* 382–402.

Pavlov, I. P. *The work of the digestive glands* (W. H. Thompson, trans.). London: Charles Griffin, 1902.

Scott, W. E. Activation theory and task design. *Organizational Behavior and Human Performance,* 1966, *1,* 3–30.

Skinner, B. F. *Science and human behavior.* New York: Macmillan, 1953.

Skinner, B. F. *Contingencies of reinforcement: A theoretical analysis.* Englewood Cliffs, N.J.: Prentice-Hall, 1969.

Thorndike, E. L. *Animal intelligence.* New York: Macmillan, 1911.

Tosi, H. L., & Hamner, W. C., (Eds.). *Organization behavior and human performance: A contingency approach.* Chicago: St. Clair Press, 1974.

4

Punishment and Discipline in Organizations

What are the arguments for and against the use of punishment in organizations?

What is the process by which punishment affects behavior?

Under what conditions is punishment most likely to have desirable effects on behavior?

It is remarkable how little is written or said about the topic of punishment in organizational settings. Extended discussions about job motivation illustrate the methods of *eliciting desired behavior* but lead one to forget that organizations also have the task of *eliminating undesired behavior.*

Yet surely punishment and disciplinary measures are, in fact, very frequently used in organizations. For many first-line supervisors and managers who have little control over organizational rewards (such as salary raises, promotions, and benefits), punishment and discipline (or their threat) are the most immediately available tools for shaping the behavior of subordinates. Indeed, one could plausibly argue that, day in and day out, punishment is used (whether intentionally or unintentionally, effectively or ineffectively) far more often than reward in attempts to influence behavior.

Why, then, the relative silence on this seemingly important topic? There are probably several reasons. First of all, punishment is a rather controversial topic. Few people debate the issue of whether to reward people for good behavior or performance, but heated arguments are touched off by the question of whether to punish ineffective or undesirable behavior. This controversy is reflected in popular discussions about child rearing, the penal system, our "permissive" society, and even in theoretical dialogues among psychologists. Second, punishment is not as pleasant a topic as rewards or positive reinforcement. It tends to suggest problems, disagreements, tensions, tyranny, and a host of other unpleasant matters. Finally, as we shall soon see, punishment is considerably more complex and unpredictable than rewards in its effects on behavior. There are more qualifications that have to be specified before we can predict whether the effect of punishment on behavior will be constructive, undesirable, or nonexistent.

Punishment occurs when an *aversive stimulus* (S^{av}) follows a response. An aversive stimulus is one whose removal is reinforcing; the removal of an aversive stimulus reinforces the behavior which precedes the removal. The next time you are in a crowded elevator, notice the behavior of the people around you. What do they do? Generally they stand transfixed gazing at the lighted numbers above the elevator door; moreover, they do this even when their destination is several floors away. What conceivable interest could people have in doing this? Quite simply, it represents behavior sustained by the removal and avoidance of an aversive stimulus: close eye contact with strangers. In our culture at least, we ordinarily experience some discomfort in face-to-face encounters with strangers in close quarters. Looking up at the numbers removes this discomfort, and consequently this behavior is strengthened in such settings.

Schematically, we may represent a punishment episode as follows:

$$S^D \rightarrow R \rightarrow S^{av}$$

Given some situation or S^D (crowded elevator), some response (close eye contact) is followed by an aversive stimulus (embarassment, awkwardness). The S^D is important here: it signifies that the behavior is followed by an aversive stimulus on certain well-defined occasions. Walking around a city square or in a long corridor, eye contact with strangers several yards away arouses less discomfort. Even in crowded quarters, eye contact poses no problems if those around you are close friends.

Discipline is a conscious attempt to punish. The boss who "chews out" a tardy employee is clearly making a deliberate attempt to make that person experience aversive consequences for such behavior; the official who calls a technical foul on an unruly coach consciously imposes a penalty for unsportsmanlike conduct.

Not all instances of punishment (even in organizations) constitute discipline, as we have defined it. Punishment occurs, for example, when a student asks the instructor a question and the instructor responds in such a way as to put the student "on the spot." The instructor may not have intended to do this (at the very least, we try not to punish intellectual curiosity, since that is the presumed goal of educational systems), but the answer had that effect. Many constructive behaviors that organizations hope for occur less frequently than desired simply because of unintended aversive consequences that follow such behaviors.

By the same token, not all disciplinary measures really constitute punishment. In some organizations, excessive unexcused absenteeism is disciplined by suspending the person from work for a few days—the person is disciplined by doing more of what he or she was disciplined for to begin with! When disciplinary measures involve consequences that actually are not aversive to the person disciplined, then no punishment has actually occurred.

THE PSYCHOLOGICAL DYNAMICS OF PUNISHMENT

Psychologists are in general agreement about *how* punishment affects behavior. In order to illustrate the process by which punishment works, let us use the example of an office clerk who likes to prop his feet up on the desk. This is the response. To the clerk's supervisor, this is an undesired response; perhaps the supervisor doesn't think it looks appropriate to visitors and management officials who occasionally pass through. So the supervisor walks over to the clerk's desk and gives him a verbal reprimand. Thus far, we have the situation shown below.

$$S^D \text{ (work environment)} \rightarrow R^x \text{ (undesired behavior of propping feet on desk)} \rightarrow S^{av} \text{ (reprimand)}$$

An aversive stimulus, such as the reprimand, usually triggers an emotional response of some kind. The emotional response may be felt or experienced as fear, guilt, or anxiety. When we add this unconditioned emotional response to the sequence, we have

$$S^D \rightarrow R^x \rightarrow S^{av} \rightarrow R^{uc}$$

An emotional response such as fear or anxiety is itself aversive. That is, anything we do that terminates or avoids such feelings will be reinforced by the removal of the aversive feeling.

Recall from the previous chapter that an emotional response to an unconditioned stimulus (in this case, the reprimand) can come under the control of other stimuli that immediately precede the unconditioned stimulus. Thus, if the clerk feels guilt or anxiety as a result of the reprimand, the emotional response should also be triggered in the future by those events which preceded the reprimand. So, the next time the clerk props his feet on the desk, either the raising of the feet or the feel of the heels on the desk should trigger the emotional response previously evoked by the reprimand. In other words, the initial components in the response sequence of propping the feet produce stimuli (in the form of sensations) that trigger the conditioned emotional response. Since this emotional response itself is felt as aversive, any act which terminates it will be reinforced. If the clerk lowers his feet and moves the chair closer to the desk or stands up, he no longer feels anxiety. He is reinforced for doing something else that eliminates or avoids the aversive stimuli created by a negative emotion.

The key to understanding the punishment process is the emotional response evoked by the aversive stimulus. The aversive stimulus suppresses the undesired response in *that* situation *if* it evokes an unpleasant emotion which becomes conditioned to the sequence of events that led to the response (and its consequence, the aversive stimulus).

Now let us see what can go awry in this complex process. First, consider the reprimand itself. Can we be certain that it is aversive? To some people it may not be; since it gives the offender some attention, it could conceivably act as a reinforcer, especially if the clerk had a very dull job and any break in the routine offered a bit of variety. If the reprimand is not aversive, it will not generate the emotional response that suppresses the undesired behavior.

Second, even if the reprimand is indeed aversive, it may occur too late after the response to come under the control of stimuli immediately preceding the undesired behavior. If the clerk had his feet propped up on the desk for 45 minutes before the supervisor intervened, the events leading up to propping the feet may be totally unaffected by any resulting emotional response.

Third, let us assume the clerk is a very nervous, anxiety-prone sort of person. The reprimand may trigger a very strong emotional response—indeed, much stronger than the supervisor intended. The anxiety response may be so strong and intense that it "spreads" to much of the surrounding work environment—that is, the entire immediate work setting acquires the power to evoke an anxiety response. The anxiety may prevent the foot-propping but also may prevent the clerk from effectively concentrating on his job.

The clerk may discover, on the other hand, that propping the feet is followed by a reprimand only under certain conditions—when the supervisor is nearby, when the supervisor is not preoccupied with other matters, when the supervisor seems to be in a foul mood. So the clerk simply learns to discriminate between the S^D's that define occasions when a particular response is or is not punished, and the foot-propping is suppressed only in the presence of certain well-defined cues.

In the conditions described above, punishment either would not have its intended effect of suppressing the response or would have unintended effects perhaps more than offsetting the value of any deterrent effect. Seldom can one confidently predict what the net effect will be, precisely because of the complexity of the process.

THE CASE AGAINST PUNISHMENT

Many people, including quite a few psychologists, argue that punishment should be avoided as a means of trying to influence behavior. Their objections to punishment are prompted, at least in part, by humanistic considerations or ideology but also include the following arguments:

1. For punishment to be at all effective, there must be continued monitoring or surveillance, which is a very wasteful use of high-priced managerial time.

2. Punishment never really extinguishes or eliminates undesir-

able response tendencies but only temporarily suppresses them. These tendencies reappear with full force when the threat of punishment is removed.

3. Punishment has undesirable side effects. It may cause resentment and hostility toward the punisher, with a motive of trying to "get even" later through sabotage, output restriction, or doing things that make the punisher "look bad" or cause him inconvenience. The fear associated with the punishing agent may lead the punished person to avoid the manager's very presence; this, in turn, makes it more difficult for the manager to play the desired role of coach, teacher, or counselor. Or the reaction to punishment may be more extreme, resulting in a rigidly cautious posture on the part of the offender because of the anxiety aroused. This can make it more difficult for the person to learn new behavior, including very desirable behavior, or to adapt to change.

If punishment is so ineffective in changing behavior and has such undesirable side effects, why, then, do people make so much use of it? Why haven't they learned over the centuries to make more frequent use of other methods in place of punishment? Skinner (1953) believes that punishment is still used mainly for one reason: its use is reinforcing to the punisher. Since the application of an aversive stimulus does *immediately, although temporarily,* suppress the undesired behavior which is noxious to the punisher, the punishing behavior is reinforced by the cessation of the undesired behavior. Since the immediate consequences of one's behavior are the most influential in shaping it, the punisher continues to punish when confronted by subordinate behavior that is disapproved.

One could also argue that if the controlling agent feels angry and frustrated by subordinate performance, the act of punishment may be reinforcing to the agent by providing an opportunity to "blow off steam" and ventilate feelings; that punishment gives some people a feeling of power, which is reinforcing; and that in many cases punishment is the "easiest" thing to do, since it does not require a great deal of thought.

If punishment is to be avoided, what do the critics suggest that we use in its place? They offer several possibilities:

1. Try extinction. Find out what reinforcers (sometimes subtle ones) are sustaining the undesired behavior. What does the subordinate "get from doing that"? The unruly one may be getting praise and recognition from peers. Then get those peers to cooperate with you (sometimes easier said than done) by ignoring the unruly behavior. When such behavior is not reinforced, it will eventually lose strength and become extinguished.

2. Use environmental engineering—rearrange the features of the environment so that the stimulus situation doesn't evoke the undesired response but some other response.

Skinner (1953) tells the story of a manager who had a traffic problem caused by women hurrying down the corridor as soon as the end of the workday was signaled. The manager solved the problem by placing wall mirrors along the corridor. The stimulus situation that had evoked stampeding down the hallway was transformed into one which encouraged a more leisurely and orderly walk-and-stop sequence.

One of the authors was once in a cafeteria and had to use the rest room facilities while waiting for lunch to be prepared. On the inside of the door to the toilet stall was a small blackboard, with a piece of chalk attached by a string. Apparently, the owner was trying to use environmental engineering to encourage behavior less costly and troublesome than the usual obscene graffiti semipermanently etched on the walls and doors.

3.   Along lines similar to the strategy offered above, reward either desirable or neutral behavior which is *physically incompatible* with the undesired behavior. If children are rewarded for exercising or for performing light outdoor chores before dinner, they are prevented from excessive snacking and TV watching.

4.   Simply allow adjustment, development, or maturation to take its course. With biological maturation, young children eventually learn not to throw fragile objects, cry, or wet the bed; punishing such behavior may not speed up this process at all and may cause emotional problems if it is applied to behavior over which the child has insufficient biological control or discrimination. Similarly, new or inexperienced employees make many mistakes and do many wrong things that they will learn to avoid, given a reasonable period of adjustment; punishment may not hasten this process, and if it causes undue anxiety, it can actually retard the process.

These, then, are the suggested alternatives to the wholesale use of aversive control. Skinner's novel *Walden Two* presents a vision of a utopian society in which punishment has been made obsolete by the effective use of nonaversive procedures.

REBUTTAL TO THE CASE AGAINST PUNISHMENT

It has probably already occurred to the reader that, however desirable the use of nonaversive control may be, there are nevertheless some possible weaknesses in the case against punishment.

1.   As Bandura (1969) points out, much of our healthy behavior is in fact acquired due to *naturally punishing* contingencies. We learn how to ride a bike, not to run on slick floors, not to drive fast on icy roads, not to wear heavy clothing in the summer, not to run immediately after a heavy meal, all because nature punishes us. Furthermore, we learn these things rather quickly and without any resultant emotional scars, hang-ups, or neuroses. Apparently, then, nature uses

Figure 4–1

Much of what we learn is due to naturally occuring aversive control.

punishment very effectively, and as we shall soon see, there may be some clues in natural punishments for the effective use of punishment and discipline in organizations.

2. Some of the recommended alternatives to punishment are not always feasible, economical, or equitable. For example, if the undesired behavior is *intrinsically* reinforcing, it will be difficult, if not impossible, to use the extinction procedure. There is no way you can allow the response to occur without its being reinforced. If a kid plays with matches or a worker goes to sleep on the night shift, it is hard to imagine how these things can be allowed to occur in the absence of reinforcement, for in a sense such activities are *their own* reinforcement. Rearrangement of the physical environment may be out of the question due to technological constraints or economic considerations. Singling out the frequent offender and rewarding him for doing other things may appear inequitable to the majority of subordinates who have been conscientious all along. And the maturation or adjustment period may simply take too long for the manager who is pressed for immediate results.

FACTORS DETERMINING WHETHER PUNISHMENT IS EFFECTIVE

Solomon (1964) contends that the critics of punishment have sometimes been too dogmatic in their denunciation of its use. While punishment *may* sometimes be ineffective in changing behavior or may produce unwanted by-products, there is nevertheless considerable evidence that punishment *can* be an effective tool *under certain conditions.* What are the conditions which make for efficacious punishment?

1.   Punishment is more effective if it is applied before an undesired response has been allowed to gain strength. The longer an undesired response is allowed to occur unpunished, the stronger it becomes, and thus the more resistant it becomes to *any* method of behavioral control. The irony is that many well-intentioned managers will "look the other way," or "try to be patient," or forestall any kind of confrontation, when they witness a rule violation. Their hope is that "things will take care of themselves" and that the subordinate will stop doing it. When the subordinate doesn't stop but persists in repeating the offense, the manager finally runs out of patience and "moves in" to correct the situation with discipline. Unfortunately, the offense may now be a strongly ingrained response and highly resistant to external control. The manager should have "moved in" earlier.

2.   Other things being equal, punishment is generally more effective when it is *relatively intense* and *quick*—that is, administered as soon after the undesired response as possible. When punishment is applied in a program of gradually increasing intensity, people can adapt to the punishment. Ironically, many official disciplinary programs—well intentioned and apparently based on very humanitarian considerations—begin with very mild and sometimes delayed punishment, with gradually severer punishment (culminating in dismissal) after repeated occurrences of the offense. This may be much less effective (and ultimately less humanitarian) than moderately severe punishment of early instances of the offense.

Punishment should quickly follow the undesired response in order to maximize the association between the behavior and its consequences. The speedier the punishment, the greater information value it has to the recipient and the more it seems like a natural and automatic result of his behavior.

3.   Punishment should focus on a specific act, not on the person or on his general patterns of behavior. Punishment should be dispensed in an impersonal manner, not as a means of "revenge" for the manager or as a way of venting his own frustrations. The more impersonal the administration of discipline, the less likely is the person punished to experience the kind of humiliation or rage which strains the relationship between manager and subordinate.

Unfortunately, the tactic frequently used by supervisors—ignoring early offenses, trying to be patient in the hope of preventing an "incident"—almost guarantees that when the offense occurs repeatedly, the manager will finally run out of patience and that when discipline finally is applied, it will be in an emotional, personal manner. The manager in fact is likely to feel resentment at having his or her patience tried, and discipline then has all the overtones of arbitrariness and pettiness. No wonder, then, that the person punished feels a need to "even the score" or to reassert strength and status. On the other hand, the manager who takes some disciplinary action—however mild—when a violation first occurs is more apt at that point to be in control of his or her own emotions and to be able to punish in an impersonal manner.

4. Punishment should be consistent across persons and across time. The more consistently discipline is administered, the less it will appear to be prompted by ulterior motives. Unfortunately, as Rosen and Jerdee (1974) have found, organization officials tend to be inconsistent. They tend to let minor infractions pass unnoticed when things are running smoothly otherwise, when there is a big push to speed up production, or when the supervisor is not experiencing much pressure from above. Also, managers quite understandably (though often regrettably) apply different patterns of enforcement against those with longer job tenure as opposed to those with shorter job tenure, or against employees with hard-to-replace skills as opposed to employees who are easy to replace. The net effect of such selectivity in discipline, whether across persons or time, is that when persons are punished, they believe "It's not what I did, it's who I am." Consequently, it is not surprising that there are unwanted emotional side effects of punishment.

5. Punishment should have information value. In part, this is accomplished when discipline meets the above criteria—is administered following early instances of undesired behavior; follows quickly after such behavior; is intense; is consistent. In addition, disciplinary measures should ideally be accompanied by explanation of why the behavior is not desired, how it can be corrected, and the expected consequences of continued violations (this does not imply that discipline should be carried out either apologetically or threateningly). Again, the importance of supervisors or managers acting *before* losing patience is emphasized: they are better able to make discipline an educational experience if they have control over their own emotions.

Another ingredient of the information value desired in discipline is guidance of the offender into acceptable modes of behavior that will be rewarded. One of the criticisms cited earlier against punishment is that it only suppresses rather than extinguishes unwanted behavior. The answer to this criticism is that punishment can be used to temporarily suppress an unacceptable response in order to create an opportunity for guiding the person into different behavior that will then be strengthened by rewards (Solomon, 1964).

6. Punishment is most effective when it occurs in the context of

a warm or nurtured relationship. Among other things, this means that the manager should be a source of rewards (for example, good feedback, friendly interaction) as well as punishment. This offsets the tendency for punishment to cause avoidance of the punishing agent. If the manager's behavior is generally such that it represents fairness and personal consideration and concern for subordinates, and if it is consistent and focused on people's specific responses rather than their personalities or their general worth as human beings or employees, punishment is less likely to cause festering emotional problems.

7. Punishment should *not* be followed by *noncontingent rewards.* How often have you seen a parent discipline a small child, then feel remorse when the kid cries, and end up showering the tot with all manner of goodies to assuage the remorse? This is, of course, especially likely to happen when the person doing the disciplining does so in an emotionally aroused state. The person probably feels more guilty about his or her manner of punishing than about the punishment itself. In any case, when noncontingent reinforcers systematically follow punishment, the punishment can have the effect of strengthening the very behavior it was designed to weaken—because the aversive stimulus can become a conditioned reinforcer by virtue of its temporal relationship with other reinforcers.

THE "HOT STOVE RULE"

Much of what we have said about the factors maximizing the effectiveness of punishment can be summarized in Douglas McGregor's "Hot Stove Rule" of discipline (see Strauss & Sayles, 1967). McGregor observed that nature, as we noted earlier in this chapter, seems to apply punishment very effectively to our behavior. We learn quickly from nature, and we learn without serious emotional problems. If we get too close to the hot stove and accidentally touch it, the reaction is immediate. What is it about the hot stove that makes it such a good teacher? It is swift: the association between our behavior and its consequences is undeniable. It is relatively intense on the very first instance of our improper response. It is impersonal: the hot stove has nothing against us as persons and doesn't lose its temper; our behavior, our specific response, is singled out. The hot stove is unerringly consistent: regardless of who touches it or when, the result is the same. Finally, an alternative response is available: move away from the stove.

The point, then, is to strive to emulate nature in carrying out disciplinary measures.

THE IMPORTANCE OF EXPLAINING THE RULES

A study by Walters and Cheyne (1966) demonstrates that *cognitive structuring*—providing a clear, cogent rationale for the punishment contingencies—determines to a great extent the effectiveness of punishment procedures. In their study, 84 first-grade boys were given some toys to play with. Some of the boys were told beforehand that there were some toys they should not handle; others *were given reasons* why they should not play with them. In addition, the boys were punished either "early," as soon as they began to reach for the prohibited toys, or "late," three seconds after they had picked a prohibited toy off the table. The intensity of the punishment was also varied: the punishment was either a 54-decibel noise or a 96-decibel noise. When *no* cognitive structuring had been provided—when no reasons were given why the boys should refrain from playing with certain toys—then late punishment or low-intensity punishment had little effect on the subjects' behavior, compared to early/high-intensity punishment. However, when cognitive structuring had been provided, even late/low-intensity punishment was highly effective.

The implications of the Walters-Cheyne study for punishment in organizational settings should be obvious. High-intensity punishment is often ruled out for practical reasons arising from labor contracts, legal constraints, and other factors; in addition, there are numerous reasons why punishment cannot be administered as quickly as theory would suggest. It becomes all the more important, then, for administrators to provide, in advance, clear and persuasive reasons why certain rules exist or why certain behaviors cannot be tolerated. The study by Walters and Cheyne suggests that if this step is taken, mild, delayed aversive stimuli can be quite effective in reducing the frequency of undesired responses.

VICARIOUS PUNISHMENT

Albert Bandura has concluded from many years of research into behavior modification that "virtually all learning phenomena resulting from direct experience can occur on a vicarious basis through the observation of another's behavior and its consequences for them" (Bandura, 1969, p. 118). We learn from observing competent models what kinds of behavior meet with success or other forms of reward. Similarly, we learn much about the contingencies of aversive control by observation of others. We are less likely to imitate those behaviors for which we see others punished.

A study by Di Giuseppe (1975) of boys five to eight years old showed that vicarious punishment is governed by much the same principles as directly experienced punishment. Boys who were reprimanded for touching a toy (supposedly belong to another child) were less likely to handle that toy when the experimenter left the room (as recorded by an observer behind a one-way glass); those reprimanded "early" (as soon as they reached for the toy) were less likely to return to it (when the experimenter left) than those who were reprimanded "late" (after actually handling the toy). Other subjects saw a film in which a boy like themselves was either not reprimanded, reprimanded late, or reprimanded early. When each of these subjects was left in the room with the toy, the effects of vicarious punishment were almost identical to the effects of direct punishment. Those who had seen the boy in the film punished were less likely to handle the toys later; and those who had witnessed immediate punishment were less likely to transgress than those who had seen delayed punishment administered.

The results of Di Giuseppe's study underscore the importance of consistency and timing on the part of organizational officials in administering discipline. The effects extend beyond that of the person being disciplined; they influence, for good or bad, those who observe the discipline.

CASE STUDY

In an article published in the *Harvard Business Review* in 1964, John Huberman recounts the experiences of a large plywood mill with disciplinary measures. His narrative nicely illustrates some of the points discussed above. The company had originally been a small one, but over a period of years it experienced a gradual increase in the size of its operations and in its work force. As increased size led to greater distance between top management and first-line foremen, many policy issues became uncertain. One of these was the issue of how to deal with work performance and disciplinary matters.

1. As a result of the uncertainty, foremen had a "tendency to delay action." They would "let minor infringements of the rules go by." Presumably, their underlying motive was to avoid unnecessary confrontations in the hope that their benign inaction would be appreciated and reciprocated with good behavior. Of course, the opposite effect occurred. "A few individuals . . . would then start to test just how far they could go."

2. "After several annoying incidents, a foreman would get sufficiently angry to decide on immediate discharge." When failure to discipline early offenses led to repeated offenses, the foreman lost patience and felt personally wronged; when he finally took disciplinary action, he did so without having control over his own emotions. Predictably, the reaction of the individual being disciplined was anger and resentment.

3. "Vigilant supervision was required to make sure that the . . . individual [who had been disciplined] would not act out his annoyance over the punishment by lowering production or quality. . . . Upon return from suspension, the man obviously had to save face

. . . to inform everyone how pleasantly and usefully he spent the 'time off.' " The disciplined person sought vengeance at being treated in a way he perceived as arbitrary, personal, and capricious. Discipline was noncontingently followed by reinforcement: first, from the union, in the form of full benefits and, in effect, a paid vacation; and later from being able to tell peers how he had given the company its comeuppance.

Eventually the company turned to a program that Huberman calls "discipline without punishment." Actually, the program was more like "punishment without discipline." Essentially it was a series of steps involving, on a first offense, a casual reminder and a note of correction (except for such severe violations as theft and fighting); on a second offense, a discussion with the individual in the foreman's office; on a third offense, a repetition of step two, but with the shift foreman also present and posing questions about alternative placement through vocational counseling provided by the personnel office. If unsatisfactory work behavior persisted, the offender was sent home for the day, with full pay—the latter being an expression of the company's sincere wish to see him become a productive member of the organization. If this measure proved unavailing, any future incident within a reasonably short time period would result in dismissal, not as a punitive act but as a realistic recognition that the individual and the organization did not have a viable relationship with each other.

The results in the first few years following the introduction of this program were considered highly satisfactory by plant management. Only three workers had experienced the fourth stage of being sent home with pay, and no workers had to be terminated (though two of the three left voluntarily a few weeks after returning to work from the suspension).

Several features of the new program should be noted. The program made very clear what steps foremen had to take at each stage of worker violations; they had a definite, companywide policy to follow. Thus there was no reason for foremen to let early incidents go by without taking some action. The steps could be taken without the need for emotional involvement by the disciplining parties. The basis for revenge and one-upmanship was rendered rather hollow by giving suspended workers their day's pay in advance. The possibilities for subsequent noncontingent rewards from the union and peers were largely eliminated.

And yet the steps prescribed for countering employee infractions were, in fact, aversive. Being reminded of an offense, conducted to the boss's office (some unions will not allow this unless the union steward is also present), counseled to consider other employment possibilities, sent home (even at cost to the company) are hardly cause for rejoicing. When your rationale for hostility and recrimination is cut out from under you, you can focus your negative feelings only on yourself.

STYLES OF DISCIPLINE

Shull and Cummings (1966) found evidence of considerable variation among managers in their philosophy and style of discipline. The authors presented a number of executives with a written case in which four workers all committed the same infraction—arriving late for work for the third time—but had different lengths of service, previous work performance records, and reasons for being late. The executives responded to the question of whom they would dock (the plant rule was a $5 fine for three late shows within a six-month period) and why. Some of the respondents—dubbed "pure humanitarian" by the authors—would fine none of the men. Others—the "pure legalistic"—would follow the rule to the letter, fining all four workers, regardless of the extenuating circumstances. These two groups accounted for most of the responses. A few executives, however, believed in a more clinical or judicial approach to discipline. They seemed to recognize the need for maintaining standards but could not accept a mechanical enforcement of rules, which they regarded primarily as general principles that were not necessarily applicable to every individual case. The violations were interpreted in the context of the worker's probable intentions and past service and the probability of repeated offenses considering what was known about the worker's character.

With such a diversity of managerial codes of justice, it is no wonder that disciplinary judgments are so frequently matters of controversy. Depending on one's orientation, one can cite disciplinary precedents based on *parity* (all violations treated alike, whether all enforced or all glossed over) or *equity* (a person's outcomes should correspond to his or her inputs in the form of service, effort, and value). Either standard can be eloquently defended or vigorously challenged, because our legal system and cultural norms seem to endorse both. Since neither standard will be universally accepted as fair by all parties, the administration of discipline is never likely to be a favorite managerial responsibility.

CONCLUDING COMMENT

The reader should not conclude that we are advocating the indiscriminate use of punishment to whip subordinates into shape. As we implied in Chapter 3, wherever and whenever there are feasible alternatives to its use (for example, the positive approach of rewarding acceptable behavior or of changing the conditions which evoke the undesired response), these are much to be preferred to punishment. Punishment, despite the best efforts of well-intentioned managers to follow the principles outlined in this chapter, remains a risky and still unpredictable enterprise because of the complex manner in which aversive stimuli affect behavior.

A basketball coach was asked why he chose to emphasize defense rather than offense. His answer was, "Offense is very complicated, whereas defense is basically simple; and I'm not too smart, so I emphasize the simple things." If a manager keenly feels the limitations of human intelligence in administrative matters, he or she is well advised to emphasize the "simpler" positive reinforcement strategies (although it often requires considerable thought and planning to discover ways of using the simple methods).

For obvious reasons, empirical research on the effects of punishment on human behavior has been somewhat limited. The professional ethics which govern the conduct of research on human subjects rule out the use of anything but mild, innocuous punishment in experiments. Thus, what we know about the effects of punishment—aside from our naturalistic observations—derives mainly from studies with lower organisms and studies which use mild electric shock, loss of bonus money accumulated during the experimental period, verbal rebuke, or similar aversive stimuli in experiments with children and college students.

Nevertheless, the fact remains that administrators do use punishment and sometimes have to, even if only as a last resort. For some time to come, discipline in organizations is likely to be one of the responsibilities of managers. If the administrator can closely imitate the hot stove, the exercise of discipline can have a constructive effect on the behavior of organization participants and *need not* result in hostility, rigidity, or the alienation of subordinates from organization goals.

SUMMARY

Punishment of a response occurs when the response is followed by aversive consequences. The processes by which punishment affects behavior are quite complex, and thus the overall effects of punishment on behavior are harder to predict than are the effects of reward. Critics of aversive conditioning techniques argue that punishment requires surveillance to be effective, that punishment only suppresses rather than extinguishes undesired response tendencies, and that it frequently causes destructive side effects. These critics suggest that the prevalence of punishment is sustained primarily by its immediate but temporary reinforcement of the punisher. Alternatives to punishment in eliminating undesired behaviors include extinction, environmental engineering, reinforcing competing but acceptable responses, and allowing maturation to occur at its natural pace.

Punishment tends to be more effective when it is applied to weak responses, when the aversive stimulus is relatively intense and quickly follows the response, and when punishment is focused on the act rather than the person, is consistent across time and persons, contains or is accompanied by information, and occurs in the presence of a warm relationship. These conditions are summarized in McGregor's Hot Stove Rule of discipline in organizations. These conditions also explain why naturally occurring punishment is effective without producing dysfunctional side effects.

CONCEPTS TO REMEMBER

Hot Stove Rule	clinical/judicial
cognitive structuring	disciplinary style
vicarious punishment	parity
pure humanitarian	equity
pure legalistic	

QUESTIONS FOR DISCUSSION

1. Some behaviors in organizations are rewarded by one set of reinforcing agents (such as peer groups) and punished by another set of agents (superiors). What determines whether the behaviors in question will be maintained, strengthened, or weakened?

2. Some individuals seem to respond positively (in the desired direction) to disciplinary measures, some negatively, others to "shrug it off." How can we account for these differences?

3. What does the label *permissiveness* as applied to the home, the courts, the schools, or other institutions imply to you? Is an agent who forswears the use of punishment necessarily "permissive"?

4. "In the long run, punishment, unlike reinforcement, works to the disadvantage of both the punished organism and the punishing agency" (Skinner, 1953, p. 183). Discuss.

5. Unions, legislation, and the bureaucratization of organizations have limited or proscribed the use of a number of punitive measures by managers. What techniques of punishment—what kinds of aversive stimuli—are generally available to managers? Which of these can be tailored to fit the Hot Stove Rule?

CASE 1

Ralph Gilliam had worked in the shipping department of the Sampson Paper Products Company for over 12 years and had generally been regarded by those around him as a steady, dependable, hard-working employee. Last Friday, while working in the area of the department in which a No Smoking sign was conspicuously posted (because of the concentration of flammable materials in the area), he lit up a cigarette. Just as he lit up, a co-worker pulled back the sliding door to the loading dock and a strong gust of wind blew the cigarette from Ralph's lips onto the floor near some combustible chemicals. Ralph, responding with a speed and agility that belied his age of 53, pounced on the cigarette and extinguished it before any damage was done. Meanwhile, the foreman, Sid Robeson, saw what had happened.

Question

If you were Sid, which of the following actions would you take?

(a) Do nothing; ignore what happened; *(b)* go over to Ralph, point out that he has committed a serious violation, and promise him that you will have to penalize him if he ever does it again; *(c)* prepare a written reprimand to be placed in Ralph's personnel file; *(d)* levy a $10 fine; *(e)* suspend Ralph from work for one day without pay; *(f)* discharge Ralph from the company.

CASE 2

Now, go back to the story above, and revise the story to read: "Ralph had worked for less than a year in the company and was generally regarded by those around him as an indifferent worker who needed constant pressure to do what was expected of him in the job; he also was absent more often than anyone else in the department." The rest of the details of the story remain the same.

Question

If you were the foreman and had the same set of alternative responses available to you as before, what would you do?

CASE 3

Assume the same version of the story as in Case 2 above, with this additional change: ". . . a strong gust of wind blew the cigarette into some combustible materials and ignited a fire. By the time the fire had been extinguished, over $300 worth of finished paper goods had been damaged."

Questions

Again, what would you do if you were Sid? Does your course of action vary among the three versions of the case? Why or why not? What are the effects of varying or not varying the form of discipline imposed on the offender as a consequence of either the person's previous work history or the damage caused by the offense?

REFERENCES

Bandura, A.   *Principles of behavior modification.* New York: Holt, Rinehart & Winston, 1969.

Cummings, L. L., & Scott, W. E., Jr. (Eds.).   *Readings in organizational behavior and human performance.* Homewood, Ill.: Irwin-Dorsey, 1969.

Di Giuseppe, R.   Vicarious punishment: An investigation of timing. *Psychological Reports,* 1975, *36,* 819–824.

Huberman, J.   Discipline without punishment. *Harvard Business Review,* 1964, *42,* 62–68.

Reese, E.P.   *The analysis of human operant behavior.* Dubuque, Iowa: Wm. C. Brown, 1966.

Rosen, B., & Jerdee, T. H.   Factors influencing disciplinary judgments. *Journal of Applied Psychology,* 1974, *59,* 327–331.

Shull, F. A., & Cummings, L. L.   Enforcing the rules—how do managers differ? *Personnel,* 1966, *43,* 33–39.

Skinner, B. F.   *Walden two.* New York: Macmillan, 1948.

Skinner, B. F.   *Science and human behavior.* New York: Macmillan, 1953.

Solomon, R. L.   Punishment. *American Psychologist,* 1964, *19,* 239–253.

Strauss, G., & Sayles, L.   *Personnel: The human problems of management.* Englewood Cliffs, N.J.: Prentice-Hall, 1967.

Walters, R. H., & Cheyne, J. A.   Some parameters influencing the effects of punishment on social behavior. Paper presented at the Annual Meeting of the American Psychological Association, New York, 1966.

5

Perception

How do we process stimulus information from the environment?

How do we reduce the complexity of the stimulus world to a simpler basis for action?

How do we form impressions of people?

How does our own behavior enter into the process of perceiving others?

Do you regard yourself as a rather perceptive person, more observant than most other people? If so, test your powers of observation and recall on the questions below:

1. Which way does Abe Lincoln face on a penny?
2. In which hand does the Statue of Liberty hold her torch?
3. What is the highest number on an AM radio dial?
4. How many tines are on a standard dinner fork?
5. Which two letters do not appear on a standard telephone dial?
6. Most U.S. postage stamps give their denominations with a number plus:
   a. cents   b. ¢   c. c
7. On the back of a $5 bill is the Lincoln Memorial; on a $10 bill it's the Treasury building; on a $20 bill the White House. What's in the center of the back of a $1 bill?
8. If a common pencil isn't cylindrical, how many sides does it most likely have?
9. Does it say "Coke" or "Coca-Cola" on every can of the stuff?
10. How many geometric shapes are in the CBS "eye" logo?

Chances are, you have "seen" all of these objects (or pictures of them) hundreds of times. Yet few readers will have much confidence in their answers to the question. And this lack of confidence tells us something very basic to an understanding of the perceptual process: We do not make use of all the information in the environment surrounding us.

Perception is the process by which individuals select, organize, store, and interpret sensory stimulation into a meaningful and coherent picture of the world around us (Berelson and Steiner, 1964). Our brain does not passively "register" all stimuli that surround us. We take an active role in selecting what we perceive, as suggested by Figure 5–1.

First of all, human beings have a limited *span of perception*. Some persons have the apparent gift of attending to more stimuli than others, and certain conditions affect the breadth of attentional span over time for any one individual. But there is a definite upper limit to the amount of sensory stimulation that a person can process. The immediate effect of this limitation is that we have to *select a sample* of the stimulus situation for active scrutiny.

Secondly, even that limited sample of stimuli must undergo some transformation. The sense organs have the potential capacity for greater discrimination and differentiation than our information-processing center can interpret. We have to recode the "raw data" into a simpler form of organization. The human ear, for example, has the potential capability to distinguish 11,000 separate tones, and the eye can discriminate 35,000 different hues, but in the immediate act of

Figure 5–1
A General Model of Perception of the Physical Environment

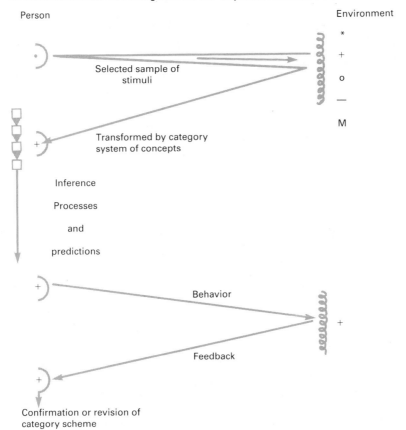

perceiving we cannot possibly make use of this potential. Further-more, George A. Miller, an expert in the study of human information processing, argues convincingly from his findings (Miller, 1956) that we generally can deal with only about seven bits of information at one time. The result of this disparity between what the sense organs can register and what the mind can process is that we have to *orga-nize* raw data into categories of thought. Call these categories words, labels, concepts, constructs, or whatever; the important point is that we use these categories to summarize and record what seem to rep-resent to us the most "important" aspects of the otherwise over-whelming amount of sensory stimulation.

At this point we irretrievably lose some information. Having used the category "fifteen-cent stamp" for collapsing the voluminous data contained in a small rectangular piece of paper (and if you doubt that such a volume of data exists, you have never talked to a serious stamp-collecting hobbyist), you cannot retrieve the information about whether there is a *cents, ¢,* or *c* on it. That information was not important and was "processed out." [Oh, yes. The answers to the quiz: (1) He's looking left, which means to us his nose points right; (2) right hand; (3) 1600 (or 160); (4) usually four; (5) *Q* and *Z*; (6) c; (7) no picture, just the word *ONE* in large letters; (8) six; (9) both; (10) three—a circle inside a football inside a circle. If you answered more than five or six correctly, you did better than the average person. Source: *Indianapolis Star Magazine*, January 6, 1980.]

The nature of the category system used by the perceiver will determine how much, and which kinds, of stimulus information will be accessible in short-term memory. The category scheme also affects the perceiver's sensitivity to subtle differences between similar stimuli. The Hanunuo natives of the Philippines have names for 92 different varieties of rice and consequently are able to note the differences among these varieties. English-speaking persons have only one word—*rice*—and would have trouble noting any distinctions among those varieties (Brown, 1965).

Generally, we develop rather complex, highly discriminating category schemes for objects that are important to us. The skiier, for example, develops a richer mental vocabulary for snow than would other people because a difference in the texture of snow on a downhill slope has some bearing on the appropriate skiing technique. Put another way, we develop concept names as internal cues because distinctions among them are important in order to respond correctly.

It should occasion no surprise that the richness of a person's *total* category scheme determines to a considerable extent that person's powers of observation, recall, problem solving, and creativity. In fact, the most consistent predictor of a manager's income and career mobility is vocabulary. The reason for this association is not that more successful managers impress others with big words but that they have better equipment for observing, interpreting, storing, and recalling subtle distinctions.

Having categorized a portion of the sense data, the perceiver can proceed on the basis of certain built-in assumptions to make inferences about the perceived object. Having categorized from limited visual contact an object as a desk, I can infer that it is solid, would support my weight, would hurt me if I fell against it, would provide a firm level surface for writing. Perception invariably entails numerous leaps of faith; we always go beyond the given data to draw inferences. To do otherwise would bring behavior to a screeching halt. If I had to examine the details of every desk I encountered, I would have no time for making good use of any desk. We capitalize on the *economizing* process in perception by proceeding from categorization to inference.

Of course, not all such inferences are correct. The desk may actually be nothing but papier-mâche, and if so I will tumble to the floor should I try to lean against it. If this happens, I recode the object based on new information generated by my own behavior—the object is redefined as "paper desk," and different inferences (it will tear, burn) result. But the inference-generating process never stops, and we do it so instinctively that *we often mistake our inference for direct observation*, especially when conditions for perceiving are not optimal.

Laboratory experiments have demonstrated this confusion between inferences and direct observation. Such studies make use of the *tachistoscope*, a device for studying characteristics of human visual perception under less-than-optimal conditions. It projects images on a screen for very short duration, usually tiny fractions of a second. The experimenter can manipulate the characteristics of the image to see what subjects "see." In one such study (Bruner and Postman, 1949), the experimenter projected ordinary playing cards but reversed the conventional association between suit and color for some of the cards—spades and clubs were red, hearts and diamonds black. Most subjects reported "seeing" the cards as they had always previously seen them. They had *inferred* that a three of diamonds would be red, because that is the normal inference that follows from that category. But they apparently had no awareness that they had made such inference; the inference was experienced as direct observation.

To summarize: we attend to a selected sample of available stimuli; we recode the raw sense-data into a category system; we use the "rules" of the category system to make predictions; we act on the basis of such predictions; and the results of our actions may or may not alter our original perceptions.

STIMULUS SELECTIVITY

The sample of available stimuli to which we attend does not represent a random sample. Characteristics of the stimulus setting interact with characteristics of the perceiver to determine the focus of attention.

Stimulus Characteristics.   In a crowd of people most of whom are of average height, we tend to notice more easily the one tall person; in a living room filled with people wearing white dinner jackets, we attend most immediately to the one person in a blue cardigan sweater; on a printed page, the one word that is in all capital letters or italics will most quickly catch our notice. A noise that has been screened out of awareness is again noticed if the pitch, rhythm, or volume of the noise changes. In short, *differential stimulus intensity* of an object in relation to other objects tends to bias the sample of stimuli selected. Stimuli that are similar to each other tend to fade into the background, while a few stimuli dissimilar to the others will stand out as "figures" against the "ground."

Motion, especially against a static background, also draws attention. Long ago, merchants realized that drivers will more easily notice a neon sign in which sequential lighting of adjacent bulbs creates the illusion of motion. (As numerous store owners competitively copied this practice, the resulting esthetic effect has led many communities to ban this form of advertising). Magicians usually keep their hands moving in flourishing gestures to distract the audience from any cues that might give the trick away.

Novelty in the stimulus field also directs the perceiver's attention. Advertisers continually seek unusual and unexpected images to command the attention of the jaded eye of the TV watcher or magazine reader.

Characteristics of the Perceiver. To some extent, hereditary or physiological differences lead to characteristic tendencies to more readily perceive certain stimuli. Left-handed instructors, for example, tend to focus more on that part of the classroom to their left; people vary in the kinds of sounds to which they are most sensitive. But *motivational state* undoubtedly represents the most important perceiver characteristic in influencing the focus of perception. A hungry person entering a hotel dining room will tend to ignore the finer points of the tapestries on the walls or the chandeliers, looking only for the varieties of food or food-related stimuli available. The stronger the need or incentive state that is aroused, the greater the tendency to ignore irrelevant stimuli. In one study (Organ, 1977), the experimenter gave subjects typewritten copies of an essay strewn with grammatical and typographical errors, and he asked the subjects to identify and correct as many errors as they could. Half the subjects were given additional bonus points contingent upon how many of the errors they found; the other subjects were not given this incentive. After collecting the essays, the experimenter administered a multiple-choice test of the content (facts, names, numbers) of the essay. Those who proofread for the contingent bonus scored significantly lower on this test. Thus, *motivation has a dual effect on perception:* the *type* of motive influences the *direction* of the perceptual focus. The *strength* or intensity of the motive affects the *breadth of perceptual span*—the stronger the motive, the more narrow the perceptual focus becomes. Ironically, intense levels of motivation on a task can impair performance *if* performance requires sensitivity to subtle stimuli. Strong motivational states apparently activate the category systems most relevant to dealing with those motives and simultaneously suppress those coding schemes irrelevant to the motive. The hungrier you become, the less perceptive you become of objects unrelated to food.

PERCEIVING PEOPLE: FORMING IMPRESSIONS OF OTHERS

One could argue that we do not really "perceive" others at all. We perceive only their immediate behavior and their most obvious physical characteristics. Yet our real interest in others concerns their traits, motives, abilities, and other stable attributes. If we wish to assess someone in terms of a future relationship—as friend, ally, client, employee, someone to do business with, a partner in some nontrivial activity—we clearly have to go beyond the immediately available information and make some inferences about that person's abiding dispositions.

The Attribution Process. In piecing together an impression of someone, our first requirement is to assign some cause to the person's immediate behavior. We must go beyond the behavior itself to make inferences about underlying traits. Trait names are our important constructs in perceiving people. As Brown (1965) notes, it is easier to recall a few trait names than the complex myriad of behavior data that we actually observe. Therefore our information processing concerning other people quickly recodes observations of behavior into trait names. Chances are, if you think of someone you now know very well, you think of that person almost totally in terms of adjectives (warm, sociable, easygoing) rather than specific actions.

Before you can move from the observation of behavior data to trait inferences, you have to *attribute* the various behaviors either to *external* causes (e.g., situational factors) of the behavior or to *internal* causes (e.g., traits, motives, or abilities). The basic rule of attribution is that behavior judged to be externally caused is not informative about the traits of the person (Heider, 1958; Jones and Davis, 1965). Put another way, behavior which is consistent with, and therefore can be explained by, external factors, tells us little about the underlying dispositions of a person. Suppose, for example, that you enter a restaurant and the host greets you with a bow, a wide smile, and expansive gestures of concern for your comfort. Do we thereby infer that this host is a warm, kind person? Hardly. Of course, he *could* be warm and kind, but even if he were cold and selfish, he would probably act in the manner described. He is *supposed* to act that way, because external influences dictate this behavior. The expectations of his boss, the desire to have satisfied customers who will come back, the hope for a generous tip, and various other factors could induce such deferential behavior. Consider another example, this one from work: you supervise someone very closely, taking special effort to monitor how hard she is working, and also making sure *she* knows you are keeping a close check on her. As you monitor her work, she keeps at the task, not goofing off. What inference can you draw about her diligence or conscientiousness? She is working diligently, but that *could* be explained by the fact she knows you have her under close surveillance. Therefore you cannot assume with confidence that diligence represents one of her stable attributes. In fact, a study by Strickland (1958) shows that close supervision by a superior over a subordinate has precisely this effect, namely, a lack of confidence that the subordinate would work as hard if not closely supervised.

We can confidently assign internal causes to a person's behavior only under certain conditions: when no obvious external forces in the situation could account for the behavior; when the person's behavior actually runs *counter* to the direction of any such situational forces; or when two or more strong external forces would exert roughly equal but opposite effects on behavior so that the balance is determined by internal dispositions. If the host greeted us in a surly, insulting fashion, we might well figure that that reflected a cold or uncaring disposition, since the situational forces would have had the opposite influence. On the other hand, if you passed this person on the street when he was wearing his street clothes, not his tux, and he stopped to pick up a dropped parcel for you, you would feel that his behavior originated from a kind nature, since no overpowering forces in the situation demanded such behavior.

While the attribution rule seems logical, we often fail to use it. In observing others' behavior, we seem to have a strong bias toward an inference of internal causation. Heider (1958) concluded that a major bias in social perception is the tendency to see *persons* and not situations as the cause of action. This is especially the case when the situational forces are subtle or complex. Our attention is drawn toward the person, and our limited attentional span may not incorporate other stimuli in the situation that might cause the behavior.

Recall our earlier statement that a condition of strong motivational or emotional arousal tends to narrow our perceptual focus, rendering our perception less sensitive to subtle or motive-irrelevant cues. This principle applies to person perception. If another's behavior has direct effects on your emotions, chances are that your attention span will exclude the information pertaining to situational explanations of that behavior. For example, when you as a detached observer see a policeman carrying out his duties of directing traffic, and in the process gesturing and speaking sharply to pedestrians and motorists, you probably make no inferences about the policeman's personal motives or traits. He simply does what his job requires; who knows what he may be like as a husband or bowling partner? But suppose *you* are a pedestrian, perhaps crossing the street prematurely, and the same policeman calls out to you. Now his behavior has a personal impact— and now his clipped admonition represents not what "a policeman has to do in his job," but a reflection of a more sinister personality, perhaps arrogance: a bully with latent fascist tendencies. As Roethlisberger and Dickson (1964) noted five decades ago in their analysis of worker attitudes, the arousal of strong emotions reduces our ability to make fine perceptual discriminations.

Research evidence (e.g., Walster, 1966) also suggests that the seriousness of the consequences of a person's behavior affects our weighting of its internal versus external causes. The more serious the consequences, the less we consider external causes. If a driver parks her car on a hill without applying the emergency brake and the car rolls a few yards before coming to rest against the curb or a tree, we may dismiss it as "one of those things, could happen to anybody." If it gathers momentum and crashes into someone's living room or, worse, injures a child playing in his front yard, our perception of the driver becomes a matter of identifying the traits—carelessness, stupidity, inconsiderateness—that account for such tragedy.

Physical Cues. Our inferences concerning others' traits derive, not only from observations of behavior, but to some extent from their observable physical characteristics. Such inferences often rest in part on prevailing *stereotypes* of questionable validity—such as the notions that red-haired people have a volatile temperament, people with blue eyes are somewhat cold and restrained, tall people have more self-confidence, chubby people are easygoing and self-indulgent. Physical cues that reflect gender or ethnic group membership may suggest (with questionable validity) certain stereotypic trait configurations. But the most pervasive influence of physical cues on trait inferences involves the general perception of *physical attractiveness* of another.

Physical attractiveness has a *halo effect* on our impressions of others. A halo effect occurs when we allow some generally favorable or unfavorable characteristic to color our evaluative impressions about other characteristics. Certainly in our culture, pysical attractiveness (or its opposite) represents a value-tinged characteristic of others. And we speak here of not only the attractiveness of the opposite sex but of the more general aspect of the esthetic qualities of a person's appearance. Upon seeing someone for the first time in virtually any context, our first evaluative judgment tends to involve physical attraction.

The evidence mounts from social psychological studies that we tend to ascribe more desirable traits to attractive than to unattractive people. Good-looking children are assumed to have better personalities, to be better behaved, to be more honest (Dion, 1972). In another study (Landy & Sigall, 1974), male college students read essays to which a picture of the female student author was either attached or not attached; half of the pictures showed an attractive author and half showed an unattractive author. The essays, in fact, had been prepared by the experimenters as either well written or poorly written. When quality of the essay was held constant, subjects rated the essay better for the attractive women and rated the presumed ability of the attractive women higher. The differential advantage of physical attractiveness had its strongest effect on the ratings when the essay itself was poor. As you might expect, physical attractiveness also has an effect on interviewers' judgments when they assess resumes of applicants for a managerial position (Dipboye, Fromkin & Willback, 1975).

Height also appears to exert a pervasive halo effect on our impressions of others—especially our impressions of men, but perhaps increasingly so of women as well. One study (cited in Keyes, 1980) of starting salary offers extended to a university's graduates found that men 6 feet, 2 inches tall averaged 12 percent more in pay than those standing 5 feet, 11 inches (the pay advantage for above-average academic standing, by contrast, was only 4 percent!). Another study (also cited in Keyes, 1980) showed that sales recruiters chose the taller candidate when given a choice among two equally qualified candidates, one over six feet tall and the other only five feet, five inches. The results indicated that 72 percent of the recruiters chose the six-footer, 27 percent expressed no preference one way or the other, and only 1 percent picked the shorter applicant. Stogdill's (1948) review of traits associated with leadership status showed that taller people have an advantage in attaining the leader role. And, in this century, only once (1976) has the shorter of the two major-party candidates won a presidential election. Apparently we ascribe to taller people the characteristics of strength, competence, good judgment, and he ability to command respect and influence.

Trait Configurations.   Thus far we have discussed how perceivers ascribe a trait to the perceived other on the basis of inferences drawn either from observed behavior, from physical cues that trigger stereotypic conceptions, or from halo effects. Our inference processes seldom rest, however, with a single trait. Each of us tends to think in terms of clusters of traits that go together. As Bruner, Shapiro, and Tagiuri (1958) described it, people have *implicit personality theories* about the relationships between one trait and another. For example, you may believe that people who are generous are usually also honest and happy; that someone who is very neat is also likely to be punctual and efficient. Some implicit personality theories appear to be widely shared; others reflect more idiosyncratic notions. The effect of such theories is that, correctly or not, we use evidence of one trait to infer the existence of others. More important, we often do not realize that such second-order inferences (first-order inferences being those drawn from observed behavior or physical cues) were actually made without directly observed data. In other words, if you observe that Walter keeps his desk and work area very tidy and uncluttered, your impression may move so quickly and instinctively from the inference "he is a neat person" to "he is also efficient and punctual" that you do not realize you have no evidence of his efficiency or punctuality.

Implicit personality theory represents an economizing device in forming impressions of others. It enables us to take a little information a long way. Obviously this facilitates interaction with others and making the judgments on which such interaction proceeds. The other side of the coin is that the more we go beyond the information given to us, the greater the probability of error. But so what? Can we not revise our impressions of others in the light of new information?

First Impressions.   The bulk of the evidence from experiments in person perception argues for a *primacy effect* in our impressions of others. Impressions formed from initial encounters with someone exert a disproportionate influence on the way you continue to perceive them. Experiments (such as Luchins, 1957) studying this phenomenon show that, when subjects receive "contradictory" information about a stimulus person, the effect of the earlier information dominates the overall impression that they form. For example, if your first exposure to someone suggests an outgoing nature and subsequent observation indicates an aloof quality, you will think of the person as more outgoing. As Brown (1965) comments, "first impressions appear to be as critical as secretarial schools have always said they were."

This does not mean that first impressions are permanent, or that we ignore subsequent data about people. Rather, the initial trait inferences act as a baseline to which subsequent observations must be assimilated. Suppose, for example, that your first encounter with a newly hired employee leads you to think that he has rather limited abiliies. Then you observe his work in the next few days and you see that it looks pretty good. Rather than discard your initial impression altogether, you find one means or another to reconcile these subsequent observations with that impression. You might, for example, imagine this new worker as one who has modest ability but works very hard to realize the full potential of those limits. Or you could resolve the contradiction by regarding the work as requiring thoroughness and neatness rather than mental ability. Or you could hold to your impression of *generally* limited abilities but with a narrow, specific sort of aptitude for this specialized task. Eventually, of course, the effect of continued observations of objectively high-caliber work on an array of important jobs may alter your original impression quite a bit. But the point is this: The first impression filters and retards what the effect of subsequent observations would otherwise be.

The Self-Fulfilling Prophecy

Our perception of an object does not affect the object itself. But our impressions of people can, at least indirectly, affect their behavior. Moreover, initially erroneous impressions by a perceiver can shape the behavior of the target person so that it conforms with the original impression.

Psychologists Robert Rosenthal and Lenore Jacobsen (1968) selected an elementary school in a lower-class neighborhood and gave all the children a nonverbal intelligence test. They explained to the teachers that the test could identify "intellectual bloomers," or children whose intelligence would show a sudden surge in development. Rosenthal and Jacobsen then randomly picked 20 per cent of the children in each room and gave their names to the teachers. The teachers were told these pupils would become "intellectual bloomers." In fact, of course, there was no real basis, from the test or otherwise, for expecting any greater intellectual development on the part of these children, since they had been chosen randomly; any difference between these children and the others (controls) resided solely in the teachers' impressions. Eight months later, the researchers retested the pupils. Those whom the teachers had thought would "bloom" showed an overall IQ gain of four points, while the control children did not increase their IQ on the average.

This study sparked an intense controversy, and some critics pointed to possible flaws in the research procedures. A number of subsequent studies, however, have generally supported the generalization that teachers' expectations affect student achievement.

Impressions and expectations per se do not actually affect the targets of the impressions. Rather, our impression of someone influences how we behave toward that person. Our behavior provides cues toward which the person responds, and following such responding, our subsequent behavior provides stimuli which reinforce, fail to reinforce, or possibly punish the response. The point is that our initial impression may well determine the nature of the cycle of responses and counterresponses that follows. The original perception, even if unfounded, triggers a sequence which makes the perception a self-fulfilling prophecy.

Later studies by Rosenthal and others have explored the behavioral mechanisms that mediate the effect of teacher expectancies on student achievement. First of all, teachers enact a *generally warmer interpersonal climate* with those whom they expect to excel scholastically. Second, the warmth they provide to such pupils is *given for different reasons* than the warmth given to others. The teacher smiles fondly at the expected bloomer who asks a profound question or offers an insightful comment. The student already labeled as "slow" receives warmth for being just that; if he or she makes a perceptive comment, the teacher reacts with veiled defensiveness. Third, teachers actually *spend more time* with those already pegged as "fast"— that is, the teachers teach them more, provide greater input. Finally, teachers give such children *more opportunities* for practicing and displaying their learning—they call on them more, give them more time to answer, assign them to important roles in class projects, and so on.

In the Rosenthal-Jacobsen study, the researchers planted the seeds of expectancies that later bore fruit. Would such impressions have formed without the intervention of psychologists? If so, would "naturally occurring" expectancies have been more valid? The best evidence we have suggests that the answers are: Yes, teachers do form such impressions very early, and No, they do not form such impressions on any particularly objective or valid basis. They tend to expect more rapid development from physically attractive children. They expect it more from children of parents with higher socioeconomic status. They expect it if older siblings whom they previously taught showed it. And, as we have seen, the effect of such expectations is to generate a course of events which transforms them into reality.

You should have no difficulty imagining how self-fulfilling prophecies operate in other kinds of organizations. Given a group of subordinates, a manager can form initial impressions of their potential as employees on the basis of physical attractiveness, the reputation of the school or college they attended, their sex, the timbre of their voices, or the impressions described on their resumes by the personnel officer who interviewed them. Regardless of the source of the impression, the manager tends to act more warmly toward those of whom much is expected, reinforcing any sign of professional growth while ignoring or misinterpreting the same behavior by others. The manager will spend more time with the "best and brightest," teaching them more, introducing them to other key figures, providing more feedback (and providing it in a different fashion), giving them a closer look at the "inner face" of operations in the organization. Finally, the manager will provide more "response opportunity" to those seen as bloomers—giving them more nonroutine assignments, more visible roles to play, more time at center stage.

PERCEPTION AND THE JOB INTERVIEW

Perhaps no other job-related situation makes such stringent demands on one's fragile perceptual abilities as the initial placement interview. The outcomes are obviously of critical importance for both the interviewer and the applicant; the cost of error looms ominously over the thoughts of both parties. As we have already seen, the motivational arousal created by this pressure tends to narrow rather than broaden our span of perception, leaving us somewhat insensitive to subtle stimuli. On the other hand, both interactants have a vested interest in managing, or contriving, the impressions they put forward, which means the most salient stimuli tend to convey somewhat limited and unrevealing information. Finally, the typical job interview lasts for 30 minutes or less, and the recruiter may have to interview

122

Figure 5–2

The person-to-person interview places overwhelming demands on the tenuous process of social perception.

as many as a dozen applicants in succession. What effects do these demands have upon the information processing of the recruiter?

Evidence suggests that the interviewer will be more influenced by negative information than positive signs (Kanouse & Hanson, 1972). If the applicant frequently interrupts the recruiter, this evidence of "impoliteness" tends to dominate the interviewer's impression even if other cues have suggested several desirable traits such as personal neatness, articulate speech, candor, and industriousness. To some extent, one can appreciate why negative information would dominate the impression formed by the recruiter: it serves to narrow potential candidates to a smaller number of persons who can be more intensively compared with each other; also, the personal cost (in terms of embarrassment, at least) to the recruiter of eventually hiring a dud exceeds the cost of the other type of selection error of turning away someone who *would have* done well in the job. Yet the implication is that the somewhat bland, weakly positive applicant with no obvious faults clearly has the edge over someone of possibly much greater potential who simply presents one glaring aspect of a negative nature.

Perhaps more alarming is the finding that interviewers usually reach a judgment in the first five minutes of the interview (Springbelt, 1958). This suggests that the recruiter is using the remainder of the interview merely to "confirm" the impression already formed.

The initial inferences have led to expectancies which color subsequent observations. If the judgment is negative, the interviewer may unconsciously communicate this evaluation through tone of voice, body language (e.g., avoiding eye contact, leaning away from the direction of the applicant), or actually probing for more negative information. These cues, in turn, may put the applicant on the defensive, making his or her behavior more awkward or even slightly hostile. Such responses, of course, only serve "to fulfill the prophecy" of the recruiter's expectations.

On what basis could an interviewer reach a decision (even if it is only implicit) in such a short time? The recruiter may have previously examined the candidate's résumé or written application. Preliminary inferences about overall ability from this source may predetermine the direction of the interview. Should recruiters avoid looking at the résumé until after the interview? A study by Tucker and Rowe (1977) suggests that such a procedure does not significantly increase the decision time of the interviewer and probably would not make the interviewer any more open-minded.

One must assume that interviewers are strongly influenced by halo effects. You have doubtless heard many a self-styled "shrewd judge of people" argue that the firmness of a person's handshake tells a lot about that person. To date, we know of no instance in which handshake predicts job performance, other than how a person will subsequently shake other people's hands. We have already seen that physical attraction and height can influence impression.

Even if the interviewer scrupulously weighs only the most relevant information, evaluative impressions of a candidate can be strongly influenced by *contrast effects*. The recruiter will probably evaluate very strong or very weak applicants on their own merits. But a study (Wexley, Yukl, Kovacs & Sanders, 1972) in which college students rated applicants in videotaped interviews showed that assessments of "average" candidates were strongly influenced by who preceded them in prior interviews. Those who followed low-suitability applicants received much higher absolute ratings than those who followed high-suitability applicants. In fact the differences were nearly as great as the difference between ratings given to the high- and low-suitability applicants themselves.

In view of these findings, it is not surprising that experts in personnel and industrial relations regard the interview as a poor diagnostic tool unless the interviewer has been well trained.

CONCLUSION

The more complex, ambiguous, and dynamic our surrounding environment becomes, the more we rely on our own devices to support the perceptual process. Behavior in organizations typically scores high in complexity, ambiguity, and dynamism: Therefore, those who observe behavior in organized settings resort to shortcuts in perception, even at the risk of error. It would be unrealistic for us to tell you to base your impressions only on valid data. What seems more appropriate is to counsel a somewhat tentative, flexible style in forming impressions of the physical and social reality around you. The conviction that most of our "knowledge" derives from economizing processes—which aid perception but also lead to errors—should at least make us more sensitive to cues that contradict such knowledge. We also become more likely to qualify any knowledge conveyed by others, even if ostensibly based on "direct observation," for we realize the frailty of their perceptual systems, too. In short, we realize that we may know a great deal, but we know very little for sure.

SUMMARY

In perceiving the world around us, we do not take account of all potential stimuli. Our sense organs practice a selective focus, determined in part by the characteristics of stimulus objects and in part by our own characteristics, such as motivational state. We actively use category systems to transform and simplify sensory stimulation. Using such category schemes, we make inferences and predictions that guide behavior.

Perception represents a process in which we use observations of behavior and physical cues to infer traits. We work through the attribution process of assigning internal or external causes to behavior. Typically, we have a bias toward overestimating the person (as opposed to the situation) as a causal force. We draw upon physical cues—such as personal attractiveness or ethnic group membership—to use halo factors or stereotypes in forming an impression of certain traits. Furthermore, our conceptions of how traits go together as packages (implicit personality theories) lead us to infer some traits from evidence concerning other traits.

Our impressions of people, unlike those of objects, can indirectly shape their behavior through the manner in which we act upon our impressions. This effect forms the basis of the self-fulfilling prophecy, in which originally erroneous impressions lead to response-counter-response sequences that seem to confirm the original impression.

CONCEPTS TO REMEMBER

motivational effects on perception
span of perception
attribution process
stereotypes
halo effect
implicit personality theory

primacy effect
self-fulfilling prophecy
contrast effects in interviews
negative evaluative set in interviews

QUESTIONS FOR DISCUSSION

1. In a study conducted by Dearborn and Simon (1958), researchers presented a group of 23 managers a detailed case about a steel company. The managers—who represented a variety of functional areas such as sales, accounting, and production—were asked to identify and define the single most important problem facing the company. Dearborn and Simon found that the managers generally defined the major problem in terms that corresponded to their own functional areas—e.g., sales executives saw the major problem as one of marketing, personnel managers defined the critical issue as one of human relations, and so on. How can you account for these findings using some of the principles underlying the perceptive process?

2. How do you account for the persistence of stereotypes and implicit personality theories? Choose an example of each to illustrate your reasoning.

3. Physical attractiveness and height were noted as two frequently occurring halo effects in forming impressions and evaluations of others. What others come to your mind? Try to think of halo effects that might significantly influence the perceptions of a corporate recruiter in an interview or a manager appraising a subordinate's performance.

4. In what sense do we "perceive ourselves"? How would the process of self-perception resemble the process of perceiving others? How do you think it would differ? (*Hint*: Social psychological research strongly suggests that the attribution bias in perceiving the behavior of others does not operate the same way in perceiving our own behavior.)

5. Can you think of an instance when the self-fulfilling prophecy has worked to your disadvantage? In your favor? Describe as pre-

cisely as you can the mediating *behavioral* linkages—your own behavior as well as that of others.

CASE

Refer back to the case following the preceding chapter on punishment and discipline. Discuss the implications of the worker's seniority, his past performance, and the seriousness of the consequences as they affect one's perception of the incident and how such perceptions would probably influence a supervisor's disciplinary measures. How do the notions of implicit personality theory, halo effect, primacy effect, and attribution apply here?

REFERENCES

Berelson, B., & Steiner, G. A. *Human behavior: An inventory of scientific findings.* New York: Harcourt Brace & World, 1964.

Brown, R. *Social psychology.* New York: Free Press, 1965.

Bruner, J. A., & Postman, L. On the perception of incongruity: A paradigm. *Journal of Personality,* 1949, 18, 206–223.

Bruner, J. A., Shapiro, D., & Taguiri, R. The meaning of traits in isolation and in combination. In R. Tagiuiri & L. Petrullo (Eds.), *Person perception and interpersonal behavior.* Stanford: Stanford University Press, 1958.

Dearborn, DeWitt C., & Simon, Herbert A. Selective perception: A note on the departmental identifications of executives. *Sociometry* 1958, *21,* 140–144.

Dion, K. Physical attractiveness and evaluation of children's transgressions. *Journal of Personality and Social Psychology,* 1972, *24,* 207–213.

Dipboye, R. L., Fromkin, H. L., & Willback, K. Relative importance of applicant sex, attractiveness, and scholastic standing in evaluation of job applicant resumes. *Journal of Applied Psychology,* 1975, *60,* 39–43.

Heider, F. *The psychology of interpersonal relations.* New York: John Wiley & Sons, 1958.

Jones, E. E., & Davis, K. E. From acts to dispositions: The attribution process in person perception. In L. Berkowitz (Ed.), *Advances in experimental social psychology* (Vol. 2). New York: Academic Press, 1965.

Kanouse, D. E., & Hanson, L. R., Jr. Negativity in evaluations. New York: General Learning Press, 1972.

Keyes, R. *The height of your life.* Boston: Little, Brown, 1980.

Landy, D., & Sigall, H. Beauty is talent: Task evaluation as a function of the performer's physical attractiveness. *Journal of Personality and Social Psychology,* 1974, *29,* 299–304.

Luchins, A. S. Primacy-recency in impression formation. In C. I. Hovland (Ed.), *The order of presentation in persuasion.* New Haven, Conn.: Yale University Press, 1957.

Miller, G. A.   The magical number seven, plus or minus two: Some limits on our capacity for processing information. *Psychological Review*, 1956, *63*, 81–97.

Organ, D. W.   Intentional vs. arousal effects of goal-setting. *Organizational Behavior and Human Performance*, 1977.

Roethlisberger, F. J., & Dickson, W. J.   *Management and the worker*. New York: Wiley Science Editions, 1964.

Rosenthal, R., & Jacobsen, L.   *Pygmalion in the classroom*. New York: Holt, Rinehart & Winston, 1968.

Springbelt, B. M.   Factors affecting the final decision in the employment interview. *Canadian Journal of Psychology*, 1958, *12*, 13–22.

Stogdill, R. M.   Personal factors associated with leadership: A survey of the literature. *Journal of Psychology*, 1948, *25*, 35–71.

Strickland, L. H.   Surveillance and trust. *Journal of Personality*, 1958, *26*, 200–215.

Tucker, D. H., & Rowe, P. M.   Consulting the application form prior to the interview: An essential step in the selection process. *Journal of Applied Psychology*, 1977, *62*, 283–287.

Walster, E.   The assignment of responsibility for an accident. *Journal of Personality and Social Psychology*, 1966, *5*, 508–516.

Wexley, K., Yukl, G., Kovacs, A., & Sanders, R.   Importance of contrast effects in employment interviews. *Journal of Applied Psychology*, 1972, *56*, 45–48.

6

Attitudes and Behavior

What is the structure of attitudes?

How are attitudes and behavior related?

How are attitudes acquired?

What functions do attitudes serve?

How are attitudes changed?

Mark Twain observed that "differences of opinion make horse races and missionaries." He might well have noted that differences in sentiments give rise to labor unions, work group allegiances, product markets, and office politics.

In the work setting as elsewhere in life, reality is never totally defined by the objective physical characteristics of people and things. As we noted in the previous chapter, people take an active role in perceiving their environment. Even more important than the perceptual process, however, is the process by which people attach *meaning* to what they perceive. Objects are not merely perceived; they are related to other objects, they are interpreted, and they are evaluated. Ultimately we respond as much to this internal construction of meaning as we do to the object itself. We can scarcely hope to understand behavior in organizations without reference to this covert process by which meaning is constructed. Therefore, we must examine the role of *attitudes* in mediating overt responses to external stimuli.

Figure 6–1
Mediating Role of Cognitive Processes

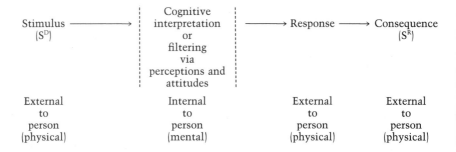

WHAT IS AN ATTITUDE?

We use the word *attitude* in casual conversation to indicate "how we feel about something." However, the social psychologist finds it useful to conceptualize an attitude as something more complex than feelings. First of all, the psychologist regards an attitude as a *hypothetical construct*. In psychological terms, a hypothetical construct is something which we cannot directly observe but *infer* from behavior. A *motive* for example, is a hypothetical construct; so is an *instinct*. We do not see an attitude, a motive, or an instinct; we see, at most, their effects. By using the term *motive*, you are, in effect, saying something like, "there must be some underlying force which causes a person to behave like that, and I'm going to call that force a motive." Thus, the term *attitude* means essentially "an unseen force which we presume exists in order to explain certain behavior."

Second, the social psychologist finds it useful to regard an attitude as an organization of emotional, belief, and action-tendency components. That is, an attitude consists of feelings, beliefs, and predispositions to behave in certain ways. Furthermore, these components are tied together, psychologically, in the sense that each component has implications for the others.

Describing an attitude this way explains why attitudes form the basis for the construction of the meaning we attached to objects and events. We relate an observed stimulus to others through a system of beliefs. We evaluate these relationships by how we feel about them. We are predisposed to respond in certain ways by the implications of these beliefs and feelings.

COMPONENTS OF AN ATTITUDE

The Affective Component

The *affective* or *emotional component* of an attitude develops as a *conditioned response* by association with stimuli that have either rewarding or punishing effects. Thus, affective components are learned through classical conditioning methods (see Chapter 3). For example, McGinnies (1970) points out that expressions of warmth and affection from one's parents are probably among the earliest unconditioned stimuli for positive affective responses and that the stimuli for many negative affective responses are probably derived from parental disapproval or neglect. Any behavior by either parent or child that immediately precedes these rewarding or punishing stimuli gains some measure of control over the elicited reaction. Thus the term *love*, because it is often preceded by physical demonstrations of affection, becomes a conditioned stimulus to reactions that most persons would describe as pleasant. On the other hand, a word such as *hate* elicits other reactions, generally reported as unpleasant because they have characteristically preceded some aversive event. Thus certain words become cues for emotional reactions, and we may assume that the context in which the words are used comes to serve the same functions. In addition, the words help us understand our *feelings* about the object in question.

In 1966 Dickson and McGinnies used questionnaires to survey the attitudes of a sample of university students toward the church. They then presented these students with tape-recorded statements that either praised or disparaged the church, while simultaneously recording their emotional responses (as measured physiologically with the galvanic skin response, or GSR). Both prochurch and antichurch students responded with greater emotion (as shown by elevations in GSR) to statements that contradicted their attitudes than to those that reflected their attitudes.

Since the affective component of an attitude is a classically conditioned response, it has many of the properties of other classically conditioned responses. For example, once an emotional response has been conditioned to an object, that object may in turn generate similar responses to other objects often associated with it. An emotional response to certain facial expressions (such as frowns) of others may develop because such expressions immediately precede actions by others that give us discomfort. Thereafter, words that are characteristically uttered in accompaniment with frowns also can acquire control over emotional responses of fear, anger, or loathing. Thus, many words acquire negative connotations because of the social and physical cues associated with them. Finally, any other word that is regularly combined with existing words already possessing negative affect acquires such a connotation. A person who usually hears the word *business* associated with words such as *greed, exploitation, arrogance,* and so on is likely to have a negative attitude toward business. On the other hand, someone who usually encounters the same term with positive words such as *jobs, opportunity, service,* and *benefits* will develop a positive attitude toward business.

Many of our attitudes thought to be rationally derived may simply represent a long chain of classically conditioned emotional (or "gut") responses. You may have a positive or negative attitude about something you have never seen or something you actually know very little about, so long as you have seen the word in the context of other words that have already come to control certain responses. Osgood, Suci, and Tannenbaum (1957) have shown that the affective or emotional component of words accounts for about 50 percent of their connotative meaning. Perhaps this is the reason bureaucrats, administrators, and politicians like to develop new but ungainly terms and phrases when they propose specific policies. An unfamiliar term is less likely to evoke widely prevalent emotional reactions that might otherwise cause resistance. During the 1962 Cuban missile crisis, President Kennedy used the term *naval quarantine* rather than *blockade,* because the latter term —due to its historical association with acts of war—would have triggered a more powerful emotional response among our own citizens as well as among the Soviets. President Nixon referred to the movement of U.S. troops into Cambodia in 1970 as an *incursion* rather than an *invasion,* for the same reason.

Conditioned emotional responses also generalize to objects that are similar in some fashion. Thus, if you have a strong positive emotional response to your father, you are likely to have a positive attitude even toward strangers who resemble your father. It is well known that sub-jects will express positive and negative attitudes about people just from looking at their pictures.

The Cognitive Component

The *cognitive component* of an attitude represents the *beliefs* that a person has about a person or object. Your attitude toward labor unions, for example, includes your beliefs about the effects that union activities may have on the economy, beliefs about what unions do for their members, beliefs about whether their actions promote liberal or conservative causes, and so on. These beliefs may come from personal observation, from what you read or hear, or from your own infer-ences; they may be factual, speculative, or fiction. A belief has atti-tudinal implications, however, only if the belief has reference to something you have *feelings* about. Your belief that unions belong to the AFL-CIO probably exerts little attitudinal force. But if you believe unions protect the worker from exploitation, or believe that unions

Figure 6–2
Belief systems underlying three different attitudes toward labor unions.

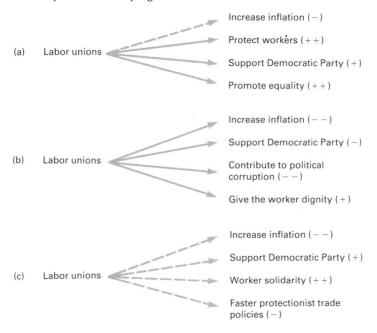

contribute to corruption in politics, and you have feelings about either of these effects, then the beliefs have attitudinal implications.

Fishbein (1967) argues that your attitude toward an object or person is determined by the weighted sum of your beliefs about that object or person. Each belief represents a level of confidence or certainty about the connection between the object and some other object toward which you already have a favorable or unfavorable disposition. Thus, the overall attitude is determined by the *strength* of the beliefs, the *proportion* of the beliefs that connect the object with "good" or "bad" things, and the *intensity of feeling* about these things. Figure 6–2 illustrates three hypothetical belief systems about unions. Solid lines represent strong or confident beliefs, dotted lines represent less-certain beliefs. A single + or − designates objects of moderately favorable or unfavorable evaluation, and a double + + or − − indicates strong dispositions. How would you characterize the overall attitude toward unions in these instances?

The Behavioral Component

Any attitude, *taken by itself*, implies some predisposition to behave one way or another toward its referent object. The behavior, however, refers, not to a single response, but to a broad array or class of *potential* responses. If your overall attitude toward labor is positive, then—other things being equal—you are more likely to:

Say nice things about labor unions

Act friendly toward a union member

Vote for a candidate supported by organized labor

Defend a union criticized for going on strike

Purchase products made by unionized workers

than would someone whose attitude toward unions is negative. You may not *actually* do any of these, because other factors may override your attitude, or you may do something other than these. The point is that we can imagine a set of behaviors that expresses to one degree or another a favorable disposition toward unions, and a person with such a disposition is more likely to display some of the responses in that set.

ARE ATTITUDES (BELIEFS AND EMOTIONS) RELATED TO BEHAVIORAL RESPONSES?

During the early 1930s a sociologist named Richard LaPiere traveled throughout the United States in the company of a young Chinese couple. Unknown to the young couple, LaPiere maintained a record of their travels noting especially how the two Chinese were received by clerks in hotels and restaurants. In a 1934 article, LaPiere reported that only once was the couple not treated hospitably.

In addition to recording how the Chinese couple was treated, La-Piere obtained information about attitudes toward Chinese. Six months after visiting each establishment, he sent a letter to the hotel or restaurant asking whether Chinese clientele would be accepted. Over 93 percent of the responses said no—Chinese would not be accommodated.

LaPiere thus obtained extremely discrepant information about prejudice toward the Chinese. People *acted* one way (friendly, hospitably) but reported that they would respond to Chinese in a different manner (negative affect and beliefs about Chinese).

The study by LaPiere poses the important question of whether or not internal attitude components (beliefs and emotions) are related to behavior. It seems logical that we would *intend* or *prefer* to behave consistently with our feelings and beliefs. But do our intentions and preferences always predict our actual behavior?

Figure 6–3
Conceptual Scheme for Relating Attitudes to Stimuli and Responses

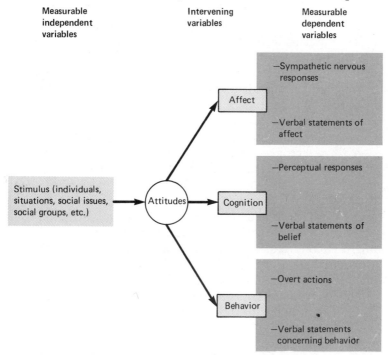

Source: From M. J. Rosenberg and C. I. Hovland, "Cognitive, Affective, and Behavioral Components of Attitude," in *Attitude, Organization, and Change*, ed. M. J. Rosenberg, C. J. Hovland, W. J. McGuire, R. P. Abelson, and J. H. Brehm (New Haven: Yale University Press, 1960).

Wicker (1969) examined the relationship between verbally expressed attitudes and overt behavior. After reviewing a sizable portion of the research evidence, he concluded that there is little evidence to support the assumption that verbally expressed attitudes correlate highly with the overt behaviors implied by those attitudes.

Mann (1969) noted that the discrepancies between attitudes and behavior are not really surprising and should be expected. He offers three reasons for these discrepancies. First, Mann agrees that behavior is determined not only by attitudes but also by external factors in the immediate social situation. Mann says, "Consider the non-prejudiced behavior of the seemingly prejudiced proprietors in LaPiere's study. Perhaps at the time of the visit of the Chinese the proprietors needed the money, were reluctant to become involved in an argument, or were impressed with LaPiere; these factors may have prevented the prejudiced attitude from influencing their behavior" (p. 111).

A second reason given by Mann as to why attitudes and behavior are often discrepant is that many different attitudes are relevant to a single action. Rokeach (1966) contends that attitudes toward the object as well as attitudes toward the situation in which the object is encountered determine the individual's behavior. Attitude objects are almost always encountered in situations in which there are already strong, overriding attitudes toward other components of the situations. Therefore, inconsistency between behavior and internal attitudes might be a function of orientation to a situation. Mann noted, "In public places, such as restaurants and hotels, there are socially defined and regulated codes of conduct. One is not supposed to make a scene, embarrass the guests or scream racist obscenities in the foyer of a hotel. The attitude that politeness and decorum is the appropriate behavior in a hotel supersedes the attitude of prejudice toward Chinese, and La Piere's companions are made welcome" (p.112).

A third factor, according to Mann, is the type of attitude underlying the prejudice. He notes that "intellectualized" attitudes are rich in beliefs and stereotypes but have no real action tendencies. "Just because the proprietor expresses a negative evaluation or intention about Chinese in general, it cannot be assumed that he has committed himself to a corresponding form of behavior to every Chinese he might encounter. . . . If there is no action orientation in a particular attitude there is little reason to expect consistency among beliefs, feelings, and behavior" (p. 112).

A very sizable literature has now accumulated concerning the predictability of behavior from measures of attitudes. While the findings are by no means wholly consistent, the following conclusions seem to have much support:

1. Measures of *general* attitudes seldom predict specific behaviors very well. Your attitude toward labor unions in general might have

little to do with your overt behavior toward a particular union local president in your community. On the other hand, when the attitude measure and the object of your behavior are matched in specificity, the correlations improve. Measures of attitudes about conservation do not predict consumption of unleaded fuel, but attitude measures about unleaded fuel do predict quite well the frequency of buying such fuel.

2. Attitude measures predict behavior only to the extent that situational constraints do not limit the freedom of behaving in the manner suggested by the attitude. If you have an unfavorable view of unions, but membership in the union is a requirement of your job and supporting it is a precondition for maintaining good relations with co-workers, then your behavior will not likely reflect an anti-union attitude. If you moved to a different area and obtained a job in a nonunionized plant, there would be more freedom to express the attitude in overt behavior.

3. Attitudes may remain latent until situational stimulus cues activate them. You may have a very strong attitude about unions, but your day-to-day environment may contain nothing to trigger that attitude—you do not encounter union members, you do not get involved in discussions of politics or the national economy, you purchase products that do not identify whether they come from unionized plants, you are not affected by any disruptions due to strikes or other work stoppages. Clearly there would exist no basis for predicting any important aspects of your behavior from a pencil-and-paper measure of your attitude.

WHERE DO ATTITUDES COME FROM?[1]

Attitudes reflect a person's previous reinforcement history. As such, attitudes are *learned.* The determinants of a person's attitude system include societal influences, major group memberships, the family, peer groups, and prior work experience.

Societal Influences. Our culture and language provide us with the experiences and boundaries for our initial attitudes. We are taught at a very early age that certain attitudes and beliefs are more acceptable than others. The attitudes of Americans toward Communism are very different from those held by the average Russian.

In the area of international management and multinational organizational exchanges, it is important to understand the value system (attitude framework) of the society or culture one is in before making judgments or taking action. What seems appropriate in one's own cul-

---

[1]Adapted from T. W. Costello and S. S. Zalkind, *Psychology in Administration* (Englewood Cliffs, N.J.: Prentice-Hall, 1963), pp. 260–263.

ture may be totally unacceptable in another culture. For example, in South America attitudes toward punctuality are not nearly as intense as they usually are in urban North America.

Major Group Memberships.　Within our own society, each of us is strongly influenced by the major groups to which we belong. Our geographic region, religion, educational background, race, sex, age, and income class all strongly influence how we view the world. Students familiar with marketing surveys learn that *target markets* are generally based on these categories. *Playboy*, for example, claims to be the magazine of highest readership among males between the ages of 18 and 30 with incomes over $15,000 annually. If one were interested in influencing the attitude of young adult males toward a new product, then *Playboy* might well be a good place to advertise the product.

The Family.　The family is the major influence on the initial core attitude system held by a person. Obviously the family influences early learning patterns and controls the groups and culture to which a person is initially exposed.

Peer Groups.　As we approach adulthood, we rely increasingly on our peer groups for approval. Initially other children, acquaintances, playmates, and friends influence our attitudes. As we enter the world of work, our co-workers and others influence what we say, how we feel, and how we respond. How others judge us determines to a certain extent our self-image and our approval-seeking behavior. We often seek out others who share attitudes similar to our own, or else we change our attitudes to conform to the attitudes of those in the group (fraternity, dorm, club) whose approval is important to us.

Prior Work Experience.　A person just starting to work already has a host of attitudes developed and acquired from the culture, the family, and the peer group. By the time the person goes to work in a specific organization, he or she will hold many attitudes toward the type of job which is acceptable, the pay expected, working conditions, and supervision. As noted in Chapter 3, the manager will have to understand these individual differences when administering rewards and punishments and when assigning jobs.

In a study of the attitudes of skilled and semiskilled workers to job enrichment (the process of increasing the responsibility and variety of a job) Davis and Werling (1960) surveyed a West Coast plant employing 400 operating personnel and 250 clerical and administrative personnel. The interests of skilled workers, which were similar to those of management, included company success, self-improvement, and improvement of operations. Semiskilled workers, on the other hand, lacked concern for company goals and attached little importance to job content. Blood and Hulin (1967) suggested that workers in large cities were alienated from the work norms of the middle class (positive affect for occupational achievement, a belief in the intrinsic value of hard work, a striving for the attainment of responsible positions, and a belief in the Protestant work ethic). Rather, they adopted the norms of their own particular group, seeing work as a necessary evil and emphasizing fulfillment away from work and a primary concern about pay and benefits.

ATTITUDE STRUCTURE AND CONSISTENCY

In our examination of the relationships among the components of attitudes, we noted that people strive to maintain consistency among these components (beliefs, feelings, and actions) but that apparent contradictions often occur. In addition to the question of the internal structure of attitudes, there is the question of the structure of attitude *systems*—clusters of attitudes about a set of related objects which fit together in an interconnected, integrated whole. Social scientists have spent a considerable amount of time studying the extent to which consistency exists among the attitudes in a cognitive system, what happens when attitudes become inconsistent with one another, and how adjustments are made to restore consistency to the system.

In seeking answers to these questions, a number of theories of cognitive consistency have been developed. These theories go beyond attitudinal consistency to a more general cognitive consistency in the image or "map" of the world held by the individual. That image includes thoughts, values, and actions as well as attitudes about some object or some set of events. At the core of the interest in cognitive consistency is the assumption that people need to attain harmony and congruity among their cognitions of objects and persons in the environment. Brown (1965) observed that "the human mind expects good things to cluster together and to be opposed to the cluster of bad things . . . positively valued objects should be linked by associative bonds and, similarly, negatively valued objects should be linked by associative bonds. Between positively valued objects and negatively valued objects there should be only disassociative bonds" (p. 553). Whenever these rules are violated, a state of disequilibrium exists and a tension is generated that is reduced only when equilibrium is restored.

If an individual has formed an attitude and has engaged in some behavior, what are the psychological implications of any discrepancy between the attitude and the behavior? Like Brown, Festinger (1957) notes that a state of disequilibrium, which he calls *dissonance*, exists when there is a discrepancy between the attitude and the behavior of an individual. Although several other theories have been advanced to explain the psychological processes employed in reaching equilibrium, Festinger's Cognitive Dissonance Theory will be discussed here because it relates to *both* the attitude-behavior consistency argument and to the more generic problem of cognitive consistency mentioned earlier.

Festinger's Cognitive Dissonance Theory

The term *dissonance* refers to a psychological inconsistency among cognitions associated with internal attitudes and behaviors. Two cognitions are in a dissonant relation if one implies the opposite of the other. For example, the cognition "I smoke a pack of cigarettes a day" is psychologically inconsistent with "Cigarette smoking is extremely hazardous to one's health, and I could die of cancer!"

The *Cognitive Dissonance Theory* predicts that a person will experience discomfort or tension (dissonance) when two cognitions are psychologically inconsistent. Because the occurrence of cognitive dissonance is unpleasant, the individual acts to reduce or eliminate it.

The individual reduces dissonance arousal by restoring consistency between cognitions. This may be done in several ways. The person may alter personal behavior, change beliefs, change feelings, or add new cognitions that explain the previous inconsistency (Calder & Ross, 1976). The smoker may reduce dissonance by giving up smoking, or, if he or she is not willing to do this, the person can choose to believe that "smoking is not dangerous if you don't inhale," or believe that "when your number is up, it's up."

When a behavior is fully justified by external circumstances (for example, to avoid pain or to acquire rewards), little or no dissonance is aroused by an inconsistency between that behavior and the person's attitude. On the other hand, if the behavior cannot be explained by a reference to external circumstances, the person will experience dissonance and be motivated to reduce the inconsistency. A study by Staw (1974), who studied male students enrolled in the ROTC in 1969–71, illustrates how people alter their original attitudes to restore consistency when external forces do not apparently justify behavior. Many of his subjects had joined the ROTC, in part, to avoid being drafted and sent to Vietnam. When they joined the ROTC they signed a contract requiring them to continue in it for the remainder of their stay at the university and to become reserve officers in the Army if such appointments were offered. After these students had made their commitment to ROTC, the Selective Service System conducted a draft lottery. Each of the ROTC cadets, like all other males of draft-eligible age, received a number that would have been his had he not joined ROTC. The number indicated a high, medium, or virtually no chance of being drafted.

Staw reasoned that students who won numbers that would have allowed them to avoid the draft should have experienced cognitive dissonance. They had made an irrevocable commitment to the ROTC when their chances of being drafted were very low. In other words, they had not needed to join the ROTC to escape the draft. One way these students could reduce dissonance was to decide that they enjoyed the ROTC, that the ROTC was a valuable experience in its own right. Accordingly, Staw had the cadets complete questionnaires that assessed their satisfaction with the ROTC. As dissonance theory predicted, those students who had the least to gain by being in the ROTC (those with high draft numbers and little probability of being drafted) indicated the most satisfaction. Interestingly enough, those students also averaged the highest grades in the ROTC.

Cognitive dissonance theory has important implications for the relationship between the effort a person exerts to attain a goal and the person's attitude toward the goal once it is achieved. Specifically, any undesirable aspects of the goal are dissonant with the knowledge that a considerable amount of effort was exerted to attain it. The more effort, in any form, an individual exerts to achieve a goal, the more dissonance is aroused if the goal is less valuable than was expected. The individual may reduce this dissonance by concentrating on the positive aspects of the goal or distorting its value.

Essentially, then, cognitive dissonance theory argues that, not only do beliefs and feelings affect behavior, but behavior affects beliefs and feelings. Social psychological experiments (see Aronson, 1973) show that, when we are induced to hurt someone, we tend to attribute negative characteristics to the victim—especially if we wish to preserve an image of ourselves as decent individuals who do not go around hurting innocent others. By the same token, we tend to like people whom we have befriended. Benjamin Franklin in his *Autobiography* told of a political opponent who was personally antagonistic to Franklin. Franklin, as it happened, wished to obtain a certain book and no one in Philadelphia except his antagonist had it. Franklin went to the man's house and asked if he might borrow the book. The man lent him the book, and thereafter he and Franklin got along famously. Franklin derived a rule from his experience: If you want to convert an enemy into a friend, *ask* a favor of him. A person who acts benevolently toward you will be predisposed to think well of you.

There are other implications of the dissonance principle. An emotional response toward some object will exert a force toward beliefs that are consistent with the emotion. Experiments (e.g., Rosenberg, 1960) show that subjects who are conditioned through hypnosis to have positive or negative emotional responses toward objects will later derive beliefs that are consistent with the emotion. People who have an instinctive loathing for snakes believe they are slimy (actually they are not); those who flinch at the sight of cockroaches believe they are filthy (actually they are very fastidious and clean).

As Aronson (1973) concluded, Man is as much a *rationalizing* as a rational animal. We are uncomforatble with apparent discrepancies among our feelings, beliefs, and actions. Either the discrepancies have to be explained by strong forces beyond our control, or the appropriate attitude components must be adjusted to restore harmony.

FUNCTIONS SERVED BY ATTITUDES

Regardless of how attitudes are formed, there is little dispute among psychologists that people do have attitudes and that it is important to understand those attitudes. Organizations, especially their personnel and marketing departments, spend millions of dollars to measure the attitudes of employees and consumers. Why? Because attitudes influence other important psychological processes, such as the formation of simple social judgments, the perception and interpretation of ambiguous stimuli, the learning and retention of controversial material, and receptivity and openness to new information. Moreover, while attitudes do not invariably predict specific responses to specific situations, attitudes do suggest the more general patterns of behavior that will occur if the person is not constrained by external forces. Not everyone who dislikes the job or boss will quit immediately, but sooner or later many of those who have these feelings will leave when the opportunity arises.

In addition to helping us predict the behavior of others, attitudes, according to Katz (1960), serve functions for the personality and help us adapt to our environment. Katz suggests that four personality functions are served by the maintenance and modification of social attitudes: *adjustment, value expression, knowledge,* and *ego defense.* Unless we understand the psychological need which is met by holding an attitude, states Katz, we are in a poor position to predict when and how the attitude will change. The same attitude may perform different functions for the different people who express it. Let us see how Katz perceives the differences in the various functions served by attitudes.

The Adjustment Function. This function is a recognition of the fact that people strive to maximize the rewards and to minimize the penalties in their external environment (the hedonistic principle discussed in Chapter 3). Attitudes acquired in the service of the adjustment function are means for reaching desired goals or for avoiding undesirable results, or are associations of sentiments based on experiences in attaining motive satisfactions.

Attitudes serve as steering devices. A positive attitude about a restaurant where you have enjoyed the food, the service, the clientele, the atmosphere steers you in the direction of maintaining your patronage of the place and thus continued reinforcement. Expressing certain attitudes leads to respect, support, and liking from those around you. Attitudes that serve adjustment functions have a pragmatic character: you like the things and the people who lead to positive outcomes for you, and you dislike those which lead to pain, frustration, or discomfort.

The first author once worked for a luggage manufacturer and sent out to the sales force a questionnaire asking them to compare various brands of luggage in appearance, style, functional properties, and design. Their rank-orderings of competitive brands on these characteristics correlated almost perfectly with the rankings based on sales! In effect, the salespeople were saying that a suitcase has a good design if it sells; has a good appearance if it sells; even has a good color if it sells.

The Ego-Defensive Function.   People expend a great deal of their energy learning to live with themselves. Many of our attitudes have the function of defending our self-image.

We noted earlier that often our attitudes emerge or change so as to be consistent with our actions. If we act in ways that harm people, and have no prior basis of justifying such acts, we have a dilemma. How can we think well of ourselves, on the one hand, yet know that we have without good reason hurt others? The tension created by such dissonance may prompt us to derogate those whom we hurt. We impute crass motives, inferior qualities, or undesirable traits to such persons—"they deserved it." Such beliefs allow us to defend our own egos from the damaging implications of our actions. Undoubtedly many decent middle-class citizens who acquiesced in the Nazi treatment of Jews felt pressured to defend their self-images by groping for beliefs that Jews were Communist sympathizers, enemies of the Reich, or at least mercenary parasites. In our own country, those who supported the quarantining of Japanese-Americans in the panic on the West Coast that followed Pearl Harbor felt similar needs to rationalize their treatment of innocent people. Those who have actively or passively discriminated against women or against blacks or other ethnic groups may defend their self-images by belief systems that ascribe inferior traits or abilities to them.

Ego-defensive attitudes may arise when we feel threatened by others. Older managers are often intimidated by brash, young graduates with awesome technical skills—especially if the Young Turks make a point of emphasizing these differences. The older manager, to fend off the painful (and perhaps unfounded) implication that he has become "inferior," in defense may impute to these junior officials "lack of judgment and common sense," "arrogance," or "narrow focus."

Unfortunately, unfavorable attitudes held by people in one group often cause the "self-fulfilling prophecy" to occur in the behavior of the stereotyped group. The self-fulfilling prophecy, in turn, provides a justification for actions toward the stereotyped group. If you, as a male, say that women are unqualified for top management positions and that therefore you won't train them for such positions, sure enough, women remain unqualified for the positions, and they know it as well as you do. Women thus may come to believe that they are unqualified because they have been discriminated against, and both men and women are then justified in their attitudes—the men for believing that women are inferior at certain tasks and the women for feeling that men are biased and prejudiced. The research of Rosen and Jerdee (1976) has shown that older people are perceived to be significantly less capable of effective performance with respect to creative, motivational, and productive job demands, even though the actual performance of older people does not support this belief.

The Value-Expressive Function. Although many attitudes have the function of preventing individuals from revealing their own true nature to themselves and others, other attitudes have the function of giving positive expression to one's central values and to the type of person one conceives oneself to be. Katz (1960) says, "Value-expressive attitudes not only give clarity to the self-image but also mold that self-image closer to the heart's desire" (p. 170).

Many of the attitudes espoused by professional groups—such as scientists, physicians, writers, accountants—serve to articulate the fundamental values to which their vocation subscribes. Scientists, for example, place a premium on the free and unencumbered pursuit of knowledge. This value becomes the point of departure for assessing many dimensions of work, organizations, and relationships. Similarly, a person who strongly endorses the Protestant work ethic (Chapter 9), which pervasively values hard work and self-denial, will tend to voice attitudes toward specific persons or practices as a means of reflecting this value.

The point we strive to make here is that values deeply embedded in a person's self-image remain somewhat ill formed and inchoate until expressed in some fashion. Expression is easier when values are attached to specific objects in the form of attitudes. The consistency and interconnectedness of these attitudes define the value and, in a very real sense, enable the person to communicate his or her self-image.

The Knowledge Function An old adage says that the only people who have no opinion about a specific issue are those who know absolutely nothing about it—neutrality equals ignorance, in other words.

Most readers would acknowledge that we have a better memory for the things we feel strongly about than we do for those matters toward which we are indifferent. In much the same fashion, some attitudes provide perspective on the assemblage of facts, experiences, observations, inferences, and speculations that comprise our cognitive domains. Attitudes provide structure to these domains, giving them meaning and coherence. When facts are sorted out according to how they fit our beliefs and emotions, those facts have more meaning (even if, inevitably, the result is some bias in the way in which facts are sought out and emphasized). The very drive to seek new information is largely prompted by the need to experience consistency and rationality in attitude systems.

Biographer Ronald Steel (1980) attributed the success and influence of the legendary political columnist Walter Lippmann to the need of an audience for attitudes that unified knowledge:

> The personal editorializing of "Today and Tomorrow" (Lippmann's column) rested on a frank recognition that . . . journalism was not about facts, but about interpretations of what seemed to be "facts." Lippmann attributed his success . . . to the growing complexities of public life and the need . . . for someone . . . who could put the news into perspective [Steel, 1980, p. 281].

THE PROCESS OF CHANGING ATTITUDES

According to Katz (1960), an attitude that no longer serves its function will cause the individual holding that attitude to feel blocked or frustrated. Modifying an old attitude and replacing it with a new one is a process of learning, and learning always starts with a sense of being thwarted in coping with a situation. However being thwarted is a necessary, but not a sufficient, condition for attitude change. See Table 6–1 for an overview of the growth and change dynamics of attitudes serving different functions.

Arousal and Change of Adjustment Attitudes

Katz states that the two basic conditions for the arousal of existing attitudes are the activation of their relevant need states and the perception of the appropriate cues associated with the content of the attitude. To change attitudes which serve an adjustment function, one of two conditions must prevail: (1) the attitude and the activities related to it no longer provide the satisfactions they once did; or (2) the individual's level of aspiration has been raised.

Since the prejudices of employees serve the function of meeting *current needs* by following the rewards and avoiding punishment, one way to change such attitudes is to change the environment and its rewards. Changes in attitudes occur more readily when people perceive that they can accomplish their objectives by revising their existing attitudes. Hovland, Janis, and Kelley (1953) state that attitude change is contingent upon some incentive that is provided by the

Table 6–1
Determinants of Attitude Formation, Arousal, and Change in Relation to Type of Function

Function	Origin and Dynamics	Arousal Condition	Change Condition
Adjustment	Utility of attitudinal object in need satisfaction; maximizing external rewards and minimizing punishments	1. Activation of needs 2. Salience of cues associated with need satisfaction	1. Need deprivation 2. Creation of new needs and new levels of aspiration 3. Shifting rewards and punishments 4. Emphasis on new and better paths for need satisfaction
Ego defense	Protection against internal conflicts and external changes	1. Posing of threats 2. Appeal to hatred and repressed impulses 3. Rise in frustrations 4. Use of authoritarian suggestion	1. Removal of threats 2. Catharsis 3. Development of self-insight
Value expression	Maintenance of self-identity; enhancing favorable self-image; self-expression and self-determination	1. Salience of cues associated with values 2. Appeal to individual to reassert self-image 3. Ambiguities which threaten self-concept	1. Some degree of dissatisfaction with self 2. Greater appropriateness of new attitude for the self 3. Control of all environmental supports to undermine old values
Knowledge	Need for understanding, meaningful cognitive organization, consistency and clarity	Reinstatement of cues associated with old problems or of old problems themselves	1. Ambiguity created by new information or by change in environment. 2. More-meaningful information about problems

Source: From T. W. Costello and S. S. Zalkind, *Psychology in Administration* (Englewood Cliffs, N.J.: Prentice-Hall, 1963), p. 274.

communicator or is implied as a consequence of accepting the communicator's message. Kelman (1961) refers to this acceptance as *compliance*; that is, the individual accepts influence because he or she hopes to achieve a favorable reaction from another person or group. In face-to-face situations in which an individual is put under group pressure to adopt an opinion contrary to what he or she believes, yielding to the influence attempt is based on the desire to conform to the expectations of others in order to receive rewards or avoid punishment. For Kelman, this is an instance of compliance in which the opinion is adopted publicly without actual inner acceptance. In such instances, as soon as the group releases its arousal pressure, the individual reverts to his or her initial opinion.

Arousal and Change of the Ego-Defensive Attitude

Katz (1960) notes that attitudes which help protect the individual from internally induced anxieties or from facing up to external dangers are readily elicited by any form of threat to the ego. As implied in Table 6–1, the threat may be external, as in the case of a highly competitive situation, a failure experience, or a derogatory remark. Prejudice, as noted earlier, is a major type of ego-defensive attitude. Most prejudices are maintained because the group to which one belongs gives support to them. Since many prejudiced attitudes are learned through classical conditioning (association) and are *emotional* in basis, they are harder to change than are attitudes based on information (beliefs) and learned by instrumental conditioning methods.

Katz lists three factors which can help change ego-defensive attitudes. First, the source of threat, real or imagined, must be removed. Social approval is important to the individual's self-image, and people have less need of ego-defensive attitudes in a supportive climate. Second, catharsis, or the ventilation of feelings, can help set the stage for attitude change. Third, ego-defensive behavior can be altered as the individual acquires insight into his or her own mechanisms of defense. Stotland, Katz, and Patchen (1959), for example, found that involving people in the task of understanding the dynamics of prejudice helped arouse self-insight and reduce prejudice. The manager who is faced with the need to hire more women could *involve* the biased foreman in their selection. Instead of saying "You must hire Sally Jones," the manager might allow the foreman to interview five or six qualified women and to select the one he thinks is suitable for the job.

Frontal attacks on ego-defensive attitudes often boomerang. The attitude, after all, protects the person from threat; attacks on such attitudes simply increase the threat and therefore increase the need for the attitude. Feminists who indulge in such sports as selecting "male chauvinist pig of the week" may enjoy the ventilation of their righteous indignation but probably have little prospects for changing the attitudes of prejudiced managers about women and work. All that will be accomplished is to make them more defensive about any past sex discrimination. They will have even greater need to rationalize their actions so as to defend their own conceptions of themselves as decent and fair-minded.

Arousal and Change of the Value-Expressive Attitude

Katz (1960) suggests two conditions which are relevant to changes in an aroused value-expressive attitude. First some degree of dissatisfaction with one's self-concept or its associated values is the opening wedge for fundamental change. Dissatisfaction with the self can result from failure or from the inadequacy of one's values in preserving a favorable image of oneself in a changing world. Second, dissatisfaction with old attitudes as inappropriate to one's values can also lead to change. Such dissatisfaction with old attitudes may stem from new experiences or the suggestions of other people.

Kelman (1961) labels this process of change *identification*. Identification occurs when an individual adopts the attitudes of a person or a group because his or her relationship with the person or group is satisfying and forms part of his or her self-image. An illustration of the role reference groups play in changing value-expressive attitudes is provided by observations made at Bennington College in the 1930s by Newcomb. Questionnaires measuring political-economic progressivism were given to members of the student body each year to determine how these attitudes changed during their four years at Bennington. A steady decrease in conservatism, with a concurrent increase in progressivism, was found in students as they advanced from the freshman through the senior years. For example, 62 percent of the freshmen, 43 percent of the sophomores, 15 percent of the juniors, and 15 percent of the seniors favored Alfred Landon, the conservative Republican presidential candidate of 1936. Interestingly, 66 percent of the students' parents favored Landon, a figure most closely associated with the results for the freshmen. It was apparent that the political-economic attitudes of the students became increasingly divorced from the attitudes of their parents as the students proceeded from freshman to senior (Newcomb, 1943).

Arousal and Change of the Knowledge-Function Attitude

The knowledge-function attitude should be the easiest attitude to change since it is based on information and beliefs which are open to examination and dispute. The means for changing this attitude are persuasion and the use of new sources of information. Kelman (1961) sees the knowledge-function attitude as being based on the *internalization* of attitude-related information contained in persuasive communication delivered by reliable and trustworthy sources. The central idea is that an opinion or attitude becomes accepted because its adoption and expression satisfy a desire for consistency and structure in one's framework of knowledge.

FACTORS DETERMINING THE EFFECTIVENESS OF PERSUASION

Persuasion is a process in which a source effects change in a target's attitude by changing key beliefs relevant to that attitude. This process has engaged the interest of public officials and commentators for many years, since they are so concerned with public opinion. Social psychologists have perhaps invested more of their resources into researching persuasion than any other single topic. The research has focused mainly on characteristics of three factors: the source, the message, and the target.

The Source. Not surprisingly, sources with high credibility are more effective in changing beliefs than are less credible sources. A respected nutritionist such as Dr. Jean Mayer has a better chance of changing your thinking about a high-fat diet than would a disc jockey or a garage mechanic.

The credibility of the source appears to have its greatest effect at the time the target actually receives the message. Some studies offer disturbing evidence of a "sleeper effect" in persuasion: as time passes after initial receipt of the message by the target, highly credible sources lose some of their impact, while less credible sources exert *greater* effect on attitude change. The sleeper effect is shown graphically in Figure 6–4. After a few weeks, the target may be affected almost equally by messages from more or less credible sources. One possible explanation for this occurrence is that, with the passage of time, targets disassociate the content of the message from its origin. This phenomenon gives cause for some concern, since it suggests that rumormongers and charlatans, in the long run, may influence opinion nearly as much as experts.

Some recent studies and reanalysis of earlier ones, however, raise some question about the genuineness of the "sleeper effect": Gillig and Greenwald (1974) suggest that the decreased effectiveness of a high-credibility source is *not* matched by a corresponding increase in the effectiveness of the low-credibility source.

Qualifications and reputed competence, of course, bear very strongly on the credibility we impute to a source. In addition, however, there arises the question of whether the source stands to benefit from the target's change in attitude. Even granting the expertise of

Figure 6–4
The "sleeper effect" of source credibility on persuasion.

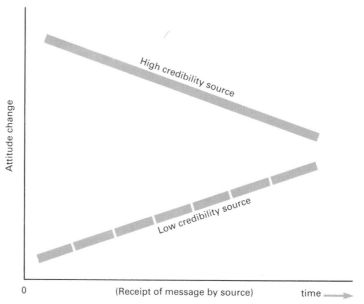

Dr. Jean Mayer in matters of nutrition, his credibility might well suffer if he were known to have financial interests in some brand-name food that he publicly endorsed. We suspect that most managers who experience little success at persuasion do so, not because subordinates question the superior's expertise, but because they wonder about his or her motives.

Other things equal, the communicator increases the chances of effective persuasion by doing or saying something at the outset that suggests a kinship with the recipient or audience. This is a time-honored technique among politicians, public officials, commencement speakers, and probably effective managers. The political candidate visiting a rural hamlet almost invariably remarks upon his or her own small-town roots and usually opens the speech with some kind words about the community. In 1967, the Vice President Hubert Humphrey visited the campus of the University of North Carolina at Chapel Hill to make a speech in defense of the Johnson administration—which had begun to lose support of student and academic groups because of the war in Vietnam. Humphrey not only stressed his own early career as a professor but also noted the analogy between his own number two status and the Tarheel basketball team (then ranked number two in the nation behind UCLA).

Such "warming up" to the recipient or audience presumably lowers the defenses of the latter. It increases the probability that the recipient will actually try to comprehend the communicator's arguments and inhibits the audience from a dogged, covert resistance. Of course, if the warming-up technique comes across as blatant, insincere ingratiation, the effect may be just the opposite.

The Message. Should an advocate present only one side of the issue or acknowledge the contrary view as well? The research record suggests that, in most instances, a two-sided message is more effective at changing the recipient's beliefs. This is likely due to the fact that a two-sided message has more credibility. Furthermore, the two-sided approach has a particular advantage over the one-sided attempt when the recipient is *(a)* intelligent, *(b)* familiar with the issue, or *(c)* clearly in initial opposition to the communicator's position. Any advantage of the one-sided approach seems to be limited to an audience not familiar with the issue (and therefore having few strong existing beliefs to begin with) or already in agreement with the source. Even in these situations, the effectiveness of a one-sided message may be short-lived; a series of studies by McGuire (1964) strongly suggests that exposing the recipient to contrary views and *simultaneously refuting them* works as an *inoculation* to lessen the vulnerability of the recipient to future arguments supporting a different view. Therefore, organizational officials will experience maximal effectiveness in persuasion, especially in the long run, by acknowledging the logic and evidence supporting other viewpoints as well as the ones they seek to establish and maintain among employees.

Will the persuasiveness of a message be enhanced by playing upon the fears of a recipient? The reader will have no difficulty recounting instances in which advocates have used this technique. Political candidates have sketched grim pictures of nuclear holocausts and starvation among elderly citizens that will come about if their opponents attain office; managers and owners have on occasions predicted that their pleasant environs would turn into vacant, rusted-out factories and wind swept ghost towns if workers voted in a union; voluntary health-care organizations have shown smokers the charred lungs of a deceased, two-pack-a-day addict. What is the effect of such appeals to emotion?

Janis and Feshback (1953) lectured to three groups of high school students on the importance of good dental hygiene. The first group heard a presentation with minimum use of fear-arousing tactics; the second heard a talk with a moderate appeal to fear; and the third group was exposed to rather scary pictures of the consequences of neglecting dental hygiene (e.g., bleeding gums, rotten teeth). A fourth group served as control subjects. The results, as measured by students' responses to a questionnaire one week later about their conformity to good dental hygiene habits, showed the minimum-fear appeal to be most effective (36 percent net change in conformity with prescribed practice), followed by the moderate-fear appeal (22 percent); the strong-fear message was least effective (only 8 percent net change).

The authors reasoned that arousal of strong emotion in the form of fear arouses the recipient's defenses; it interferes with the covert rehearsal of the arguments presented. The recipient, in a sense, "blocks out" the threatening stimuli. One suspects this would happen most frequently among those people most predisposed to emotional upset to begin with. Recently one of the authors asked an acquaintance if she had seen pictures shown by animal protection groups of dogs caught in leg-traps or commercial hunters bludgeoning baby harp seals in the Arctic. She replied that she always tried to avoid looking at such ads because they upset her. As a consequence, the ads never had the intended effect of inducing her to mail a contribution to the animal protection group or otherwise become active in their cause.

In some instances, however, research has demonstrated effectiveness of a strongly fear-arousing approach. The situations favoring this approach appear to be those in which the communicator can somehow prevent the recipient from screening out the threatening stimuli and can specify immediate constructive steps to alleviate the fear. Such situations would require an unusually high level of control by the source (e.g., one-on-one doctor-patient interaction) and are not representative of most environments in work organizations. At the very least, we suspect that managers who use such appeals may either tarnish their credibility or acquire a generally threatening aura that leads to avoidance behavior by subordinates.

The Recipient.   With source and message characteristics equated, what kinds of people are most likely to bend to persuasive arguments?

The research on personality factors that might correlate with persuasibility has produced few consistent findings. The evidence suggests that persons with low self-esteem yield to persuasive messages more often and to a greater extent than high–self-esteem individuals; also, high–self-esteem people characteristically attempt to exert more influence via persuasion than do their low–self-esteem counterparts. McGinnies (1970) suggests that low self-esteem and high persuasibility "stem from the same type of previous experience, namely negatively reinforced instances of argument with others. That is, individuals who have systematically been punished for disagreeing with . . . others may come to agree . . . with greater frequency" (pp. 393–394).

Research through the mid-1960s also suggested that females were more persuasible than males. Again, this difference probably derived from differential contingencies of social reinforcement in the culture;

females were more apt to have been reinforced for acquiescence (especially to male authority figures) than for assertiveness. The evidence of changing cultural demands and expectations in this respect suggests that any sex difference in persuasibility has diminished in the last decade or two.

Studies reviewed by McGinnies (1970) show that the initial attitude of the target determines to some extent how successful a persuasive message will be. Those who previously hold extreme attitude positions tend to show more resistance to a persuasive message. Moreover, the *discrepancy* beween the position advocated in the message and the position of the target is important. If the discrepancy is minor, little change in attitude results—apparently because the target, in order to fend off pressures to change beliefs, *displaces* the *perceived position* of the source in the direction of his or her own presently held attitude. In other words, the recipient interprets the message as supporting his or her own position. On the other hand, if the position advocated represents *one extremely different* from the target's, the recipient may exaggerate the discrepancy so as to reduce the credibility of the source. Therefore, the source must take some account of the present attitude extremity of the audience in order to fashion a message that has an optimal degree of discrepancy—not too little, not too great—with the attitude of the audience.

ATTITUDE CHANGE: A WORD OF CAUTION

Perhaps we would not be out of order in emphasizing here that, ultimately, it is people themselves who change their own attitudes. Persuasive messages and alterations in the stimulus environment might initiate the sequence that results in attitude change, but in the final analysis people change their attitudes when they are quite good and ready to do so. We emphasize this point as a precaution to the reader against viewing attitude change as a matter of artful manipulation or quick and easy exercise in propaganda. To be sure, some individuals have more talent than others at "selling" a point of view, at least in a series of "hit-and-run" encounters. But when you have to live with people in a sustained relationship, influencing attitudes of those involved in these relationships does not lend itself to machine-like simplicity. In a democratic culture, people are conditioned to think of their attitudes and opinions as matters of rights, and attacks upon them in whatever form are not taken lightly.

We should note, too, that many persons look upon attitude change as an instance of the broader pattern of *reciprocity* in social exchange between individuals. This suggests, as Costello and Zalkind (1963) have noted, that managers should stand ready to amend their own attitudes when it is timely and appropriate to do so. Such a posture increases the chances that they will find their subordinates more receptive to influence in the form of persuasion. Attitude change is a two-way street; subordinates expect a measure of reciprocity to prevail.

SUMMARY

An attitude is an individual's predisposition to evaluate an object in a favorable or unfavorable manner. The structure of an attitude consists of affective (emotional), cognitive (belief), and behavioral components. Attitudes as measured by pencil-and-paper instruments do not necessarily predict the respondent's behavior very well; just how closely attitudes and behavior correlate depends on the specificity of the attitude object, the situational constraints on the person's behavior, and whether or not situational cues make the attitude salient. Furthermore, behavior may precede the attitude; individuals, when induced to act in a form that has implications about attitudes, arrange subsequent attitudes to be consistent with the behavior. A functional approach to attitudes emphasizes the needs they serve for individuals; attitudes may serve adjustment, ego-defensive, value-expressive, or knowledge functions. Attiudes change, then, in response to changes in needs or functions they serve. The effectiveness of persuasive messages in changing attitudes depends on characteristics of the source, the message itself, and the recipient.

CONCEPTS TO REMEMBER

hypothetical construct	knowledge function
affective component	persuasion
cognitive component	compliance
behavioral component	identification
cognitive dissonance	internalization
adjustment function	"sleeper effect"
ego-defensive function	inoculation
value-expressive function	

QUESTIONS FOR DISCUSSION

1. Sears, Roebuck and Company since 1939 has had a department for surveying employee attitudes. This unit surveys the attitudes and opinions of all stores and their employees every three years, an undertaking which is very costly in time and money. Why do

you think Sears would spend millions of dollars to do this? How do you think Sears uses this information?

2. How do advertisements for consumables (such as cigarettes, soft drinks, beer, paper towels) differ from those for durables (such as automobiles, cameras, lawn mowers)? Why do you think these differences exist? Try to account for these differences in terms of the components of attitudes, the functions attitudes serve, and the appropriate strategies for influencing different types of attitudes.

3. Why do political campaign managers concentrate their resources on the uncommitted voters?

4. One can point to a number of concerted attempts to influence attitudes in the general population that were not successful. Cases that come to mind include the early Vietnam War protesters in the mid-1960s; the appeal to the public to drive at a maximum speed of 55 miles per hour; efforts of some large corporations to improve their "images"; efforts of unions to gain acceptance in certain clerical and professional occupations. Can you identify specific reasons for some of these failures?

5. In what instances should a manager *avoid even trying to change* a subordinate's attitude?

REFERENCES

Aronson, E.   The rationalizing animal. *Psychology Today,* May 1973, 46–52.

Blood, M. R., & Hulin, C. L.   Alienation, environmental characteristics, and worker responses. *Journal of Applied Psychology,* 1967, *51,* 284–290.

Brown, R.   *Social psychology.* New York: Free Press, 1965.

Calder, B. J., & Ross, M.   *Attitudes: Theories and issues.* Morristown, N.J.: General Learning Press, 1976.

Costello, T. W., & Zalkind, S. S.   *Psychology in administration.* Englewood Cliffs, N.J.: Prentice-Hall, 1963.

Davis, L., & Werling, R.   Job design factors. *Occupational Psychology,* 1960, *34,* 109–132.

Dickson, H. W., & McGinnies, E.   Affectivity and arousal of attitudes as measured by galvanic skin responses. *American Journal of Psychology,* 1966, *79,* 584–589.

Festinger, L.   *A theory of cognitive dissonance.* Evanston, Ill.: Row-Peterson, 1957.

Fishbein, M.   A behavior theory approach to the relations between beliefs about an object and the attitude toward the object. In M. Fishbien (Ed.), *Readings in attitude theory and measurement.* New York: John Wiley & Sons, 1967.

Gillig, P. M., & Greenwald, A. G.   Is it time to lay the sleeper effect to rest? *Journal of Personality and Social Psychology,* 1974, *29,* 132–139.

Hovland, C. I., Janis, I. L., & Kelley, H. H. *Communication and persuasion: Psychological studies of opinion change.* New Haven, Conn.: Yale University Press, 1953.

Janis, I. L., & Feshback, S. Effects of fear-arousing communications. *Journal of Abnormal and Social Psychology*, 1953, *48*, 78–92.

Katz, D. The functional approach to the study of attitudes. *Public Opinion Quarterly*, 1960, *24*, 163–204.

Kelman, H. C. Processes of opinion change. *Public Opinion Quarterly*, 1961, *25*, 57–78.

LaPiere, R. T. Attitudes vs. actions. *Social Forces*, 1934, *14*, 230–237.

Mann, L. *Social psychology.* New York: John Wiley & Sons, 1969.

McGinnies, E. *Social behavior: A functional analysis.* Boston: Houghton Mifflin, 1970.

McGuire, W. J. Inducing resistance to persuasion. In L. Berkowitz (Ed.), *Advances in experimental social psychology.* New York: Academic Press, 1964.

Newcomb, T. M. *Personality and social change.* New York: Dryden Press, 1943.

Osgood, C. E., Suci, G. J., & Tannenbaum, P. H. *The measurement of meaning.* Urbana: University of Illinois Press, 1957.

Rokeach, M. Attitude change and opinion change. *Public Opinion Quarterly*, 1966, *30*, 529–548.

Rosen, B., & Jerdee, T. H. The nature of job-related age stereotypes. *Journal of Applied Psychology*, 1976, *61*, 180–183.

Rosenberg, M. J. Cognitive reorganization in response to the hypnotic reversal of attitudinal affect. *Journal of Personality*, 1960, *28*, 39–63.

Rosenberg, M. J., & Hovland, C. I. Cognitive, affective, and behavioral components of attitude. In M. J. Rosenberg, C. I. Hovland, W. J. McGuire, R. P. Abelson, & J. H. Brehm (Eds.), *Attitude organization and change.* New Haven, Conn.: Yale University Press, 1960.

Staw, B. Attitudinal and behavioral consequences of changing a major organizational reward: A natural field experiment. *Journal of Personality and Social Psychology*, 1974, *29*, 742–751.

Steel, R. *Walter Lippmann and the American Century.* Boston: Little, Brown, 1980.

Stotland, E., Katz, D., & Patchen, M. The reduction of prejudice through the arousal of self-insight. *Journal of Personality*, 1959, *27*, 507–531.

Wicker, A. W. Attitudes versus actions: The relationship of verbal and overt behavioral responses to attitude objects. *Journal of Social Issues*, 1969, *25*, 41–78.

7

Needs, Goals, and Motives:

Theories of Motivation

How is behavior energized?

How is behavior directed?

How is behavior maintained?

When organizational behaviorists discuss motivation, they are primarily concerned with (1) what energizes human behavior; (2) what directs or channels the behavior; and (3) how the behavior is maintained or sustained. Each of these three components represents an important factor in our understanding of human behavior at work. First, we see that an energizing force within individuals "drives" them to behave in certain ways. Second, a goal orientation directs their behavior *toward* a goal object. Third, forces in individuals and their environments either reinforce the intensity of their drive and the direction of their energy or discourage them from their course of action and redirect their efforts.

WHAT ENERGIZES HUMAN BEHAVIOR?

As noted above, one of the things that managers need to understand about the motivation of their subordinates is what energizes human behavior. A comprehensive review of all motivational theories is clearly beyond the scope of this text. There is, however, a popular theory that can provide the student with an understanding of what energizes a worker's behavior. That is need theory (Maslow, 1943; Alderfer, 1969).

Need Theory

Maslow has suggested that the underlying needs for all human motivation can be organized in a hierarchical manner on five general levels, as shown in Figure 7–1.

Figure 7–1
Maslow's Need Hierarchy

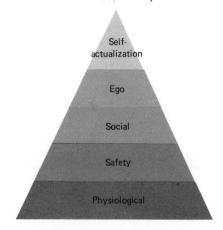

At the lowest-order level are *physiological needs*, which include the needs for food, water, sex, and shelter. For a human being who lacks everything, the major motivation would be such physiological needs. For example, an extremely hungry man would define utopia as a place where there is plenty of food. Human beings live by bread alone where there is no bread.

When the physiological needs are satisfied, the *safety needs* become the most important in the hierarchy. These are the needs for protection against danger, threat, and deprivation. McGregor (1960) has aptly summarized the potency of the safety needs:

> Arbitrary management actions, behavior which arouses uncertainty with respect to continued employment or which reflects favoritism or discrimination, unpredictable administration of policy—these can be powerful motivators of the safety needs in the employment relationship at every level, from worker to vice president. In addition, the safety needs of managers are often aroused by their dependence downward or laterally. This is a major reason for emphasis on management prerogatives and clear assignments of authority.

The third level in the hierarchy comprises the *social needs*, that is, the giving and receiving of love, friendship, affection, belonging, association, and acceptance. If the first two levels are fairly well gratified a person becomes keenly aware of the absence of friends, or of a sweetheart, and will be motivated toward affectionate relations with people in general and toward a place in his or her primary group relations in particular.

At the fourth level in the hierarchy are the *ego needs*, which are generally classified into two subsets, The first subset includes the needs for achievement, adequacy, strength, and freedom. In essence this is the need for autonomy or independence. The second subset includes the needs for status, recognition, appreciation, and prestige. In essence this is the need for self-esteem or self-worth.

The fifth and highest level in the hierarchy is the *self-actualization need*. This is the need to realize one's potentialities for continued self-development and the desire to become more and more of what one is and what one is capable of becoming. For example, a musician must create music, an artist must paint, a poet must write in order to achieve ultimate satisfaction. Unfortunately, the conditions of modern industrial life afford only limited opportunity for the self-actualizing need to find expression.

Certain assumptions and qualifying statements should be noted with respect to Maslow's hierarchy: (1) The hierarchy is dynamic in the sense that the most prepotent need takes precedence in motivating behavior. For example, to the extent that one has been deprived of food, physiological needs become more important than all other needs. But when a given need is fairly well satisfied, the next-higher need emerges to motivate behavior. (2) Any behavior tends to be determined by several or all of the basic needs simultaneously rather than by only one of them. For example, eating may be partially for the sake of filling the stomach and partially for the sake of comfort and the amelioration of the other needs; or one may make love not only for sexual release but also to convince oneself of one's sexual prowess, to make a conquest, or to win more basic affection. (3) The basic needs are only one class of behavioral determinants. While behavior is almost always motivated, it is also almost always biologically, culturally, and situationally determined as well. (4) There are relative degrees of satisfaction in these basic needs, and the hierarchy should not be interpreted in an all-or-none sense. In 1943 Maslow suggested that in our society, on the average, the physiological needs are generally 85 percent satisfied, the safety needs 70 percent satisfied, the social needs 50 percent satisfied, the ego needs 40 percent satisfied, and the self-actualization need 10 percent satisfied.

Two major postulates follow from Maslow's need hierarchy: (1) A satisfied need is not a motivator of behavior. A person lacking economic security will devote much time and effort to attain it; but once this goal has been reached, it will have little or no effect on behavior. (2) As lower-order needs are satisfied, higher-order needs become more-important determinants of behavior. A work force that has come to take job security for granted will increasingly seek to satisfy the needs for self-esteem, achievement, or self-fulfillment.

A second need theory, similar to the one offered by Maslow, has been presented by Alderfer (1969). Alderfer argues for three levels of needs: existence, relatedness, and growth. *Existence* needs are those required for physical survival, security, and comfort. *Relatedness* needs include those pertaining to affiliation with others, love, friendship, and the urge to belong. *Growth* needs refer to the striving for independence in thought and action and the need to experience a feeling of competence. Like Maslow, Alderfer argues that the extent to which a lower-level need is satisfied influences its importance and the importance of higher-level needs. He agrees with Maslow's hypothesis that the satisfaction of growth needs makes them more important to people, and that the lack of satisfaction of higher-order needs can make lower-order needs more important to people.

Need theory is very difficult to test empirically, and only a few studies have attempted to either prove or refute the models. Some support has been found for the following conclusions. (1) In the United States and Great Britain, studies find the hierarchical satisfaction of needs that Maslow postulates. (2) Across all managerial levels the least-satisfied needs are seen as most important. (3) Security and social needs tend to be better satisfied in higher-level managerial jobs than in lower-level jobs. (4) Higher-order needs are usually activated and satisfied after lower-order needs are fulfilled.

A review of the relevant research by Wahba and Bridwell (1973) found little support for Maslow's model as originally formulated. Empirical studies do not confirm the existence and identity of five distinct need categories; the data suggest rather that there are a cluster of related lower-order needs and a different cluster of overlapping higher-order needs. A longitudinal field study by Lawler and Suttle (1972) argues for modifying the hierarchical character of Maslow's model.

Their data indicate that lower-order needs (e.g., physiological and security needs) as a group must generally be satisfied before higher-order needs are activated. However, once lower-order needs are met, *any* of several higher-order needs—such as the need for autonomy, self-esteem, relationships, or growth—may be activated. The higher-order needs need not operate in sequential fashion or in the manner of a hierarchy. Furthermore, Lawler and Suttle suggest that, while lower-order needs become less important as they are satisfied, this relationship does not necessarily hold for higher-order needs.

The general concept of a need hierarchy has considerable relevance to the successive life stages and career stages of adults. Hall and Nougaim (1968), who built upon the work of Erik Ericksen on stages of adult development, found in a five-year study of 49 young managers that career concerns change in a systematic pattern. Early career stages were characterized by a concern for security and gaining acceptance within an organization. During the first five years, concern gradually shifted from security to professional identity, achievement, and autonomy. In later career stages managers are more apt to seek *generativity*, a need that does not have any obvious fit in Maslow's hierarchy. The need for generativity is a quest for some contribution or influence that will endure after one's death. It may be sought by influencing the careers of younger professionals or founding a new organization with a distinctive mission.

Regardless of which theory of needs we subscribe to, it seems to be intuitively plausible that most of our waking hours are spent in the service of some need. Perhaps the dominant philosophical and religious themes in some cultures are able to instill a "peace that passeth all understanding," a state in which needs or goals have no urgency. But everything we know about life in the Western world suggests that it is a restless existence, a continual striving for something. A need may be satisfied, but always a different need takes its place. For some individuals, this cycle repeats itself until an insatiable need—perhaps some form of "impossible dream"—takes hold.

WHAT DIRECTS ENERGIZED BEHAVIOR?

Motivated behavior not only has *force*, derived from some wellspring of tension or energy, but also a *direction* or pattern. Individuals in work organizations seldom scatter their behavior in a random fashion; they focus it. We find that some people focus and direct their behavior into rather high levels of work effort, while others direct much of their behavior toward task-irrevelant activities.

Expectancy theory, the operant model, and goal-setting theory are the major conceptual frameworks that attempt to explain how people at work direct their energies.

Expectancy Theory

The *expectancy theory* of motivation (often referred to as *instrumentality theory*) was originally proposed by Tolman in 1932 as part of his *purposive psychology of behavior.* In essence, he argued that a person's purpose in behaving must be analyzed with respect to the person's *perceived likelihood* that an action will lead to a certain outcome or goal and with respect to the stated *value* or *attractiveness* of the outcome or goal. Several theorists subsequently offered further conceptual additions to this theory (see, for example, Porter and Lawler, 1968). Vroom (1964) was the first to specifically relate the theory to motivation in the work environment. Among today's industrial and organizational psychologists, expectance theory is a widely accepted theory of motivation.

A number of different versions of an expectancy model of work effort have been offered by motivation theorists and researchers. While these different models share certain basic concepts and assumptions, they differ substantially in terminology, scope, and notation. We have chosen not to survey all of these models but to present one which is notationally simple and direct, yet expresses the core assumptions of expectancy theory.

Staw (1977) has offered a very appealing and useful scheme for grasping the essential notions of an expectancy model of job motivation. The scheme is shown in Figure 7–2.

Figure 7–2
An Expectancy theory model of the determinants of level of work effort (adapted from Staw, 1977).

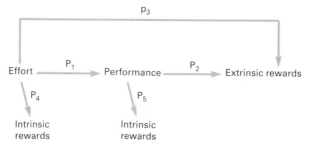

The principal elements in the scheme are the classes of rewards and the subjective probabilities (P's) of obtaining them. An individual who directs effort toward a particular level first takes into account the various reward outcomes that may follow. These include extrinsic rewards (such as possible salary increases, promotions, benefits) made contingent on superior performance or possibly even given to those who put forth a great deal of effort. Outcomes also include the intrinsic rewards inherent in outstanding performance on *certain* tasks; for example, feelings of pride in craftsmanship or satisfaction of achievement. Finally, certain tasks—especially those that afford a considerable degree of variety, autonomy, novelty, stimulation, or pleasant social encounters—provide intrinsic rewards of effort itself. In sum, an individual may exert considerable effort because effort itself is rewarded by the organization, because the effort leads to outstanding performance that is rewarded by others, because the effort leads to accomplishments valued in themselves, or because the effort (or *process* of working) itself is stimulating regardless of what it might lead to. Obviously, a person's effort might be sustained for combinations of these reasons, too; but if *none* of these rewards is anticipated, effort will be minimal.

For simplicity of illustration, we omit negative outcomes, such as supervisory criticism, fatigue, or peer group disapproval. A person would, however, take both positive and negative outcomes into account.

Rewards do not tell the whole story, however. It is not only the *amount* of contemplated rewards, but also the *perceived probability* that a particular level of effort would result in those outcomes. If the individual thinks there is a very low probability of differential pay for outstanding performance, the size of the pay difference may not induce extra effort beyond a minimum or average level. Furthermore, even if P_2 is fairly high that will make little difference if P_1 is very low. Even if you think outstanding performance is virtually certain to be generously rewarded, it won't make much difference to you if you think there is little likelihood of your attaining such a performance level no matter how hard you work. (We have all known students who can make Bs and would like to make As but say they "could study twice as hard and still would get the same grade.")

One of the major contributions of expectancy theory is identifying two very different kinds of "motivational problems"—those cases in which P_2 is low versus those in which P_1 is low.

Why Would P_2 Be Low? Why would a person think that differential performance is not likely to be recognized by the reward system? One reason, of course, could be that such a perception is very accurate. While organization officials may give lip service to the idea of matching pay or other benefits to performance level, in practice they may seldom do so. Suppose the organization does stand ready to reward outstanding performance—could P_2 still be low? It could if co-workers convinced a person from the outset that any performance above a standard level is not rewarded. It could be low if the organization kept its salary schedules secret; Lawler (1973) has found that secrecy leads employees to *underestimate* the pay differentials that exist. Finally, if performance levels must be rated by superiors, some people may not believe they will be given due credit for extra performance.

Why Would P_1 Be Low?   Some employees simply have average or below-average skills for a given job; others (low–self-esteem persons) may believe this even when it is unfounded. In either case, a person who thinks he or she is already performing as well as possible is not likely to think extra effort will improve performance.

If an employee is not sure how performance is defined, or doesn't know what activities or allocations of time result in superior performance, the results are a feeling of job ambiguity and a sense of hesitation. These, in turn, tend to inhibit effort because of the fear of wasting one's time and energies on matters that may prove to be trivial or irrelevant to performance.

These different types of motivational problems call for different remedies. A low P_2 level calls for steps toward a reward system that establishes credibility among workers. Low P_1 may call for extra training, reassignment, or structuring of the job by supervisors and others so that the "path" to better performance becomes clearer.

We should not overlook the importance of the other Ps in Figure 7–2. These become especially important as P_2 diminishes. The anticipation of a sizeable psychic reward from some job achievement may evoke significantly high levels of exertion. A high P_4 is associated with tasks that are at least moderately difficult, that clearly represent a significant contribution, and that use aptitudes or traits which the individual values.

We hasten to emphasize that these Ps are *subjective* probabilities. They represent levels of confidence or certainty as they exist in the person's thinking; they need not, and often do not, correspond closely to "true" probabilities as they really exist. An individual arrives at such probabilities by some mixture of observation, inferences, hearsay, and experience. They may change over time. Rarely do people actually think in precise quantitative terms of a .15 or .60 probability, but they do discriminate between future outcomes that they regard as "almost a sure thing," "very likely," "maybe," "possible, but I doubt it," and "ain't no way."

The expectancy model is essentially a decision-making approach to motivation. The thrust of this theory is that people process information available to them about the magnitude and probability of future outcomes of their behavior and act rationally according to the conclusions of such information processing. People may be unrealistic or biased in making decisions about their work behavior, but that does not invalidate the model.

The Operant Model

Operant concepts were described in Chapter 3 to account for the acquisition of behavior. Operant concepts also provide a model for explaining the direction of motivated behavior.

According to the operant model, behavior is distributed across classes of responses as a function of the *contingencies of reinforcement* of those responses. Recall that the contingency of reinforcement involves the situation, the response, and its immediate consequences. Positive reinforcers are those consequences which strengthen, and thus make more probable, the responses which immediately precede those consequences in a particular situation. Any important stimulus in the situation which differentiates the occasions for reinforcement versus nonreinforcement of a particular response is the discriminitive stimulus.

Thus, in the operant model, a person who puts forth a great deal of work effort is one who is reinforced for so doing. The reinforcement may be noncontrived, that is, a naturally occurring consequence of the behavior; or the reinforcement may be contrived. In either case, it must follow soon after the behavior in order to strengthen that behavior rather than some other behavior.

Recall, too, the *Matching Law*, or the *Law of Relative Effect*. According to this principle, the frequency of a response is determined, not only by its own rate of reinforcement, but also by how this compares to the rate of reinforcement for competing responses in that situation. A response may be reinforced at a low rate yet occur with considerable frequency if competing responses are reinforced at a still lower rate. Conversely, a response that is reinforced at a fairly high rate might still occur infrequently if competing responses are reinforced at a still greater rate. Thus, the distribution of a person's behavior in work versus nonwork responses will be determined by the relative reinforcement rates for these classes of behavior. Furthermore, we note that, even within the class of work-relevant responses, these are likely to be reinforced at differential rates. Some parts of the job may be more interesting than others, some activities provide more feedback than others, some lead to more social reinforcers (such as interaction or approval) than others. The Matching Law asserts that people will concentrate their work efforts toward those parts of the job that yield greater relative rates of reinforcement.

Differences between the Expectancy and Operant Models

What, you may ask, is the practical difference between expectancy theory and operant concepts? Clearly, they bear substantial similarity to each other. Both emphasize the consequences of behavior; both are *process* models that take consequences (rewards, reinforcers) as given and do not concern themselves about *content*, or *why* a given reward or reinforcer matters to a person.

The two approaches differ, however, in some respects. Expectancy theory assumes that people allocate their behavior according to *anticipated consequences* of actions. People weigh the information available to them and *make decisions* according to the value of those consequences and the subjective probabilities of their realization. Expectancy theory is forward-looking; it views behavior as a product of what people think will happen in the future.

The operant model, on the other hand, views present behavior as *shaped by previous reinforcement histories.* The operant framework accords no explicit role to decision making or cognitive forecasts of the future, but looks to the past to account for current strength and frequency of responses. To change these responses in the future, we have to alter the contingencies of reinforcement as they now exist. Very well, you may argue, but is not previous experience the major determinant of what one anticipates in the future? Probably so. But expectancy theory at least implies that a person may choose to ignore entirely the past if present information suggests the environment has changed. The operant model would still accord a significant effect of reinforcement history on present behavior.

On a more pragmatic level, the two approaches differ on the importance of *timing.* Expectancy theory assumes that a reward anticipated far into the future as a result of present behavior can influence that behavior now. It assumes that people will work now for outcomes not realized until weeks, months, even years ahead: provided, of course, that the value of the outcome is not cognitively "discounted" by the length of waiting and that the subjective probability of the outcome's occurring is not diminished by the length of the anticipated interval. The operant model, on the other hand, argues that present behaviors will *extinguish* if not soon reinforced in *some* fashion. The future, distant outcomes cannot affect the long chain of responses unless they are presently sustained by more immediate outcomes, such as symbolic representations of the ultimate reward (e.g., feedback).

A clue to reconciling these models is to recognize expectancy theory for what it is—namely, a model of *decision making.* Expectancy theory offers a plausible account of why you *decide* to work at certain levels of effort, *decide* to embark on a weight-reduction program, *decide* to begin a jogging regimen, or *decide* to work toward some long-run objective. In other words, expectancy theory says something about our initial choices or tentative commitments. The operant model, however, speaks convincingly to the question of just how durable these decisions or commitments actually turn out to be in ongoing behavior. You may decide to work hard for next year's promotion, but if specific instances of such work behavior go unreinforced in the short run, the behavior will weaken, whether or not you are aware of any cognitive revocation of the decision.

Goal-Setting Theory

Although expectancy theory has been the most popular explanation of worker motivation it has not had as much impact in on-the-job settings as has goal-setting theory. According to Locke (1976), expectancy theory as currently formulated is nothing more than a theory of cognitive hedonism which posits that the individual cognitively chooses the course of action that leads to the greatest degree of pleasure or the smallest degree of pain. Locke criticizes expectancy theory for failing to see that hedonistic cognitions alone are insufficient to determine a person's value system, but he also notes that values alone are insufficient to determine a person's behavior. Following the teaching of Tolman (1932), he states: "If individuals cannot properly be described as pursuing pleasure, then what does guide their action? With respect to motivation, it would be more accurate to say that individuals strive to attain goals, values or purposes than to say that they strive for pleasure. Even when pleasure is a causal factor in choice, an individual's focus in acting is typically on the object of the action (the goal) rather than on pleasure" (Locke, 1976, p. 2).

Thus, in goal-setting theory there seem to be two cognitive determinants of behavior: *values* and *intentions* (goals). Locke offers two definitions of values: "A value is that which one acts to gain and/or keep" (Rand, 1964); "It is that which one regards as conducive to one's welfare" (Branden, 1966). Locke goes on to state that the form in which one experiences one's value judgments is emotional. For Locke, therefore, the most fundamental effects of goals on mental or physical action are directive in nature. They guide people's thoughts and overt acts to one end rather than another. Locke further asserts that not every goal leads to an activity or end specified by the goal. A particular goal may not lead to an efficacious action because it conflicts with the individual's other goals. Moreover, the situation at a given time may be perceived as inappropriate for action. An individual may not have sufficient knowledge, ability, or determination to carry out a plan of action. Even abortive action, however, is typically initiated and guided by conscious goals, and such action may be highly correlated with the action intended. Schematically, a goal-setting model of performance appears as shown in Figure 7–3.

A considerable amount of work has tested the linkage between goal setting and action. Although this work has been confined to a few investigators and some rather constrained settings, the support is impressive. Locke and his associates (see Locke, 1968) conducted a series of laboratory experiments to test the effects of goals on performance. They found that the higher the intended level of achievement among their subjects, the higher the level of performance. Even individuals who tried for goals so high that the goals were rarely, if ever, reached, performed better than did individuals who set relatively easy goals.

Figure 7–3
Goal-Setting Model of Motivation

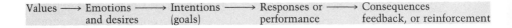

Values ⟶ Emotions ⟶ Intentions ⟶ Responses or ⟶ Consequences
        and desires   (goals)   performance   feedback, or reinforcement

Although most of the support for goal-setting theory has come from laboratory experiments, work by Carroll and Tosi (1973), Latham and Kinne (1974), Latham and Baldes (1975), and Kim and Hamner (1976) has also established the external validity of goal setting as an important motivational tool.

Thus there seems to be no dispute that goal setting is a cause of performance. If a manager knows what a person expects or values, what goals the person has, and what rewards the person finds reinforcing, then the manager has the tools needed to channel the energy of the person in a given direction.

ONCE BEHAVIOR IS CHANNELED, HOW IS IT MAINTAINED?

You will recall that at the beginning of this chapter we said that the study of motivation implies an understanding of how to *energize*, *channel*, and *maintain* behavior. Just as there are several theories which explain how behavior is energized and channeled, there are also several theories which explain how behavior is maintained. These theories are all similar in nature since they deal with the internal and external reward structure. They include reinforcement theory, social comparison theory, attribution theory, and two-factor theory.

The Operant Model

According to the operant framework, the *schedules of reinforcement* of a class of responses determine the durability of those responses. As you will recall from Chapter 3, *variable, intermittent* schedules of reinforcement not only lead to more consistent and higher rates of responding than fixed schedules, but also have the effect of promoting resistance to extinction over periods of nonreinforcement.

When a response is very weak to begin with, reinforcement must occur frequently. This is especially true if we seek to *shape* the behavior toward some ultimate criterion; we have to use the method of successive approximation and reinforce liberally any small increase in rate or quality of the behavior until it stabilizes at the criterion level. At that point, it is important to make reinforcement more variable. We can gradually *stretch* the ratio of occurrences of behavior per unit of reinforcement. If artificial reinforcers have been used to strengthen the behavior, these can be gradually phased out if the behavior now has the capacity for generating its own reinforcement on a variable basis.

To summarize, operant principles assert that strong levels of responding are best maintained on a variable, intermittent schedule of reinforcement.

Equity Theory

We argued in Chapter 6 that the meaning of a stimulus depends on more than its objective properties. The meaning of a reward or reinforcement is not totally determined by its amount or frequency; it is also determined by how we interpret it in relation to some context. Equity theory explains how we interpret social rewards and how this interpretation affects the maintenance of a given level of work effort.

According to Equity Theory (Adams, 1961), we seek social justice in how we are rewarded for our job performance. We take into account, first of all, the total set of *outcomes* we experience from work. Outcomes include pay, benefits, status, pleasant relationships, privileges, intrinsic interest in the job, and any other desired consequences or work. We also consider the *inputs* we provide to the job. Inputs include any activity or contribution which we regard as relevant: expenditure of time and effort, experience, skills, sacrifices, stress level experienced, loyalty, and commitment. We expect our outcomes and inputs to be, in some sense, appropriate to each other. But how do we judge appropriateness?

Equity theory argues that we evaluate the equity or justice of our outcomes by a process of social comparison (Festinger, 1954). We compare the *ratio* of our outcomes to inputs with the ratio of out-comes to inputs for some "comparison person." The comparison person may be a co-worker or a group average (such as prevailing stand-ards in a department, organization, community, or industry). Our comparison, then, is

$$\frac{\text{Outcomes (own)}}{\text{Inputs (own)}} \quad \text{versus} \quad \frac{\text{Outcomes (others')}}{\text{Inputs (others')}}$$

For example, if your outcomes are twice as great as the comparison person's, they are equitable if you judge your inputs also to be twice as great. Similarly, if your outcomes are only half that of the compar-ison person, they would be equitable if you regarded your inputs as only half as much.

If you consider your ratio of outcomes to inputs to be less than that of the comparison person, you experience inequitable compen-sation. Equity theory states that you will attempt to bring the ratios into balance. You will try to have your outcomes increased or, if un-successful, reduce your inputs, perhaps by decreasing your level of work effort. Alternatively, you could reevaluate your outcomes (es-pecially those that are intangible) and decide your outcomes are greater than you originally thought. Similarly, you may reevaluate the inputs of the comparison person, concluding that they included more hardships or sacrifices than you first thought.

If your ratio of outcomes to inputs exceeded that of the comparison person, you would regard yourself as unfairly overcompensated. To achieve equity you could increase your inputs (for example, by in-creasing the quantity or quality of your work) or seek to increase the outcomes of others.

Most of the research testing equity theory has focused on pay. Pay is only one of the relevant outcomes, but pay lends itself more easily to social comparisons than other outcomes do, and people seem to be especially sensitive to such comparisons. Experimental studies strongly suggest that perceived inequity in the form of underpayment leads to a reduction in work effort. However, those studies did not permit subjects to restore equity by certain other means, such as in-creasing their pay. Many groups in industry, especially those in unions, probably seek first and foremost to increase wage levels. The major weakness in equity theory at the present is the inability to predict *which* method(s) people will try to use to restore equity. Re-duction of work effort is certainly one method, but anecdotal evi-dence and casual observation strongly suggest that at least some per-sons resist any major change in work effort. It is also conceivable that some people will tolerate a certain degree of inequity, neither making a concerted effort to change any outcomes or inputs nor altering their perceptions.

The available evidence also suggests that people will increase their quantity or quality of work when this is the most obvious means of correcting a situation of inequitable overpayment. Again, however, this evidence comes from controlled experiments in which other methods of restoring equity were either not feasible or made very difficult. More naturalistic field studies suggest that feelings of inequitable overpayment are either rare or that they are easily and quickly dispelled by perceptual reappraisal.

Some practical recommendations follow from equity formulations. First, it would seem that the entire process of performance evaluation must be made an explicit, public process, perhaps even with some form of adjudication or appeal. Organizations should make explicit exactly what inputs are valued highly for individual employees. Similarly, outcomes within organizations should be overtly tied to such inputs. Lawler (1973), for instance, reports that employees tend to overestimate the pay others receive. From a social comparison point of view this may be harmful if it leads individuals to reduce their own inputs in order to remedy perceived inequity. Thus policies of pay secrecy should be reexamined. Managers should also be aware that different types of employees select different types of people as a basis for comparison. Salaried individuals tend to compare themselves to values that they themselves have established. Professionals, on the other hand, compare their inputs and outcomes to those of other professionals (Goodman, 1977). The fact that an individual may be well rewarded by intraorganizational standards does not ensure high levels of employee inputs if the comparison persons are external colleagues who are much better rewarded.

Attribution Theories

Another class of motivation theories which has gained prominence of late is the attribution approach. The most well-developed theoretical notion of this approach is what Kelley (1971) has termed the *discounting principle*. Simply stated, "the role of a given cause in producing a given effect is discounted if other plausible causes are also present" (Kelley, 1971, p. 113). There have been many demonstrations of this principle within both interpersonal and individual task situations.

Within the interpersonal area, Heider (1958) noted that the causes of another's actions are a function of personal and environmental forces, and that one will infer personal causation to the extent that environmental forces are absent.

More recently, Bem (1972) extrapolated the discounting principle of causal attribution to the study of self-perception—or how one views one's own behavior—within a social context. Bem hypothesized that the strength of external pressures will determine the likelihood that a person will attribute his or her own actions to external or internal causes. Thus, a person who acts under strong external rewards or punishments is likely to assume that such behavior is under external control. However, if extrinsic contingencies are not strong or salient, the person is likely to assume that this behavior is due to his or her own interest in the activity, or that the behavior is intrinsically motivated. De Charmes (1968) has made a similar point in his discussion of individuals' perception of personal causation: "As a first approximation, we propose that whenever a person experiences himself to be the locus of causality for his own behavior (to be an Origin), he will consider himself to be intrinsically motivated. Conversely, when a person perceives the locus of causality for his behavior to be external to himself (that he is a Pawn), he will consider himself to be extrinsically motivated" (p. 328).

Although such a distinction between intrinsic and extrinsic motivation may be of academic interest, the impetus for increased concern by organizational psychologists stems from the practical possibility that intrinsic and extrinsic motivation may not be strictly additive. Deci (1971), for instance, suggested that the use of extrinsic rewards may lower intrinsic motivation on a positively perceived task activity. His studies show that if you pay people for doing something they already enjoy doing, they will soon enjoy it less, and that if the pay is later withdrawn, they will expend less effort in doing it.

Some boundary conditions have been established for the negative relation between intrinsic and extrinsic motivation. Deci (1972) suggests that extrinsic rewards may not lower intrinsic motivation if the rewards are not contingently administered according to individual level of performance. Ross (1975) claims that external rewards must be salient in the task situation. Staw, Calder, and Hess (1976) maintain that external rewards must be inappropriate or counter to situational norms in order to find an inhibitory effect.

Although the above moderating variables would appear to lessen the concern of managers intent on organizational motivation, the attribution approach remains troublesome to organizational psychologists. It is probably evident to the reader by now that the causal attribution theory of Deci (1972) and de Charmes (1968), known as *cognitive evaluation theory*, is somewhat in disagreement with reinforcement theory and expectancy theory concerning the impact of contingent reinforcement (especially monetary rewards) on worker motivation. While the latter two theories differ greatly on the origins of behavior and/or the reasons why contingent reinforcement has a positive impact on future performance, they do agree that contingent rewards, including money, enhance the motivational level of a person involved in an interesting task assignment. This is not the case with cognitive evaluation theory. As de Charmes (1968) notes:

> Intrinsically motivating tasks are those in which a person feels that he is in control, that he originated the behavior (as an Origin) with the concomitant feelings of free choice and commitment. Introduction of extrinsic reward, however, places the person in a dependent position relative to the source of the reward. To the extent that the person expects a reward for his task he is unfree and has not chosen the task for its own sake alone. The source of the reward is an external causal locus for his behavior. When rewards are important, dependence on the source of reward places a person in the position of a Pawn. Put in a more commonplace way, the highly paid employee is less free to dissent [p. 329].

Although there is some anecdotal support for the theory that money is not a motivator of performance or is a negative motivator of performance, there is little empirical support. Indeed, as we have discussed in this chapter and in Chapter 3, contingently administered rewards are positively related to high levels of performance. It is possible, however, that money and other external rewards can be so strong that the intrinsic aspects of the task itself are ignored, to the detriment of future performance. It is also possible that offering strong external rewards, such as money, is inappropriate in certain situations (for example, in return for friendship, to obtain sexual favors, and so on). In those situations, offering such rewards may have detrimental effects on the performance and the relationship. However, cognitive evaluation theory seems to relate only to those special circumstances. In work situations, it seems to have less relevance. It does make a contribution, however, in that it highlights the need to understand both the rewards of the task (intrinsic rewards) and the rewards of the outcomes (extrinsic rewards).

Two-Factor Theory

A theory of work motivation which has aroused a good deal of comment, support, and controversy in recent years and one whose terminology is now ingrained in modern management literature is Herzberg's (1959) two-factor theory (also known as the motivation-hygiene theory). The theory is based on the assumption that dissatisfaction leading to the avoidance of work and satisfaction leading to attraction toward work do not represent the end points of a single continuum. Rather, two separate, unipolar continua are required to reflect people's dual orientation to work; hence, the two-factor theory. On the one hand, people seek to avoid anything painful or unpleasant. Hence, unpleasant factors which cannot be avoided produce degrees of increasing job dissatisfaction. That is:

–	0

| Increasing job dis- satisfaction | No dissatisfaction |
| Negative orientation to work | Neutral orientation to work |

On the other hand, people are attracted toward anything agreeable or pleasant. Hence, pleasant or attractive factors which are potentially attainable lead to degrees of increasing job satisfaction. That is:

0	+

| No satisfaction | Increasing job satisfaction |
| Neutral orientation to work | Positive orientation to work |

As discussed below, the independence of these two scales results from two distinctive sets of job factors that apply to only one continuum or the other.

Herzberg's theory was derived from a study of need satisfactions and the reported motivational effects of those satisfactions on 200 engineers and accountants employed by firms in the Pittsburgh area. Each of these employees was asked to recall a time at work when he felt particularly *good* about his or her job. Interviews were then conducted to determine why the employees felt as they did, and whether their feelings of satisfaction had affected their performance, their personal relationships, and their feelings of well-being. The same respondents were then asked to recall a time when they felt particularly *bad* about their jobs. Interviews followed to determine the nature of the events which led to the negative expressions.

On the basis of the data provided by the employees' recall, by the subsequent interviews, and by analysis of the information obtained, the following conclusions were derived: (1) Factors associated with the job itself (intrinsic, content, or psychological factors) tend to lead to job satisfaction (on the positive side, or to the right of zero, as noted above). The intrinsic factors associated with job satisfaction are achievement, recognition for work well done, the work itself, responsibility, and advancement. Low levels of the intrinsic factors result in little satisfaction (near 0) but not dissatisfaction. (2) Factors associated with the environment surrounding the job (extrinsic, context, or physical factors) tend to lead to job dissatisfaction (on the negative side, or to the left of zero, as noted above) or prevent dissatisfaction.

As shown in Figure 7–4, the extrinsic factors associated with job dissatisfaction are company policy and administration, supervision, salary, interpersonal relations, and working conditions. Good working conditions prevent dissatisfaction but do not cause satisfaction. (3) Job satisfiers are generally determiners of long-term changes, and job dissatisfiers are generally determiners of short-term positive changes of attitude. (4) Job satisfiers are called *motivators* since they fulfill an individual's need for psychological growth. Job dissatisfiers are called *hygienes* since they merely serve to prevent an individual from getting "sick of work"; hence, the motivation-hygiene theory.

Herzberg's theory has been one of the most researched theories in organizational behavior. Evidence refuting the theory is almost as extensive as the evidence confirming it. Herzberg himself, in a review of 10 studies of 17 populations through 1966, all of which used the "story-telling method," found general confirmation for the theory. However, House and Wigdor, in a review of 31 studies through 1967, some of which did not use that method, found a general lack of confirmation for the theory. In their own reinterpretation of Herzberg's original data, House and Wigdor (1967) found that lack of achieve-

Figure 7–4
The Components of
Herzberg's Two-Factor Theory

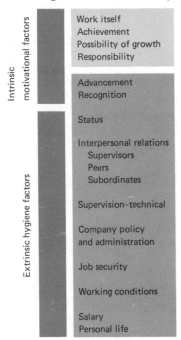

ment and recognition were more frequently identified as job dissatisfiers than were working conditions and relations with supervisors.

Herzberg's theory does not suggest that hygiene factors are trivial. They *are* important. Salary, company policy, administration, and working conditions must not be neglected, but they must be held in perspective. The hygienes have always been—and probably always will be—easier to measure, control, and manipulate than the motivators. The motivators are more complex and subjective, and often too elusive to measure. But to the extent that management concentrates on hygienes, while at the same time neglecting motivators, then workers are probably going to seek more of the hygienes—higher salaries, better working conditions, more fringe benefits, shorter hours, and so on.

It seems that both cognitive evaluation theory and Herzberg's two-factor theory point out the need to examine the rewards of the task itself as a sustainer of performance. We should note here, however, that both task rewards (How pleasant is my task? How challenging is my job?) and outcome rewards (praise, promotion, pay) should be used by management as tools for maintaining channeled behavior.

SUMMARY

Motivation is a concept used to explain why a person performs at the level that he or she does. Because performance is assumed to be a function of motivation and ability, if an able person fails to perform as we expect, then we tend to attribute the lack of performance to low motivation. This low motivation can stem from a lack of drive, inadequate goals, or a negative task assignment. A major point made in this chapter is that a manager needs to understand, from the point of view of the employee, (1) what energizes behavior, (2) what directs or channels behavior, and (3) how channeled behavior can be maintained. A manager can partially influence all three of these dimensions; therefore, when a worker is "unmotivated" in a task situation, the low productivity which results is partially the fault of the manager.

If we draw upon the material presented thus far in this text, we can now depict a general model of performance as shown in Figure 7–5.

In Figure 7–5 we see that a person's cognitive state and environmental situation influence current and future levels of performance. Number one (1) items are *drive-producing* (energizing) motivators. Number two (2) items are *channeling* motivators. Number three (3) items are *maintaining* motivators. Thus, although motivation is a complex phenomenon, by directly or indirectly controlling these var-

Figure 7–5
General Model of Performance

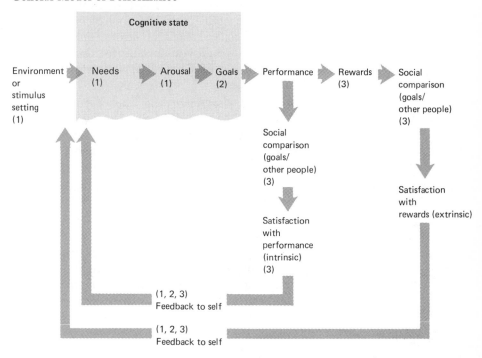

ious components, a manager can have a great influence on a worker's performance level. However, since the worker is also influenced by persons other than the manager, the manager can never expect to be able to exercise complete control over the motivation of the worker.

CONCEPTS TO REMEMBER

need hierarchy	schedules of reinforcement
career stages	social comparison
expectancy theory	equity
contingencies of reinforcement	two-factor theory
Matching Law	attribution
	hygiene factors

QUESTIONS FOR DISCUSSION

1. The need hierarchy model of Maslow continues to influence thinking about both conceptual and applied issues of job motivation—despite the general lack of strong empirical support for such a model. How would you account for this? (You might want to review the portion of Chapter 2 concerning the criteria for evaluating theories.)

2. Suppose you are a supervisor and one of your people shows a chronically low level of work effort. How would you deal with this problem? How would your approach differ depending on whether you subscribed to expectancy theory or the operant model?

3. As noted in the text, expectancy theory and the operant model differ on the importance of *timing* of rewards. Would they differ on the importance of *frequency* or *consistency* or rewards? Explain.

4. Suppose we accept Herzberg's findings concerning the effects of motivation and hygiene as valid. How might we *explain* these results in terms of *(a)* an operant model *(b)* expectancy theory or *(c)* social comparison theory, rather than the two-factor theory?

CASE

Bill Butterfield, marketing manager of the Topeka Manufacturing Company, had just completed a two-week trip during which he audited customer accounts and prospective accounts in the northeastern states. His primary intention was to do follow-up work on prospective accounts contacted by sales staff members during the previous six months. The prospective clients were usually dealers or large department stores.

To his amazement, Butterfield discovered that almost all of the so-called prospective accounts were fictitious. The sales staff had obviously turned in falsely documented field reports and expense statements. Company sales personnel had actually called upon only 6 of 32 reported dealers or department stores. Thus Butterfield surmised that the sales staff had falsely claimed approximately 80 percent of the goodwill contacts. Further study showed that all members of the sales staff had followed this general practice and that not one had a clean record.

Questions

How would reinforcement theory, expectancy theory, goal-setting theory, and equity theory be used to explain this situation? How would two-factor theory and cognitive evaluation theory explain this situation? How do you explain the fact that all sales personnel followed this practice?

REFERENCES

Adams, J. S.   Wages inequities in a clerical task. Unpublished study, General Electric Company, New York, 1961.

Alderfer, C. P.   An empirical test of a new theory of human needs. *Organizational Behavior and Human Performance,* 1969, *4,* 142–175.

Bem, D. J.   Self-perception theory. In L. Berkowitz (Ed.), *Advances in experimental social psychology* (Vol. 6). New York: Academic Press, 1972.

Branden, N.   Emotions and values. *Objectivist,* 1966, *5,* 1–9.

Calder, B. J., & Staw, B. M.   Interaction of intrinsic and extrinsic motivation: Some methodological notes. *Journal of Personality and Social Psychology,* 1975.

Carroll, S. J., & Tosi, H. L.   *Management by objectives.* New York: Macmillan, 1973.

deCharmes, R.   *Personal causation: The internal affective determinants of behavior.* New York: Academic Press, 1968.

Deci, E. L.   Effects of externally mediated rewards on intrinsic motivation. *Journal of Personality and Social Psychology.* 1971, *18,* 105–115.

Deci, E. L.   Intrinsic motivation, extrinsic reinforcement, and inequity. *Journal of Personality and Social Psychology,* 1972, *22,* 113–120.

Festinger, L.   A theory of social comparison processes. *Human Relations,* 1954, *7,* 117–140.

Goodman, P. S.   Social comparison processes in organizations. In B. M. Staw & G. R. Salancik (Eds.), *New directions in organizational behavior.* Chicago: St. Clair Press, 1977.

Hall, D. T., & Nougaim, K. E.   An examination of Maslow's need hierarchy in an organizational setting. *Organizational Behavior and Human Performance,* 1968, *3*(1), 12–35.

Heider, F.   *The psychology of interpersonal relations.* New York: John Wiley & Sons, 1958.

Herzberg, F.   *Work and the nature of man.* Cleveland: World, 1966.

Herzberg, F., Mausner, B., & Snyderman, B.   *The motivation to work* (2nd ed.). New York: John Wiley & Sons, 1959.

House, R. J., & Wigdor, L. A.   Herzberg's dual-factor theory of job satisfaction and motivation: A review of the evidence and a criticism. *Personnel Psychology,* 1967, *20*(4), 369–389.

Kelley, H. H.   *Attribution in social interaction.* New York: General Learning Press, 1971.

Kim, J., & Hamner, W. C.   The effect of goal setting, feedback, and praise on productivity and satisfaction in an organizational setting. *Journal of Applied Psychology,* 1976, *61,* 48–57.

Latham, G. P., & Baldes, J. J.   The practical significance of Locke's theory of goal setting. *Journal of Applied Psychology*, 1975, *60*, 122–124.

Latham, G. P., & Kinne, S. B.   Improving job performance through training in goal setting. *Journal of Applied Psychology*, 1974, *59*, 20–24.

Lawler, E. E. III.   *Motivation in work organizations.* Monterey, Calif.: Brooks/Cole, 1973.

Lawler, E. E. III, & Suttle, J. L.   A casual-correlational test of the need hierarchy concept. *Organizational Behavior and Human Performance*, 1972, *7*, 265–287.

Locke, E. A.   Toward a theory of task motivation and incentives. *Organizational Behavior and Human Performance*, 1968, *3*, 157–189.

Locke, E. A.   Personnel attitudes and motivation. Working paper, University of Maryland, 1976.

Maslow, A. H.   A theory of human motivation. *Psychological Review*, July 1943, 370–396.

McGregor, D.   *The human side of enterprise.* New York: McGraw-Hill, 1960.

Porter, L. W., & Lawler, E. E.   *Managerial attitudes and performance.* Homewood, Ill.: Irwin-Dorsey, 1968.

Rand, A.   The objectivist ethics. In A. Rand (Ed.), *The virtue of selfishness.* New York: Signet, 1964.

Ross, M.   Salience of reward and intrinsic motivation. *Journal of Personality and Social Psychology*, 1975, *32*, 245–254.

Staw, B. M.   Motivation in organizations: Toward synthesis and redirection. In B. M. Staw & G. R. Salancik, (Eds.), *New directions in organizational behavior.* Chicago: St. Clair Press, 1977.

Staw, B. M., Calder, B., and Hess, R.   Intrinsic motivation and norms of payment. Working paper, Northwestern University, 1976.

Tolman, E. C.   Purposive behavior in animals and men. New York: Century, 1932.

Vroom, V. H.   *Work and motivation.* New York: Wiley, 1964.

Wahba, M. A., & Bridwell, L. G.   Maslow reconsidered: A review of research on the need hierarchy theory. From proceedings of 1973 Academy of Management meetings, Boston.

8

Job Motivation:
Methods of
Application

What are the most popular programs for applying motivation concepts?

What are the theoretical bases for these programs?

What are the limitations of these programs?

In the preceding chapter, we examined a number of conceptual approaches to understanding motivation at work. Undoubtedly many organization officials have their own intuitive versions of these theories and use them with varying degrees of success. Beyond the informal application of motivational concepts by individual managers, many organizations have constructed formal programs, on a relatively large scale, in order to increase employee motivation to perform various constructive behaviors. In so doing, these organizations and their leaders have been strongly influenced by one or more of the theoretical models discussed in the previous chapter.

Over the last two decades, the most widely adopted formal programs for improving patterns of individual worker motivation have been (in no particular order) *Organizational behavior modification*, or programs emphasizing positive reinforcement; *Job redesign*, sometimes called job enlargement or job enrichment; and *Management by objectives* (MBO). The majority of firms among *Fortune's* top 500 have had experience with one or more of these programs, on varying scales of involvement. Public, nonprofit organizations—such as state and local governments, hospitals, and school systems—have also experimented with versions of these programs. All three of these approaches have gone through periods of "faddism," and none of them today attracts either the publicity or management interest accorded to them when they were the "in" thing to do. However, they continue to be widely used.

In this chapter we seek to examine the conceptual rationale for these programs, describe the methods used to implement them, and offer tentative assessments of how these programs have fared in practice.

ORGANIZATIONAL BEHAVIOR MODIFICATION: USING POSITIVE REINFORCEMENT

Organizational behavior modification (OB Mod) represents the application of operant concepts and principles to organized settings. These concepts, which we discussed in Chapter 3 and reviewed in the previous chapter, come primarily from the work of B. F. Skinner (e.g., 1953). Long before these concepts became popular in industry, they had been systematically and effectively applied in mental health and educational institutions. Nord (1969) drew attention to the broad relevance of operant principles for the work environment, and Luthans and Kreitner (1975) demonstrated the compatibility of reinforcement concepts with the more popular schools of management thought.

OB Mod, in contrast to other motivational programs, actually does not concern itself directly with "motivation" as an explanatory construct. Nor does it have recourse to other internal states such as "attitudes" or "personality traits" as representing "ultimate causes" of behavior. First and foremost, it concerns the observation of behavior itself. Second, it assumes that such behavior is lawfully related to the observable antecedent stimuli of that behavior and the immediate consequences of behavior. To modify behavior, you modify the contingencies and schedules of reinforcement rather than trying to change attitudes. Otherwise, OB Mod makes no global assumptions about human nature or human needs.

Stages in Program Development

The methods used to implement a program of organizational behavior modification (OB Mod) have been amply described and illustrated by Lawrence Miller (1978), who has served as a consultant to many companies in the design of such programs. As Miller notes, the first step is *pinpointing*, or defining very precisely in operational terms the work behavior which is to be modified. OB Mod cannot be applied to such vague, catchall goals as "working harder" or "more effective service." Miller observes that many managers are unsatisfied with employees' performance but have not analyzed their dissatisfaction to the point of identifying specific behaviors they would like to see changed. This process may often prove to be the most difficult step in OB Mod. Only when officials can define the target behavior in concrete terms, such as "return a customer's call within 90 minutes," or "wear your safety visor," will OB Mod be feasible.

The second step consists of a *baseline audit*. Officials must determine how frequently the target behavior occurs before there is any intervention. This knowledge is needed in order to serve as a comparison for any subsequent performance levels. Such information enters into any cost/benefit analyses of potential gains. Finally, it documents in convincing, quantitative terms the state of present performance and may supply the "shock treatment" needed for managers who have complacently overestimated the performance of their units.

Next, a *criterion* or standard must be set. This is the ultimate goal toward which subsequent efforts are aimed. A standard may already exist; if not, one has to be set on the basis of observation and judgment. The standard should be realistic and attainable but sufficiently higher than present practice to make the OB Mod program cost effective.

The next step is to *"consequate"*—choose a reinforcer. Officials have to specify a consequence for reinforcing an instance of the desired behavior. Several considerations enter into this choice: The reinforcer must be flexible and timely so that it can be delivered as soon after the behavior as possible; it must be something which does not lead quickly to satiation on the part of the employees; it must have broad appeal to the group in question. In many OB Mod programs, foreman and supervisors are trained to use social reinforcement in the form of praise coupled with quantitative feedback—e.g., "Roy, I see you're now holding scrap rates to less than 5 percent, and that's just super." In other programs, improvements are posted conspicuously on wall charts or bulletin boards. Some elaborate programs translate the feedback into points or stamps which can be accumulated and later exchanged for merchandise or privileges of the employee's choice. Miller (1978) suggests that "reinforcer surveys" be periodically administered (possibly by inclusion in a more general survey) with questions such as:

I would work harder if _____.
If my boss would _____ I would
    enjoy working here.
My job would be more rewarding if _____.

Responses to such items offer clues as to the types of reinforcers that may prove effective.

Whatever the reinforcers chosen, it is desirable that they be mediated by the supervisor. This practice makes the supervisor's attention a conditioned reinforcer; it strengthens the social reinforcement by the manager for those later occasions when it has to serve as the major source of ongoing reinforcement.

At the onset, the reinforcers chosen may have a very *contrived* tone; that is, they are "artificial," not naturally occurring consequences of the behavior. Some critics of OB Mod call this the "gumdrop" syndrome and consider the use of Green Stamps, tokens, or gold stars as demeaning, much like a trainer using pellets of food to reward animals. Often, however, somewhat contrived reinforcers are necessary if the desired behavior does not have the initial strength required to generate more natural reinforcers.

From this point, the program moves to the *shaping* stage. If the target behavior occurs only 50 percent of the time and the standard is 95 percent, it would be unrealistic and futile to wait until the standard is reached before providing reinforcement. The likelihood is that such an immediate improvement will not occur; therefore, any intermediate gains will go unreinforced and the efforts made to achieve such gains would undergo extinction. Rather, officials have to use the method of successive approximations. As Miller (1978) notes, two conditions are required for doing this: (1) some variability in present rate of responding, and (2) selective reinforcement. Initially, any improvement, no matter how small, over the average baseline value is reinforced liberally and frequently. As responding begins to stabilize at a slightly higher rate, only further improvement beyond that level is reinforced. By stages, the criterion of reinforcement is gradually moved toward the ultimate standard.

Once the target behavior approaches the standard or criterion level with some consistency, an important decision arises. Should the contrived reinforcers used up to this point be continued, or does the target behavior now have the strength to generate more noncontrived reinforcers—such as pride in one's work, covert self-reinforcement, respect from peers and superiors, the gleaming smile of a customer, a high-quality finished product? At the very least, OB Mod practitioners recommend *stretching the ratio* of contrived reinforcers. This means using them less frequently on a variable ratio schedule. A given amount of reinforcement is contingent on increasingly larger numbers of responses. This step offers several advantages: More economical use of the reinforcer; less likelihood of satiation; and, as we noted in Chapter 3, promoting greater resistance to extinction.

Contrived reinforcers may be gradually phased out as the target behavior begins to generate sufficient noncontrived reinforcement. Contrived reinforcers may still be needed, however in some amount or frequency in order to sustain the effect of naturally occurring reinforcers. Whether contrived reinforcers can be completely eliminated is an empirical question which can be answered only by continual monitoring of performance.

Example: Emery Air Freight[1]

This company realizes significant savings when small shipments intended for the same destination are shipped together in containers rather than separately. Company policy strongly encouraged this procedure, and many operating officials believed it was being followed almost all the time.

A performance audit showed, however, that containers were, in fact, used only about 45 percent of the time. Emery set a target goal of using containers 95 percent of the time, representing a savings of $650,000 annually over baseline performance.

Emery provided its operating managers with programmed instruction workbooks on the use of positive reinforcement. Managers began a systematic program of awarding praise and other social reinforcers to workers for any improvements over baseline performance level. In addition, workers were given printed forms for recording their own behavior, thus providing a continuous record of feedback. In the early stages, supervisory praise was given frequently; as performance in-

---

[1]At Emery Air Freight: Positive reinforcement boosts performance. *Organizational Dynamics*, 1973, 1, 41–50.

creased and approached the target level, praise was given with gradually decreasing frequency, and the self-recorded feedback provided most of the reinforcement.

Emery tried positive reinforcement in other operations, too, such as sales and customer service. In each case, the result was dramatic improvement over initial performance levels. In three years of applying positive reinforcement principles, Emery estimates it saved over $3 million.

Emery found that eventually praise from supervisors began to lose its effect. In fact, sheer repetition led in some cases to the risk that praise would become an irritant rather than a reinforcer. To overcome this problem, the company encouraged operating managers to diversify their portfolio of reinforcers. Supervisors made use of other reinforcing options, such as letting a worker switch temporarily to a more enjoyable task after completing a less enjoyable one, providing release time contingent on good performance, and sending personal letters of commendation from executives to the employee's home. Still, however, the bread-and-butter reinforcer that sustained the performance was the immediate, precise feedback which workers received as they made their own comparison of current performance to the standard.

Criticisms of OB Mod

Formal programs of positive reinforcement have generated a certain amount of controversy, whether in spite of or because of their apparent success. Some critics see such practices as demeaning— much like conditioning a bar press response by laboratory rats. They argue that the extension of operant concepts to social systems constitutes a form of manipulation that deprives people of their human dignity and promotes a slavish subservience to artificial rewards.

There can be no argument to the assertion that positive reinforcement is a form of manipulation—if, indeed, it is successful. Any tactic that influences behavior must, by definition, be considered manipulation. But organizations, in order to function, must exert influence on the behavior of their members. Thus, the charge of "manipulation" would apply to any organization that succeeds in coordinating collective effort to some common goal.

Skinner (1972) has reminded us that we inevitably control each other's behavior. We respond to each other in ways that either strengthen prior behavior, punish it, or extinguish it. We cannot avoid exerting such influence even if we wish we could. The important criterion is not whether we influence, but whether such influence is constructive to the parties affected. Skinner suggests that we should not leave such influence to operate in an unsystematic fashion. It is far more rational for a social system to plan its contingencies of reinforcement. This makes it possible for all parties—managers and workers alike—to be positively reinforced, and the organization contributes to the larger culture.

OB Mod uses artifical reinforcers, not as ends in themselves, but to strengthen constructive behaviors that eventually will generate their own noncontrived reinforcers. Thus, contrary to what some critics argue, OB Mod does not overlook the importance of intrinsic rewards from work. The "gumdrop stage" is not seen as a permanent condition but a means of reaching a more desirable state in which people experience satisfaction from the constructive consequences of their own competence.

Curiously, OB Mod consultants hear more objections to operant applications from managers than from hourly workers. Some managers apparently adhere to the philosophy that if a worker is paid a fair wage, "then he *ought* to do what is expected of him without any extra reward." Unfortunately, good wages, distributed in an across-the-board fashion, function primarily to attract and hold workers. In the absence of some more precise contingency, the paycheck at the end of the week has little effect on job behavior earlier in the week. History teaches us that when organization officials do not have the use of immediate positive reinforcement, they inevitably resort to aversive forms of control, which often have longer-run ill effects for both the manager and those managed. Organizations cannot count on idealistic conceptions of what is "right" to sustain constructive behavior except in very special circumstances: when the expressed, operational goal of the organization is itself clearly idealistic, and when the organization can pick its participants very selectively so as to admit only those who internalize such goals. General Motors can scarcely hope to emulate the Salvation Army.

The most conspicuous limitation of OB Mod concerns the type of work behavior for which it is suited. It has its most straightforward application to work behavior that can be *precisely defined, quantitatively measured,* and *frequently repeated.* Thus it pertains most readily to simple, routine, recurring task responses. Formal programs of positive reinforcement could not be easily applied to more unstructured tasks, to jobs that require creative responses, or to significant but rarely occurring job behaviors. Operant concepts, in a theoretical sense, do have relevance to such dimensions of work, but it would be difficult to design and administer a program applying the concepts to such types of work.

We must remember, too, that contingencies of reinforcement never exist in a vacuum. In practice, workers and managers experience varying degrees of conflicting contingencies. Most jobs, even simple ones, are governed by competing criteria (e.g., quality versus quantity; pleasing the customer versus satisfying a superior), and operant concepts in themselves do not provide any answer as to optimal resolution of these conflicts. Furthermore, the reinforcers used by managers may pale in comparison to the resources of others who seek to strengthen behaviors at variance with those desired by management. We strongly caution the reader against a narrow and simplistic view of the effects of formally administered reinforcers in a complex environment. Some OB Mod programs have experienced limited and temporary effectiveness (some have even had counterproductive effects) because of the failure to analyze the strongly embedded social contingencies in the system.

Whyte (1972) has reminded us that organizations represent complex networks of interlocking behaviors, and increasing the rate of a specific response by one individual or group is sure to have repercussions elsewhere in the system. The very acts that produce reinforcement for some may indirectly produce aversive consequences for others. Waiters and waitresses who do their utmost to serve the customer may bring undue pressure to bear upon the harried cook; increased production by a work crew may disrupt routines of shipping, inventory control, inspection, or other segments of the materials flow.

Reppucci and Saunders (1974) have drawn from their own experiences as behavior modification consultants to point out problems of implementation in natural settings. One such problem arises from the fact that the OB Mod consultant does not deal directly with the target subjects; rather, he or she must rely upon indigenous-setting personnel to observe and reinforce behavior. Thus, the consultant must first modify the behavior of the staff—the supervisors and other officials who manage the behavior of others. This task is far from simple. Staff behavior is itself the product of complex contingencies inside and outside the host organization. Attempting to alter these contingencies touches upon competing definitions of ultimate criteria and challenges vested interests. Repucci and Saunders conclude that realistic OB Mod must be founded, not only upon principles of operant psychology, but also with some political and economic astuteness.

Nonetheless, numerous corporations claim to have made good use of basic operant concepts. While objective evidence is scant, reports in popular and trade publications suggest that OB Mod—in the right circumstances—can enhance the effectiveness of operations as well as improve the quality of work life. Hamner and Hamner (1976) reported on the experiences of about a dozen large organizations that have tried OB Mod and found results to be generally very positive, though not entirely unmixed.

JOB REDESIGN

The major premise underlying job redesign as a motivational program is that job motivation is sustained primarily by the job itself. Put another way, the important rewards are the *intrinsic rewards* generated by task effort.

A number of partially overlapping conceptual and philosophical frameworks converge in the notion of job redesign. But without question the most direct and immediate implications for this approach come from Herzberg's (1966) Two-Factor Theory. Herzberg maintained that job-extrinsic factors—such as salary, conditions surrounding the job, supervision, relations with co-workers—serve mainly hygienic functions: when well-managed, they prevent the "disease" of dissatisfaction that arises from feelings of inequity or physical discomfort. In doing so, the hygiene or extrinsic factors meet the basic, lower-order needs to feel secure and to avoid pain. Having met such needs, they can do no more. Only the job itself, the task, can provide the means of satisfying the higher-order needs for stimulation and psychological growth. And the job can do this only if it is "enriched."

Herzberg questioned the trend in modern industry toward work simplification. The techniques introduced by Frederick Taylor and other apostles of "Scientific Management," then carried forward by industrial engineers, had called for a fractionization of work into jobs that consisted of highly repetitive cycles of simple operations. When used on a vast scale—as in the assembly lines of automobile plants— these techniques boasted, not only the advantages of mechanical efficiency, but very short training times for new workers. The increased production made possible by this system, in turn, made it possible to pay higher wages to workers.

By the mid-1950s, some observers began to wonder if work simplification had begun to cause certain dysfunctions which more than offset the virtues of mechanical efficiency. At this time, concern centered around the problem of repetition. British psychologists had explored the industrial applications of the phenomenon of *response-produced inhibition*. When an organism repeats a stereotyped response, an inhibition builds up against further repetition of that response. This inhibition has nothing to do with muscular fatigue; rather, it is a feedback mechanism from the central nervous system. British studies had shown that, on certain repetitive tasks, many workers showed intermittent deficits in responding that could be accounted for only by this principle.

The obvious antidote to response-produced inhibition was some opportunity for *alternating response*. Response-produced inhibition dissipates rapidly when an alternative response is performed. Thus, the first attempts at job redesign (actually preceding Herzberg's the-

Figure 8–1

Advocates of job redesign point to the assembly line as the classic modern instance of work devoid of intrinsic rewards.

ory) introduced variety into the task by *job enlargement*. Programs of job enlargement required the worker to alternate periodically between different responses, giving the worker more different things to do. Early studies suggested that job enlargement (or *horizontal job loading*) produced generally positive results, at least initially, in the form of better morale, less absenteeism, and greater production. The casual, uncontrolled nature of the studies, however, precluded any confident conclusions. Moreover, a few of the published studies described disappointing results, and a selective bias may have led companies to report only successful programs.

Herzberg (1966) contended that job enlargement offered little in the way of motivational potential. The job must be "enriched." It must provide the worker an opportunity to experience a sense of achievement on the job. This meant building into the job complexity, autonomy, and challenge. Whereas job enlargement called for horizontal loading, job enrichment implied *vertical job loading.* The latter involves, not only alternating operations, but responsibility for *planning* the operations and *evaluating* the product of the operations.

Supporting Theories

Robert White (1959) suggested that a basic motivational drive of human beings is to acquire and demonstrate *competence.* This drive, which he called "effectance motivation," is the urge to make the environment behave, to produce an effect upon the environment. This motive appears very early in life in a diffuse, undifferentiated fashion; one sees it even in infants as they find that they can turn on a flashlight, knock over a pile of blocks, or prick a soap bubble. With maturity, this need for competence takes more specific forms in the compulsion toward a craft, the arts, the professions, or entrepreneurship. White felt, however, that its full expression and development depended upon the satisfaction of more basic needs related to survival and avoidance of pain.

Argyris (1957) noted the natural direction of growth patterns from infancy through adolescence to adulthood: from a passive being to whom things happen toward an active stance of making things happen; from dependence on others to increasing independence; from a limited repertoire of behavior to one increasingly extensive; from a shorter to a longer time horizon; from a subordinate status toward equal status with others. People possess strong motives toward further psychological growth along these dimensions. But Argyris was convinced that most work environments place barriers in the way of further growth. Tasks that take away discretion and emphasize simple, repetitive work operations thwart the growth motives and produce frustration. In response to the pain of frustration, most workers suppress the urge toward further psychological growth and regress to earlier developmental stages. They become passive, they deemphasize the role of work in their lives, they live for the short run, they focus on shallow rewards available through creature comforts and unchallenging forms of entertainment. Argyris, in sum, indicted the bureaucratic form of work organization. He called for new approaches to structuring the work environment, including new designs of jobs.

deCharms (1968) and Deci (1975) have carried forward the theoretical development of the construct of intrinsic motivation. The essence of this motivation is the desire to see one's self as an "Origin" rather than a "Pawn." Tasks that capture intrinsic motivation are those from which people can derive evidence of their competence and a sense of personal causation (as opposed to external inducement).

Thus, a number of theoretical streams converge toward the conclusion that jobs must possess certain attributes in order to provide intrinsic rewards that satisfy growth needs.

Characteristics of Motivating Jobs

Research by Turner and Lawrence (1965), Hackman and Lawler (1971), and others has identified four attributes of tasks that largely determine the degree of intrinsic rewards from job effort. These attributes are: (1) variety—the extent to which the job requires different operations; (2) autonomy—the degree of worker latitude in choosing work methods, deciding the sequence of operations, and pacing the work; (3) task identity—the extent to which the worker does an "entire piece of work" and can identify the results of the work; and (4) feedback generated by the task itself. Studies generally show that workers' *reported perceptions* of these attributes correlate positively with job satisfaction and reported levels of work effort. To a somewhat lesser extent, workers' descriptions of job characteristics correlate with attendance and independent measures of performance (e.g., supervisory evaluations). Other research has shown that subjects' reported descriptions of these task attributes are capable of discriminating between jobs officially classified at different salary grades.

Programs of job redesign, therefore, attempt to increase the extent to which existing jobs possess the core attributes of variety, autonomy, task identity, and feedback. In addition, many programs also attempt to increase the level of *job-relevant interaction with others* in order to enrich the social dimension of work. While this attribute is not consistently related to the usual measures of motivation and performance, it does appear to have an effect on attendance and general job satisfaction.

Hackman and Oldham (1975) have identified another attribute, *task significance*, that determines the intrinsic rewards of job effort. Task significance is the degree to which the job, as perceived by the worker, "really counts"—i.e., has a considerable impact on other people in or outside the organization.

Finally, worker participation in managerial decision making has been included in some approaches to job redesign. Many advocates of job enrichment believe that this dimension of work is essential to promote employee involvement in the job. European experiments in job redesign have been more concerned with this factor than American programs. Worker participation, indeed, has become a controversial political issue in several European countries. Furthermore, unions have provided for more worker participation in job redesign itself in Europe, while these programs in the United States have been initiated, implemented, and evaluated almost entirely by management.

Stages in Program Development

The leading advocate of job enrichment in the United States today is probably Robert Ford, personnel director of work organizations and environmental research at AT&T. From 1965 to 1968 AT&T conducted 19 formal field experiments in job enrichment, and since then it has expanded the program to many additional areas of the Bell system. On the basis of AT&T's success with its job enrichment program, Ford (1973) sees the job enrichment strategy as involving three stages. The *first* stage is designed to improve work through systematic changes in the modules of work. During this stage each worker is given a whole, natural unit of work and is assigned specific or specialized tasks which enable him or her to become an expert in this expanded work module. Ford says that in defining modules that give each employer a natural area of responsibility, AT&T tries to accumulate modules (units) of work until one of the following has been assigned to the worker: (1) a customer outside the organization; (2) a client within the organization; or (3) a manufacturing task in which an individual can produce a complete product or large portions of a complete product.

In order to improve morale and upgrade performance, AT&T has recently begun to "nest" jobs together during this stage. This method goes beyond enriching *individual* jobs by putting together people whose work modules complement one another. Job nesting is therefore the opposite of job pooling (for example, a secretarial pool), in which workers who perform a similar task are located together.

The *second* stage enriches the work through systematic changes in the control of the work module. During this stage, as an employee gains experience, the supervisor turns over responsibility to the employee until the employee is handling the work completely. The ultimate goal is to let the worker have complete control over the job. This increases the accountability and control of individuals over their own work, and indeed, makes each employee a manager of the project.

The *third* and final stage is perhaps the most important to the success of the job enrichment program. During this stage the job is enriched through systematic changes in feedback signaling whether something has been accomplished. During this stage periodic reports are made directly available to the worker rather than to the supervisor. Like the positive reinforcement program, this stage allows the worker to monitor the quality and quantity of work in order to make the corrections necessary. Ford (1973) says, "Definition of the module and control of it are futile unless the results of the employee's effort are discernible. Moreover, knowledge of the results should go directly to where it will nurture motivation—that is, to the employee. People have a great capacity for midflight correction when they know where they stand" (p. 99).

Unlike a positive reinforcement program, job enrichment requires a big change in managerial style. It calls for moving controls downward. A positive reinforcement program, on the other hand, is not intended to change managerial style but to increase the manager's ability to give varied kinds of feedback as it relates to worker performance. Therefore, the job enrichment program involves, not only changing the feedback received by the worker and the worker's task involvement, but also changing the traditional relationship of the supervisor with subordinates.

Results of Job Redesign Programs

Scores of firms have undertaken some form of job redesign. Notable examples include Texas Instruments, Corning Glass, IBM, AT&T, Proctor & Gamble, Maytag, Buick, Motorola, Monsanto Chemical, Donnelly Mirror, Exxon, Polaroid, Xerox, and Scott Paper Company. In Europe, programs by Volvo and Saab-Scania (Sweden), and Philips (Netherlands) have attracted much attention and discussion. Some experiments have been carried out on a small scale, with selected groups thought to be most in need of radical improvement; in other instances, as with the Gaines Foods Company and Scott Paper Company, entirely new plants have been designed and constructed in order to carry out comprehensive reforms in job structure.

The majority of firms that have experimented with job redesign describe the projects as "successful." Of course, this is to be expected. A management team that has invested large sums of stockholders' money in *any* project, attracted media attention, and put the prestige of the firm on the line will certainly want to interpret the results as justifying the costs. Since most assessments of these programs come from uncontrolled case studies, the evidence for success or failure is generally ambiguous. Therefore, it would not be surprising if officials overestimated the benefits of the programs.

Culling the evidence available from studies that used fairly objective measures of relevant criteria before and after job redesign, the following seems to be a fair statement:

1. Results do not support the case for a consistently strong improvement in productivity. In many of the instances in which productivity did improve, the increase could have been largely accounted for by nonmotivational factors, such as newer and better plant and equip-

ment, greater flexibility of operations, and improved scheduling of materials flow in the work process.

2.   Somewhat more consistently, studies report an improvement in quality of finished products.

3.   The majority of instances show some improvement in work attendance, and the inference is that increased worker satisfaction mediates this effect.

After more than 15 years of job redesign projects by scores of organizations, the checkered pattern of results precludes any unqualified evaluation. The experiences of some programs have been positive, some inconclusive, and at least a few negative. Part of the problem in sorting out the results stems from the realistic observation that management can hardly redesign jobs without changing other variables in the work environment at the same time. To restructure jobs usually means that you also change equipment, the nature of supervision, elements of the formal reward system, patterns of interaction, frequency and quality of communication between management and workers, and so forth. Neither positive nor negative effects of the program as a whole can easily be attributed to any one variable; positive effects due to increased intrinsic rewards from the task may be offset by perceived inequities in new compensation arrangements, and positive effects attributed to changes in tasks may actually result from other changes made.

Some would argue that job redesign seldom gets a "fair chance" to prove itself. Unions have offered, at the most, lukewarm support for the concept. Leaders of organized labor have been known to criticize "demeaning work" and to call for work that preserves the worker's dignity. But in serious collective bargaining the definition of "quality of work life" zeroes in on pay, benefits, safety, hours of work, and job grades. Some unionists, such as William Winpisinger (1973), are frankly and outspokenly suspicious of management's ulterior motives behind the push for job enrichment; they wonder if it is not merely a disguised effort to get more work for less pay, or even to undercut the influence of the union. Certainly job redesign plays havoc with the well-defined job descriptions that presently limit management's ability to manipulate work assignments and responsibilities. Furthermore, if management and labor find it hard to agree on concrete issues such as pay and benefits, it would be much more difficult to agree on something as elusive as "intrinsic job rewards." Therefore, unionists have not generally embraced programs for job enrichment.

In some instances, the initial success of job redesign programs has threatened lower-level supervisors and managers. As we have noted, job redesign builds into the job certain dimensions of work that previously were in the domain of supervisory responsibilities. Naturally, if this downward shift in responsibility "works," lower-level managers wonder if they may soon be expendable. At the very least, redesigned jobs that give workers more autonomy and discretion affect a manager's sense of control. Foremen and supervisors might interpret job enrichment as simply one more step in the erosion of their authority, while their responsibilities remain as great as ever. Not surprisingly, lower-level managers, after initial endorsement of job-redesign programs, often become less cooperative in the extension and consolidation of the changes made.

Beyond the question of enlisting the active support of organized labor and lower levels of management looms a more fundamental issue brought to light by results of some programs: it appears that at least a very sizeable minority of the labor force still places greater priority on the *extrinsic rewards* of pay, benefits, and working conditions than on the intrinsic rewards of work. Consider, for example, a study by Simonds and Orife (1975) of job transfers initiated by employees through a job-posting system. Out of 71 transfers, 51 were for higher-paying jobs. More interesting, employees initiated transfers to 15 jobs which offered more pay but were also more routine. In no transfer was a more enriched job preferred at lower pay. Only if an enriched job also offered higher pay did an employee seek the transfer.

Locke, Sirota, and Wolfson (1976) introduced a job enrichment program in three clerical work units of a federal agency. Productivity increased, but it soon became clear that this was not due to motivational or attitudinal forces. Instead, the productivity increase was due to more efficient use of manpower. elimination of redundant operations, feedback, and competition. Attendance improved initially because workers expected higher pay would also be forthcoming. When workers realized that pay would not increase, many of them were irate. The authors concluded:

> It was clear . . . that these employees viewed their jobs *instrumentally*, that is, as a means to an end . . . .
>
> It was not that they were indifferent to the work itself, they clearly preferred interesting to dull work. But in their hierarchy of values, the extrinsic rewards came first [p. 710].

Our conclusion, then, is that increasing the intrinsic rewards of task effort still holds vast potential for enhancing job motivation, but that realizing this potential involves coming to grips with prickly political, institutional, and cultural dilemmas. It is not the theoretical framework supporting job redesign that is in question; rather, we have underestimated the difficulties of applying that framework in complex settings. Results of the more successful programs have been sufficiently encouraging for us to believe that efforts along these lines will continue and that some of the major problems will be resolved.

MANAGEMENT BY OBJECTIVES

Programs of OB Mod and job redesign evolved in response to conceptual frameworks that preceded them. By contrast, management by objectives (MBO) represents a case in which practice ran far ahead of formal theory and research. Indeed, much of the research supportive of MBO not only came after years of implementation by hundreds of organizations but was actually independent of any concern with MBO.

Credit is usually given to Peter Drucker for the embryonic formulation of MBO. Drucker, in his *Practice of Management* (1954), stressed the importance of having managers at every level working for clearly defined objectives that were integrated across levels. Integration and consistency of these objectives would result from collaboration between superior and subordinate officials in setting quantitative performance goals.

Carroll and Tosi (1973) give credit also to Douglas McGregor for popularizing a goal-oriented approach to managing. McGregor (1960) criticized many existing methods of appraising the performance of managers. He argued that, all too often, managers were evaluated on the basis of style, personality characteristics, or irrelevant "halo" factors rather than results. Furthermore, performance review discussions often made both superior and subordinate officials uncomfortable, since they focused on weaknesses rather than strengths. McGregor suggested that a more positive motivational climate would result from evaluating performance against well-defined quantitative goals, worked out in advance by boss and subordinate in discussion. This would leave subordinates latitude for using their own "style" or methods for achieving the goals. The criterion of performance would be measurable results. Appraisal would provide feedback of actual performance in comparison to the goal.

Numerous versions of MBO (also called "management by results" and "goals management") were already being practiced when theoretical and empirical work on goal setting came to light in the late 1960s. Locke (1968) argued that the immediate determinant of task behavior is conscious intentions, which in turn derive from values and from cognitive maps that link behavior and its outcomes to the realization of those values. Goals serve the purpose of making intentions clear and explicit. Feedback and incentives are important because they stimulate goal setting or lead a person to accept an external goal. Participation in setting a goal is important, also, if it leads to acceptance of the resulting goal.

Results of laboratory experiments by Locke and his associates, using simple tasks, support the hypothesis that specific, precise goals ("increase your output by 10 percent") lead to greater productivity than general ("do your best") goals. Demanding goals ("increase your performance by 20 percent") result in higher productivity than easy goals ("increase your output by 5 percent"), *provided* the subject accepts the goal. So long as the subject does not reject or abandon the goal as impossible or unrealistic, difficult goals lead to higher performance, whether or not the goal itself is actually reached. A recent study (Latham and Saari, 1979) supports the prediction that whether a subject is assigned the goal or personally sets it makes little difference as long as goal difficulty is the same. Some evidence from field studies (e.g., Latham and Yukl, 1975) suggests that participation results in more demanding goals.

McClelland's (e.g., 1961) work on the theory of achievement motivation (discussed in greater detail in the next chapter) also supports the basic concepts of MBO. Managers as a group usually score rather high on this motive. Two characteristics of people who are strongly motivated by the need to achieve are (1) a tendency to set moderately difficult, but attainable, personal goals and (2) a compulsive need for quick, precise feedback on the performance. MBO, then, creates a task environment that capitalizes on the motivational characteristics of managers.

The MBO Process

There is no such things as a "pure" or "definitive" prototype for MBO. The format and structure of the program invariably include features to fit the prevailing conditions in an organization. Nonetheless, MBO consultants typically base the design of a program on a framework that has as its core the following sequence of events:

1. The subordinate manager works up a written statement as a provisional draft of his or her objectives for the coming period (year, six months, or quarter). This statement anchors the objectives in measurable terms. Any objective judged to be important is linked to a quantifiable index. The subordinate, in effect, says "these are the criteria by which I choose to be judged."

2. The subordinate submits this statement to the superior for review. Their joint discussion, which may lead to modifications of the subordinate's original statement, results in the final and formal statement of the objectives.

3. Periodic but frequent joint reviews by superior and subordinate discuss progress to date and assess the distribution of time and effort toward various component goals. This provides feedback to the subordinate concerning which objectives need more or less emphasis. A regional sales manager, for example, may confirm that he or she is making rapid strides toward meeting the overall sales objectives but

is running behind in progress toward the objective of securing orders from 25 new industrial customers. These interim review sessions help to "fine-tune" the direction of subsequent efforts.

4. At the end of the period for which goals were set, superior and subordinate discuss in a more comprehensive fashion the latter's performance. Analysis concerns the reasons why some or all goals were not met—ideally in a constructive fashion for purposes of future planning. Some goals may, in retrospect, be judged as unrealistic; unforeseen developments (e.g., a strike, an economic downturn, a change in corporate policy by top management) may have led to constraints that handicapped the subordinate's performance; or the subordinate might have pursued the wrong strategies. The review provides the basis for defining objectives for the upcoming period.

A major dimension of variation in the implementation of MBO concerns whether the process starts from the bottom up or top down. If the latter is chosen, the chief executive officer and top management first define the overall, companywide objectives for the period (which may go beyond a year to include much longer-range target goals.) As the process works down, each subordinate manager formulates objectives consistent with the goals and constraints of the larger unit.

According to Webber (1979), the initial conception of MBO was just the opposite: objectives were to flow from the bottom up, with succeeding levels of management integrating and coordinating goals of subsidiary units into a larger framework. This approach has the advantage of providing more autonomy and a greater sense of involvement by junior officials but makes it more difficult for top management to exert systemwide control. On the other hand, the top-down approach, while more realistic, may lead lower-level managers to feel that goals have been imposed upon them.

Another variation deals with the question of whether MBO is tied to decisions about compensation. On one hand, it seems logical that managers will be more personally involved in the setting and pursuit of goals if their performance in comparison to the goals determines their salary. On the other hand, one can argue that to tie compensation to MBO may subvert and distort the goal-setting process. Subordinates might concentrate the goal-setting upon areas of operation where they knew they could "look good" rather than honestly aiming at target goals that would benefit the organization as a whole.

Assessment of MBO

Research in the form of correlational field studies has sought to determine which elements of the MBO process have the most favorable effects on participants. Findings reported by Carroll and Tosi (1973) suggest that the *degree of subordinate influence* is *not* an important factor in the perceived success of the program. *Difficulty* of goals set has an uneven relationship with participant motivation: difficult goals seem to stimulate the more mature and self-confident manager but have a discouraging effect on less-experienced subjects. More consistently positive relationships with program criteria are noted for the *clarity* of goals set, the perceived *relevance* of the goals, and the *frequency of feedback*.

Other research has attempted to evaluate the overall effect of MBO. Many studies report increased productivity, better planning, improved attitudes toward performance appraisal, and increased morale of managers. Unfortunately, virtually all of these findings come from uncontrolled case studies comparing pre-MBO data with trends immediately after MBO. Also, many of the criterion measures come from responses to interviews. This does not mean that we should ignore such findings, but clearly we have to qualify them.

Perhaps the most amibitious and rigorous test of an MBO intervention is that conducted by Muczyk (1978). His study compared the performance of 13 branch banks which underwent MBO to an identical number of "control" branch banks not exposed to MBO. The criteria were "hard" measures of overall financial performance, as well as attitudinal measures. Measures were taken at the beginning of the study, 6 months after the start of the experiment, and 12 months after the start. The experimental and control banks were matched for market area and size in order to minimize any differential advantage of one group over the other. Muczyk found no significant effects attributable to MBO at either the 6-month or 12-month checkpoints, in either financial performance or attitudinal criteria. Banks that underwent MBO did improve their performance over baseline levels, but so did the other banks. Muczyk qualified his findings by noting that MBO was introduced only from the middle-management ranks down; the preferred strategy is to include top-level management as well. Moreover, officials participated on a voluntary basis, so that "the normal pressures exerted by top management on behalf of the success of a program introduced on a more permanant basis were absent" (p. 327).

Limitations of MBO

We might note first of all that MBO, in both its conception and application, is virtually entirely for managers. OB Mod and job redesign have found readiest application to operative, nonmanagerial employees. MBO, by contrast, has found little or no application with nonmanagerial, nonprofessional workers. Of course, there is nothing inherent in any of these programs that would logically and necessarily exclude any groups from treatment. But the thrust of MBO as typically designed lends itself more easily to subjects with some minimal levels of responsibility and authority.

Even among MBO interventions otherwise judged successful, a consistently voiced objection is to the amount of paperwork involved (Carroll & Tosi, 1973; Webber, 1979). The mechanics of the goal-setting, feedback, and review processes generate an enormous number of forms for documentation. Most managers consider this result an irritant and a distraction. On the other hand, it seems to be more of a burden at the beginning of the program than later, as subjects become accustomed to the process and acquire some proficiency at expediting the process.

Participants often feel that MBO distorts the nature of their performance by placing excessive emphasis on performance dimensions that easily lend themselves to quantitative expression. They feel that they hurt their personal interests if they spend much time on tasks that are important but difficult to measure. A regional sales manager can set precise goals for total sales, number of new accounts, administrative costs per dollar of sales, and sales revenue from new products. On the other hand, it is not so easy to set specific goals for customer service and subordinate development. A half day spent in consultation with a potentially big customer may be more important than a dozen routine phone calls to existing clients, but there is no obvious means of measuring and documenting this. Ridgeway (1956) found that whatever is formally measured attracts attention and effort at the expense of whatever is not measured. People assume that what is measured is what "really counts." While MBO programs include intensive training on how to set clear goals for all areas of performance, it does not provide magic formulas for measuring intrinsically subjective or qualitative dimensions.

In some organizational climates, MBO—if imposed upon subordinates resentful and distrusting of the hierarchy—may be viewed as a "club" to *force* people to unreasonable levels of effort toward unrealistic goals. The numbers associated with the objective-setting and review process exert a special tyranny of their own without consideration of mitigating circumstances. The result is that managers direct their ingenuity toward finding methods of beating the "statistics game" rather than making substantive contributions.

As with OB Mod and job redesign programs, the results produced by MBO probably depend very much on *how* it is introduced and implemented, on the support demonstrated by top-level managers, and on the existing climate of the organization. Evaluating the program itself apart from these other variables in field settings is well nigh impossible. The best that can be said is that MBO *can* produce increased job motivation among managers, but there is no guarantee that it *will* do so if barriers work against it.

Nonmotivational Objectives of MBO

Here we have focused on MBO as a program for increasing managerial job motivation. However, there are other purposes addressed by MBO. Many practitioners see it primarily as an effective means of ensuring managerial *control* over system performance. Others view it foremost as an aid to planning over time horizons intermediate between long-range plans and day-to-day operations. Many consultants stress its benefits as a *developmental* tool for junior managers. As we have noted earlier, some emphasize the *performance-appraisal* feature of MBO. Of course, motivation enters into all of these issues to some extent. Nonetheless, numerous instances of MBO, while not ignoring its motivational implications, emphasize its impact on planning, control, and development of subordinate managerial skills.

CONCLUDING OBSERVATIONS

While we have discussed these programs as if they were totally distinct from one another in both practice and philosophy, they do overlap to some extent. OB Mod, for example, clearly contains elements of goal-setting and feedback emphasis that are most often associated with MBO. Job redesign attempts to increase the total amount of reinforcement for work effort by drawing upon the non-contrived reinforcers made possible by job enrichment. MBO, in some respects, "redesigns" or "enriches" the jobs of junior managers and captures the reinforcing quality of precise feedback.

We draw attention to these underlying similarities in order to forewarn the reader against partisan claims that any one model or program of job motivation has a monopoly on validity or practical benefits. OB Mod, job redesign, and MBO do not reflect antagonistic concepts but rather different points of emphasis. There is no reason—philosophical or practical—why they cannot complement each other.

Furthermore, like the character who was shocked to realize he had been "speaking prose all his life without knowing it," many organizations practice the core components of one or more of these programs without either calling them by their popular names or even knowing that such programs exist. It would represent a wild oversimplification to say that one firm practices MBO and another absolutely does not, or that one company has "adopted" OB Mod and another "avoided" it. One could scarcely imagine an organized setting in which, at least informally, officials were not setting goals, reinforcing superior efforts, or "enriching" the jobs of promising employees who are capable and desirous of greater challenges.

SUMMARY

Organizational behavior modification, job redesign, and management by objectives represent the most widely practiced formal programs for increasing job motivation. OB Mod procedures draw from the concepts of operant psychology; job redesign springs from the assumption that employees seek to satisfy psychological growth needs at work; and MBO is supported by the demonstrated effects of goal setting. Each program, however, can also be supported by other theoretical frameworks. Empirical assessment of these interventions has produced inconclusive results; none of these approaches has a guarantee of success, in part because so much depends on the institutional context in which they are introduced. They represent not cookbook formulas, but guidelines that must take account of the technological and political constraints specific to the organization.

CONCEPTS TO REMEMBER

OB Mod	job redesign
pinpointing	intrinsic rewards
baseline audit	Two-Factor Theory
reinforcer survey	response-produced inhibition
contrived reinforcer	job enlargement
shaping	job enrichment
noncontrived reinforcer	effectance motivation
stretching the ratio	MBO

QUESTIONS FOR DISCUSSION

1. Some critics of OB Mod have argued that it "reeks of authoritarianism." Is this a fair criticism? Why or why not?
2. Are OB Mod and job redesign incompatible with each other? Frame your answer in both theoretical and practical terms.
3. If a job-redesign program leads to increased productivity and profits, should the increased earnings be shared with those performing the redesigned jobs? Why or why not?
4. Compare and contrast MBO with job redesign.
5. Discuss the difficulties of *evaluating* the effectiveness of any intervention aimed at increasing job motivation.

CASE[2]

Jim Anderson, the director of the Deep River office of a large insurance company, had for some time been concerned with problems of absenteeism, turnover, and generally poor morale. Job enrichment was suggested as a possible solution, and he decided to pursue this course of action.

The Program

Originally, Anderson proposed to conduct a program in the home office data input departments and possibly Deep River keypunch, but as of June 1972, he was actively promoting the possibilities of a much broader project encompassing all Deep River operations. While top management gave this proposal serious consideration, by the end of 1972 it was decided that a more limited program should be conducted in the Deep River office. To that end, an attitude survey was administered in the spring of 1973 to all Deep River clerical employees. The survey was designed to measure employees' attitudes toward 10 major aspects of their jobs: (1) advancement, (2) responsibility, (3) workload, (4) job content, (5) salary, (6) supervision, (7) communication, (8) working conditions, (9) training, and (10) management. The results identified three problem areas: job content, responsibility, and communication. It was decided that a job enrichment program would effectively address itself to these issues.

The coding services department was chosen to participate in the program for several reasons. Attitude survey scores from this department were decidedly negative on all three problem areas. Moreover, in coding services no other major problems were identified through the survey, and there were enough task functions to make enrichment possible. After discussions with local area administrators and the superintendent of the department, a final "go" decision was made.

Early in May 1973, a four-day off-site workshop was conducted to provide a better understanding of the principles of job enrichment. Participants included all first-line supervisors and their assistants, Deep River management, organizational development personnel, and an outside, hired consultant. Upon the recommendation of the consultant, worker participation was rejected on the basis that (1) it was management's prerogative to restructure jobs, (2) it would be awkward for supervisors and subordinates to jointly plan changes in subordinates' jobs, and (3) the expectations of the subordinates might be

[2]Paul J., Champagne, "Deep River Insurance Company," in J. E. Dittrich and R. A. Zawacki (Eds.), *People and Organizations* (Plano, Tex.: Business Publications, Inc., 1981) pp. 307–315. Reprinted by permission of the author and publisher.

unrealistic and the actual changes, therefore, disappointing. Workshop members began to apply the principles of Herzberg's motivation-hygiene theory, working out ways of translating responsibility, achievement, recognition, and growth into work-related items. During "greenlighting" or brainstorming sessions, supervisors contributed ideas for improvement of subordinates' jobs without criticism or comment. During "redlighting" sessions, priority items based on what had to be done first were listed, including possible barriers within management's control and possible steps to overcome them. Subgroups composed of pairs of supervisors and assistant supervisors then selected those items they wished to implement in their units.

At the conclusion of the redlighting and implementation sessions, five items were recommended: (1) coders would take turns handing out work; (2) individual coders would begin requisitioning materials directly from filing units; (3) coders were to become experts in their own areas of responsibility; (4) branch offices would be assigned to coders; and (5) coders would begin reviewing their own error sheets returned by the branch offices. Following the workshop, the supervisory teams met with internal and external consultants every two weeks through the early summer of 1973 to plan the implementation.

Early on, the problem of possible loss of earnings under the company's existing wage incentive plan was discussed by management. Under wage incentive, every job was studied, using time and motion techniques, to determine efficient work cycle times. When an employee produced at a rate equal to 70 percent of maximum possible efficiency a bonus was added to the employee's base salary. For some this amounted to $40 or more per week.

The basic problem was that enrichment training time would not count toward the weekly bonus. Therefore, employees participating in a job enrichment program involving extensive retraining would be penalized. A number of possible solutions were suggested, including dropping the wage incentive and increasing base salary. It was finally decided to deal with the problem by (1) lengthening the overall training time to minimize time off measurement, and (2) giving participating employees a bonus equal to the amount lost under the wage incentive during training. Each trainee was compensated for the time off measurement with a single payment of $20 to $40. While this amount was small it was sufficient to induce 55 percent of the coding services employees to participate in the program. Until this solution was proposed, only 28 percent of the eligible employees had volunteered for the program.

Once retraining was completed, jobs were retimed so that each participating employee's weekly wage incentive bonus would remain at about the same level as it had been prior to retraining. No attempt was made to reclassify the "larger" jobs (i.e., increase the weekly base pay) since management did not perceive the issue of money as a possible source of trouble.

Most job enrichment programs involve some anticipated changes in the job time cycle; not so here. Under enrichment, coders were expected to handle an entire unit of work, including correction of errors, but no change was made in the wage incentive time standards. For example, if an auto-liability coder performed all the 44 separate tasks required on one unit of work, the time standard for 100 percent efficiency was 33.42 minutes. During the enrichment program this did not change; 100 percent efficiency was still 33.42 minutes. The only difference was that participating coders were required to know and (if necessary) perform each and every task in a unit of work while nonparticipating coders were not. Participating coders were also accountable for errors made by the branch office or keypunch. If an error was detected in incoming work, the coders would contact the branch office by telephone, teletype, or memo. When an error was detected by the company computer, the coder was expected to pull the file, reconcile the error, and see that it was processed correctly by the keypunch operators. All of this took time and required that the coders work harder and faster than before in order to stay within the wage incentive time standards. Management did not seem to realize the negative effect of this on coders' attitudes toward enriched work.

On October 1, 1973, the program was officially launched using the training schedule devised during the workshop. Membership was strictly voluntary but everyone was encouraged to participate. The program was presented by management as a method for increasing employee interest and job satisfaction. All those who participated in the program were female high school graduates (average age, 22).

Coding services were composed of three basic units: special multiperil (SMP); loss; and auto and liability coding (ALC), with each responsible for coding premium or loss evidence on all types of casualty insurance—i.e., marine, fire, auto, personal liability, etc. The coded information related to the billing, accounting, and statistical experience of the branch offices. This information was then forwarded to the keypunch department for input into the company's computer system.

Prior to job enrichment, work was distributed to individuals without regard to the branch office that initiated it. Under the program, task modules were established, providing complexity, completeness, discretion, and feedback for a unit of work. After employees had been retrained, all work forwarded from branch offices was assigned to specific individuals, requiring them to perform all tasks and functions necessary to process the work. This created continuing individual accountability for a whole unit of work, and clearly associated individual workers with particular branch offices.

At about the same time that job enrichment was getting under way, a number of other changes were being implemented which affected the entire Deep River staff. Late in 1973 and early in 1974 a number of steps were taken in an effort to deal with a variety of other problems identified by the 1973 attitude survey. For example, carpeting was installed, employees were given better explanations of the company bonus plan, job classifications in a number of departments were revised, improved vending machines were installed in the lunchrooms, rest room facilities were improved, open posting of jobs was begun, greater effort was made to open communication channels between supervisors and subordinates, and a modified flexi-time program was instituted. Since management was attempting to deal with several pervasive problems, no incongruity was seen between these changes and the ongoing job enrichment program.

By the early part of 1974, 41 out of 75 eligible employees were performing enriched jobs. In March 1974, a follow-up attitude survey was conducted focusing on the same issues as its predecessor. To management's surprise and dismay, there was little or no change in employee attitudes. Responsibility, job content, and communication were still reacted to negatively. The results were particularly disappointing in view of the ongoing job enrichment program. Management had expected that enrichment would improve employee attitudes and when it did not, faith began to wane in its ability to produce the desired outcomes.

The final evaluation at the end of one year's operation of the program indicated some reduction in turnover and absenteeism. The productivity figures were less conclusive, however. While the situation in coding services had improved, the rest of the Deep River staff showed even greater gains. Based on these findings, management labeled the program a failure and decided to discontinue all job enrichment activity. They felt that the results of the program were not sufficiently impressive to justify the expense of job enrichment.

Anderson and his staff decided not to expand the program to other units in the Deep River office. But even though future job enrichment programs were shelved, branch coders were allowed to choose whether or not to retain their enriched jobs. Among the three units, SMP chose as a group to continue under the program; in ALC and loss, only 4 of the 28 participating employees chose to remain and were still in the program one year and three months later (see Exhibit 1).

The Results of Job Enrichment

Absenteeism

During the program absenteeism among participating employees showed marked improvement, as shown in Exhibit 2.

Exhibit 1
Employees Who Opted to Retain Enriched Jobs after Completion of the Trial Program

Unit	Number Eligible for Program	Number Opting for and Participating in Program	Number Opting to Remain in Program Three Months after End of program	Number Opting to Remain in Program One Year and Three Months after End of Program	Percent Remaining in Program One Year and Three Months after End of Program
Auto-Liability Coding	31	23	9	3	13%
Loss Coding	31	5	2	1	20
Special Multiperil Coding*	13	13	13	13	100
Total	75	41	24	17†	41

*Special multiperil coders decided as a group to retain enriched jobs.
†The attrition from the program was not the result of turnover; two employees initially in the program quit the company in the spring of 1975, while two others quit in the spring of 1976. All had opted to retain the enriched jobs before quitting.

Exhibit 2
Annual Absenteeism*

	October 1, 1972, through October 1, 1973 (before Enrichment)	October 1, 1973, through October 1, 1974 (during Enrichment)
Coding Services		
Enriched Job Participants .... (n = 41)	5.6	3.4
Nonenriched Job Participants .... (n = 34)	7.0	9.9
Deep River Clerical Staff (Exclusive of Coding Services) .... (n = 400)	7.8	7.2

*The average number of days absent per employee: the total number of absences in a year among the employees in a department divided by the average number of employees in that department.

From October 1, 1974, average absenteeism in the enriched group dropped 2.2 days per year while among nonparticipating personnel it increased 2.9 days. During this same period the overall Deep River staff also experienced some improvement, but only 0.6 day.

According to the three unit supervisors in coding services, job enrichment had its most noticeable impact on absenteeism. When an enriched employee was absent for any period of time, the person's work was distributed to other members of the unit. This had an impact on the absent employee since errors made by someone else could interfere with the ongoing relationship established between the coder and the branch offices. Errors or delays, though made by someone else, were nevertheless the responsibility of the employee assigned to the branch. Rather than have to deal with problems created by others, employees apparently made a greater effort to be present.

Turnover

Turnover among participating employees was also reduced (see Exhibit 3). Turnover in the enriched group was reduced by 50 percent from the previous year. In addition, among employees on enriched tasks turnover was 10 percent less than among other personnel in coding services. However, this gain was overshadowed by the overall improvement in the Deep River office where turnover was 3 percent less than among the enriched group. To management it appeared that better results had been obtained without job enrichment.

Exhibit 3
Annual Turnover*

Coding Services	October 1, 1972, through October 1, 1973 (before Enrichment)	October 1, 1973, through October 1, 1974 (during Enrichment)
Enriched Job Participants .... (n = 41)	72.4%	32.6%
Nonenriched Job Participants .... (n = 34)	72.4	43.1
Deep River Clerical Staff (Exclusive of Coding Services) .... (n = 400)	67.1	29.6

*The percentage of employee turnover per year: the total number of quits in a year divided by the total number of employees in the appropriate units.

Even though absenteeism had improved dramatically, turnover made a stronger impression on management. It was apparently viewed as much more important in terms of the company's operations.

Productivity

Management expected job enrichment to have a dramatic impact on productivity, but as Exhibit 4 indicates, the results of the program were inconclusive. Productivity through the third quarter of 1974 among enriched employees was 14.8 percent higher than the nonenriched group, but the overall trend in coding services was downward. From January 1, 1974, through October 1, 1974, productivity in the enriched group had dropped 2 percent (97.3 to 95.3). During the fourth quarter of 1974 this trend was reversed slightly. The enriched group increased to 97.5 percent by the end of 1974. During the first three quarters of 1974 productivity among the nonenriched employees declined from 88 percent to 81 percent, a drop of 7 percent, and the fourth quarter of 1974 showed a further decline to 80 percent.

Even though the overall experience of the enriched group was better than that of the nonenriched employees in coding services, the lack of a clear trend was disturbing to management. It was particularly so in comparison with the rest of the Deep River staff, where productivity through the third quarter of 1974 had been almost stable.

When third-quarter productivity for enriched employees was examined by unit only SMP showed any improvement. Loss was down

Exhibit 4
Productive Efficiency in 1974 by Unit*

Unit		1st Quarter 1974	2nd Quarter 1974	3rd Quarter 1974	4th Quarter 1974
Loss Coding	Enriched .... (n = 5)	94.8%	89.8%	94.0%	100.8%
	Nonenriched .... (n = 26 to 28)	98.8	90.0	92.5	89.0
Auto- Liability Coding	Enriched .... (n = 23 to 24)	97.7	97.0	91.7	94.0
	Nonenriched .... (n = 7 to 8)	95.8	86.8	69.7	73.6
Special Multiperil Coding	Enriched .... (n = 13 tp 18)	99.4	95.5	100.1	97.8
	Nonenriched .... (n = 0)	—	—	—	—
Total Coding Services	Enriched .... (n = 41 to 48	97.3	94.1	95.3	97.5
	Nonenriched .... (n = 33 to 34)	88.0	88.5	81.1	80.0
Total Deep River Clerical Staff (Exclusive of Coding Services .... (n = 400)		94.0	96.0	93.0	unknown†

*Productivity was measured by how effectively a unit of employees utilized its time: the unit's average efficiency (i.e., how much work it processed in a given period of time) multiplied by the average percentage of time on measurement (i.e., the amount of time the employees engaged in measured work. This excludes lunch breaks, rest breaks, training time, etc.).

†The utilization for the fourth quarter of 1974 was not computed for the total Deep River clerical staff by the company.

slightly, as was ALC. Even though productivity among nonenriched employees in loss and ALC was also down, this offered management little solace. The productivity trends further reinforced management's growing skepticism about the utility of job enrichment.

Exit Interviews

Shortly after the formal end of the program on October 1, 1974, company organizational development personnel conducted interviews with 28 employees, selected at random from among those involved in job enrichment. The results showed that 82 percent of those interviewed felt the enriched tasks to be more interesting, but a large majority (79 percent) also felt participants should be paid more. Bonus-making ability during enrichment was a major problem for 71 percent of these employees (see Exhibit 5).

Exhibit 5
Follow-up Interviews with Randomly Selected Participants in the
Enrichment Program*

	Response	Percentage Agreeing (Total n = 28)
1.	The job was more interesting and enjoyable	82
2.	Should be paid more	79
	a. Job classification should be raised	29
	b. Bonus-making ability was a major problem	71
	c. The job should be retimed	54

*Content analysis of interviews with 28 of the 59 participants in job enrichment.
Source: Interviews conducted by home office organizational development personnel.

While these data reveal the basic problem encountered by management, comments made by the employees interviewed indicated even more forcefully the primary reason for their continuing discontent. The one item of greatest concern to the coders performing enriched tasks was the problem of lost bonus money during the program.

Comments like the following were common:

I like the idea of branch coding, but thank goodness I don't depend on the bonus money.

I like branch coding but because you get such a variety of work it is very hard to make your efficiency. I think the rates [basic job classification] should be raised.

I don't like branch coding, because without my bonus money my base pay is nothing. I find myself becoming very disgusted and not even caring about my work. You work harder now and have nothing to show for it.

I like branch coding because of the variety of work, but I find I have nowhere near the efficiency I used to. If someone offered me a job that paid about the same as my base pay right now, I'd take it. Before, I never would because of my great bonus money. But now, I'd jump at the chance.

I like branch coding because I like the variety of work . . . [but] I also think we do a lot of work for our pay—I mean I really work harder now than I did when I was a regular coder.

Within the individual units, employee reaction to job enrichment was much the same. For example, SMP branch coders felt the training was good, but the training payment was too low to adequately compensate for lost bonus earnings.

In response to the question "How do you feel about the changes?" all four people interviewed in SMP responded that they were generally more satisfied with the enriched job. They liked having responsibility for particular clients. Most (three of four) felt they had more control over the work. All mentioned the increased task variety of the enriched job as a favorable feature. Their major gripes centered around the loss of bonus money which accompanied job redesign. They felt they should be paid a higher base salary since it was definitely harder to earn the same bonus on the new job.

ALC branch coders felt that their training payments had been inadequate when compared to the bonus they could have made on the old job during the same time period. Four of the coders interviewed in this unit were making significantly less bonus money than they had on the old job. The problem was not due to the intrusion of extra jobs into their work by the supervisors, but rather was seen as the need for adequate retiming of work standards to allow for the numerous new tasks involved. As one of the employees put it, "They (management) didn't look at the whole picture before putting it in (job enrichment)." Or as another stated, "It's more mental work for less money."

The comments from the loss department were much the same. One coder, for example, said that her bonus had slipped from approximately $40 to $13 per week. This eventually caused her to drop out of the program, since, as she put it, "I'm working here for money."

Questions

Do you share the apparent conclusion of Deep River management that the job enrichment program was a failure? How do you account for the results? What might management have done differently? What are the implications of the Deep River experience for *(a)* the theory supporting job redesign? *(b)* the practice of job redesign? *(c)* the empirical evaluation of such programs?

REFERENCES

Argyris, C. *Personality and organization.* New York: Harper & Row, 1957.

Carroll, S. J., Jr., & Tosi, H. L., Jr. *Management by objectives.* New York: Macmillan, 1973.

deCharms, R. *Personal causation: The internal affective determinants of behavior.* New York: Academic Press, 1968.

Deci, E. L. *Intrinsic motivation.* New York: Plenum Press, 1975.

Drucker, P. *The practice of management.* New York: Harper & Row, 1954.

At Emery Air Freight: Positive reinforcement boosts performance. *Organizational Dynamics,* 1973, *1,* 41–50.

Ford, R. Job enrichment lessons at AT&T. *Harvard Business Review,* 1973, *73,* 96–106.

Hackman, J. R., & Lawler, E. E., III. Employee reactions to job characteristics. *Journal of Applied Psychology,* 1971, *55,* 259–286. (Monograph)

Hackman, J. R., & Oldham, G. R. Development of the Job Diagnostic Survey. *Journal of Applied Psychology,* 1975, *60,* 159–170.

Hamner, W. C., & Hamner, E. P. Behavior modification on the bottom line. *Organizational Dynamics,* Spring 1976, pp. 2–21.

Herzberg, F. *Work and the nature of man.* Cleveland: World, 1966.

Latham, G. P., & Saari, L. M. The effects of holding goal difficulty constant on assigned and participatively set goals. *Academy of Management Journal,* 1979, *22,* 163–168.

Latham, G.P., & Yukl, G. A. A review of research on the application of goal setting in organizations. *Academy of Management Journal,* 1975, *18,* 824–845.

Locke, E. A. Toward a theory of task motivation and incentives. *Organizational Behavior and Human Performance,* 1968, *3,* 157–189.

Locke, E. A., Sirota, D., & Wolfson, A. D. An experimental case study of the successes and failures of job enrichment in a government agency. *Journal of Applied Psychology,* 1976, *61,* 701–711.

Luthans, F., & Kreitner, R. *Organizational behavior modification.* Glenview: Ill.: Scott, Foresman, 1975.

McClelland, D. C. *The achieving society.* Princeton, N.J.: D. Van Nostrand, 1961.

McGregor, D. *The human side of enterprise.* New York: McGraw-Hill, 1960.

Miller, L. *Behavior management.* New York: John Wiley & Sons, 1978.

Muczyk, J. P. A controlled field experiment measuring the impact of MBO on performance data. *Journal of Management Studies,* 1978, *15,* 318–329.

Nord, W. R. Beyond the teaching machine: The neglected area of operant conditioning in the theory and practice of management. *Organizational Behavior and Human Performance,* 1969, *1,* 375–401.

Repucci, N. D., & Saunders, J. T. Social psychology of behavior modification: Problems of implementation in natural settings. *American Psychologist,* 1974, *29,* 649–660.

Ridgeway, V. F. Dysfunctional consequences of performance measurements. *Administrative Science Quarterly,* 1956, *1,* 240–247.

Simonds, R. H., & Orife, J. N. Worker behavior versus enrichment theory. *Administrative Science Quarterly,* 1975, *20,* 606–612.

Skinner, B. F. *Science and human behavior.* New York: Macmillan, 1953.

Skinner, B. F. *Beyond freedom and dignity.* New York: Alfred A. Knopf, 1972.

Sorcher, M., & Goldstein, A. P. A behavioral modeling approach in training. *Personnel Administration,* March–April 1972, pp. 35–41.

Turner, A. N., & Lawrence, P. R. *Industrial jobs and the worker.* Cambridge: Harvard University Graduate School of Business Administration, 1965.

Webber, R. *Management: Basic elements of managing organizations.* Homewood, Ill.: Richard D. Irwin, 1979.

White, R. Motivation reconsidered: The concept of competence. *Psychological Review,* 1959, *66,* 297–334.

Whyte, W. F. Skinnerian theory in organizations. *Psychology Today,* April 1972, 67–68, 96, 100.

Winpisinger, W. W. Job satisfaction: A union response. *AFL-CIO American Federationists,* 1973, *80,* 8–10.

9

Personality:
Dimensions of Individual Differences

What are the important dimensions of personality?

How can the organization accommodate diverse personalities in an effective manner?

You have to be cut out for this job. Some people can get along in it, others couldn't. It depends on what you're cut out for.

These words came not, as you might think, from a highly specialized professional such as a stockbroker or air traffic controller. They were spoken by a janitor who worked in a residence hall where the first author lived during graduate school. In their utter simplicity, they express something we all instinctively feel: everyone is different from everyone else, and this uniqueness must somehow be addressed by models of organizational behavior.

What accounts for the uniqueness of the individual? To begin with, every individual—except pairs of identical twins—has a unique set of genes. Heredity sets the boundaries within which later stages of development occur. To the extent that the central nervous system, hormones, and sense organs govern overt behavior, the individual's unique genetic base will account for some differences among people. To just what extent "nature" or heredity determines individual differences is a matter of considerable controversy (especially with respect to the determination of intelligence); some theorists accord it a substantial role, others believe it to be much less significant than environment, or "nurture."

Each person also has a unique history of reinforcement, or "background," if you will. It has long been recognized, for example, that the same parents respond differently to later-born children than to the firstborn, if for no other reason than that they are really different parents the second time around. They themselves have been changed by the experience of parenting the first new member of the family. As individuals are drawn into the expanding circles of different peer groups, subcultures, and institutions, these differences in reinforcement history accumulate. Some of these early effects will wash away; others will leave imprints that resist the tides of time.

The ultimate effect of both heredity and reinforcement history, as far as organizations are concerned, is that organizational environments do not write on a blank slate. Such environments will have their effects, but the effects will be stronger on some than others, and the effects will vary. Differences in organizational environments—in reward systems, job design, supervisory styles—will account for some proportion of the variance in observed behavior, but neither research nor informal observation has shown such factors to account for all of the behavior in organizations. Lay people and scientists alike assume that much of the remaining variance must be chalked up to fairly stable differences in characteristics of people. In sum, there is no way to argue with the oft-cited dictum of Kurt Lewin that $B = f(P, E)$: behavior (at a given time) is a function of both the individual personality and the environment. A more current and much preferred rendering of this statement asserts that behavior is a function of the *interaction* between the personality and the environment. Neither one by itself tells the whole story; we have to consider their joint effects.

The Concept of Personality

You have doubtless discovered that the concept of personality is indispensable to everyday thinking. You probably cannot imagine what other terms you would use to think about the people you know. And, like most concepts that we use so instinctively, it is frustratingly difficult to define what we mean by *personality*. But we must be explicit and self-conscious about this construct if we are to bring it into a conceptual approach to organizational behavior.

The concept of personality, as we ordinarily use it, seems first of all to imply something about the characteristic *internal states* of persons. As Brown and Herrnstein (1975) note:

> . . . we seek to explain the fact that a given constant stimulus has varying effects on the same organism at different times, which leads one to believe that the effect is mediated by changing internal states . . . people differ in the readiness with which they fall into one state or another, and these readinesses are summarized as abiding properties of the organism—traits, temperaments, dominant needs, skills, and so on [p. 529].

Second, these internal states are inferred from *consistency* in behavior across different situations. Obviously no one behaves the same way in every situation. We pray in church, whistle in the shower, yell at football games, and argue over the dinner table. But the characteristic differences among persons do seem to carry over across a variety of situations. The individual who is quieter than most in church *tends* also to be more reserved at dinner. In other words, it is the *comparative*, not absolute, qualities of behavior that seem to have some consistency.

Third, our native concept of personality includes the quality of *stability*. Personality is, by our definition, something that endures in its basic elements. Again, this is not an absolute characteristic. Personality—a person's *self*— consists of "layers" of habits and predispositions. The surface layers may exhibit considerable change over short time intervals, as reflected perhaps in changing preferences for such things as style of clothes, entertainment, hobbies, or foods. Other predispositions, such as those reflected in political leanings or job interests, change only gradually over longer periods of time, perhaps measured in years. Still more fundamental constituents of the self— temperament, moral values, ultimate purposes—typically change very little except over an appreciable portion of one's life span. To be sure, we can all point to exceptions, to those occasional individuals who seemingly undergo "total conversions" as a result of some extraordinary experience. Yet, we refer to such rare instances with some proper degree of astonishment, as "like a sudden but total personality change." Nonetheless, such radical changes occur so seldom that we assume considerable stability in the structure of personality.

Finally, our concept of personality involves the notion of *uniqueness*. Whatever the "readiness toward internal states," whatever the consistencies in behavior across situations, whatever the underlying characteristics that may persist, they are different for each individual.

Conceptual Approaches to Uniqueness

Yes, we take it for granted everyone is unique. But do we, in fact, consciously *attend* to the uniqueness of every person with whom we interact? No—because, as we have argued elsewhere (Chapters 2, 5), our information-processing capabilities do not permit it. In a sense, we "recognize" that people are individually unique, yet in practice we cannot deal with the extraordinary, perhaps infinite, number of mental categories that this recognition would logically require. We share with science the incapacity for dealing with the discrete, unique event or object as unrelated to everything else. Like science, we work out a compromise. We conceive of uniqueness in terms of a limited number of contributing dimensions. The difference is that some of us find certain dimensions more useful for understanding and classifying people; others use other dimensions. Think, for example, of someone whom you have just met in the last few days. What categories did you immediately use for "storing" or "filing" your impression of the person? Was it in terms of the warm-cold category? Or in terms of neat-sloppy? Passive versus active? Chances are, you made use of just a few dimensions of thought. Yes, you recognize that person is unique, but the total extent of that uniqueness would never in fact be made known to you, no matter how much time you subsequently spent with the person. For your working purposes, that person is defined for you in terms of a few dimensions, susceptible to "cross-referencing" in your mental files. Depending on your lay theory of personality—that is, your conception of what characteristics tend to go together (e.g. the assumption that warm people tend to be more honest, kind, courteous, etc.), your impression may go beyond the behavior you observed and draw some tentative inferences about other aspects of the person. And, with extended interaction, you will no doubt feel the need to use other categories of thought as a useful basis of defining the individual. The point is this: we use a limited number of dimensions or categories in order to construct an impression of personality.

Theories of personality do essentially the same thing. All schools of thought in personality theory subscribe to the notion that some, most, or all of the important differences among individuals can be explained by a limited set of constituent elements. These elements may be described as values, motives, traits, types, developmental stages, or unconscious forces, depending on the approach taken and the individual differences presumed to be important. Since each element is conceived as a continuum, with an infinite number of points lying upon it, using even a single element does no violence to our notion of uniqueness. Every individual could be characterized, in principle, as corresponding to a different point on the continuum, even if we can in practice never measure the element with such precision, and even though we will in practice cut the dimension into a few chunks (high, low, medium) for comparing any one person to others.

Personality Theory and the Manager

Within reasonable constraints of time and space in a volume such as this, we cannot hope to do justice to the full scope of personality theory and research. A single chapter could not possibly incorporate the contributions of such prolific theorists as Sigmund Freud, Gordon Allport, Carl Rogers, Erich Fromm, Karen Horney, Henry Murray, and Kurt Lewin, to name just a few. What we have tried to do below is to sample some schools of thought which appear to contribute most to an understanding of work behavior and at the same time illustrate various approaches to understanding individual differences.

We have chosen not to provide any account of approaches based on the Freudian psychoanalytic model of unconscious forces. We do not believe that a capsule review of this approach will aid the administrator in observing individuals at work; in fact, we suspect that to try to do so would do more harm than good if readers were tempted to try off-the-cuff analysis of others' unconscious forces. This position constitutes no judgment on the worth of psychoanalytic theory in the general sense; it merely notes realistically that the administrator is not a clinician and the work organization is no place for psychoanalysis.

We have also excluded from the discussion those approaches which, implicitly or otherwise, postulate what the "healthy" or "mature" personality *should* be. Again, we do not reject these clinical points of view; quite to the contrary, we applaud the humanitarian values and concern by which they are inspired. But, once again, we fear that in such a case the adage "A little knowledge is a dangerous thing" applies. We simply do not want to encourage simplistic judgments by ill-formed laymen as to who is "sick" and needs "mending."

Finally, we have not addressed ourself to individual differences based on sex, age, race, or ethnic origin. We do not by our silence mean to suggest that there are no such important differences. But the last decade or more has called into question many such differences that were previously assumed to exist, especially as reflected in work behavior.

The sampling below is thus quite selective, omitting so much as it does of alternative points of view. However, each of the approaches reviewed has shown some utility for organizational behavior in both theory and practice.

APPROACHES TO STUDYING PERSONALITY

A Motive-Based Approach

Some motives or needs—such as those for food, water, sleep, and shelter—are quite temporary in nature. Our need for food persists only until we have ingested enough of it to satiate ourselves, and then our behavior is directed toward other goals until hunger pangs strike again or until some delicacy (for example, chocolate cream pie) appears in our perceptual field. Other motives, however, are more enduring, more chronic, and less likely to be quickly satiated. The persistence and stability of such motives suggest one approach to studying personality. A stable motive is by definition a preoccupation with certain types of goal objects and thus a predisposition to respond in certain directions.

Atkinson (1958) and McClelland (1961), among others, have discovered a technique for identifying such motives in human subjects. Their technique, called the Thematic Apperception Test (TAT), consists of presenting the subject with a still picture and asking the subject to make up a story about that picture. For example, the picture might show an architect seated at a desk, with blueprints, drafting materials, and a photograph of the architect's family on the desk. The subject is asked to make up a story explaining what has led up to that scene, what the architect is thinking, and what will happen later.

The use of this projective technique is based on the assumption that, given such an ambiguous stimulus, people will *project* into it their own longings, desires, and goals. Motives are identified by the kinds of imagery or themes which emerge strongly in the subject's story.

Need for Achievement

A strong achievement motive is identified by themes in the subject's story which relate to striving for some standard of excellence in task accomplishment. Need for achievement (or *n Ach,* as abbreviated by McClelland) reflects a strong goal orientation, an obsession with a job or task to be done. Someone with strong n Ach, making up a story about the picture mentioned above, would talk about a challenging assignment that the architect is working on, such as the need to design a bridge which would withstand strong winds, yet also meet other criteria.

McClelland (1961) has identified a number of reliable behavioral manifestations of this need. People with high n Ach are attracted to tasks which challenge their skills and their problem-solving abilities; they have little interest in games in which luck is a major determinant of success. These persons set difficult but realistic goals which present an objective prior probability of about .3 to .5 of success. They avoid setting goals that they believe are almost impossible to achieve or that guarantee a virtual certainty of success. They prefer tasks whose outcomes depend on their own individual efforts; if help is needed, they select people on the basis of competence in the task rather than people who are socially congenial. They have a compulsive need for quick, concrete feedback on how well they are doing, and they especially like feedback in quantitative form, such as percentages, number of units, and so forth.

Achievement, then, has a special meaning in this context. Scientists, teachers, and artists do not score high in n Ach, even though they may realize substantial achievement in a more general sense. They neither need nor obtain quick, unambiguous feedback about their efforts.

McClelland finds that entrepreneurs and managers are especially likely to have high n Ach. Whether in a socialist or a capitalist country, in private business or in government, the more effective managers tend to have a sharply focused goal orientation, a drive to compete either with peers or according to some standard of excellence. They make moderately risky decisions in settings in which they believe they can exert some control over the outcomes, and they constantly gauge the effectiveness of their decisions and effort by some unambiguous index. McClelland suggests that it is no accident that most cartoons set in a business office show in the background a chart with a curve depicting sales, profits, or production.

McClelland believes that the need for achievement is shaped rather early in life—in part by the culture, through such media as children's readers, and in part by parental styles which encourage children to take responsibility, promote independence in action, and reinforce achievement. He further asserts that the economies of entire nations rise or fall over the years as a consequence of the culture's influence on the need for achievement, reflected in the development of the entrepreneurial "instinct."

Need for Affiliation

A second motive identified in subjects' stories is the need for establishing, maintaining, or restoring pleasant emotional relationships with other people. Persons with strong needs for affiliation (n Aff) want primarily to be liked by others; "getting along" with co-workers is more important to them than how much the group accomplishes. In response to the picture of the architect, such persons would emphasize the architect's thoughts about the family in the portrait on the desk: the good times they have had together, how much they mean to one another. Persons with high n Aff would be more sensitive to other people's feelings than would persons with high n Ach. They would be attracted to tasks involving groups, while the high n Ach person would prefer being a loner with a job that depends on him or her alone. As managers, high n Aff persons might avoid task decisions that would engender emotional or social conflict.

It would be tempting to infer that high n Ach persons make the best managers and that high n Aff individuals would make ineffective managers. However, some concern for affiliation is important if the manager is to develop the group structure and climate necessary for long-run effectiveness.

Need for Power

A third motive is the desire to exert control or influence over people. Unfortunately, this need tends to suggest, to most people, something sinister about a person's motives. However, a strong need for power does not necessarily result in an autocratic or tyrannical leadership style. Winter (1967) found that this need (n Pow) could take either an *unsocialized* or a *socialized* expression in college students. In the former case, it was reflected in a desire for sexual conquest or physical aggression. In its socialized form, it was manifested by active membership in, or leadership of, student and community groups or organizations which sought constructive ends, such as civil rights, campus reform, and student government.

There is reason to believe that a manager should have at least a moderate level of n Pow in order to be effective. Otherwise, he or she would shrink from making decisions and would allow the group to develop in an aimless, uncharted direction. As Chapter 3 pointed out, managers must inevitably accept the responsibility for influencing the behavior of the people who work for them. A manager's need for power has been shown to be quite compatible with a leadership style which stresses the development and participation of subordinates; it is not the exclusive mark of the bully or the manipulator.

Finally, it should be noted that the actual expression in behavior of these various motives depends to a large extent on the stimulus cues in the environment. For example, even a very strong need for achievement will not be manifested in an environment in which there is little opportunity for achievement (as we have defined it). *Motives are latent or dormant unless aroused by salient stimulus cues.*

A Trait-Based Approach

Allport and Odbert (1936) searched the dictionary and found over 3,000 words to describe personal characteristics—the exact number depending on how many of the trait adjectives were judged to be roughly synonymous. A trait-based approach to personality assumes that these *surface traits* can be accounted for by a much smaller number of *factors* (see Figure 9–1). This assumption draws support from repeated observation that many surface traits correlate to some degree with each other within clusters. For example, people who are impulsive also tend to be outgoing, active, prone to take risks, and talkative. Thus, underlying these traits is the hypothetical construct of some personality factor, whatever we choose to call it.

The personality researcher using this approach typically starts with a questionnaire or what is commonly called an *inventory.* Each item or question in the inventory asks the respondent how accurately a statement characterizes his or her behavior; each item is, in a sense, a question about a trait as expressed in one's behavior or likes and dislikes. The total number of questions may range from about 20 to several hundred. When a large sample of subjects responds to the

Figure 9–1
The Trait-Based Approach to Personality

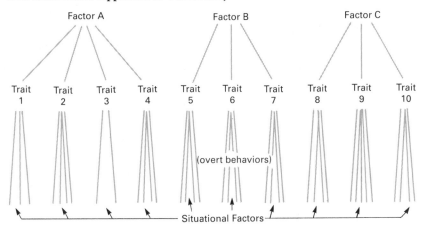

questions, the results are submitted to a statistical treatment known as *factor analysis*. Factor analysis, taking account of the patterns of correlations between answers, identifies a small number of factors, each of which underlies a cluster of traits. However, the exact number of factors which emerges depends somewhat on judgment; it is not wholly determined by the data. Because of this, advocates of a trait-based approach differ among themselves as to the number of factors that should be regarded as separate and distinct.

Hans J. Eysenck (1967) believes that two factors deal adequately with the important variance in measured personality traits. He has called these factors *neuroticism* and *extraversion*.

Neuroticism

Eysenck has interpreted this factor as degree of emotional stability. One might also think of it, without doing great violence to Eysenck's writings, as predisposition to anxiety. A number of other researchers besides Eysenck have also found this construct useful in tying together a number of correlated traits.

The person who scores high in neuroticism can be characterized as one who is quite sensitive to conditions of threat—be they real or imagined. Such a person, the High N, has a lower threshold than the Low N for the stimulus events which trigger emotional arousal in the forms of fear, guilt, or worry. In the work environment, the High N syndrome often manifests itself in the following ways:

1. *Low tolerance for job ambiguity.* The High N much prefers a work situation with explicit supervisory expectations, clear ground rules, and a well-structured task. This need for structure increases as pressure—in the form of serious consequences contingent on success or failure—also increases. Of course, all of us desire some minimum degree of clarity in our jobs, and we all fret when we are not clear what our responsibilities are or what we need to do to meet them. But the High N is much more apt to experience acute anxiety when confronting an unstructured job situation.

2. *Need for reassurance.* The High N's discomfort with unstructured work situations arises, at least in part, because such situations do not provide reassuring feedback about the appropriateness of one's activities or efforts. The High N needs such feedback, even if only to know that he or she is not royally screwing things up. In the absence of such reassurance, the High N worries about possible mistakes and tends to undervalue his progress. The High N is very much motivated by the *need to avoid failure* and its consequent embarrassment, self-reproach, and guilt feelings. While the Low N adheres to the motto "In the absence of information to the contrary, I can assume I'm doing

just fine," the High N tends to fear the very worst until reassured that this is not the case. Often such a person will "fish" for such consoling words from the supervisor or colleagues.

3. *Unstable, job-related self-esteem.* All of us sustain bruises to our egos when we experience failure (in either an absolute sense, or relative to our own standards or others' progress), just as we have our egos uplifted after an episode of success. For the Low N, this fluctuation of self-esteem occurs only to a moderate degree around a fairly stable estimate of self-worth. For the High N, self-esteem is much more sensitive to episodes of success or failure, especially the latter. Also, the High N's self-esteem is likely to be less "compartmentalized"; disappointments in job performance affect not only vocational self-esteem but easily spread over to affect feelings of adequacy in other aspects of the self.

4. *Sensitivity to threat.* Sooner or later, every administrator has justifiable cause to use some degree of threat in communicating to subordinates. The threat may be implicit, such as presenting factual negative feedback about someone's performance without further comment; it may take the form of an honest warning; or it may become an angrily delivered ultimatum. Mild threat is likely to arouse little anxiety for the Low N; in fact, it may hardly even register. The High N, on the other hand, is likely to evince a considerable measure of concern, even reading into the message something more serious than was intended. Strong threat, on the other hand, may be just enough to get the Low N's full attention so that he or she responds in a constructive fashion, but it could absolutely cripple the High N. In the latter case, anxiety may lead the person to focus so much on the anxiety itself that he or she cannot concentrate adequately on a complex task.

Have you ever noticed that some people, when strongly rebuked for committing some error, then work so hard at avoiding that same mistake that they proceed to make five *other* kinds of mistakes? Such people fit our description of the High N. Their easily aroused anxiety causes "tunnel vision," a reduced span of perceptual attention. In such a state, a person loses the ability to detect nonobvious cues. On simple tasks, this effect may actually help performance, because it helps block out irrelevant distractions. But on tasks that require a wide attention span—which require one to attend to a variety of quickly changing events in different parts of the perceptual field— this arousal usually impairs performance.

Ironically, the High N can be said to be "overmotivated" at times, especially by the concern for avoidng real or imagined aversive stimuli. The adverse consequences of such overmotivation take such familiar forms as forgetting one's lines because of stage fright, drawing a blank on the final exam even though one "knows" the material,

228

Figure 9–2

The worker who scores high in neuroticism is sensitive to even mild criticism and corrections.

jumping from the sixth-story window instead of taking the fire escape, or (in the case of a good basketball team) committing a plethora of turnovers in the opening game of a postseason tournament.

We should hasten to emphasize that high neuroticism, or proneness to anxiety, bears no relationship to intelligence or any kind of general aptitude that we know of. In and of itself, this trait is neither good nor bad (nor, for that matter, is its opposite at the other end of the dimension). High N's as a group are in no general sense more or less adjusted than others and no better or worse prospects for any responsible position of employment. It all depends on whether they accept in a mature fashion that this is the way they are and how they deal with it. Some people simply lower their sights and try to avoid situations that present any prospect of failure—yet, if inescapably caught in such a situation, may work so hard to avoid failure that they back into success. Others cope with the frequently aroused anxiety by withdrawal, or escape into fantasy, procrastination, or drugs. Still others become perfectionists, fearing that any little mistake or overlooked detail will contain the seeds of disaster. Some students for example, study for an exam three times as hard as they really need to, just to provide a margin of safety, while others still the raging demon of anxiety with a couple of six-packs the night before the exam or by seeking permission to withdraw from the course.

One cannot help wondering about the origins of high neuroticism and whether or not organizational attempts to reduce it would be fruitful. One school of thought, supported by some empirical evidence, suggests that neuroticism is linked to hereditary biochemical and physiological factors. A hypothesis advanced by Eysenck, which seems to fit a number of findings but has not been demonstrated by direct test, is that differences in neuroticism are related to differential thresholds of arousal in the visceral brain, which integrates the autonomic functions of the sympathetic nervous system (Eysenck, 1967).

If neuroticism in behavior is indeed a product of physiologically based factors, then organizational environments could not appreciably change this personality dimension. On the other hand, Kahn and his colleagues argue that the "presence of environmental stress seems to produce 'neurotic' emotional reactions in those who score low on the neurotic anxiety scale" (Kahn et al., 1964, p. 260). Such symptoms, they admit, may be temporary rather than chronic. Nevertheless, they regard it as plausible that persistent job stress may amplify the individual's tendencies toward the generalized trait of neuroticism.

There is some speculation that susceptibility toward neurotic anxiety is a function of early reinforcement histories (that is, in childhood) emphasizing threat, aversive conditioning, and avoidance learning. If this argument has validity, then one could argue that organizational environments which are supportive and nurturant could, over a long period of time, reduce levels of neuroticism for those who are located at the extreme upper ends of the distribution. Whether such environments would have a beneficial effect, a dysfunctional effect, or no effect at all on low-neuroticism individuals is another question. In any case, any changes in neuroticism that could be effected would seem to require rather long periods of time. However, the organization official can anticipate how this trait will affect responses to threat, job ambiguity, and lack of feedback.

How can the manager identify organization members who may be quite high on the dimension of neuroticism? One way, of course, is to have people take one of the various questionnaires for measuring this trait. A more direct, but cruder judgment may be made by observing in people's behavior or self-descriptions the qualities which have been associated with high neuroticism. Frequent references to guilt feelings about trivial matters, expressions of worry about health that seem exaggerated or unconfirmed by medical examination, a habit of working feverishly to complete minor projects long before their deadlines, obsessive concern with possible traumatic events in the distant future, inability to shrug off past mistakes or failures, are all possible clues. The perceptive executive can notice when a patterning of such symptoms suggests an individual relatively high in neurotic emotionality and then make reasonable predictions about how such a person would react to various types of motivational systems, leadership styles, or environmental stressors.

Extraversion-Introversion

The dimension of extraversion-introversion is a second broad, underlying trait which historically has figured very prominently in the theoretical and empirical work on personality. The dimension has had a stormy history, however, and there has been more confusion and disagreement about its meaning than has been the case with neuroticism.

In everyday parlance, we typically use the terms *extravert* and *introvert* in a manner that relates primarily to sociability: extraverts are more outgoing and gregarious, introverts shier and more retiring. The meaning of extraversion in the psychological literature has been broader than this, although sociability may be one of a cluster of surface traits related to extraversion. Jung used the concept *extraversion* to refer to "the kind of outward orientation that makes a person highly aware of what is going on around him and causes him to direct his energy toward objects and people outside himself" (Tyler, 1965). "Introversion" referred to the opposite tendency—sensitivity to one's own feelings, memories, consciousness, and inner life.

A contemporary interpretation of extraversion as a personality dimension, as typified in the writings of Hans J. Eysenck (1967), is that extraversion relates to individual differences in the need for external sensory stimulation. In general, extraverts have a greater need for stimulation—in the form of social activities, crowds, adventures, frequent change in the environment, intensity of colors or noises, or drugs. Introverts need less stimulation, and are more often concerned with reducing stimulation from the environment than increasing it.

Of course, this dimension is a continuous one, and the terms *introvert* and *extravert* are used only in a relative or comparative sense. Most of us experience both needs, but at different times or in different proportions; that is, there are occasions when we need to shut out stimulation in order to avoid overstimulation and other occasions when we feel a bit starved for stimulation. We try to regulate the flow of stimulation in order to maintain some comfortable level of "subjective excitement." Quiet, restful vacations at secluded spots appeal to us when we are being bombarded by the events of a hectic workday; but usually after a few days or weeks of escape to such havens, we become restless, and our appetite for stimulation reasserts itself. Furthermore, the level of "subjective excitement" that is comfortable for us tends to vary with the time of day (receptivity to stimulation for most of us being greater in the late morning or the early afternoon than in the early morning hours or late in the evening) and with the task that preoccupies us.

Eysenck believes that differences in the need for external sensory stimulation correspond to individual differences in the functioning of the *reticular brain stem formation.* The latter is a dense nerve network in the lower central part of the brain. It acts as a gatekeeper by which external stimulation "sprays" the entire brain cortex with the energy to function—to see, hear, think, or react (French, 1957). The reticular formation is somewhat like a battery for the working parts of the brain. Two components within the reticular formation work in antagonistic functions to regulate this generalized current: a facilitator, which "amplifies" the stimulation; and an inhibitor, which tends to "muffle" it. Eysenck suggests that the extravert's "muffler" is stronger than the "amplifier," and that the reverse is true for introverts. Thus, extraverts need more generalized stimulation to overcome the inhibitory or muffling tendencies, whereas introverts have a greater need for holding stimulation within bounds due to the stronger excitatory tendencies of the facilitator. Eysenck's hypothesis has not been directly proved, but he has traced the converging lines of a host of different studies to this appealing explanation.

Given Eysenck's interpretation of this personality factor, we would expect extraverts and introverts to differ in those forms of behavior that aim at enhancing or reducing stimulation. The extravert, for example is attracted to risk taking, especially physical risks. The extravert is more likely to be drawn toward such endeavors as skydiving, downhill skiing, motorcycle racing, fast driving, and contact sports. Living close to physical danger, even the possible threat of death itself, is no doubt terribly stimulating; the extreme extravert would probably agree with the words of the poet Robinson Jeffers, "Life and death upon one tether, running beautifully together"—but the introvert scarcely needs such stimulation.

Extraverts prefer job environments that provide novelty, variety, intermittent bursts of intensity, unpredictability, and spontaneity. Even occasional crises have their appeal. If their jobs or the surrounding context are bland, extraverts will soon look around for job-extraneous sources of stimulation—practical joking, petty gambling, making up little games to play, and the like. Within limits, such distractions probably do no harm, and they help pull the extravert through the day, although they may occasion some irritation for introverts.

Extraverts sometimes satisfy their need for stimulation from interpersonal and intergroup conflicts. Such conflicts, whatever good or harm they do, undoubtedly have the effect of providing stimulation. While it might sound extreme to suggest that extraverts might deliberately provoke conflict in order to satisfy a pent-up need for excitement, one can easily imagine that in dull times they will make the most of incidents that provide a pretext for feuding, grievance, and in-house intrigue. The introvert would tend more easily toward emotional exhaustion if such conflicts became very frequent or intense.

The major job-related problem for the introvert is sensory overload—for example, introverts are much more likely to be bothered by excessive noise (Weinstein, 1978). Introverts prefer predictability, orderliness, and stability in the job environment.

Of what importance is the extraversion-introversion dimension to the study of behavior in organizations? Some implications are perhaps obvious. On repetitive tasks or on tasks performed in environments that offer very little sensory stimulation, the introvert will usually do better; the extravert will spontaneously engage in task-irrelevant behaviors to increase stimulation. On tasks performed in environments in which sensory overload threatens (for example, variable noise, random stimulus changes that require unpredictable shifts in the focus of attention, distractions), the extravert will get along better. In short, extraverts are more apt to suffer—either in terms of lower satisfaction or deterioration in performance—from sensory deprivation or understimulation; introverts more often fall prey to overstimulation, sensory overload, and excitation. As with other dimensions of personality, the differences do not become striking until one compares groups at opposite ends of the distribution.

There is a less obvious—though ultimately perhaps much more important—implication of this personality variable for the theory and practice of organizational behavior. Research findings have shown that introverts may be *more conditionable* than extraverts, especially when conditioning occurs on variable schedules of reinforcement and when the reinforcing stimulus is low in intensity. The issue is not completely settled, but the evidence points in this direction, and it is a crucial issue for organizations. Organizations are very much involved in the conditioning process, inasmuch as they seek to shape individual behavior toward designated ends. Much of this conditioning is unplanned and subtle, using the mildest reinforcers; these, however are precisely the conditions under which introverts demonstrate greater conditionability. One study showed that introverts had longer job tenure and fewer unexcused absences, and were generally rated as better adjusted to the job (Cooper & Payne, 1967). Another study found that introverts in graduate business courses reacted more positively to small bonuses contingent on maintaining day-to-day preparation for classes (Organ, 1975b).

To date, extraversion has received little attention in studies investigating such topics as motivation, performance, and leadership in ongoing organizations. Perhaps future research integrating this variable into theories of organizational behavior will increase their explanatory power.

Eaves and Eysenck (1975) report findings from a study of 837 adult pairs of twins which they interpret as strongly supporting the hypothesis of a genetic link to extraversion. Roughly half of the variance in extraversion scores could be attributed to heredity. Moreover, their data also supported the position that both sociability and impulsiveness are traits which derive from the broader dimension of extraversion.

If neuroticism and extraversion are basic yet separate and independent dimensions of personality, one might wonder what sorts of surface-trait personality profiles might result from a combination of high neuroticism and extraversion, low neuroticism and extraversion, high neuroticism and introversion, and low neuroticism and introversion. Eysenck (1973) suggests that Figure 9–3 presents a plausible classification of traits that emerge. For example, persons high in neuroticism

Figure 9–3
Trait Patterns Related to Combinations of Levels of Neuroticism and Extraversion

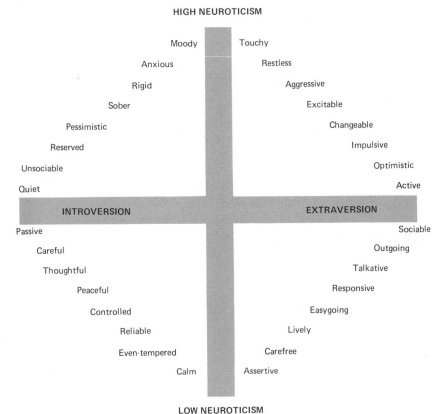

Source: Adapted from H. J. Eysenck, *Eysenck on Extraversion* (New York: John Wiley & Sons, 1973), p. 27.

will display different patterns of behavior, depending on whether they are introverts or extraverts. The highly emotional introvert copes with psychic turbulence by turning inward on it—withdrawing from social relationships and dwelling on his or her fears and anxieties. The unstable extravert copes by expressing his or her emotions, snapping at people, or becoming hyperactive.

Other Trait Approaches

R. B. Cattell and J. P. Guilford, two of the more prominent theorists of the trait-factor school of personality, believe that Eysenck has gone too far in reducing data from trait inventories to only two major factors. Cattell (1972) argues that, after identifying 16 major dimensions of personality from a very long inventory of questions, no further reduction is possible without serious distortion of the available data. Guilford (1975) proposes a scheme of 13 first-order factors and four second-level factors: social activity, introversion-extraversion, emotional stability, and paranoid disposition. Guilford also takes exception to Eysenck's formulation of the extraversion dimension, which Guilford calls a "shotgun" wedding of the traits of sociability and impulsivity—which he (Guilford) believes do not belong together as a factor.

Most of the other eminent trait theorists also believe that Eysenck is premature in pressing for a genetic explanation of these traits and factors, especially in the case of extraversion. They do not rule out the general proposition that heredity in some fashion may account for some predispositions of individuals toward certain behavior patterns. But, given the present uncertainty over the number and identification of the underlying dimensions of behavior, they regard any hypothesis about precise physiological origins of these dimensions as speculative at best.

A Belief-Based Approach

We take it for granted that differences in *cognitive* variables—beliefs, opinions, perceptions, expectations—underly much of the differences in people's behavior. Many of the elements of our cognitive structures are transitory in nature, altered by new information. But might there not be broad, underlying factors to people's cognitions? Could it be the case that some people are predisposed to certain types of belief structures? If so, are these predispositions stable?

Julian B. Rotter (1966) seems to have isolated such a belief system and has developed an instrument for measuring it. It is *locus of control:* the degree to which a person believes that his actions can influence his outcomes in life. *Internals* believe their behavior to be relatively decisive in determining their fate. *Externals* believe their behavior to be less decisive in this respect; they believe that chance, luck, or powerful agencies (persons or institutions) exert a very strong influence on what happens to them, an influence which supersedes any effects due to their own actions. Note that the issue here is *not* differences in the amount of reinforcements, success, or rewards experienced. The external may consider himself very well off in terms of what he is actually getting out of life. Nor do the differences refer to the amount of power possessed by other entities in the environment. Rather, the differences refer to beliefs about whether outcomes (good or bad) are *contingent on one's behavior.*

Rotter's locus of control construct derives from his theory of social learning. Rotter asserts that reinforcers and incentives shape our behavior only to the extent that we believe our behavior actually causes—not merely precedes—such reinforcers. In many cases, such beliefs are based on experiences in those situations. The individual who has spent many years in photography knows that a good picture is not a matter of happenstance; it depends on good composition, proper exposure, and the subsequent chemical processing of the film and paper. The greater our experience with a certain activity or class of situations, the greater the extent to which our beliefs about personal control are specific to those particular activities and situations.

Rotter believes that in addition to specific beliefs about personal control over outcomes, there is a generalized expectancy of internal versus external locus of control. These generalized beliefs exert their greatest effects when we are thrust into novel or unfamiliar situations about which specific beliefs are likely to be weak and uncertain. For example, the generalized internal and the generalized external who are seniors in high school will tend to have similar notions (other things being equal) about their degree of personal control over the grades they receive. But when they arrive on the college campus as freshmen, the internal tends to assume that his or her own behavior will, somehow, be the dominant factor in how things work out. The external, by contrast, will be impressed by the role of forces beyond his control as determinants of his effectiveness. As time goes by, these generalized beliefs about personal control will become less important determinants of their academic behavior as repeated specific experiences shape their beliefs. In sum, our beliefs about personal control are a mix of specific beliefs based on experience and a generalized tendency to view one's own behavior as either a strong or weak force in determining one's outcomes. The latter—internal versus external locus of control—tends to be somewhat stable, while the specific beliefs change more quickly.

An early study (Seeman & Evans, 1962) found that hospitalized internals made more persistent inquiries to the medical staff about the nature, origins, and treatment of their illness than did the externals. Since then, a number of studies have found internals to be more informed about their respective occupations and to experience less ambiguity about their jobs. This difference between internals and externals makes sense. The more that you believe you can affect your own outcomes, the more likely that you will place a premium on information concerning the type of behavior that is appropriate. On the other hand, the greater the weight you attach to forces beyond your control, the less likely that you will regard further information as worth the costs of search. Furthermore, note that these differences in information-seeking habits could act to reinforce the original beliefs about locus of control. The more you use strategic bits of information to your own advantage, the more you confirm the assumption that you can take charge of your outcomes in life.

A recent study (Anderson, Hellriegel, & Slocum, 1977) demonstrated how internals and externals differ in response to an unfamiliar situation. The authors interviewed the owners and managers of 102 businesses seriously affected by flooding during the onslaught by Hurricane Agnes in 1972. In general, externals experienced greater emotional stress. Moreover, externals were more concerned about coping with their own tension and frustration, tending to withdraw from the task of rebuilding and to express bitterness and aggression about the "rotten hand they had been dealt." Internals went immediately to work to acquire new loans, resources, and personnel; to maintain their clientele; and to restore previous levels of production. Obviously, no one could have prevented the storm itself. But the internals had faith that a proactive, problem-solving stance could determine whether the flooding was a conclusive tragedy or only a temporary setback.

Internals, in general, perceive more order and predictability in their job-related outcomes. Compared to externals, internals have more confidence that their own level of effort determines how well they perform, and they believe that performance level determines how well they are rewarded (Mitchell, Smyser, & Weed, 1975). Internals usually report greater levels of overall job satisfaction. While internals and externals both prefer to be supervised in a participative fashion, it matters more to internals. Again, this seems logical: the more you generally believe your own behavior causes your outcomes, the more latitude and scope you would seek for doing things your way.

However, a person's locus-of-control beliefs could be so internal as to constitute, in effect, a denial of the very real forces that lie beyond anyone's practical control. A failure to take a realistic account of such forces could lead to a very inefficient, fruitless expenditure of time and energy. A study by Behrman, Bigoness, and Perreault (1980) of industrial sales personnel found that the best performers were neither the most internal nor the most external, but intermediate in generalized expectancies for locus of control. Thus, we can hardly assume that "the more internal, the better."

Determinants of Internal-External Locus of Control Beliefs. Although researchers have identified a host of correlates of locus of control, little evidence has been found that addresses the more specific question of what causes the belief system covered by this construct. One can speculate by drawing tentative inferences from the correlational studies that have been conducted, but only longitudinal studies that trace the changes in subjects' belief systems over a considerable period of time—ideally from childhood into the early adult years—will shed much light on the origins of internal and external locus of control. Nevertheless, the question is worthy of attention for the theory and practice of organizational behavior, for several related reasons: (1) Locus of control, being a cognitive variable, is presumably amenable to alteration, even if the process requires months or years. Unlike neuroticism and extraversion, which are probably rooted in relatively permanent physiological factors, belief systems are necessarily acquired and are the product of exposure to some type of social and physical environment. (2) Many of the behavior patterns that go along with internal locus of control—the search for information, attempts to control the environment—would appear to be positively related to the effectiveness of organizational functioning. If internal locus of control is the *cause* (rather than the effect) of these behavior characteristics, and if the organization can learn how to influence people's locus of control beliefs (for example, by the reward contingencies or other components of the organizational climate), our understanding of organizational effectiveness could be enriched considerably.

In all probability, there are a variety of causal antecedents of locus of control. The simplest explanation would be that internals and externals are rather accurate in their perceptions, that internals are simply products of an environment in which their behavior has actually been the determinant of their outcomes and that externals have experienced futility in trying to determine their own lots. Some support for this argument comes from studies showing that minority groups and disadvantaged socioeconomic classes score more external on the Rotter questionnaire than do white middle-class groups. It certainly seems plausible that such individuals actually do exert less leverage in the way of choice or voluntary behavior for affecting their fates. Nevertheless, economic, social, and political disadvantages do not seem to tell the whole story, for even within relatively homogeneous groups there is considerable variation in locus of control, from extreme internal to extreme external.

A number of researchers have focused on parental antecedents of locus of control as a causal explanation. Predictability and consistency of parental discipline, parental support and involvement, and parental encouragement of autonomy and self-control have been hypothesized as causes of internal locus of control. However, the evidence is sketchy, and it is derived from retrospective descriptions by college students of what their parents' behavior was like.

Wolk and DuCette (1974) have presented evidence in favor of a radically different explanation of the origins of locus of control. Their studies indicate that internals display a significant superiority over externals in amount of *incidental learning*—that is, in the ability to pick up incidental, apparently unrealted cues and relationships while concentrating on material relevant to some other task for which they have been given instructions. Internals seem to be blessed with a cognitive style that organizes stimuli into structures or chunks preserving maximal amounts of the originally embedded information.

Their explanation fits well with operant concepts. Recall that the three important components of a contingency are the S^D (the discriminative stimulus), the R (the response), and the S^R (the consequence). In real-life situations, a given R never gets rewarded under all conditions, but only in certain stimulus situations—in other words, when certain stimuli are present. Furthermore, the nature of the stimulus, the elements which define it and which differentiate it from stimulus situations in which the response is not rewarded, can be very subtle and elusive. It could be that externals habitually use a cognitive style which often fails to capture subtle differences in stimuli. As a result, an external sees only that he or she is sometimes rewarded and sometimes unrewarded for certain behavior, on a seemingly random basis; if this is true for a large number of classes of behavior, the person draws the generalization that his or her behavior does not have a large influence on outcomes. On the other hand, the internal—due to different methods of processing information—picks up the subtleties of the different stimuli and concludes that, *under certain conditions*, a systematic relationship does exist between behavior and rewards.

In any case, much work remains to be done before we can answer the question of whether the organization can alter the locus of control of its participants, and if so, which, if any, of the correlates of locus of control also change. In the absence of conclusive evidence, one prescription can be strongly urged. Organization officials should try to make reward systems as sensitive as possible to individual differences in behavior, to communicate the reward contingencies as clearly as possible, and to train or nurture individuals to enable them to meet those contingencies. To the extent possible, individuals should also have input into the formalizing of contingencies that apply to important areas of their work behavior.

A study by Eitzen (1974) showed that locus of control becomes more internal as a result of exposure to certain environments. Twenty-one juvenile delinquent boys were assigned in groups to foster homes in which adult couples had been trained to use a comprehensive, systematic program of behavior modification using contingencies of positive reinforcement. The foster parents shaped socially constructive behaviors by reinforcing the boys with points that could be accumulated and exchanged for certain privileges and desirable objects. Over a three-year period from the start of this project, the average locus of control score of the group became steadily more internal, while a control group of high school students showed no such change. We may tentatively conclude, then, that organizations *can* foster a somewhat internalized sense of control by systematically administered contingencies of reinforcement. We suspect that, by giving the individuals affected by such contingencies a chance to help design them, one might compound the effect on locus of control.

Value-Based Approaches

Among the more enduring characteristics of adults are the *values* they hold. Values have been defined as "conceptions of the desirable that are relevant to selection behavior. . . . a special kind of attitude functioning as standards by which choices are evaluated" (Smith, 1963). Values, in short, are ideals, the reference points by which we measure the goodness of our actions, our aims, and our experiences.

A number of theorists have offered taxonomies of values. Allport, Vernon, and Lindzey (1951) drew from the writing of the German philosopher Spranger, who identified six basic values:

Theoretical: interest in the abstract truths that unify knowledge.

Economic: an orientation to pragmatic, workable, useful things.

Esthetic: interest in beauty.

Social: an orientation toward and concern for people.

Political: the pursuit of power and influence.

Religious: interest in spiritual and moral realms.

Allport, Vernon, and Lindzey devised a questionnaire which gives an index of the relative strength of these values for the respondent. This measure, called the Study of Values, has been used extensively in research on differences among occupational, ethnic, and religious groups. For example, people who enjoy sales and related types of work tend to have stronger economic, political, and social values. According to Tyler (1965), the Study of Values "has been a useful instrument for identifying aspects of personality not readily measurable in other ways."

Donald Super (1962), in the context of his research on vocational counseling, has developed a scheme for the analysis of job-related values. At the broadest level, a person's work values can be characterized largely as *intrinsic* or *extrinsic*. Intrinsic values focus on altruism, creativity, autonomy, intellectual stimulation, esthetics, achievement, or management. Extrinsic values center not on the work itself but on those ends for which it is instrumental—such as life-style, pleasant surroundings, congenial associates, security, status, and purchasing power. Needless to say, most people have both intrinsic and extrinsic work-value orientations, but one or the other predominates—a fact of which we become painfully aware when we have to decide on how much of one to trade off for the other. There are probably legions of workers at all levels who would like more freedom or the chance to do something more interesting than their current job affords but would not accept a 25 percent reduction in annual income in order to do so.

The Protestant Ethic

The German sociologist Max Weber argued that the doctrines of Calvinism promoted industrial capitalism in Western Europe by inculcating a certain set of values. These values included, first of all, an emphasis on the inherent goodness of work itself. A person's work was regarded as a calling, in the very literal rendering of the concept of vocation. Moreover, the experience of financial rewards from one's work was regarded as a manifestation that one was blessed by God, a member of the Elect few predestined to share His grace. However, money created temptations to the flesh, whose yearnings were to be suppressed. Protestant values called for self-restraint and deferral of gratification. By investing one's earnings in the form of capital, one could practice such self-denial. Over a period of many years, repeated investment of earnings created the capital base for the takeoff of Western societies into the economic breakthrough of the Industrial Revolution.

Thus, the Protestant ethic represents a cluster of values which define a "work conscience" of sorts. The values hold that people are obligated to work and that honest work—no matter how humble—is its own reward. Conversely, these values condemn laxity, idleness, and self-indulgence. Even a person's leisure pursuits should be useful, not idle play. Inner restraint dictates that enjoyment of nonwork activities must be postponed until one has "earned" that right.

A number of recent studies suggest that a secularized version of this set of values represents a useful construct in understanding stable differences among individuals. One study (Mirels & Garrett, 1971) found that people who generally endorse the Protestant ethic (PE)—as determined by their reactions to statements about work and the pleasures of the imagination and the flesh—tend to be more accepting of authoritarian leadership than nonendorsers of such values. Those who endorse the PE also tend to express interest in occupations demanding a concrete, pragmatic orientation to work, such as carpentry or veterinary medicine, but not in occupations that emphasize theoretical or abstract values or which require a capacity for creative, playful fantasy, such as music or writing.

In another study (Merrens & Garrett, 1975), subjects were given 100 sheets of paper, on each of which were pictured 250 circles in rows of 10. Each subject was told to draw an X in each circle with his or her nonpreferred hand and to keep working until too tired to continue. Note that subjects had no financial incentive to spur them to work, nor did the task provide much in the way of intrinsic appeal. The experimenters simply waited to see how long subjects would work until quitting (the experimenters terminated the work if the subject had not quit after 30 minutes). Those who previously had scored high on a PE measure spent an average of 23 minutes on the repetitive task, compared to less than 17 minutes for low scorers. Endorsement of the PE predicted not only the amount of time worked but also the amount of work completed, which was about 60 percent greater for those who scored high on the PE scale.

A number of possible explanations, none of them mutually exclusive to each other, could account for such findings. The high scorers on the PE measure may have been more driven to suppress feelings of fatigue or boredom, an explanation consistent with the value placed on self-control and discipline. High scorers might also have felt more of a moral obligation binding upon them due to having committed themselves as subjects—an explanation consistent with other findings that high PE scorers accept more personal responsibility for their own actions. Finally, those who endorsed the PE might have accepted to a greater extent the legitimate authority of the experimenter, since those who value PE show a general tendency to accept systems of external authority.

A more recent study (Greenberg, 1977) found that not only did high PE endorsers work harder on a boring task, regardless of the motivational conditions, but they increased their output following negative feedback (defined by the experimenter's report that they were doing poorly in comparison to most other subjects); on the other hand, performance by low PE scorers declined following such feedback. Both groups increased their performance following positive feedback, but for high PE scorers, the increase did not match that which occurred after negative feedback. These findings support the position of those (Wollack Goodale, Wijting, & Smith, 1971), who suggest that work and self-esteem are closely linked in the value network of the PE. In other words, high PE scorers tend to experience

242

Figure 9–4

Are Protestant ethic work values dying out with the older generation of workers?

guilt or loss of self-esteem when given reason to think they are not working as hard as they should. Regaining a sense of self-esteem becomes contingent on working harder.

Recent surveys by Cherrington (1977) suggest that older workers are more apt to endorse the PE values than are their younger counterparts. Such values may be affected by stages of adult development. Alternatively, the affluence and liberating tendencies of our culture in recent decades may have made it more difficult to endorse the values of self-restraint and deferred gratification. Only time will tell whether the PE syndrome is a vanishing legacy of the peculiar set of forces which have shaped our history or a dimension of individual differences which transcends historical relativism. Undoubtedly, these, like any other values, are influenced by the contemporary character of certain institutions, such as the church, family, schools, and community. That does not, however, rule out the possibility that some individuals—for whatever reasons, including innate endowment—may at any time be more susceptible than others to these influences.

A CONCLUDING CAVEAT

We have discussed several dimensions of personality and shown why these have some logical relationships to job behavior. However, we have stopped short of asserting that a particular personality measure would *generally* predict superior or inferior job performance. In general, we would caution managers against using such measures in order to select among job applicants. The fact is that very little evidence exists to show that personality tests reliably predict quality of job performance. Rulings by courts and federal officials have therefore discouraged the use of these tools in making hiring decisions.

Why do most personality measures not predict performance very well? One reason is that most of them can be faked by respondents who have sufficient incentive for doing so. If you seek a sales position and are given a questionnaire attempting to measure your extraversion, you could probably tell right away that certain answers would be more consistent with widely held notions of what makes someone good at sales. If you wanted the job badly enough, you might answer, not in a candid fashion, but in the way you thought would make you look like the right person for the job. This, of course, would destroy the validity of the measure.

However, there is a more basic reason why personality measures, no matter how reliable and valid in themselves, do not predict job performance very well. Most jobs permit varying styles or approaches toward achieving final results. For example, one person may achieve success in sales because of an easygoing, affable nature which promotes smooth interaction with potential clients. Another person may succeed, even though reserved and formal in demeanor, because of a very professional, analytic approach to markets, customer needs, and product specifications. Still another individual, while essentially shy, "forces" an outgoing nature because the financial incentives make the discomfort of doing so worthwhile. In short, personality differences have to do with *predispositions* toward various job behaviors. These predispositions may be overriden by compelling incentives, or they may be adapted toward varying approaches to achieving good results on the job.

The more appropriate role of reliable, valid personality measures occurs in a context of individual counselling. Ideally, they should help people discover more clearly for themselves their basic predispositions and how these predispositions relate to the demands of various occupations. Given this information, people have a more informed basis for *self-selection* into different jobs. The Strong Vocational Interest Blank, for example, is a counselling tool which compares respondents' descriptions of themselves (their likes and dislikes) with those of people who have apparently experienced reasonable levels of satisfaction in different professions and occupations. It cannot tell a person whether he or she will be successful in any given occupation, but it can suggest whether a person is likely to be comfortable working for very long in that occupation.

SUMMARY

Individuals do not respond alike to the same organizational environments, and the study of behavior in organizations must take account of the dimensions underlying these differences. The trait-based approach to this issue seeks to derive empirically a small number of factors, such as neuroticism and extraversion. Another approach examines differences in stable, enduring motives such as needs for achievement, power, and affiliation. A belief-based approach focuses on a person's generalized expectancy that one's own behavior does or does not control important outcomes. Finally, the Protestant ethic represents an example of a value-based approach to individual differences. Various approaches have their distinctive measurement methodologies, which are useful in research and counselling but are seldom justified as a basis for making hiring decisions.

CONCEPTS TO REMEMBER

projective test	thematic apperception test
neuroticism	n Ach
extraversion-introversion	n Aff
reticular brain stem	n Pow
internal-external locus of control	Protestant ethic
incidental learning	

QUESTIONS FOR DISCUSSION

1. Describe some person you know who is probably high in neuroticism. What characteristic of his or her behavior leads you to believe that this is so?
2. Describe some person you know who would probably score high in extraversion. What characteristics of that person lead you to suspect this?

3. Would a very strong need for achievement ever be dysfunctional for a manager's performance?

4. What situational factors might affect the level of a person's need for affiliation?

5. Some observers of the contemporary work scene believe that the Protestant ethic, as defined in this chapter, is on the wane. If so, what forces might account for this? Can you argue the case that it is still "alive and well" in the 1980s?

CASE[1]

Del Rice is the assistant manager of Sac County Federal's largest branch. He is 31 years old and has been employed by the institution for six years. After a brief orientation period as a teller he was given further training and assigned to his present position, in which he has worked for nearly five years. Two years ago he was elected by the board to become an assistant vice president. He does a good job in planning work and in supervising his employees. As an administrator he is competent. He gets along unusually well with his employees, the customers, the general public, and his branch manager. He is president of the local Savings and Loan Institute chapter, where he has taken many courses. Civic duties make time-consuming demands on him.

The branch manager, Amos Turner, is 68 years old. He is a senior vice president and director of the association, one of the few remaining members of the initial investors who founded the association almost 40 years ago. Turner is one of the most widely respected and popular members of the community in that section of the city where the branch office is located. He has literally hundreds of personal friends and acquaintances and is strongly motivated by a desire to have the association render the best possible customer service tailored to suit their individual needs.

Following Rice's assignment to the branch, Turner assigned more and more of the internal functions to the young man. Now he does little but talk to people who come to him for personal services, and he takes some loan applications. Turner has been pleased with Rice's work and has recommended salary increases for him at the end of each salary review period.

More than one of the vice presidents at the main office object strongly to Rice's attitude concerning matters affecting their respective departments. The chief loan officer maintains that Rice does not

[1] Reprinted with permission from Edgar G. Williams, *People Problems* (Bureau of Business Research, Indiana University Graduate School of Business, Bloomington, Ind.), 1962.

obtain sufficient information about the property or the credit of loan applicants on which to make a reasonable decision, despite continuing requests on his part for the assistant manager to obtain more information. He also says that Rice wants to process every loan application that originates at his branch as a prime loan with respect to the terms offered the borrower even though the risks involved may be marginal.

The personnel manager says that Rice constantly harasses him to provide additional personnel for his branch, maintaining that his employees have to work harder and longer than others in the association, although there is a work load as nearly equitable as the personnel manager has been able to devise.

The controller says that Rice too readily breaks minor rules that have been established for internal control in order to accommodate unusual requests from his customers. These men summarize their views by saying that Rice has a bad case of "branchitis."

The supervisor of branch operations, Rex Daily, receives these complaints from the department heads. He says that he has checked out all of the complaints, found most of them to be true, and has spent many hours with Rice trying to explain to him how he can improve his management of branch affairs and at the same time be more consistent with the established policies of the association. Like the department heads, he has found Rice's responses to be argumentative or consisting of wisecracks about the "experts" at the main office who "pick on" the branch personnel.

A new branch is to be opened within two months in an area that is a logical extension of the general area now being served by the branch headed by Turner and Rice. Rice has informed Daily that he wants very much to be named as the manager for the new branch. (Other branches have been opened since he has been with Turner, but he has never before requested consideration.)

Rice told Daily that all of the people in his community and especially his personal friends expect him to get the appointment. He also said that he considers this to be a turning point in his career with the association.

Turner has told Daily that he considers Rice to be one of the two best-qualified men for the job and will consent to but not urge his selection for the post because of the difficulties that losing the young man would cause him in his own branch.

Rice apparently knows his superior's attitude because he referred to it when making his request that Daily recommend him for the job at the new branch manager's office. Daily realizes that with Turner taking a neutral position, his recommendations will undoubtedly be accepted by the managing officer.

Questions

Which personality constructs do you find useful for understanding the behavior of Del Rice? Illustrate with specific examples.

If you were Rex Daily, could you—and would you—recommend Rice? Explain the reasoning behind your judgment.

REFERENCES

Allport, G. W., & Odbert, H. W.   Trait-names: A psychological study. *Psychological Monographs*, 1936, 47(i).

Allport, G. W., Vernon, P. E., & Lindzey, G.   *Study of Values*. Boston: Houghton Mifflin, 1951.

Anderson, C., Hellriegel, D., & Slocum, J.   Managerial response to environmentally induced stress. *Academy of Management Journal*, 1977, 20, 260–272.

Argyris, C.   *Personality and organization*, New York: Harper & Row, 1957.

Atkinson, J. W.   *Motives in fantasy, action, and society*. Princeton, N.J.: D. Van Nostrand, 1958.

Behrman, D., Bigoness, W., & Perrault, W.   Sources of role ambiguity and their consequences upon salespersons' satisfaction and performance. *Management Science*, 1980, in press.

Brown, R., & Herrnstein, R.   *Psychology*. Boston: Little, Brown, 1975.

Cattell, R. B.   The 16PF and basic personality structure: A reply to Eysenck. *Journal of Behavioral Science*, 1972, 1, 169–187.

Cherrington, D.   The values of younger workers. *Business Horizons*, 1977, 20, 18–20.

Cooper, R., & Payne, R.   Extraversion and some aspects of work behavior. *Personnel Psychology*, 1967, 20, 45–57.

Eaves, L., & Eysenck, H.   The nature of extraversion: A genetical analysis. *Journal of Personality and Social Psychology*, 1975, 32, 102–112.

Eitzen, S.   Impact of behavior modification techniques on locus of control of delinquent boys. *Psychological Reports*, 1974, 35, 1317–1318.

Eysenck, H. J.   *The biological basis of personality*. Springfield, Ill.: Charles C Thomas, 1967.

Eysenck, H. J. (Ed.).   *Readings in extraversion-introversion* (Vol. 3). London: Staple Press, 1970.

Eysenck, H. J. (Ed.).   *Eysenck on extraversion*. New York: John Wiley & Sons, 1973.

French, J. D.   The reticular formation. *Scientific American*, May 1957, pp. Reprinted in T. J. Teyler (Ed.), *Altered states of awareness*. San Francisco: W. H. Freeman, 1972.

Greenberg, J.   The Protestant work ethic and reactions to negative performance evaluation on a laboratory task. *Journal of Applied Psychology*, 1977, 62, 682–690.

Guilford, J. P.   Factors and factors of personality. *Psychological Bulletin,* 1975, *82,* 802–814.

Joe, V. C.   Review of the internal-external control construct as a personality variable. *Psychological Reports,* 1971, *28,* 619–640.

Kahn, R. J., Wolfe, D. M., Quinn, R. P., Snoek, J. D., & Rosenthal, R.   *Organizational stress.* New York: John Wiley & Sons, 1964.

McClelland, D. C.   *The achieving society.* Princeton, N.J.: D. Van Nostrand, 1961.

Merrens, M., & Garrett, J.¯   The Protestant ethic scale as a predictor of repetitive work performance. *Journal of Applied Psychology,* 1975, *60,* 125–127.

Mirels, J., & Garrett, J.   The Protestant ethic as a personality variable. *Journal of Consulting and Clinical Psychology,* 1971, *36,* 40–44.

Mitchell, T., Smyser, C., & Weed, S.   Locus of control: Supervision and work satisfaction. *Academy of Management Journal,* 1975, *18,* 623–631.

Organ, D. W.   Effects of pressure and individual neuroticism on emotional responses to task-role ambiguity. *Journal of Applied Psychology,* 1975, *60,* 397–400.(a)

Organ, D. W.   Extraversion, locus of control, and individual differences in conditionability in organizations. *Journal of Applied Psychology,* 1975, *60,* 401–404.(b)

Organ, D. W., & Greene, C. N.   Role ambiguity, locus of control, and work satisfaction. *Journal of Applied Psychology,* 1974, *59,* 101–102.

Porter, L., Lawler, E., & Hackman, R.   *Behavior in organizations.* New York: McGraw-Hill, 1975.

Rotter, J. B.   Generalized expectancies for internal versus external control of reinforcement. *Psychological Monographs,* 1966, *80,* (1, Whole No. 609).

Runyon, D.   Some interactions between personality variables and management styles. *Journal of Applied Psychology,* 1973, *57,* 288–294.

Seeman, M., & Evans, J.   Alienation and learning in a hospital setting. *American Sociological Review,* 1962, *27,* 772–783.

Silverman, R., & Blitz, B.   Learning and two kinds of anxiety. *Journal of Abnormal and Social Psychology,* 1956, *52,* 301–303.

Smith, M. B.   Personal values in the study of lives. In R. W. White (Ed.), *The study of lives.* Englewood Cliffs, N.J.: Prentice-Hall (Ch. 14), 1963.

Super, D. E.   The structure of work values in relation to status, achievement, interests, and adjustment. *Journal of Applied Psychology,* 1962, *46,* 231–239.

Tyler, L. E.   *The psychology of human differences.* New York: Appleton-Century-Crofts, 1965.

Weinstein, N. D.   Individual differences in reaction to noise: A longitudinal study in a college dormitory. *Journal of Applied Psychology,* 1978, *63,* 458–466.

Winter, P. G.   *Power motivation in thought and action.* Unpublished doctoral dissertation, Harvard University, 1967.

Wolk, S., & DuCette, J.   Intentional performance and incidental learning as a function of personality and task dimensions. *Journal of Personality and Social Psychology,* 1974, *29,* 90–101.

Wollack, S., Goodale, J., Wijting, J., & Smith, P.   Development of the survey of work values. *Journal of Applied Psychology,* 1971, *55,* 331–338.

10

Stress in Organizations

What are the different meanings of stress?

What is the relationship between stress and health?

What is the relationship between stress and emotions?

What is the relationship between stress and performance?

What are the major stressors in organizations?

What is involved in managing stress?

In your mind's eye picture a 48-year-old male executive, graying at the temples, seated at a desk. His shirtsleeves are halfway rolled up; his collar is open, his tie is loosened. His facial muscles appear taut; he props his elbows on the desk with hands clenched together tightly so that the veins in his forearms stand out boldly. He looks away from his desk—which is littered with papers in disarray, an ashtray overflowing with squashed cigarette butts, and four coffee-stained Styrofoam cups—and winces at the relentless sweep of the hands on the wall clock. Picking up a pencil, he snaps it in impotent rage.

In one fashion or another, you have seen this image countless times before. It represents the stereotype of job stress. As such, it illustrates some widely held assumptions about stress: stress increases with the level of responsibility of the job; stress is an uncomfortable state of mind marked by tension and anxiety; stress causes a breakdown in performance; stress is caused by the pressures of time and other people's demands upon us.

These assumptions are, at best, oversimplified. Just how valid they are depends on what we mean by *stress*—and the word means many different things to different people. Part of our task in this chapter will be to sort out these varying meanings and put them into a framework such that these meanings have some consistent relationship to each other. The vernacular and technical meanings of stress have become thoroughly confused, probably because they overlap somewhat. As a result, many people seem to misunderstand the relationship between stress and feelings, stress and illness, stress and adaptation, stress and performance—even stress and life.

STRESS AS AN EVERYDAY TERM

In everyday usage, stress generally connotes something unpleasant. We may use the term to describe something *environmental*, such as a traffic jam on the morning commute to work or the task of completing a term paper due the next morning. At the same time, we use the word to denote the *emotions* aroused by the external problem— the emotions of anxiety, fear, irritation, or frustration. Finally, we associate with stress certain *physical* symptoms—a clutching of the gut, a stiffened neck, sweating under the arms, jittery hands.

In sum, our popular "model" of stress resembles that of Figure 10–1. We think of stress as referring to any or all of the elements in a sequence defined by an undesired circumstance, an uncomfortable state of mind, and an unpleasant mixture of physical sensations. We would probably acknowledge, as well, some feedback effects: as we

Portions of this chapter draw extensively upon a previously published paper by one of the authors: D. W. Organ, "The Meanings of Stress," *Business Horizons*, June 1979, 32–40.

become aware of the physical sensations (e.g., clammy hands, racing pulse), our emotional states (e.g., anxiety) become more acute; as we become more anxious, we find ourselves doing things (acting impulsively, making mistakes) which aggravate the problem. In effect, we equate *stress* with *distress*.

Figure 10–1
A Model of the Popular Meaning of Stress-Distress

Unpleasant situation
↓
Uncomfortable   ——————————————→   Disturbing
state of mind   physical symptoms

There is nothing inherently "wrong" with this model. It is wrong only when we substitute this definition of stress for the technical meaning of stress as a scientific construct in statements about relationships between stress, on the one hand, and illness, performance, and adaptation. When we shift to a scientific meaning of stress, we find that pleasant events as well as unpleasant ones can cause illness; that stress can be accompanied by very positive feelings and emotions as well as negative ones; that adaptation to stress does not negate its toll on the body; that performance itself can add to stress but is not necessarily affected by it.

STRESS AS A SCIENTIFIC CONSTRUCT

Stress became a scientific construct when it was defined and elaborated by the research and writing of Professor Hans Selye. He discovered in experiments with laboratory animals that whether he subjected rats to extreme cold, injected chemical irritants into their tissue, or just held them as they struggled to get loose, there were certain common reactions in the animals' physiological processes. Of course, there were specific effects as well, associated with each particular treatment, but Selye was interested in the common denominators—the invariant response of the organism's body to any *demand* placed upon it. The common features constituted what Selye labelled the General Adaptation Syndrome, or G.A.S.—the syndrome by which a state of stress is manifested.

The nonspecific response of the body to some environmental demand, or *stressor* (which could be a germ, an overload on a group of muscles, a loud noise, extreme heat or cold) involves the body's endocrine system. It begins with the pituitary, a cherry-sized organ resting at the base of the brain. The pituitary signals the *alarm* stage of the G.A.S. by sending a chemical messenger in the form of the hormone ACTH to the adrenals. During this stage the body is, in a sense, in retreat, experiencing a temporary and minor loss of efficiency until it can rally its forces of resistance. The adrenals, in repsonse to ACTH, initiate the second stage of the G.A.S., the *resistance* stage, by secreting its own hormones, adrenaline and noradrenaline, collectively called the catecholamines. The catecholamines enter the bloodstream and trigger a succession of changes in the body chemistry—such as level of fatty acids in the blood and the blood's clotting chemistry and also alters the digestive processes. These processes during the resistance stage eventually have the effect of enabling the organism to neutralize, isolate, or minimize the damage to the integrity of the organism as a whole; the body seems to adapt to the demand.

However, Selye believes that any organism has, from birth, only a fixed, limited amount of adaptation energy. Every stress response of the body uses up some of this precious asset. Whatever is used up cannot be replaced. Thus, the resistance stage of the G.A.S. cannot continue indefinitely. Subjected to an environmental stressor of sufficient strength for a sufficiently long time, the adaptive energies of the organism are depleted, and exhaustion or collapse—the third and final G.A.S. stage—follows.

Figure 10–2
Stress as a Scientific Construct Formulated by Hans Selye

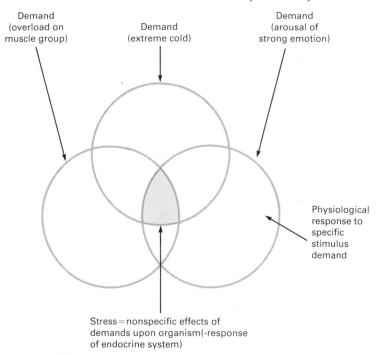

Demand (overload on muscle group)

Demand (extreme cold)

Demand (arousal of strong emotion)

Physiological response to specific stimulus demand

Stress = nonspecific effects of demands upon organism(-response of endocrine system)

The exhaustion may take the form of depression, bed rest, or some other temporary lapse. This appears to allow the body to transfer some of its fixed store of adaptation energy from "long-term reserves" (analagous to a savings account) to a short-term available supply (like a demand deposit). But this is a transfer, a borrowing, which cannot be repaid. If the process continued, eventually the entire stock of adaptation energy would drop to nothing, and life could not go on.

Therefore, "adaptation" is a costly business. To "adapt," in this sense, to a stressor does not mean that the stressor does no harm. Adaptation is the essence of stress itself, at least in a physiological sense.

To summarize, stress as a scientific construct represents the invariant, nonspecific reaction of the body to any environmental demand—whatever form that demand may take.

STRESS AND ILLNESS

As we discussed above, the adrenals play a significant role in providing resistance to agents which threaten the body. We are constantly exposed to, even transporting within us, microbes that could potentially wreak havoc to our tissues. This seldom happens because the endocrine system, in which the adrenals are involved, defends against such bacteria. But what if the endocrine system is somewhat overloaded with so many demands that it cannot deal with all of them?

To address this issue, let us examine Table 10–1. The table shows a list of changes or events which can occur in a person's life. With each event is associated a number which serves as a rough index of the relative degree of adjustment demanded by the event. The weighting scheme was derived through studies by Professors T. H. Holmes and R. H. Rahe (1968) and colleagues at the University of Washington. Their studies asked people of varying ages and from several different cultures to compare each event with each other in terms of the degree of adjustment required. It seems to be universally agreed that the death of a spouse requires more adjustment on the part of the surviving spouse than any other single event. The table provides a rough measure of the degree of adjustment required of a person in a given time period by totaling the number of points associated with each change in a given period of time.

Holmes and his coworkers found that once a person "earns" 200 or more points in a single year, there is at least a 50-50 chance of experiencing a fairly serious breakdown in health in the following year. One who totals up 300 or more points in a year runs that risk factor up to about a 75 to 80 percent chance. The illness brought on by such demand for adjustment can appear in almost every specific form:

Table 10–1
Social Readjustment Rating Scale

Life Event	Scale Value
Death of spouse	100
Divorce	73
Marital separation	65
Jail term	63
Death of a close family member	63
Major personal injury or illness	53
Marriage	50
Fired from work	47
Marital reconciliation	45
Retirement	45
Major change in health of family member	44
Pregnancy	40
Sex difficulties	39
Gain of a new family member	39
Business readjustment	39
Change in financial state	38
Death of a close friend	37
Change to a different line of work	36
Change in number of arguments with spouse	35
Mortgage over $10,000	31
Foreclosure of mortgage or loan	30
Change in responsibilities at work	29
Son or daughter leaving home	29
Trouble with in-laws	29
Outstanding personal achievement	28
Wife begins or stops work	26
Begin or end school	26
Change in living conditions	25
Revision of personal habits	24
Trouble with boss	23
Change in work hours or conditions	20
Change in residence	20
Change in schools	20
Change in recreation	19
Change in church activities	19
Change in social activities	18
Mortgage or loan less than $10,000	17
Change in sleeping habits	16
Change in number of family get-togethers	15
Change in eating habits	15
Vacation	13
Christmas	12
Minor violations of the law	11

Source: From "Scaling of Life Change: Comparison of Direct and Indirect Methods" by L. O. Ruch & T. H. Holmes, *Journal of Psychosomatic Research*, 1971, Vol. 15, 224.

digestive ailments, respiratory problems, back trouble, kidney malfunction, injuries to the bones or muscles, almost any breakdown in the body's economy. What is the explanation for this relationship? Significant changes in one's immediate life environment trigger a rapid succession of new situations with which one has to cope. The endocrine system provides the adaptation energy for the sustained arousal and vigilance needed to cope with the novelty, uncertainty, or conflict occasioned by the new situations. But remember it is this same endocrine system which provides the basis for resistance to any agent (e.g., bacteria) which threatens the body. Usually such bacteria are adequately defended against by a healthy immune system. If the endocrine system is constantly marshaling the body's energy for adjustment, the capacity for resisting those lurking microbes will be exhausted. Thus, wherever the body is most vulnerable, a breakdown can occur after a period of sufficiently great demands for social or psychological adjustment. (For a very readable account of the effect of life changes on illness, see Alvin Toffler, *Future Shock*; (1970), pp. 289–304.)

One should note that a number of the events listed in Table 10–1 are "positive"; one ordinarily thinks of them as occasions for pleasure or celebration. The layman's definition of *stress* as something to be avoided hardly seems to describe marriage, birth of a child, promotion, outstanding personal achievement, sudden drastic improvement in financial position, moving to a bigger home in a better neighborhood, or graduation from college. Yet, to the extent that these events pose demands for adjustment, they are stressful in Selye's sense, and if enough of these changes are bunched together they can produce health problems.

EMOTIONAL STRESSORS

Some of Selye's experiments with laboratory animals—subjecting them to cold temperatures or injecting a foreign substance into their tissues—seem to have little to do with stress as we think of it in organizations. But a series of his studies do have more direct relevance to us. When he held a rat so that it could only struggle in futility and not get away, Selye found some of the same physiological responses (the G.A.S.) that occurred with direct insults to their bodies. Yet in forcibly immobilizing the animal, he did not injure it. The stress response of the adrenals seemed to be mediated rather by strong emotions (in this case, something like anger or frustration). We, as human beings, are susceptible to very strong emotional responses. These may be not only of unconditioned form but also of the conditioned variety, so that emotional responses can come under the control of subtle cues in the form of words and other social stimuli.

The emotions are governed by a primitive part of the lower brain called the *hypothalamus* (which also regulates some other functions, including hunger and body temperature). Under conditions of emotional arousal, the hypothalamus sends messages to the pituitary which trigger much the same sequence of events as described by Selye's G.A.S. So, consider the example of an angry superior lashing out at a subordinate's mistakes. The words, the tone of voice, the facial expressions of the boss are the sorts of cues which (in most of us) evoke strong emotional responses—anger, fear, or anxiety. Thus, the stress response of the body is triggered. However, the stress response of the body evolved eons ago to enable the body to fight or run, and neither response is appropriate in this context. The quickened pulse, the increased sugar and fat levels in the blood, the quickened clotting time of the blood, the constriction of the blood vessels—all part of the eventual effects of the adrenal response—do no good; they are a waste of the body's fixed store of adaptation energy, and they simply wear down our own unoffending tissues.

We should emphasize, however, that:

1. The stress response *may* occur without *any* strong emotional response necessarily becoming involved.

2. *Any* strong emotion can trigger the stress response. The surprising fact to most of us is that the various emotions which we distinguish from one another—fear, anger, ecstasy, thrill, hilarity—involve virtually the same internal physical responses. The distinctions among them are made by external cues and their interpretation by the information-processing centers of the brain—not by the hormones. For example, one study (Levi, 1972) found that whether people watched a horror movie, an anger-provoking film, or a comedy, the stress response (as measured by the level of adrenaline in the subject's urine) was about the same; in all three instances, the stress response was significantly greater than that which followed a dull documentary film. Thus, it is the *strength* of the emotion, not the label we put on it, that determines the stress response.

Frustration

As an *objective condition*, the term *frustration* applies to any obstruction between behavior and its goal or any interference with ongoing instrumental behavior. Specific types of frustration include the following (Lawson, 1965):

1. Nonreinforcement after a history of reinforcement. For example, a student who has been consistently rewarded for studying in a certain way (such as rote memorizing) enrolls in a course where such behavior is no longer rewarded by good marks.

2. A delay in reinforcement. An advertising writer accustomed to receiving quick feedback about performance now has to wait days or weeks before hearing anything.

3. A change in the value of reinforcement. Office workers accustomed to receiving a $10 gift certificate for a month's perfect attendance are told that, due to the need to trim labor costs, they will now get only a $5 gift certificate.

4. Sheer failure. A salesperson does all the right things, all the things he or she is used to doing, but experiences a long string of unsuccessful calls.

5. Obstruction of a response that is otherwise strong. A welder on an automobile assembly line has a full bladder, and the urge to go to the rest room is very strong but is obstructed due to shop rules concerning rest pauses.

6. Punishment, since it temporarily suppresses a response that is otherwise strong.

7. Conflict between two or more strong but incompatible responses. Even having to choose between two equally valued alternatives (such as a Buick versus a Cadillac or a vacation in the mountains versus a vacation at the seashore) is somewhat stressful. More stressful, however, are "approach-avoidance" conflicts (desiring a promotion for its status and salary, yet being afraid of the accompanying pressure and overload) and "avoidance-avoidance" conflicts (a supervisor torn between the need to punish unacceptable performance and the desire to avoid conflict).

Frustration is obviously endemic in organizational life. The existence of a hierarchy, of competition, of constraints on behavior guarantee that frustration will be frequent. This need not be the occasion for lamentation, however, since frustration often has very desirable effects on behavior.

1. Frustration adds color and complexity to behavior. Our repertoire of instrumental responses would never change or grow if we were never frustrated; we would more nearly resemble robots than persons. We would not experiment with new methods unless the old ones were occasionally found to be unsuccessful or obstructed.

2. Frustration is a precondition for *perceptual* as well as behavioral change (Cantril, 1957). Our unexamined assumptions and built-in biases in viewing a situation are not recognized until actions based on them prove ineffectual. Reinterpretations of the world around us and different perspectives on our experience are evoked by the inability to use our accustomed behavior plans in transactions with the social and physical environment. A marketing executive may conceptualize a product in a radically different manner when the unprofitability of present methods of promotion or present target markets forces reexamination.

3. Frustration usually acts to arouse reserves of energy for use in dealing with the problem at hand. Moderate arousal usually has the beneficial effect of focusing our attention more sharply, maintaining or improving vigilance, and toning our readiness for action.

These positive consequences are more likely to occur when frustration is temporary or intermittent; when alternative responses are available or substitute goals can suffice; or when the person's past reinforcement history and socialization have led him to develop at least a moderate level of *frustration tolerance.* When frustration is prolonged and the limit of frustration tolerance has been reached and passed, we use the word *frustration* to signify an *inner emotional state.* For example, a person who prepares to leave the office and finds that the door won't open (let's say it's stuck or possibly locked from the outside) is frustrated in an objective sense: instrumental behavior is being obstructed or is unsuccessful. Initially, however, the person may not experience a sense of frustration in the inner, emotional sense. If the person coolly tries to push or pull a little harder, to pick the lock with a paper clip, or to slip a plastic ruler between the door and the jamb, he or she appears to be acting rationally, and we don't usually describe the person as frustrated in an inner, emotional sense. If this ploy fails and the trapped employee's behavior then degenerates into kicking the door, banging it with a fist, or cursing (forms of aggression), stress seems to have taken a quantum jump, and the person's behavior reflects a noninstrumental, expressive, emotional state. If the employee finally gives up—decides to spend the night in the office or to waste away from hunger, crouching in a corner in a state of torpor—the stage of resistance has given way to exhaustion, apathy, and resignation.

Frustration and Aggression. The link between frustration and *aggression,* or behavior directed toward the harm of another person or object, has attracted the attention of psychologists for quite some time. Early in the century aggression was thought to be caused by some built-in instinct in animals and humans, but this explanation soon proved unsatisfactory. Ethological studies of animals in their natural habitats showed aggression to be quite rare except in order to obtain food. Later it was argued that frustration is always a cause of aggression and that aggression is always preceded by frustration. This position seemed to be extreme since *(a)* people appear to be able to endure a variety of frustrating events daily without showing aggressive behavior, and *(b)* aggression, like other types of behavior, can be instrumental and can be strengthened by reinforcing consequences that are at best only remotely related to frustration—for example, killing people for their money or, in organizations, being an intimidating browbeater in order to gain a psychological advantage over others.

The currently held view is that frustration generates a *predisposition* to aggress (often labeled anger), but that other factors determine both whether aggression takes place and the form of aggression that is manifested if it does. It seems plausible to view aggression as a "last resort" after alternative methods of coping have failed but before exhaustion has occurred. Thus, up to a point, the tendency to aggress will vary directly with the duration of frustration, the number of responses that are blocked or unsuccessful, and the strength of the responses interfered with, and will vary inversely with the number of substitutive instrumental responses for dealing with the situation. When aggression itself is unsuccessful or completely blocked, apathy or withdrawal follows. In this light, the milder forms of aggression are a healthy sign, since they reflect a will to struggle with the environment rather than to submit resignedly to failure. Military officers have long recognized that troop morale is not at its lowest level when grumbling and griping are frequent but rather when such bitching has given way to apathy and passive acceptance of the "inevitable."

Among the factors that determine whether or not aggression will actually take place are whether or not punishment for aggression is anticipated, whether or not one's peer group or another closely related social group approves of the aggression (and offers possible support in resisting punishment or counteraggression), and the extent to which aggression has been strengthened by reinforcement in the past. The last factor is a subtle but important one, because organization officials sometime unwittingly reinforce aggressive behavior. When noisy outbursts or verbal abuse by subordinates threaten an administrator's control, the administrator may be inclined to give in—remove the source of frustration. This means, of course, that when confronted by further frustrations, these subordinates are more likely to use aggression as an instrumental response. On a smaller scale, the same thing happens when we get our Coke or our quarter after some hefty slaps and kicks at the vending machine. Aggression sometimes "gets the job done."

There is some evidence that fixed ratio schedules of reinforcement—particularly when the ratio of the reinforcements to the number of responses is very low—is associated with a greater propensity to aggress when frustrating events occur (Harrell & Moss, 1974). Many reinforcers in organizations, particularly those to lower-ranking participants, are dispensed in a manner that resembles such schedules. Rest pauses, lunch periods, and smoke breaks are permitted only after relatively long and fixed periods of responding. It would seem that industry could do far more to vary the length of reinforcement intervals yet hold the total amount of rest pauses or other reinforcers to their current levels. Although in some instances technological constraints rule out variable schedules of work breaks, more often it is the weight of tradition that fixes breaks rigidly at 9:30 A.M., 12 A.M., 2:30 P.M., and so forth. Recently, some organizations have experimented with the concept of flexi-time—allowing the individual to set not only break schedules, but even the hours of work, subject to the constraint that some fixed number of weekly hours or some fixed amount of daily output be met.

Aggression is also more likely to occur when frustration is *unan-*

ticipated or is *perceived as arbitrary*. The emphasis here is on the point of view of the person or persons being frustrated. For very good and compelling reasons, adminstrators are often forced to institute changes that are frustrating to lower-ranking participants. If the rationale behind such measures is not communicated, aggression may result. Changes are less likely to be perceived as arbitrary if participants have had some form of input (whether direct or representational) into the reasons for introducing them and are told what considerations led to the changes, or if the decision makers themselves are sharing the burdens imposed by the changes.

As noted above, the anticipation of punishment can inhibit aggression. Even a severely frustrated factory worker usually doesn't punch the supervisor in the nose because the consequences may be quite costly. However, both the target and the form of aggression can be *displaced*. The frustrated worker may throw an oily rag at the boss when the latter's back is turned. The worker may use verbal abuse or try sabotage—deliberately "gum up the works." Automobile assembly line workers, for example, have ripped car upholstery or caused the line to be halted. The person may vent aggression on a co-worker or make the co-worker's job difficult. In assembly line technology, this can start a vicious circle, as each person passes problems on to the next. Another approach is to "take it out on the wife and kids." The aggression may be directed *intropunitively*, in the form of self-incrimination, self-mutilation, or neurotic guilt. A more accepted mode of aggression would be filing a grievance with the union steward. This is a form of institutionally legitimate aggression which is channeled toward constructive purposes.

At this point we can describe the administrator's real task with respect to aggression. On the one hand, he or she must avoid reinforcing illegitimate, unconstructive forms of aggression; otherwise, the administrator will only have to face more and more of it in the future, particularly as those who have been more "reasonable" learn by observation that "it pays to get tough" or that "the squeaky wheel gets the grease." On the other hand, the administrator must be careful not to bottle up direct aggression only to have it displaced onto other persons or take the form of destructive sabotage. What is the way out of this dilemma? Levinson (1959) suggests that the answer is for the organization to provide official channels for the discharge of aggression. One example is the grievance procedure of unionized organizations. Other forms could include such things as a "corporate ombudsman"—an official flak-catcher. A Japanese firm has life-sized dummies, made to look like the boss, that disgruntled workers can clobber during breaks. Ultimately, of course, such devices are of little value unless organizational officials make a sincere and determined effort to keep participants' frustration within manageable bounds, take steps to reduce frustrations when it is feasible to do so, communicate the rationale for their frustrating changes in advance, and show a willingness to help bear the cost of organization frustrations. Grievances that never get fully processed, ombudsmen who carry no real clout, and defenseless dummies cannot stretch to infinity the frustration tolerance of lower-ranking members. If frustrated persons *never* or *very seldom* get any substantive relief by using such channels, their aggression will take other, less desirable channels.

Anxiety

Psychologists have found it difficult to reach agreement on a succinct definition of anxiety as a type of psychological or emotional stress. Attempts to define anxiety have often taken the form of distinguishing between anxiety and fear or between anxiety and frustration. Whereas fear is the reaction to immediate, present danger, anxiety is the reaction to anticipated harm, whether it be physical or psychological (such as loss of self-esteem or loss of status). Whereas frustration is blockage or interference with ongoing instrumental behavior, anxiety is the feeling of *not having* appropriate responses or plans for dealing with anticipated harm. It is very difficult to make these distinctions, since the difference between fear of present danger and anxiety due to future threat is subtle. The feeling of not having adequate responses for dealing with real or imagined threat may come on slowly as attempted responses to deal with it prove unsuccessful. Nevertheless, most people seem to understand quite well what they mean when they say that they are experiencing anxiety: the sense of dread, foreboding, and apprehension that gnaws at their insides and darkens their outlook on things in general. Sometimes the source or cause of anxiety is uncertain or hard to define; the threat is vague, and the potential danger is itself unstructured or ambiguous. This, of course, renders anxiety all the more unsettling, since it makes any instrumental coping response harder to select or organize. In fact, one frequent reaction to uneasiness about impending threat is to arbitrarily and erroneously focus the threat on some identifiable person or thing so that "something can be done." Allport and Postman (1947) found that one function served by rumors is to enable people to pinpoint their uneasiness, to give it form and structure. The grapevine in organizations may serve a similar purpose.

What are the causes of anxiety in organizations? *Differences in power* in organizations, which leave people with a feeling of vulnerability to administrative decisions adversely affecting them; *frequent changes* in organizations, which make existing behavior plans obsolete; *competition*, which creates the inevitability that some persons lose "face," esteem, and status; and *job ambiguity* (especially when this is coupled with *pressure*). To these may be added some related factors, such as lack of job feedback, volatility in the organization's economic environment, job insecurity, and high visibility of one's performance (successes as well as failures). Personal, nonorganizational factors come into play as well, such as physical illness, problems at home, unrealistically high personal goals, and estrangement from one's colleagues or one's peer group.

Business Week (May 28, 1979) reported on an "epidemic" of anxiety in one of our largest corporations. The American Telephone and Telegraph Company in 1978 announced a comprehensive plan of reorganization, shifting from an organizational structure founded upon functional lines to a realignment according to market segments. This plan necessarily involved an overhaul of existing job titles, responsibilities, and reporting relationships. This understandably created uncertainty for the 250,000 employees affected; no one could predict exactly what new problems would be encountered. The immediate effect was that medical directors throughout the system noticed significantly higher levels cf anxiety among people coming in for routine examinations. The anxiety reached such levels that AT&T decided to institute a series of seminars among managers to help them cope with anxiety and other emotional symptoms of stress.

Of course, all causes of anxiety cannot be eliminated in our imperfect world of imperfect organizations managed by imperfect people, nor is all anxiety deleterious to health or performance. Moderate anxiety mobilizes and focuses our energy, sharpens our sensitivity to information in the environment, and is often a prelude to the formulation of innovative, creative solutions to problems. Successful executives have been found to be almost chronically motivated by mild to moderate anxiety (Henry, 1949); they cope with it instrumentally by making phone calls, researching for technical or business-related information, formulating a priority of attempted solutions, assessing trade-offs or positions to fall back on, and identifying "secondary targets"—steps that minimize the damage if no feasible solutions are able to eliminate the threat.

When anxiety is severe and prolonged, dysfunctional coping mechanisms are resorted to. The individual begins to direct attention to the internal sensations of anxiety at the cost of dealing rationally with the source of the anxiety. This may lead to alcoholism, drug abuse, excessive absenteeism, or a host of other forms of escapism. Since such responses do temporarily alleviate emotional stress, they are reinforcing and can become chronic reactions when anxiety is evoked.

A complicating variable in the optimal handling of anxiety is either an unwillingness to admit to it or, even if one admits to it in one's own mind, a tendency to avoid its expression. Particularly among men, there seems to be the attitude that it is a sign of weakness to talk about the experience of anxiety. This is unfortunate, for many causes of apprehension could undoubtedly be laid to rest if they were voiced, either to one's boss or to one's colleagues.

What can administrators do to help keep anxiety within moderate, manageable bounds? One thing they can do is simply reinforce its expression, so that if it is groundless it can be dispelled. They can, where possible, avoid initiating changes that uproot people from cohesive groups. The Hawthorne studies (Roethlisberger & Dickson, 1964) showed that nagging personal worries were much less debilitating to female workers when they were allowed to coalesce into natural work groups. Increasing job performance feedback, providing advance communication prior to significant planned organization change, and avoiding unnecessary competitive stimulation are all means of mitigating stressful anxiety.

As we noted in the preceding chapter, some individuals—those characterized as high in neuroticism—seem to have a particular vulnerability to anxiety. One might even say that such persons carry a pool of "free-floating" anxiety around with them, such that even mild stimuli will trigger a strong emotional response of anxiety. These people seem to have a pronounced conditionability to this emotional response to a vast range of everyday physical and social cues. In short, anxiety may well be regarded as a trait dimension as well as a "state" reaction to a specific situation (Spielberger, 1966).

Depression

All of us experience occasional episodes of what we refer to as depression. Such episodes tend to occur either during or immediately after some illness, such as a bout with the flu; after a prolonged period of struggle with some problem, especially if the struggle has not met with some success; or after experiencing some loss—loss of a close friend who moves away, loss of a relative because of death, or loss of a job.

With most of us, the experience of depression in this *acute* stage probably serves a useful function for the mind-body system, even though the experience is hardly comfortable. Depression slows the system down, in a sense; it works like a safety valve to prevent us from engaging in continued futile struggle that can only further overtax our capacities. The depression that comes with a bad cold, for example, becomes a cue to disengage from the madding crowd, leave work a bit early, put vexing chores on "hold," let some mundane tasks go by the board. This "recess" allows the body to transfer adaptation energy from the long-term stores to an easily available pool.

For most of us, the depressive episode is self-limiting. After a few days at most, feelings of renewed energy, confidence, and optimism take hold, and life resumes its normal course. For certain people, however, such self-correction of the depressive episode does not occur. Depression for them becomes *chronic,* and they seem to sink deeper and deeper into a state of apathy and self-defeating behavior patterns. These people are the true depressives. For them, the event that initially caused the acute phase of depression was simply a trigger; chances are that sooner or later, their physical and psychological makeup would have brought forth such a response anyway.

Kline (1974) estimates that at least 1 of every 6 women, and 1 in every 12 men will experience a major, chronic depressive episode—which means that a typical manager in an organization of even modest size will, over a period of years, encounter some depressive subordinate, superior, or co-worker. While clinical depression may occur in virtually the entire age spectrum from adolescence to old age, its peak incidence appears in the middle years, i.e., ages 35–55.

Flach (1974) and Kline (1974) have provided detailed descriptions of the chronic depressive's symptoms:

Sleep disturbances, especially problems with waking up after an hour or two of sleep and being unable to get back to sleep.

Loss of appetite.

Decreased sex drive.

Aversion to social contacts.

Indecision and procrastination (a depressed patient may have extreme difficulty even deciding what to wear, what to order from a menu, or how to answer a letter).

A change in dress and appearance, especially toward untidiness or unkemptness.

Fatigue and poor concentration.

In general, and most pervasive, reduced enjoyment of all the things that used to give pleasure.

A general sense of being trapped; helplessness; guilt.

In Western culture, guilt especially figures in the depressive syndrome (this does not seem to be the case among non-Western depressives). Indeed, one notes a paradox: Depressives feel they cannot control events around them, yet at the same time they feel self-blame for the way events turn out (Abramson & Sackheim, 1977). A clue to unravelling this paradox comes from Janoff-Bulman (1979): Depressives blame themselves, not merely for their behavior, but also for their character—the kind of people they perceive themselves to be—and this they feel they cannot hope to change.

Obviously, the depressive syndrome will affect a person's work. The depressive will have difficulty summoning the energy to confront the everyday challenges of work; will be easily distracted; will put off making even routine decisions. Alcoholism may exacerbate the situation. The reactions of work associates are predictable: expressions of anger or irritation, or perhaps well-intentioned pep talks. Neither is likely to help very much.

The person who has never experienced a major episode of chronic depression has no capacity for empathizing with the depressive. The nondepressed see the problem as a lack of willpower or "get-up-and-go." They soon give up on the depressive as a "loser." They simply cannot comprehend the nature of the affliction. Of course, as work associates and even family members turn away, the depressive's vicious cycle intensifies, with deeper feelings of inadequacy, guilt, and alienation. If the cycle is uncorrected, it may develop into such extreme forms as chronic alcoholism or even culminate in attempts at suicide. Even short of such tragedies, the result will be the loss to society of the contributions of an effectively functioning member.

A major breakthrough in the treatment of depressives occurred in 1957 with the discovery of the tricyclic antidepressant drugs (Flach, 1974). These drugs are not "uppers," or central nervous system stimulants. They have no effect whatever on the nondepressed; even among the depressed, they still permit the experience of "normal" or appropriate emotional responses, such as grief for a lost loved one. Rather, the tricyclics seem to activate some biochemical processes in the brain—processes which normally occur in the nondepressed but are inhibited in the depressive—so that depression becomes self-limiting. The tricyclics, moreover, do not act as a placebo; they help even those patients who don't think they will do any good ("The medicine won't bring my wife back, will it?" "How will it get my job back?" "My failures are a fact, no drug can erase them."). At the very least, therapists find this medication gives the patient an initial toehold, emotionally, so that other forms of therapy (e.g., counseling) have a much better chance of bearing fruit.

Thus, the manager should try to recognize when these serious depression bouts are occurring in an associate, try to refrain from lowering the boom or writing off the individual as a loss, and seek intervention by a professional (especially a psychiatrist, who can prescribe drugs). With appropriate treatment, the prospects for recovery to healthy functioning are considerable.

SOURCES OF STRESS IN ORGANIZATIONS

Job Overload

Probably every member of an organization has some rough, subjective notion of what constitutes an "optimal" amount of work to do.

Even if we cannot measure this ideal quantity of work, we know when our agenda of tasks approximates it. On the one hand, we have enough to keep busy so that we don't have to go out of our way to find or make work; we don't sit idle, we don't get bored. One the other hand, we have time to attend carefully to what we are doing, we find it easy to concentrate on the immediate task at hand. We feel no sense of panic if we make a mistake or if someone interrupts us. After work is over, we have enough energy left over for taking care of personal business, running errands, and enjoying leisure-time pursuits.

When the workload grows to proportions such that these ideal conditions do not exist, we know that *overload* has occurred. Everyone experiences such overload from time to time, but in some jobs it is a chronic condition. As such, it eminently classifies as a stressor, since it represents a pressing demand upon the organism and the requirement for adaptation.

We can distinguish among different types of overload. The simplest—and probably the easiest to cope with—is just having to work *long hours* on a single task or a group of closely related tasks. Self-employed professionals, small-time entrepreneurs, and farmers come to mind here; they often have long workdays, they sacrifice some leisure time, but the work has focus and their efforts cumulate.

A more vexing form of overload arises when *deadlines* and *time pressures* enter the picture. Of course, deadlines per se do not create undue stress, but when one subjectively perceives them as "unreasonable," they do act as stressors. Kiev and Kohn (1979) found that both middle and upper level managers reported this as the single most frequent stressor in their jobs. Reporters, writers, and the editorial staffs of newspapers have to live with this condition on a daily basis; Kahn (1972), a sportswriter, described the parabola of rising tension as the deadline for written material approached, and saw two reporters "stuck for prose and near a deadline begin to cry" (p. 63).

Yet there is no question that time pressures, even when they exceed our preferences, do enhance productivity. A longitudinal study of scientist and engineers (Andrews & Farris, 1972) found such pressures to relate positively to several aspects of performance, including innovativeness and overall productivity. The study also revealed that, like many of us, scientist and engineers prefer tight deadlines to no time limits at all; we seem to recognize that we need such external prods to combine with any innate self-discipline.

Qualitative overload exists when the requirements of the job outstrip the relevant skills or aptitudes of the incumbent. This problem arises frequently when the novice—whether bank teller, nurse, or pathologist—is assigned to a position where one must deal with the "tough cases" worthy of the seasoned veteran. It results, also, of course, from errors in self-selection by individuals into jobs for which they are not equipped, although they persist in the struggles because of the financial prospects of high income or social status. Sometimes this problem represents simply unfortunate judgments of personnel decision makers. We should not console ourselves with the notion that such mismatches will invariably be corrected; while often they are—although probably at great expense to the individual's self-confidence—not infrequently a person will struggle to achieve barely acceptable performance by simply working twice as hard under twice as much tension as a fully qualified person.

Finally, there is a different type of overload: simply having so many separate, essentially unrelated, tasks to perform that the whole motley agenda becomes overwhelming. The problem is not simply long hours; it is not that any one task carries a fast-approaching deadline or strains the skill requirements of the person. The root of the problem lies in the externally imposed demands for *attentional shift* and the *interruption of response sequences*. The "start-up cost" of shifting one's concentration is, in itself, a considerable stressor. This type of stressor characterizes the job often defined as "general administration" and is especially likely to occur with lower-level supervisors. It can become a pathological condition under certain circumstances:

1. When the individual either cannot (because of insufficient resources) or will not delegate some chores to subordinates.
2. When the individual has no clear sense of where the real responsibilities of the job begin and end and accepts every new "request" from a superior or someone in another department with a "problem," thus adding further obligations to the persent work load.
3. When the individual simply cannot say no to a new imposition, because of fear of reprisal, fear of alienating someone, or fear of creating a bad image.

This type of overload typically does not develop overnight. It evolves in an insidious fashion as an individual accedes to—or even volunteers for—a series of what seem to be finite, limited services. As the person strives in good faith to perform these services effectively and expeditiously, the message comes across that "this is a person we can count on." The requesters are, in a sense, reinforced for their behavior in turning to that person, and the word gets around. What seemed to be one-shot episodes gradually become on-going expectations. The role has expanded because the individual, by adopting a flexible posture toward the "discretionary" boundaries of the job, has pushed its limits out to include a greater variety of responsibilities. Soon the individual finds the organizational role crowding into other life roles (such as the family member role), stews over the disarray of unfinished business, and becomes overburdened by the items on the "guilt shelf." It would be nice, if perhaps too idealistic in most instances, if organizations could provide occasional short-term "moratoria" for overloaded employees to take stock of accumulated commitments, prune away those that are dangling at the edges, and pare them down to a manageable set of high-priority tasks. University professors do something like this when they take sabbatical leave; they have a polite excuse for shedding a stock of obligations, and they can return with a more foresighted resolve to exercise discretion in taking on ad hoc responsibilities. Unfortunately, managers often find an extended sick leave or a resignation to be the only means of accomplishing the same thing.

Role Conflict and Ambiguity

Robert Kahn and his research colleagues at the Survey Research Center of the University of Michigan (Kahn, Wolfe, Quinn, Snoek, and Rosenthal, 1964) have found role conflict and ambiguity to represent significant sources of stress in large organizations. They define role conflict as the "simultaneous occurrence of two (or more) sets of pressures such that compliance with one would make more difficult," or impossible, compliance with the other. For example, a supervisor may be pressed by superiors to maximize production from subordinates, yet at the same time to avoid morale problems that may lead to absenteeism, turnover, or grievances processed by the union. The worker may be pushed by his supervisor to maximize productivity, yet also be pressured by engineering staff to reduce materials waste or rejects due to careless workmanship. Sales executives are sometimes put in the position of having to violate the law or business ethics in order to achieve the product market penetration demanded by superiors.

Kahn et al. found role conflict to be associated with greater levels of interpersonal tension, lower job satisfaction, lower levels of trust and respect for persons exerting the conflicting role pressures, and decreased confidence in the organization. Although role conflict cannot be totally eliminated from organizations, Kahn suggests that it could perhaps be kept within reasonable bounds if administrators viewed the *role set*—the interlocking dependences, expectations, and coordinative requirements of a given number of interacting participants—rather than the individual as the basic building block of organizations.

Role ambiguity is the uncertainty surrounding one's job definition: uncertainty concerning the expectations held by others for one's job performance, concerning how to go about meeting those expectations, and concerning the consequences of one's job behavior. As Kahn notes, "efficient goal-directed behavior is based on predictability of future events" (Kahn et al., 1964). To this might be added the observation that instrumental behavior depends on achieving some degree of clarity on what goals (long-, medium-, and short-range) are relevant and on what behavior is essential in moving toward those goals. A person with a high degree of role ambiguity simply has no plans to guide behavior.

As is true for other sources of stress in organizations, individuals seem to differ vastly in the extent to which they find role ambiguity stressful. Some people, regardless of intelligence or competence, seem to demand a high degree of structure in their lives, while others are very tolerant of—even thrive on—ambiguity.

In addition to individual differences that determine the degree of stress caused by role ambiguity, there are factors in the job environment that make ambiguity more or less aversive. One of these seems to be the general level of *pressure* induced by organizational demands. When the stakes or consequences associated with instrumental role performance are very great, ambiguity is most aversive. When the job climate is rendered more protective and supportive, ambiguity seems to be more tolerable, and sometimes even preferable to highly structured roles. This should not be surprising, since greater amounts of freedom, autonomy, and discretion in one's job must inevitably mean some increase in role ambiguity as well. Perhaps the least ambiguous organizational roles are those associated with assembly line work or clerical office work, yet these are generally not preferred to creative or managerial jobs.

Thus, where role ambiguity is unavoidable—due to the very nature of the job or task—the administrator can ameliorate the resultant stress either by trying to provide a more supportive climate or by giving special attention and guidance to those persons thought to be low in tolerance for ambiguity.

Organizational Politics

A survey of over 2,500 middle- and upper-level managers by Kiev and Kohn (1979) found that respondents pointed to the "general political climate" of the organization as the third most frequently cited source of stress (the first two were, respectively, "heavy workload" and "disparity between what I have to do on the job and what I would like to accomplish"). This finding, at bottom, reflects the inescapable reality that in organizations one depends on others. To achieve virtually anything of substance means that you have to elicit the cooperation of other people. Failure to recognize and manage these dependencies will doom one to chronic frustration and the bitter gall of resentment.

Organizational politics becomes most stressful to those who are temperamentally ill-equipped to cope with it. Often this is the type of person who has a very strong need for achievement but little need or concern for power, and a rigid set of values that defines any form of concession as "selling out." As this person runs into one obstacle after another in the pursuit of achievement, "politics" becomes the focus of nightmares and impotent rage.

This is not to say that politics serve as a source of stress only for "unreasonable" people. The point, rather, is that you cannot manage this source of stress simply by demeaning politics as something which is beneath you. It is an inevitable condition of organizations when different people want different things and reach a viable consensus only by give-and-take and forming coalitions.

Type A Behavior

Sometimes the organizational environment provides the demands which trigger the stress response. In other cases, it serves merely as the arena in which individuals place demands upon themselves. The latter circumstance seems best to characterize the stressful syndrome called *Type A behavior* by Friedman and Rosenman (1974).

The Type A syndrome is one of chronic, combative struggle with the social and physical environment. The Type A demonstrates a striving to do things quickly, to attempt to do several things at once, to "achieve" the maximum efficiency and output in the time available. The Type A eats fast, walks with a snappy pace, will try to read mail or sort through budget figures while carrying on a telephone conversation, or will dictate to a recorder while driving—anything to squeeze more from the seconds and minutes. Friedman and Rosenman describe one Type A who used two electric razors, one on each side of the face, to get a few minutes more of a head start on the workday. Any person or object that jeopardizes this pace becomes the focus of barely suppressed hostility. The Type A tends to interrupt and finish sentences for someone who speaks very slowly in a rambling fashion (Friedman and Rosenman find this a useful test for diagnosing whether a client is a Type A); to break in and finish a task for a subordinate who doesn't work quickly; to grip the steering wheel so tightly that knuckles turn white when a slow driver ahead cannot be passed; to pace impatiently when a push of the button does not immediately bring the elevator.

Glass (1977), from a series of laboratory experiments using college students as subjects, has elaborated upon this behavioral syndrome. Both Type A's and their counterparts—the more deliberate, easygoing Type B's—will work fast when given a difficult goal or time limit. But the Type A, unlike the B, works just as fast when no time pressures whatsoever are involved. Also, when placed on a treadmill to test aerobic conditioning, the Type A's tend to suppress any subjective feeling of fatigue as the angle and speed of the treadmill approach the limits of their aerobic capacity.

In his novel *The Hurricane Years*, Cameron Hawley has given us a character, Judd Wilder, who personifies the Type A. At the beginning of the narrative, Wilder, an advertising and promotion executive for a carpet company, is leaving the Pennsylvania Turnpike and trying to return from New York to corporate headquarters in Pennsylvania with proofs of the stockholders' report by 8:30 that evening. Characteristically, there is no compelling reason why the report has to arrive at that time; it is simply one of the innumerable goals Wilder instinctively and unceasingly sets to stretch himself to the limit. Behind the wheel, he experiences a massive heart attack. Rushed to a county hospital, he comes under the care of Dr. Aaron Kharr, who soon recognizes the type: " . . . inherently aggressive, competitive, energetic, and ambitious . . . naturally geared to operate at a high adrenalin level."

Not surprisingly, Type A's thrive in an atmosphere of tight deadlines and recurrent quantitative goal setting. Given such jobs, they actually do turn out quite a bit of work. They often excel in middle-management and sales jobs. But they seldom make it to the top of the organization. The reasons: they have no stomach for dwelling at length on really critical issues before reaching a considered judgment, and their easily aroused impatience and hostility produce discomfort in those with whom they have to work.

In a predictive longitudinal study of several thousand 39- to 59-year-old males, Friedman and Rosenman (1974) found that those whom they had clinically categorized at the outset as Type A's ran at least double the risk of Type B's of experiencing premature coronary artery disease. The unrelenting posture of combative struggle and the hostility and rage evoked by frustration have the consequence of maintaining high levels of adrenal hormones in the blood. These hormones, which cannot serve any useful function in the fight-or-flight response for which the evolution of the species designed them, act only to increase the clotting elements in the blood which may accelerate the formation of plaques in the arterial walls.

Certain characteristics of organizational environments clearly cater to such a stress-prone profile. However, we would indict organizations unfairly if we blamed them as *causes* of this behavior. Type A's show this cluster of traits in many settings—at parties, on a sailboat, at a backyard family outing, even in bed. On the other hand, while Type B's respond with haste and struggle to difficult, pressing circumstances, they have no problem dropping back to a more measured tempo under less-harried conditions.

STRESS AND PERFORMANCE

For many years, people have pondered the question of how "stress" affects performance. Some would argue that stress has a negative effect; they would cite the case of a young executive whose work deteriorates under the critical glare of a cruel boss, or the student whose A's drop to C's in the course of a bitterly fought separation between her parents. Others take the opposite view, that stress arouses the reserves of energy and will that bring out the mettle of a person—they give you the example of a composer who produced a masterpiece while beset by the dire circumstances of poverty and a deathly ill child, or the writer who does her best work in noisy surroundings. Still others present a more complex view: "moderate" stress improves performance while "extreme" stress makes performance fall apart. Finally, some thinkers see this issue as calling for "moderator" variables: the effects of stress depend on the situation, the task, or the person. While this position seems intuitively plausible, it remains difficult to support without more precise conceptual linkages.

What seems to be missing from these views is the consideration of performance itself as a stressor, as part of the total demands impinging on the organism. Consider, for example, a study of clerical workers conducted by Levi (1967). Preliminary observation showed that the 12 women studied normally processed about about 160 invoices per hour. Suddenly the researchers intervened and offered a steeply progressive system of incentives above the monthly wages, for increased productivity.

Production increased by over 100 percent, with no rise in errors. Urine samples taken from the workers showed a significant elevation of the stress hormones, noradrenaline and adrenaline. Also, the subjects complained of exhaustion and muscular aches after the completion of the workday. When the researchers withdrew the incentive, stress hormones returned to baseline levels, and somatic symptoms declined.

How do we interpret these findings? It would appear that an individual, given reasonable workloads and standard work conditions, establishes an optimal or equilibrium level of effort. If a person attempts to make a significant departure from this balanced condition, the result is a demand which, like any other, triggers the stress response of the body.

What if performance is not increased but simply maintained while the surrounding conditions deviate from the equilibrium? A study by Glass and Singer (1972) suggests what may happen. They gave subjects some clerical tasks to perform under conditions of random, intermittent, irritating noise, while others worked under "standard" conditions. The noise had no effect one way or the other on either quantity or quality of performance. But *after* the noise had ceased, and after the people had finished the assigned task, some interesting findings came to light. When given a puzzle to solve—and the puzzle had, unbeknownst to the subjects, no solution—those who had worked with the noise showed less tolerance for the frustration of working on the solutionless puzzle. They gave up sooner than the people who had earlier worked under less-vexing circumstances.

When you have to work in the presence of a task-extrinsic stressor—be it noise, excessive humidity, distraction, or strained relationships with work associates—you have a choice. You may elect to exert the same overall level of demand upon yourself, in which case performance probably will show deterioration to some extent (the more difficult the task, the sooner this will become manifest). Alternatively, you may expend a higher level of mental and physical effort in order to maintain (or even increase) performance level—and this increases the total demand placed on you. Eventually, there must be a letdown. But it need not show on the job. It may, instead, be reflected in less tolerance for delays on the ride home, or irritation at otherwise innocuous stimuli; it may be suggested by the otherwise unaccountable inability to remember your gym locker number or what you were supposed to get at the grocery store. Still another possibility is that you simply endure a chronic level of demand placed upon yourself to maintain normally effective functioning in all the usual ways, but eventually the accumulated demands temporarily exhaust the endocrine system, which is now overcome by a virus to which it can no longer present a solid shield of immunity. Any of an array of illnesses then results.

In sum, it is the total combination of stressors, the aggregate demand on the mind-body system, which we have to consider. Dramatic, sustained levels of performance beyond "normal" represent one such demand; so does maintenance of performance under "abnormal" conditions. The more pertinent question becomes, not, What is the effect of stress on performance? (since that can hardly be predicted), but What is the eventual effect of sustaining performance under the load of increased environmental stressors?

Figure 10–3
Origins, Forms, and Consequences of Stress in Organization

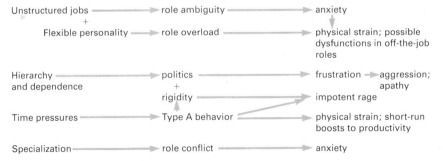

MANAGING STRESS

We can scarcely speak of eliminating stress at work. Since stress is a state of the organism under environmental demands, and since work—even the very best, most absorbing work—presents demands of some nature, we have to take the more credible tack of managing these demands.

1. *Assess the trade-off.* The essential notion of managing is allocating your resources for the best return. If something costs 50 percent more but gives you a negligible 2 percent more satisfaction, you withhold the extra cost and allocate it to some other purpose(s) which represent(s) a better bargain.

Most managers and professionals would agree, at least in principle, with the idea that 80 percent of your success comes from 20 percent of the things you do in a job. If that be the case, and if you can identify with any confidence which elements of the job represent that 20 percent, then obviously it makes sense to spare no demands on yourself to do those parts of the job well. Long hours, skipped lunches, extra coffee, worry, strain—they take some toll, but the payoff justifies it. But what about the 80 percent of the job that determines only 20 percent of your success (however you choose to define it)? Those parts of the job have to be done, but it makes no sense to wear yourself down doing them any faster or better than necessary to get on with the business at hand.

The very flexible person indiscriminately takes on added duties in ad hoc fashion without assessing the trade-off and becomes the victim of overload. The very rigid person brooks no compromises, expends inordinate energy in pitched battles without asking whether minor concessions could promote essential aims and becomes the victim of organizational politics—or, more to the point, the victim of impotent rage when thwarted by dependence on others. The Type A presses to the limit of endurance without regard to external urgency and becomes the victim of an addiction to his or her own adrenaline.

The reader may object that not all stressors are matters of choice, either in acceptance of them for oneself or in imposing them on others. True enough. But a considerable proportion of them are either of our own making or magnified by our unwitting collaboration. You probably cannot prevent the flat tire that befalls you on the way to work, but you can decide for yourself if the consequences of being more or less late call for a frenzied struggle, and when you get to work you can decide whether the day's agenda justifies a breakneck pace to make up for lost time.

2. *Compensation.* As we have emphasized above, the important consideration is the aggregate demand placed on the organism. Heavy demands on the job may be compensated by lesser demands else-

where. The executive who works long hours and competes fero-
ciously at the job but benefits from a tranquil family life and relaxing
hobby may suffer less stress than someone who glides through a nine-
to-five routine and spends the rest of the waking hours in bitter disputes with spouse and kids. Vacations and occasional long weekends
provide some compensation, but not if they are spent trying to cover
the maximum amount of territory and give no opportunity for reflection and dropping one's guard.

3. *Conditioning factors.* The organism's stress response proved
functional in the slow evolution of the species so long as the major
threats encountered were physical—such as a germ, a falling tree, or
a predator. Such threats called either for resistance via the immune
system or the quick burst of adrenaline that enabled a person to fight
or run. From time to time, we still need to fight or run, and we certainly still need our immune system. But on many occasions the
stress response is triggered by conditioned emotional responses and
other reactions to verbal, social, and symbolic stimuli. On those occasions the stress response represents a waste of the organism's resources. What the mind-body system requires is some sort of fine-
tuning to inhibit wasteful stress responses.

One such conditioning factor seems to be contacts with others.
James J. Lynch (1977) assembled data which argue strongly for the
protective role of human companionship. He found that the age-ad-
justed death rates for the divorced, single, and widowed exceed those
for married persons by a significant margin, and the difference is consistent over a large number of diseases and specific causes of death.
He cited also laboratory findings which show that the pulse rates of
animals exposed to noxious stimuli (such as loud noises previously
paired with electric shock) is substantially moderated by the physical
presence of a human being. Studies (Back and Bogdonoff, 1964) found
that a threatening interview evokes a sharper physiological stress response among subjects interviewed alone than among those accompanied by an acquaintance. A study of cardiac patients revealed that
those who had a pet were less likely to suffer a second attack within
the following year.

It is not yet clear exactly how companionship serves this protective role. But the findings suggest that the individual firmly anchored
in close, supportive relationships has a powerful ally in managing
stress. The effects are not simply psychological; they are also physiological and can be objectively quantified.

Moderate exercise constitutes a second conditioning factor. Exercise itself is a stressor. But taken in small, regular doses, there is
suggestive evidence that the effect is to tone the mind-body system
and dampen the stress response to the day's succession of minor problems and irritations. An aerobically conditioned individual not only

has a lower resting pulse rate but also responds to sudden crisis with a less-pronounced rise in heart rate. Exercise also tends to reduce the electrical conductance of the body's surface, which is one measure of organismic tension.

Herbert Benson (1974), drawing upon the evidence that various forms of meditation have beneficial physiological effects, has suggested that managers practice the "relaxation response." A session takes only 20 minutes, about the length of a coffee break. All you need to do is take a comfortable position in a quiet place, close your eyes, try to relax all your muscles, and focus your attention the the rhythmic sound of your breathing. Benson emphasizes the importance of not "forcing" the response or worrying about "how well you're doing," but simply practicing it with a passive attitude. He has used this technique with considerable success in treating high blood pressure. The practice of this relaxation response evokes many of the physiologic changes found with other forms of meditation, such as decreased oxygen consumption, lower pulse rate, and reduced muscle tension. These effects become stable, lasting well beyond the duration of the relaxation period itself; they fine-tune the body by "alleviating the effects of the environmentally induced, but often inappropriate, fight-or-flight response" of the endocrine system.

Of course, many people have their own forms of "relaxation response" or "meditation" by other names. Prayer, appreciation of simple rituals, solitary reflection in a personal "retreat," all appear to capture the essence of the relaxation response.

CONCLUSION

Managers have a dual responsibility: they must manage their own stress, and they have the charge of managing the demands placed upon others. Ethical as well as pragmatic considerations enter into any approach to balancing these responsibilities. The martyr who spares everyone else by burning up his or her own resources will probably not realize the optimal contribution of the work group; the supreme egoist who deflects every imposition upon others will sooner or later become estranged from the salubrious bonds of fellowship. With stress, as with so many issues, equity and moderation seem to represent the best guidelines.

However, we would venture to say that more administrators—especially at lower or middle ranks—err in the direction of neglecting the management of their own demands. Whether this follows from pride, a sense of noblesse oblige, or genuine concern for those around them, in the end it probably becomes a self-defeating process, because managers under inordinate stress tend to create stress for those

Figure 10–4

Aerobic exercises such as jogging help to dampen the stress response of the body to minor problems of everyday life.

around them in fashions neither foreseen nor intended. Supporting this hypothesis is the observation, from study after study, that higher level managers report less stress and enjoy better health than those of the same age at lower echelons. There are probably a number of reasons for this, but we suspect an important one is that those who manage their own demands put to better use their total resources—including the energy and vitality of others.

SUMMARY

The popular and scientific meanings of the term *stress* overlap but do not coincide. In everyday discourse, we use it to refer to situations and emotions which combine to produce *distress*. Selye developed the construct to refer to the nonspecific response of the organism's endocrine system to any demand placed upon it—regardless of how those demands are evaluated or whether they produce uncomfortable feelings. Illness follows when the total set of demands over time impair the immune function of the endocrine system. Emotional stressors include frustration, anxiety, depression, and any other strong emotion. Job-related stressors that create particular problems are job overload, organizational politics, role conflict, role ambiguity, and

Type A behavior. Such stressors may or may not affect performance, but the struggle to maintain performance under adverse circumstances adds to the total set of demands upon the organism. Approaches to managing stress include assessing the trade-offs among additional self-imposed demands, compensation, and moderating inappropriate stress responses of the body. The latter appears to be accomplished by close relationships, reasonable exercise, and various forms of meditation or related behavior.

CONCEPTS TO REMEMBER

stress

general adaptation sydrome

alarm reaction

resistance

exhaustion

endocrine system

frustration

frustration tolerance

depression

aggression

displaced aggression

intropunitive aggression

anxiety

role conflict

role ambiguity

role set

job overload

Type A behavior

QUESTIONS FOR DISCUSSION

1. Why do some individuals seem to have a greater tolerance for stress on the job? What precisely is your definition of "tolerance for stress" and how would you gauge it in the behavior of others?

2. What might cause people to view frustration on the job as arbitrary, even though there really is a good defensible reason for the events causing the frustration?

3. One author has referred to guilt and anxiety as "useless emotions." Do you agree?

4. What are the various ways in which a cohesive work group aids its members in the management of stress?

5. Over the course of this century, what development have tended to increase stress? to decrease it?

6. Explain how a person needs a mixture of both rigidity and flexibility for an optimal approach to managing stress.

CASE[1]

Frank Rogers awakened with a start. The telephone at his bedside was ringing. It was the police department reporting that the back door of the Local Savings and Loan was unlocked and that he would have to come downtown to check the office and lock the door.

Frank was secretary-treasurer and assistant manager of Local Savings and Loan. He had started work at Local after being honorably discharged from the army some 12 years before. At that time, there were only two employees: the managing officer, Al Wilcox, and himself. (At the time this case was reported the organization had a staff of 18 persons.)

As he drove toward town, the midnight air cleared his head. He began to recall the events of the hectic day he had had at the office. It was the type of day that was becoming increasingly common. Such days left him exhausted—so much so that at home he inevitably got into arguments with his wife and scolded his three children over minor things that ordinarily left him unruffled.

Today it had all started early in the morning. The chairman of the board had come into his office and created a disturbance because he had not received the statistical data for the previous month for reviewing prior to the board of directors' meeting that afternoon. Frank had intended to get the information together, but in the little time he had had between customers he had made out the monthly report for the Federal Home Loan Bank because of a fast-approaching deadline.

After the chairman of the board departed, Frank went to tell Wilcox that he needed another stenographer to help him with his work. Wilcox said that the association was overstaffed at the present and more efficient use of the personnel on hand should solve such a problem. Frank agreed with him that the quantity of personnel was adequate, but that their efficiency was poor. Wilcox took this as a direct criticism of his three relatives in the office, and a fairly heated argument between the two men developed rapidly. Tempers soon cooled, and Frank returned to his office and proceeded with his work.

About three o'clock in the afternoon Frank had stepped out of his office and seen two customers waiting at the counter. Not a single teller was in evidence. His quick investigation disclosed three tellers downstairs having coffee. Another had gone out for cigarettes and the fifth was in the supply room getting some additional supplies. Frank called Wilcox out of his office and proceeded to point out the situation to him. Wilcox heatedly told him to take care of it, walked back

---

[1]Reprinted with permission from Edgar G. Williams, *People Problems* (Bureau of Business Research, Indiana University Graduate School of Business, Bloomington, Ind.), 1962.

into his office, and slammed the door. Frank hurried the tellers out of the lunchroom with a sharp reprimand and then went to see Roger Donaldson, who was supposed to supervise the tellers.

Donaldson was about 26 years old and had worked for the association for the past five years. At first he had not exhibited much ambition, but after he had got married and his wife had had a child, his interest picked up and he was now progressing quite rapidly.

Frank asked the supervisor for an explanation of the teller situation. Donaldson advised him that he had no real control over the employees. He said that he had asked Wilcox for help but got none and, on occasions when he had attempted to discipline some of them, Wilcox had called him into his office and had reprimanded him for his actions. By this time, Frank was sorely frustrated, but he managed to keep himself under control.

At almost five o'clock, Frank's stenographer had brought him the letters to sign that he had dictated earlier that day. While signing them, he noted that there were so many errors on two of them that he stayed late and retyped them himself.

As he drove up to the office parking lot Frank thought to himself, "I wonder why the door is open? This has never happened before. The last thing that Al does is to check both doors before he leaves the building. Could I myself have forgotten?"

Questions

What are the tell-tale symptoms that Frank is operating under a considerable degree of job-related stress? What are the origins of this stress? To what extent, and in what manner, might Frank himself be contributing to the stress level? If you were a friend of Frank's, what suggestions might you offer for handling the stress of his job?

REFERENCES

Abramson, L. Y., & Sackheim, H. A.   A paradox in depression: Uncontrollability and self-blame. *Psychological Bulletin*, 1977, *84*, 838–851.

Allport, F. H.   *Institutional behavior*. Chapel Hill: University of North Carolina Press, 1933.

Allport, G. W., & Postman, T.   *The psychology of rumor*. New York: Holt, Rinehart & Winston, 1947.

Andrews, F. M., & Farris, G. F.   Time pressure and performance of scientists and engineers: A five year panel study. *Organizational Behavior and Human Performance*, 1972, *8*, 185–200.

Back, K. W., & Bogdonoff, M.   Plasma lipid responses to leadership, conformity, and deviation. In P. H. Leiderman & D. Shapiro (Eds.), *Psycho-biological approaches to social behavior*. Stanford, Calif.: Stanford University Press, 1964.

Benson, H. Your innate asset for combating stress. *Harvard Business Review*, July-August 1974, pp. 49–60.

Cantril, H. Perception and interpersonal relations. *American Journal of Psychiatry*, 1957, *114*(2), 27–29.

Cherrington, D. J. Satisfaction in competitive conditions. *Organizational Behavior and Human Performance*, 1973, *10*, 47–71.

Coping with anxiety at AT&T. *Business Week*, May 28, 1979, pp. 95ff.

Costello, T. W., & Zalkind, S. S. (Eds.). *Psychology in administration.* Englewood Cliffs, N. J.: Prentice-Hall, 1963.

Flach, F. F. *The secret strength of depression.* Philadelphia: J. B. Lippincott, 1974.

Friedman, M., & Rosenman, R. H. *Type A behavior and your heart.* New York: Alfred A. Knopf, 1974.

Glass, D. C. *Behavior patterns, stress, and coronary disease.* Hillsdale, N.J.: Laurence Erlbaum Associates, 1977.

Glass, D. C., and Singer, J. E. *Urban stress.* New York: Academic Press, 1972.

Hampton, D. R., Summer, C. E., & Webber, R. A. (Eds.). *Organizational behavior and the practice of management.* Glenview, Ill.: Scott, Foresman, 1968.

Harrell, W. A., & Moss, I. D. Two fixed-ratio schedules and their impact on aggression in humans. *Psychological Reports*, 1974, *34*, 785–786.

Hawley, C. *The hurricane years.* Greenwich, Conn.: Fawcett Publications, 1968.

Henry, W. E. The business executive: The psychodynamics of a social role. *American Journal of Sociology*, 1949, *54*, 291–296.

Holmes, T. H., & Rahe, R. H. The social readjustment rating scale. *Journal of Psychosomatic Research*, 1968, *2*, 213–218.

Janoff-Bulman, R. Characterological vs. behavioral self-blame: Inquiries into depression and rape. *Journal of Personality and Social Psychology*, 1979, *37*, 1798–1809.

Kahn, R. *The boys of summer.* New York: Harper & Row, 1972.

Kahn, R. W., Wolfe, D. M., Quinn, R. P., Snoek, J. D., & Rosenthal, R. A. *Organizational stress.* New York: John Wiley & Sons, 1964.

Kiev, A., & Kohn, V. *Executive stress: An AMA survey report.* New York: AMACOM, 1979.

Kline, N. *From sad to glad.* New York: G. P. Putnam's Sons, 1974.

Lawson, R. *Frustration.* New York: Macmillan, 1965.

Levi, L. *Stress: Sources, management, and prevention.* New York: Liveright, 1967.

Levi, L. Stress and distress in response to psychosocial stimuli. *Acta Medica Scandinavica*, 1972, Supplement 528, 119–142.

Levinson, H. The psychologist in industry. *Harvard Business Review*, 1959, *37*, 93–99.

Lynch, J. J. *The broken heart: The medical consequences of loneliness.* New York: Basic Books, 1977.

Peter, L. F.   *The Peter principle.* New York: William Morrow, 1969.

Roethlisberger, F. J., & Dickson, W. J.   *Management and the worker.* New York: Wiley Science Editions, 1964.

Ruch, L. O., & Holmes, T. H.   Scaling of life change: Comparison of direct and indirect methods. *Journal of Psychosomatic Research,* 1971, *15,* 221–227.

Selye, H.   *The stress of life.* New York: McGraw-Hill, 1956.

Spielberger, C. D. (Ed).   *Anxiety and behavior.* New York: Academic Press, 1966.

Strauss, G.   The personality vs. organization theory. In L. R. Sayles (Ed.), *Individualism and big business.* New York: McGraw-Hill, 1963.

Toffler, A.   *Future shock.* New York: Random House, 1970.

11

Job Satisfaction

Why is job satisfaction important?

What is the extent of job satisfaction in the labor force?

What groups in the labor force express the most job satisfaction?

What are the sources and consequences of job satisfaction?

What are the sources and consequences of job dissatisfaction?

As we noted in Chapter 1, one criterion by which we evaluate an organization's functioning is, of course, *performance*. For a manufacturing firm, this criterion might be share of the market or return on investment; for a hospital, the quality of health care provided; for local government, the efficiency with which services are provided to the community. Whatever the actual measure or measures might be, we evaluate the management of an organization according to some criterion of effectiveness.

To an increasing extent, especially since the 1960s, organizations are also being evaluated on the basis of the need satisfactions of their participants. When participation takes the form of a full-time job, we refer to the *job satisfaction* of the organization's work force.

Why is job satisfaction a criterion of organizational functioning? It is *not* because greater satisfaction leads in any simple or direct way to superior performance. At various times in the last four decades a number of people have justified their concern for greater job satisfaction of organization members by arguing that such satisfaction easily translates into increased productivity. However, as we shall soon see, the results of a large number of studies suggest that this argument lacks support. This is not to say that job satisfaction has no desirable behavioral consequences, but rather to disabuse the reader of any simple notion that happier people are automatically more-productive people.

Why, then, is job satisfaction so important? One reason stems quite simply from certain *value judgments*. People spend a sizable proportion of their waking lives in the work environment. From any minimally humanitarian point of view, we would want that portion of their lives to be more or less pleasant, agreeable, and fulfilling. Few people actually have the choice of working or not working; and of those who have to work for economic reasons, most have only a limited number of options as to where to work. Given such constraints, much of the population would find little cheer in their lives if the workplace offered no opportunity for satisfaction.

A second reason for attaching so much importance to job satisfaction is its relationship to *mental health*. In the realm of our subjective inner worlds, discontent about specific parts of our lives tends to have a "spillover" effect and to color our outlook even upon otherwise unrelated portions of our life space. Dissatisfaction with one's job seems to have an especially volatile spillover effect. People who feel bad about their work are apt to feel bad about many other things, including family life, leisure activities, even life itself. Psychiatrists tell us that most of their patients express negative feelings about their jobs. Admittedly, the direction of causation may sometimes run the opposite way; unresolved personality problems or maladjustment may indeed be the cause of a person's inability to find satisfaction in work. Nevertheless, anyone who has ever had to live with a parent, spouse, sibling, or roommate who didn't like his or her job knows how tense relationships with that person can be. Both casual observation and scientific study seem to provide compelling evidence that job satisfaction is an important component of overall psychological adjustment and productive living.

Evidence also points to a relationship between job satisfaction and *physical health*. According to one study (Palmore, 1969), people who like their work are likely to live longer. Again, complicating factors preclude a hasty conclusion that job satisfaction, per se, is the causal factor, since people with greater job satisfaction also tend to have greater incomes and more education, and thus may coincidentally enjoy greater advantages and knowledge which promote longevity. Nonetheless, chronic dissatisfaction with work is a stressor, and stress does eventually take its toll on the organism. Stress has been implicated as a contributing factor in the genesis of hypertension, coronary artery disease, digestive ailments, and even some types of cancer.

Level of job satisfaction does not invariably determine the general quality of life. The "spillover" phenomenon appears to characterize many of those with advanced educational attainments, as well as those who strongly identify with a profession. For many others, the "segmentalist hypothesis" (Kabanoff, 1980) more accurately describes their orientation: Some persons sharply differentiate their work roles from family, community, or personal affairs, and their enjoyment of leisure is little affected by their attitudes about work. Job satisfaction does not always generalize to satisfaction with life itself.

Later in the chapter we shall examine the reasons why employing organizations find it in their own self-interest to concern themselves with the job satisfaction of participants.

WHAT IS JOB SATISFACTION?

Essentially, job satisfaction is a person's attitude toward the job. Like any other attitude, then, it represents a complex assemblage of cognitions (beliefs or knowledge), emotions (feelings, sentiments, or evaluations), and behavioral tendencies. A person with a high level of job satisfaction holds very positive attitudes about work, and conversely, a person dissatisfied with the job has negative attitudes toward work.

Thus, like other attitudes, job satisfaction is an unobserved variable. How, then, do we measure it? How do we indirectly observe it? Probably the simplest method is to ask an individual: On the whole, are you satisfied or dissatisfied with your job? A number of surveys of job attitudes in the work force have used this technique, and for certain purposes it may suffice. For other purposes, it may be too crude a measure. A person with moderately negative job attitudes may feel too inhibited to make a direct, unqualified response of "Dissatisfied." Thus, among people responding "Satisfied," there is likely to exist a broad continuum ranging from passive dissatisfaction through indifference to strong and enthusiastic endorsement of their jobs.

To detect more subtle variations in the extent of job satisfaction, psychologists have developed a number of standardized *attitude scales* for measuring it. Different scales vary considerably in their length and format, but a typical job satisfaction instrument presents the respondent with a number of evaluative statements (some worded positively, some negatively) about various aspects of the job. The respondent is asked to indicate whether he or she strongly agrees, agrees, neither agrees nor disagrees, disagrees, or strongly disagrees with each statement. Each response is scored (for example, 5 for strongly agrees and 1 for strongly disagrees with positive statements, the opposite for negative items), and the scores on all items are summed for an overall estimate of job satisfaction. (See Figure 11–1 for representative items from such scales.)

Figure 11–1
Representative Items in Job Satisfaction Measures

Indicate whether the various statements listed below describe something that is very good, good, fair, poor, or very poor about your job.

	VG	G	F	P	VP
Management's interest in welfare of employees.					
This company as a place to work.					
Fair treatment of employees by management.					
Credit given by my supervisor for doing a good job.					
The amount of money I am paid.					
Freedom to make decisions about my work.					
Interesting work to do.					
Chances of steady work.					

Adapted from Robert P. Bullock, *Social Factors Related to Job Satisfaction* (Columbus: Bureau of Business Research, Ohio State University, 1952).

Job attitude scales were originally developed for research purposes. Industrial psychologists were interested in such questions as: How closely does level of job satisfaction correlate with individual performance? How well can job attitudes be predicted by salary? What types of leadership styles result in greater job satisfaction? More precise measures than global statements of "satisfaction" or "dissatisfaction" were needed in order to grapple with such questions. Increasingly, however, organization officials have been using job attitude scales for their own purposes, either directly or by way of consultants. By conducting periodic audits of job satisfaction, managers can spot trends in job attitudes which may not produce behavioral results until sometime later. Thus, they can take such actions as necessary to avert a rise in turnover rate or in labor grievances. Furthermore, they can isolate pockets of acute discontent in an otherwise positive climate of opinion.

The reader may object to treating job satisfaction in such a global fashion. After all, might not one feel quite good about salary and fringe benefits but be dissatisfied with one's boss? The answer is obviously yes. For this reason, most recently developed job attitude scales permit the scoring of subscales about different parts of the work environment. An overall job satisfaction score can be disassembled into scores indicating attitudes about pay, supervision, chances for promotion, co-workers, and the work itself (the intrinsic nature of the work activities performed). Although people may be expected to hold different attitudes about different aspects of the job, we find, in fact, a rather high degree of consistency in attitudes toward various aspects of the job. People who dislike their superiors show a better-than-chance probability of also complaining about working conditions such as the quality of lighting or the adequacy of rest rooms. Individuals who are bored with what they do on the job are also likely to refrain from outright positive endorsement of the organization's salary structure. Roethlisberger and Dickson (1964) noted this covariation in job sentiments nearly 50 years ago in the massive interviewing phase of the celebrated Hawthorne studies. They explained this covariation by suggesting that the logic of sentiments is different from the logic of facts. Strong sentiments do not permit as fine a degree of perceptual discrimination. Whatever the reason, tightly compartmentalized attitudes toward components of the work environment appear to be the exception rather than the rule.

THE EXTENT OF JOB SATISFACTION IN THE LABOR FORCE

What percentage of the nation's workers are satisfied with their jobs? Which groups are more or less satisfied than other groups? Are people's attitudes toward their jobs becoming more or less favorable? A number of nationwide surveys of the labor force have addressed themselves to these questions.

The longest-running series of job satisfaction surveys is that conducted by George Gallup, probably the foremost name among professional pollsters. The Gallup organization uses the simple, direct method of asking people whether they are, on the whole, satisfied or dissatisfied with their present jobs. As Table 11–1 indicates, from 1949 to the 1970s, only a small proportion of workers—20 percent at most, and usually less—responded with "Dissatisfied." These figures come as quite a surprise to most people. Contrary to many opinions, the vast majority of the nation's workers seem to feel at least moderately pleased with their jobs. They may have specific gripes about work (a favorite and traditional indoor sport of Americans), and they usually see plenty of room for improvement, but overall, they like their jobs. Furthermore, Gallup's findings are supplemented by other surveys of varying scope and representativeness (for a review of these, see Herzberg, Mausner, Peterson, & Capwell, 1955), and with almost uncanny consistency these studies show 70 to 85 percent of workers as saying that they are satisfied with their jobs.

Table 11–1
Gallup Polls of Job Satisfaction

	Satisfied	Dissatisfied	No Opinion
1949	67%	20%	13%
1963	90	7	3
1965	87	9	4
1966	87	9	4
1969	88	6	6
1971	83	9	8

Source: George H. Gallup, *The Gallup Poll* (New York: Random House, 1972).

Some critics of these findings argue that Gallup's survey method, for reasons touched on earlier, yields an inflated measure of job satisfaction, and suggest that a less-blunt way of phrasing the question would produce more realistic data. As it turns out, Gallup himself used a variation in method. In his 1950 and 1955 surveys he asked:

1. If you were to begin all over again, would you go into the same line of work or not?

   Only 55 percent said yes, 35 percent said no, and 10 percent were undecided.

2. Do you think you would be happier in a different job?

   32 percent said yes.

3. Do you enjoy your work so much that you have a hard time putting it aside?

   Only 51 percent said yes, and 45 percent said no.

4. Generally speaking, which do you enjoy more—the hours when you are on your job, or the hours when you are not on your job?

   The 39 percent who answered "on the job" were outnumbered by the 48 percent who answered "not on the job."

There seems to be a basis, then, for arguing that asking people to choose between saying that they are satisfied or that they are dissatisfied may overstate the positivity of job attitudes in the work force. Nevertheless, taking all the findings together, it appears that job satisfaction is broadly distributed throughout the nation's labor pool.

Recent Trends: Better or Worse?

In the early 1970s, the extent of job satisfaction among employed workers became a matter of some controversy. The most vocal and publicized position—portrayed in books, magazine and newspaper articles, and television documentaries—purported to show that a crisis in job morale was developing, a crisis reflected not only in surveys of job attitudes but also in such behavioral indices as increased absenteeism, higher turnover, and declining economic growth and labor productivity. *Work in America* (1973), the report of a special task force to the Secretary of Health, Education, and Welfare, commented at length on the thesis of "job alienation," with particular reference to "blue-collar blues," "white-collar woes," the dissatisfaction of younger workers, and the prevalence of negative attitudes among women and minority workers. Sheppard and Herrick's *Where Have All the Robots Gone?* (1972), based largely on a study of approximately 1,500 workers, painted an equally gloomy picture of the typical worker's job attitudes. Judson Gooding's *The Job Revolution* (1972) conveyed the same message. These three books agreed that the course of job satisfaction was spiraling downward and that the major cause of the decline was "sterile" work that offered too few people any opportunity for psychological growth and fulfillment in their jobs. The corrective approach, they urged, lay in a concerted program of job redesign in industry and business to render work more meaningful, interesting, and enriching.

Not all observers agreed that job attitudes had come to such a sorry state. Gallup's survey results, while showing a dip in the period 1963–71, suggested that the extent of job satisfaction had remained quite stable over the years since 1949, and if anything had risen between 1949 and 1971, especially for blacks. In fact, even in the Michigan study cited by Sheppard and Herrick, no more than 25 percent of any single subgroup of workers expressed negative attitudes toward work. The overall figure for the entire sample was about 14 percent—remarkably close to the 13 percent which Herzberg et al. (1955) found as a median figure in their review of studies undertaken prior to 1955.

What about behavioral indices of job attitudes, such as turnover and absenteeism? A glance at Table 11–2 shows that the quit rate among employees surveyed by government agencies did undeniably increase steadily through the 1960s. One must, however, take into account the unemployment level throughout this period to place the trend in quit rate in proper perspective. People are more apt to quit their jobs—even jobs they would otherwise be satisfied with—when they have good prospects of finding better jobs. As the unemployment figures in Table 11–2 attest, the job market became increasingly favorable for workers as the nation's economy enjoyed the longest period of sustained growth since World War II. The expansionist fiscal policies of the Kennedy-Johnson administrations, compounded by the strain upon the economy of increasing U.S. involvement in Vietnam, led generally to a shortage of workers. As the economy cooled off and entered a severe recession in 1974–75, quits became less frequent. It should be pointed out that, after correcting for unemployment level, there remains a slight trend toward a higher quit rate. For a *given* level of unemployment, turnover seems to have been slightly greater since 1963 than it was before that time. Nevertheless, most of the increased turnover between 1961 and 1970 can be attributed to the tight labor market.

Table 11–2
Turnover and Unemployment, 1960–1979

	Average Monthly Quit Rate (per 100 Workers)	Unemployment (Percent)
1960	1.3	5.6
1961	1.2	6.7
1962	1.4	5.6
1963	1.4	5.7
1964	1.5	5.2
1965	1.9	4.5
1966	2.5	3.8
1967	2.3	3.8
1968	2.5	3.6
1969	2.7	3.5
1970	2.1	4.9
1971	1.8	5.9
1972	2.2	5.6
1973	2.7	4.9
1974	2.3	5.6
1975	1.4	8.5
1976	1.7	7.7
1977	1.8	7.0
1978	2.1	6.0
1979	2.0	5.8

Source: U.S. Bureau of the Census, *Statistical Abstract of the United States*, 1963, 1970, 1974, 1980.

Figure 11–2

Are today's workers more or less satisfied than their predecessors?

National absenteeism figures are harder to come by. It is well known, though, that absenteeism in certain sectors of the economy, such as the auto industry, doubled between 1960 and 1970. Again, much of this increase stemmed from labor market conditions. When help is scarce, employers are less apt to discipline workers for excess absences (for fear that they will quit) or to discharge workers. The employers would have to compete for replacements in a diminished pool, and employees are probably aware of this. Furthermore, when plants are short of the help necessary to fill production orders, they hire more marginal employees, accepting the risk that such individuals will have less-than-desirable attendance habits. Finally, with tight labor markets forcing up basic wage rates and leading to substantial overtime earnings, people can more easily afford lost earnings from occasionally playing hooky in order to go fishing, take in a ball game, or catch up on sleep.

Nonetheless, while the evidence does not argue for anything like a "crisis" of widespread job alienation, it does appear that job satisfaction in the labor force crested sometime in the early 1960s and perhaps declined slightly thereafter into the 1970s, with little discernible pattern since the mid-1970s (see Figure 11–3). As of this writing (1981), general job satisfaction among workers probably does not match that of the early 1960s. A study by Smith, Roberts, and Hulin

Figure 11–3
Job Satisfaction in the Nation's Labor Force: Trends over Time

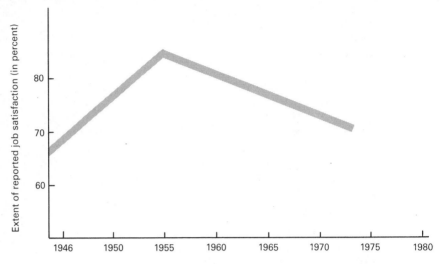

(1976) of 98,000 blue- and white-collar workers employed by an international retailing chain showed a slight decline in job satisfaction in every area of the country except the Southeast. The trend held consistently across satisfaction with such aspects of the job as supervision, pay, career future, and physical surroundings. A separate study (Smith, Scott, & Hulin, 1977) within the same organization found that job satisfaction among managerial personnel also declined between 1971 and 1974.

How can we explain the slight downward trend since 1960? Probably the strongest contributing factor derives from changes in the age structure of the labor force. Until 1960, the post–World War II labor force steadily became older. In 1960, the proportion of workers aged 20–34 numbered just over 30 percent; by the mid 1970s, members of the postwar "baby boom" had begun to mature and enter the labor force, and that figure reached 40 percent. And, as we shall see below, survey after survey shows that younger workers, particularly those under 30, tend to report less job satisfaction than older employees. It is a demographic fact of life. By the mid-1980s, however, the work force will begin to show a reversal of this trend. That factor alone would predict greater job satisfaction in the years ahead.

Other changes besides age probably figure into the post-1960 pattern of slightly lower job satisfaction. Data published by Jurgensen (1978) give us a clue as to what these changes represent. His study drew upon a 30-year practice of a large utility which asked job applicants to rank-order 10 job characteristics in terms of importance to the applicants. The steady, consistent trend throughout the 30-year period was for job security to decline in rated importance and type of work ("work which is interesting and well-liked by you") to increase in importance.

Furthermore, when Jurgensen sorted the data out by groups according to level of educational attainment, he found that both men and women with college degrees attached special importance to type of work, while those with high school diplomas or less placed more emphasis on job security.

The implications of Jurgensen's (and others') findings sum up to this:

1.   The labor force contains within its ranks an increasing percentage of workers with postsecondary educational attainments.
2.   One of the effects of increased formal education is the expectation of interesting work—work that provides intrinsic rewards.
3.   Alas, this expectation is much easier to cultivate than to satisfy. It is much easier to make work cleaner, safer, more comfortable, than it is to make work stimulating. Thus, changes in expectations about jobs have not been matched by a corresponding change in the intrinsic appeal of many jobs.

Which Groups Are Most Satisfied?

While both historical and current analyses testify to a reasonably high level of job satisfaction in the labor force as a whole, clear-cut patterns of variation exist *within* the labor force. Among the differences between groups are those pertaining to age, length of tenure, occupational level, race, and sex.

Herzberg et al.'s review in 1955 showed a rather consistent trend in job attitudes according to age and length of service (see Figure 11–4). When people begin work (typically in their late teens or their early 20s), they appear to do so with a considerable degree of enthusiasm. This enthusiasm soon wanes, however, giving way to a steady decline in job morale which reaches its lowest depths in the late 20s or early 30s. Attitudes then become increasingly positive, at least well into the 50s. The trend after that is less certain. Some studies suggest that the level of job satisfaction continues to climb or at least that it holds steady; others point to another decline—possibly due to concern about health, approaching retirement, or the end of the road as far as further promotion is concerned. In any case, the point seems well established that workers in the middle 20s to early 30s are the least-satisfied group. Sheppard and Herrick's (1972) data showed that among workers aged 20–29, 24 percent expressed negative attitudes toward work, as opposed to 13 percent in the 30–44 age bracket and 11 percent in the 45–54 range.

Figure 11–4
Age and Job Satisfaction

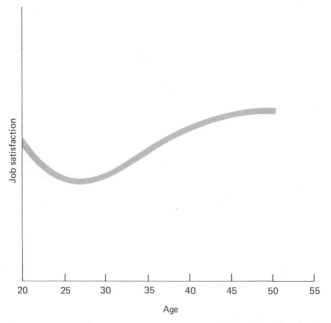

Source: F. Herzberg, B. Mausner, R. Peterson, and D. Capwell, *Job Attitudes: Review of Research and Opinion* (Pittsburgh: Psychological Service of Pittsburgh, 1955).

Why is this the case? Herzberg and his associates suggested a number of plausible reasons. When you evaluate anything—be it a job, a meal, a car, or a movie—you do so by implicitly comparing the object to others like it that you have experienced. When you take your first full-time job, you have no prior job to compare it with. How, then, do you evaluate it? Probably by comparing it with the next closest thing, school. School life is characterized by much variety, a wide circle of acquaintances, frequent opportunities for achievement, changes in activities, and a number of significant events (getting a driver's license, the first date, making a varsity athletic team, graduation, and so on). Most jobs suffer by comparison with the colorful world of academic life (more colorful in retrospect, of course). Few jobs offer that kind of variety and change of pace.

Second, and perhaps related to the foregoing consideration, is the nature of the expectations that people bring to their first job. Some people tend to expect their job experiences to be similar to those portrayed in the success stories so often encountered in movies, novels, and biographical sketches. They expect, not only good earnings, but also the kind of continual excitement and interest that might characterize, say, the fascination of a Nobel Prize–winning chemist with his researches into the mysteries of matter. In short, people begin work with unrealistic expectations and, finding that reality falls far short of their expectations, they endure the first decade of work with gradually increasing disillusionment. After some point, expectations are apparently modified and adjusted downward, and the job is seen in a more positive perspective.

We should hasten to remind the reader that even among this most dissatisfied age group, a *majority* are satisfied. Even high expectations usually seem to temper and restrain job attitudes rather than promote outright disaffection with the job.

Professional and managerial workers report the highest level of job satisfaction. Unskilled manual workers in the heavy industries, such as the automotive and steel industries, report the greatest extent of dissatisfaction. In between those two extremes are clerical and sales workers and skilled blue-collar operatives.

Blacks and other minorities are less likely to be satisfied with their work than are whites, probably because the former are overrepresented in marginal occupational categories and in unskilled blue-collar jobs. However, whereas Gallup found that in 1949 nearly half of the black workers surveyed expressed job dissatisfaction, in 1971 only about a fourth of the black workers surveyed voiced negative work attitudes.

Sex differences in job satisfaction show less consistency. Published studies up until the mid-1950s showed no clear-cut differences between males and females. Sheppard and Herrick's findings in 1972 showed females to be less satisfied than males, the difference reaching its maximum extent among workers under 30. It would appear that women, especially young women, are less likely to be satisfied with *just any* form of employment. They are more sensitive than women workers of preceding generations about working under job conditions that are inferior to those of males with the same set of qualifications as their own. Despite some years of affirmative action programs, there is abundant evidence that equality of treatment between the sexes with respect to job opportunities has not been fully achieved.

CAUSES OF JOB SATISFACTION

One analytic approach to the sources of job satisfaction is to look at the groups that seem to have the most of it—professionals and managers—and to see what they have that other workers don't have, or don't have in as great measure.

First, the most satisfied groups typically earn higher salaries than do other occupational groups. In recent years, there may have been a tendency to underestimate the role of income in determining job attitudes. This is not to say that money is the only source, or even the most important source, of job satisfaction. Many people would probably agree that insufficient pay or perceived inequitable underpay is a more decisive determinant of dissatisfaction than sufficient or fair pay is of satisfaction. Nevertheless, as Saul Gellerman (1963) has noted, money is a "complex symbol"; it represents far more to individuals than the material goods and services it can command. Income level is inextricably associated with social status, independence, lifestyle, and the worthwhileness of what one is doing. Certainly *relative* pay—one's pay as compared to significant reference groups—seems to count for something in the calculus of job satisfaction.

Second, professionals and managers enjoy much more *autonomy* in their work than do other groups. They set their own hours, their own pace, and most of the time they are free from close supervision. They unilaterally make a large number of decisions about how they do their work.

Third, and perhaps most important, professionals derive a greater measure of *intrinsic rewards* from work. Their work is varied and often stimulating. It offers a challenge to prove their mettle. It allows or requires the use of the skills and knowledge they are most proud of. It affords opportunity for continual self-development, learning, and growth. Study after study shows that professionals and managers report greater satisfaction of their needs for achievement and self-actualization than do other occupational groups.

Another method of ascertaining the major causes of job satisfaction is to ask people to rank-order various aspects of work in terms of their importance. Herzberg et al. (1955) averaged the findings of 16 such studies, involving a total of over 11,000 employees. The first-ranked factor was security; the second was the "interest from intrinsic aspects of the job"; the third was opportunity for advancement; and the fourth was considerate and appreciative supervision. Wages ranked seventh.

Almost two decades later, Sheppard and Herrick found some changes in the ranking of job dimensions. "Interesting work" was ranked first; second, third, and fourth, respectively, were enough equipment, information, and authority "to get the job done." "Good pay" ranked fifth. Job security, so important in the 1940s and early 1950s, had dropped to seventh. Workers continued to place a high value on the inherent interest afforded by the job; they remained sensitive to the leadership styles of supervision, especially with regard to consideration displayed, but also with regard to structuring the work environment;[1] and economic benefits were still accorded substantial

---

[1]An extended discussion of the effects of leadership styles on job attitudes is deferred until Chapter 15.

importance. Job security apparently matters a lot when you don't have it (the experience of many workers in the 1930s), but not when you've got it (as does more and more of the labor force).

It is important not to overlook the role of the work group in determining job satisfaction. The Hawthorne researchers in the 1920s and 1930s (Roethlisberger & Dickson, 1964) found that people working on isolated jobs were more apt to express irritation, dissatisfaction, or feelings of depression on the job. A later study of automobile industry workers (Walker & Guest, 1952) found that isolated workers disliked their jobs. Seashore (1954) noted that cohesive industrial work groups were less likely to be adversely affected by pressure for production and expressed less anxiety about their jobs than noncohesive work groups. The opportunity for pleasurable interaction with coworkers appears to atone for considerable shortcomings in other features of jobs, such as uncomfortable working conditions or tedious work. Interviews with those rare specimens who win enough money in lotteries to retire, yet soon return even to unskilled jobs, find that a frequently cited reason for going back to work is simply to be back with friends at the job.

The weights of the above-mentioned job attributes in contributing to job satisfaction or dissatisfaction vary considerably from one individual to another. For example, autonomy and the intrinsic interest of the work itself matter more to younger workers and highly educated employees than to their opposites. Job security and pay take on increased importance for workers over age 40 (Herzberg et al., 1955). Variety in the job means more to extraverts than to introverts.

Finally, individual *expectations* of the job are a crucial variable in the makeup of job attitudes. Regardless of what the job offers—the level of pay, autonomy, interest, challenge, or social gratification—if the individual expects more, he or she is less likely to be satisfied. If the general level of job satisfaction in the labor force has declined in recent years, this is almost certainly *not* due to any worsening of job conditions or characteristics. Jobs today pay more, carry more collateral benefits, are performed under better physical conditions, are freer from arbitrary or capricious intervention by employers and bosses, and probably even offer more intrinsic appeal (given the dwindling percentage of jobs in unskilled categories, such as "assemblers") than did jobs a quarter of a century ago. However, it appears that expectations have risen at a faster rate than have such improvements.

JOB DISSATISFACTION

Should we conceptualize job dissatisfaction as simply the opposite of job satisfaction? If so, do the causes of job dissatisfaction represent merely the opposite (or absence) of those things that create satisfaction? If autonomy, stimulation, and intrinsic interest lead to job satisfaction, does their absence cause dissatisfaction?

Herzberg (1966) argued that, contrary to intuitive logic, job satisfaction and dissatisfaction are not mirror opposites, nor are they generally caused by opposite things. He based his conclusions on a study which asked people to write stories about occasions on which they felt especially good about their work and similar stories about when they felt bad about the job. Analysis of the themes in the stories showed that, when achievement or the work itself were mentioned, they were much more likely to figure in an episode of "feeling good." References to conditions surrounding the job, pay, and supervision, on the other hand, were more likely to appear in stories about "feeling bad." Herzberg concluded that *job content* determined satisfaction; lack of interesting work did not create dissatisfaction, but simply prevented positive attitudes from occurring. On the other hand, *job context* determined dissatisfaction. Inconsiderate supervision, wage inequities, or poor working conditions could lead to dissatisfaction. Correcting such problems could only remove that dissatisfaction, not really bring about satisfaction.

Critics have hounded Herzberg mercilessly for methodological shortcomings of his research. Since his method consisted of the *critical incident* or story-telling technique, it did leave his findings vulnerable to the charge that subjects simply allowed defense mechanisms to distort their memories. In other words, people may have taken credit for the good times by writing about things they did themselves (achievement, advancement, the work itself), while attributing the causes of the bad experiences to people or things around them (boss, co-workers, compensation policies, irrational rules).

However, subsequent findings by other researchers lend some support to Herzberg's conclusions. Schriesheim (1978) found that the best predictors of prounion voting were critical attitudes about economic issues (pay, security, and company policy). Attitudes concerning noneconomic facets of the job (job autonomy, opportunity for accomplishment, variety) did not predict voting behavior so well. The correlation between satisfaction with economic issues and prounion voting was $-.74$, while the correlation with satisfaction on the noneconomic matters was only $-.38$.

Hamner and Smith (1978) found that the best predictors of union activity among work units were negative opinions about supervision.

A Gallup Poll survey (Gallup, 1978) asked people who described themselves as generally satisfied or dissatisfied with their jobs to give the reasons for their answers. Of those who described themselves as satisfied, more persons (39 percent) mentioned "enjoy my work" than any other reason. Those who said they were dissatisfied most frequently cited "poor wages" (34 percent). (However, 20 percent of the dissatisfied group did cite "boring job" as a factor causing their discontent.)

These studies and others suggest a model which defines four categories of satisfaction and dissatisfaction:

	Satisfied	Dissatisfied
Active	I	IV
Passive	II	III

The satisfied-dissatisfied dimension is defined by whether the person's job attitudes are generally positive or negative. The active-passive distinction refers to the frequency with which the attitude is aroused and actually becomes a force upon job behavior. A passive attitude more or less stays in the background of consciousness and is expressed only when external stimuli awaken it. For example, a person with a passive job attitude might be conscious of that attitude only when an interviewer asks about it, or when some unusually good or bad job incident occurs. An active attitude, on the other hand, is one that is more often intruding into consciousness; it has a stronger effect in filtering the perception of external stimuli and mediating the effects of stimuli on overt behavior.

We suspect that more workers would fall into Category II than any other. Such persons, if asked "On the whole, would you say that you are satisfied or dissatisfied with your present job?" would unhesitatingly answer, "Satisfied." That is, they have no serious complaints about the way the company or its officials treat them. They could see room for improvement, they might wish they had a more exciting job or prospects for a more dynamic career, but they'll take what they have and regard the intermittent periods of real involvement as a bonus. We suspect, furthermore, that workers over 35 would be disproportionately numbered in this group.

Those in Category III, the Passively Dissatisfied, represent a smaller group—a group that might actually respond "Satisfied" to a Gallup Poll, because they are not sufficiently involved with the attitude to offer even mild protest. It is a personal, somewhat private matter to them, arising from vague doubts about whether the job is as good as it ought to be.

Those in quadrant IV represent a small minority in the general labor force, although constituting a majority at times in specific organizations. They have no qualms about describing themselves as dissatisfied; they will voice their complaints, press grievances, lead the way into union activity, even engage in forms of sabotage. The reasons for their acute dissatisfaction stem not from unstimulating jobs (or at least not that alone), but because of what they regard as *inequities* in pay, benefits, supervision, or company policies.

The Actively Satisfied, in Quadrant I, represent those who genuinely enjoy what they do and are intensely involved in the job in a positive sense. Satisfaction is more than "making peace" with the job; it is a fairly characteristic *mood state* which is reflected in a number of ways, not the least of which is spreading that mood around them to some extent. These people are a sizable minority in the work force, dominated by professionals and skilled workers but well represented in all kinds of vocations. They are the ones who do the little extras, like helping others out in a pinch and working for the general welfare of the group, but not necessarily producing more in a narrowly quantitative sense.

We would not labor these distinctions too forcefully, nor do we suggest that every person unequivocally falls into only one category. We do suggest, however, that it is useful to regard some causes of job attitudes as affecting the activity versus passivity of the attitude rather than the overall positivity or negativity of the attitude. Certain job characteristics (such as task-intrinsic rewards) create active satisfaction; the absence of such factors is associated with passive job satisfaction or dissatisfaction.

CONSEQUENCES OF JOB SATISFACTION AND DISSATISFACTION

Turnover

Empirical studies have pretty well established that the satisfied worker is less likely than his dissatisfied counterpart to quit the job over a given period of time. The actual strength of the relationship between satisfaction and turnover varies considerably from one organization to another and from one time period to another. Even dissatisfied employees try to hold on to their jobs when labor mobility is low or downturns in the economy make alternative work hard to find. Conversely, even individuals who feel very positively about their present jobs can be tempted by prospects of better pay, career advancement, or other opportunities existing elsewhere. As we have already seen, the level of unemployment determines much of the variance in turnover in the labor force. On the whole, however, the satisfied tend to stay and the dissatisfied to leave. Those whom we have described as actively dissatisfied are the most likely to leave.

Absenteeism

The decision not to show up for work on a given day represents a temporary decision to quit. Thus, since turnover is inversely related to level of job satisfaction, so is absenteeism. However, just as the relationship between quit rate and job attitudes varies as a function of other complicating variables, so too the prediction of absence rate from job satisfaction must also take other factors into account. The relationship may be quite negligible when total absences for all reasons are computed. However, total absence figures are heavily weighted by long illnesses, which tend to produce large numbers of consecutive days absent. Job attitudes predict much better the *frequency* of absence—especially unexcused absence due to minor ailments—than they predict total days absent.

In some industries turnover and absenteeism account for a substantial share of total labor costs. The cost of recruiting and training new workers depends on a number of factors, including the conditions of the labor market and the length of time required to master job operations, but the figure would be in the hundreds of dollars even for most blue-collar jobs; it would be considerably higher for jobs using complex, highly specialized technology. In 1970, General Motors found that on Mondays or Fridays as many as 10 percent of production workers would be missing from work with no explanation; to avoid resultant unmanageable disruptions in the assembly line process, 2 extra workers would have to be retained for every 10 full-time jobs (Gooding, 1972). To the extent that increased job satisfaction would reduce such costs, job attitudes translate into dollars and cents.

Union Activity

As we noted above, ample evidence exists to document the relationship between job attitudes and various forms of union acitivity: signing a card in support of an election over union representation, attending meetings, supporting the union cause, and actually voting in a union. Active dissatisfaction, frequently stemming from perceptions of serious inequities pertaining to pay, supervision, and work conditions, seems to initiate and sustain these activities. Furthermore, as Schriesheim (1978) noted, these attitudes probably develop over a period of months or even years, and "it seems unlikely that they can be changed in the course of a brief election campaign" (p. 551).

Productivity?

Does increased job satisfaction lead to higher productivity? Does job dissatisfaction result in restriction of output? These haunting questions have nagged at managers and industrial psychologists alike for nearly half a century.

Popular opinion apparently views job attitudes as having a direct effect on performance. As recently as 1971, Gannon and Noon found in a survey of personnel officers that 61 percent believed happier workers to be more productive workers. Somehow it seems natural that more positive feelings about work would lead to greater output and higher quality. Unfortunately, four decades of research into this issue give little basis for drawing such a conclusion.

An exhaustive review of studies concerning the relationship between job satisfaction and job performance is beyond the scope of this chapter; the interested reader may consult a number of excellent reviews elsewhere (Herzberg et al., 1955; Brayfield & Crockett, 1955; Vroom, 1964). For illustrative purposes, however, let us cite the experiences of researchers at the Survey Research Center of the University of Michigan. In 1950, they began a large-scale investigation into the types of supervision that result in individual satisfaction and productivity. Their guiding assumption was that morale acted as an *intervening variable* between supervision and performance. That is, certain supervisory styles would affect job attitudes, and these, in turn, would affect performance. In their first study, which dealt with female clerical workers in an insurance company, the researchers succeeded in identifying certain supervisory styles which were reliably associated with higher-than-average productivity. To their surprise, however, the productive groups showed no greater job satisfaction than did the less-productive groups. Further studies of 300 railroad laborers and 6,000 workers at a tractor factory yielded the same findings. In none of these studies did satisfaction significantly predict performance; in fact, no single subcomponent of satisfaction—satisfaction with the job itself, with the company, with supervision, or with pay and promotion opportunities—accounted for any reliable share of the variance in productivity (Kahn, 1960).

Vroom's (1964) review of 20 studies disclosed only the barest of evidence supporting a direct link between job attitudes and performance. While the relationship was almost always positive, the median correlation between satisfaction and productivity was .14—meaning that job satisfaction, on the average, accounts for about 2 percent of the differences among the performance levels of individuals. Thus, while job attitudes bear a discriminable relationship with such behavior as turnover and absenteeism, the evidence suggests that a similarly strong relationship with performance is lacking.

Why are satisfaction and performance not closely related? Deficiencies in measures of performance might constitute one explanation. Many jobs do not lend themselves to objective, concrete performance measures, and subjective ratings by superiors or peers have to serve as surrogate measures. Such rating scales often exhibit unreliability and low levels of agreement among different raters. In fact, Vroom (1964) found that, in those studies using objective performance criteria, a slightly higher relationship between performance and satisfaction emerged. Nevertheless, the actual correlation was still very low.

A second explanation could be that, in many instances, individual performance level simply cannot vary to any great extent. A worker paced by an assembly line or other technological constraints can hardly work faster or harder than the total flow of work. On jobs which require coordination among several people, the fastest worker is apt to be limited by the pace of the slowest. In short, many work situations are pegged to a certain minimally acceptable performance level, with the consequence that administrators place no premium upon, or even discourage, a disruptingly higher level of performance by a few individuals.

More generally, however, the cumulative impact of empirical studies has forced organizational theorists and researchers to revise their thinking about the linkage between satisfaction and performance. That *some* linkage does exist is argued by the consistently positive, albeit very low, correlations between the two variables. The consensus of evidence and opinion on just how the two are connected is represented by Lawler and Porter's (1967) theoretical scheme (see Figure 11–5). In their model, satisfaction comes from rewards. Rewards, in turn, break down into two types: *extrinsic rewards*, such as salary increases and other reinforcements controlled by the organization; and *intrinsic rewards*, the gratifications that inhere in having done a job well or in having used one's abilities to solve a problem or meet some challenge. Rewards may or may not flow from performance in any predictable fashion, but intrinsic rewards are likely to be more closely connected to performance than are extrinsic rewards. The latter may accrue to employees in an across-the-board fashion; even if organization officials attempt to reward merit, they may find it difficult to measure performance in a reliable manner; and for many blue-collar jobs (as well as an increasing percentage of white-collar jobs), extrinsic benefits are determined by the union or by the government, leaving little flexibility in the reward system for recognizing the star performers. Finally, such determinants of job satisfaction as peer-group relations may be totally irrelevant to production.

Thus, we can see why there are many cases in which we ought not to expect much correlation between job satisfaction and performance.

Figure 11–5
The Lawler-Porter Model of the Relationship between Performance and Satisfaction

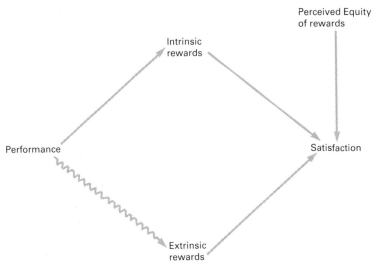

Adapted from "The Effect of Performance on Job Satisfaction" by E. E. Lawler III and L. W. Porter, *Industrial Relations*, 1967, 7, 20–28.

If a job holds little potential for intrinsic rewards, and if extrinsic rewards bear little relationship to individual performance level, the resultant connection between performance and satisfaction is weak and tenuous. In any case, whatever connection does exist is due, not to the causal effect of satisfaction on performance, but rather to the fidelity with which rewards follow performance.

Should an organization strive for a high positive relationship between satisfaction and performance? On the one hand, the answer is yes, since satisfied people tend to stay. If the performance-satisfaction connection is strong, the ones who stay will be the more productive employees, and turnover will be more likely to occur among the less-productive people. How, then, can organization officials make the connection stronger? The Lawler-Porter model indicates two methods: (1) correct the reward system so that top performers receive proportionately higher extrinsic rewards; and/or (2) modify the task so that it becomes capable of yielding intrinsic rewards for performance. The latter method amounts to a program of job enrichment.

On the other hand, we must remember that not all organizations have "performance problems." Some companies would be satisfied with routine, minimally acceptable individual performance if they could just count on having a sufficient number of people show up for work at the start of each shift. For such companies, a frontal assault on job attitude problems would clearly make more sense than would efforts to manipulate satisfactions through an indirect and discriminative strategy centered on the reward system.

Is There a Case for "Satisfaction Leads to Performance"?

Behavioral scientists seem to derive an almost perverse joy out of disproving conventional folk wisdom. The more that we can knock commonsense truisms into a cocked hat, the more we seem to justify our calling. Organizational psychologists in the last two decades have relentlessly hammered the "naive" belief that satisfied people ipso facto become better workers. Researchers have marshaled data from scores of studies demonstrating just how tenuous the empirical linkage is between job attitudes and productivity criteria.

If research evidence offers little support for the notion that "satisfaction leads to performance," why do legions of experienced managers persist in the belief? These practitioners cannot be easily dismissed as obtuse victims of their own delusions. Many of them have made successful careers from perceptive observations and good judgment. How do we square our findings with the fact that intelligent practitioners believe that greater satisfaction leads to better performance?

Organ (1977) has suggested that a key to resolving this paradox lies in the word *performance*. If by *performance* we mean something akin to quantity of output, creative solutions, or quality of craftmanship, then we are talking about the type of individual performance that industrial psychologists have, with some success, tried to measure. And for such measures, we agree with the generally accepted conclusion that satisfaction does not appear to determine—in any appreciable or straightforward fashion—the level of contribution.

But does the manager define *performance* solely in this manner? We suspect that managers have much more in mind when they use the term. They use the word as a blanket cover for a variety of *altruistic* or *citizenship behaviors* that include such "little things" as helping out a fellow employee with a job-related problem; helping a new worker learn the ropes and break in to the job; accepting temporary frustrations like a "good sport"; cooperating in carrying out changes pushed down from higher ranks; saying good things about the department, the organization, or the supervisor; "coming through in the clutch" (e.g., making a special effort to show up for work in extremely bad weather, even though there is a defensible excuse for staying home); keeping the workplace clean; acting as a "peacemaker" to defuse conflict between other workers—the list could go on and on. These things could be done "for" the supervisor, "for" the work group, "for" the organization, or simply "for" the individual's personal reasons. But they are behaviors quite valued by organization officials, and they are done to a great extent by some, less so by others, and almost not at all by more than a few. And the practicing manager apparently believes they will be done more often by satisfied people.

There are at least two different conceptual frameworks from social psychology that would support this belief. One, social exchange (Adams, 1965; Blau, 1964), asserts that people generally feel bound by the prescriptions of social justice and reciprocity. If people experience pleasurable moods on the job because of what their superiors have done for them, they feel an obligation to reciprocate. Increased productivity may represent the most obvious form of reciprocity, but many work situations make this impracticable. The individual seeking to reciprocate may not have the requisite skills for marked improvement in productivity; the person's work may depend so much on others' efforts or external constraints that greater effort toward productivity would be futile. Often, the individual rightly suspects that superiors would show more appreciation for other things: loyalty, compliance, "solid citizenship"—or all those "little things" we enumerated above.

Katz and Kahn (1966) have written convincingly on the importance of *nonprescribed*, spontaneous behaviors of people in organizations. No design of an organized system of roles can hope to anticipate all of the contingencies and urgencies that arise in day-to-day functioning. Consequently one cannot write into any job description the requirement that the incumbent respond in citizenship fashion to such urgencies. In fact, many such responses go unnoticed, or at the very least are difficult to measure and credit to a specific individual. Furthermore, it is not so much the isolated occasion of these responses but their *aggregative* or *cumulative* effect which lubricates the social machinery of organization units, making them more viable and effective. Thus, managers are doubly appreciative of consistent response as a "good soldier," since they can neither specify nor require many of such instances.

There are boundary conditions around the reciprocating motive. We feel the obligation to reciprocate only to the extent that others appear to have acted on their own volition in doing us a good turn. Moreover, we bristle at the thought that someone has tried to manipulate us, or strategically tried to put us under a sense of obligation for concealed, ulterior purposes. Overwhelming benefactions which we cannot hope to repay may arouse guilt or ego-defensive attitudes, leading us to suppress feelings of indebtedness.

Nonetheless, with due recognition to these boundary conditions, the layman's "gratitude" theory that satisfied people do more of certain valued behaviors has support from a respectable body of theory.

Bateman (1980) found empirical support as well. Supervisors of non-academic staff members of a university rated their subordinates on the extent to which they exhibited a variety of citizenship behaviors—e.g., keeping the workplace clean, helping out in a pinch, making sacrifices to work through temporary disruptions, complying with the rules, and so on. Bateman found a strong positive correlation between the ratings and the satisfaction reported by the employees.

A second body of literature that argues for a relationship between job attitudes and citizenship behaviors concerns the effects of generalized mood state. A series of studies (e.g., Levin & Isen, 1975; Isen, Clark & Schwartz, 1976) have found that an unexpected turn of good fortune disposes people to be more altruistic toward the plight of others. For example, individuals who receive a windfall in the form of finding a $5 bill on the sidewalk are subsequently more likely to help a passerby pick up dropped groceries or give a lift to a stranded hitch-hiker. It is conceivable that this tendency represents, in part, just another form of attaining equity: in this case "equity with the world" (Austin & Walster, 1975). But a study by Rosenhan, Underwood, and Moore (1974) suggests that something more is at work. They asked some third-grade boys and girls to think for one minute about a recent event that had made them happy; others to think about an event that made them sad; and a control group simply to count out loud to 30. Immediately afterward, each child was given 25 pennies. The researchers then gave the subjects an opportunity to put some of their pennies into a bag, ostensibly for their classmates who could not participate. Those children who had thought about a happy occasion donated more pennies than the ones who simply counted to 30, who in turn gave more than those who had ruminated over an unhappy experience. The authors concluded that *negative affect* (unhappiness or resentment) increases the psychological distance between the self and others, while *positive affect* (a good mood) *decreases* such distance. They described as "striking" the tendency of affect, whether positive or negative, to generalize from whatever caused it to other stimuli, notably other persons, in the immediate situation.

We suggest, then, that rank-and-file organization members characterized by frequent and enduring moods of positive affect will be more attuned to the needs of co-workers, superiors, and subordinates around them than will unhappy people. They will be more disposed to act altruistically in response to those needs that arise. These are the people we describe as "actively satisfied." Their job attitudes are not only positive but easily aroused and salient in their thinking processes; their sentiments about work are closely linked to their patterns of behaving and interacting with others. We suspect that the satisfaction of such people stems, in part, from the temperaments they bring to the job, but perhaps this type of mood can also be induced by the intrinsic pleasures of the job and other rewarding job experiences.

Contrariwise, those who fit the "actively dissatisfied" category—who chronically bear grudges and harbor resentments—would be least disposed to exhibit citizenship behaviors, except perhaps to comrades who seem to share their mood.

Unfortunately, many of the devices designed to tap job opinions do not readily permit an identification of those who fit the categories "actively satisfied" and "actively dissatisfied," as distinguished from their more passive and probably more numerous counterparts (an exception is Scott's (1967) semantic differential measure). While the measurement of job attitudes has become quite an industry in itself, the conceptual treatment of job satisfaction has not kept pace. At times we seem to have adopted a raw empirical stance regarding the construct—we paraphrase the old saw about intelligence, regarding job satisfaction as whatever is being measured by job satisfaction scales. Recently we have noted signs (e.g., Landy, 1978) of interest in a fresh theoretical approach that would link our knowledge of job satisfaction more securely to basic psychological processes. Such conceptual advances would give us a much sounder basis for devising and assessing programs to improve the quality of work life.

SUMMARY

Job satisfaction of participants is one criterion by which we evaluate organizations. The importance attached to this criterion derives from humanistic values, the effects of job experiences on mental and physical health, and the overall quality of life (although, for many persons, job experiences may not critically determine general life satisfaction).

General job satisfaction, as well as satisfaction toward specific facets of the job, is measured by standardized attitude or opinion surveys. Surveys repeatedly show that 75 to 85 percent or more of the country's labor force report being generally satisfied with the work they do. Data suggest that the current extent of satisfaction is slightly less than in the early 1960s; this decline appears to be largely attributable to the greater proportions of young workers in the labor force, and partly due to the increased level of educational attainments, which breeds higher expectations concerning the intrinsic appeal of work. The data do not support any notion of a "job alienation" crisis. Job satisfaction is highest among professional and managerial workers. Income, autonomy, intrinsic psychological rewards, and social gratification are major determinants of satisfaction; perceived inequities about pay, policies, working conditions, and supervisory treatment appear to be the major sources of active dissatisfaction.

Job attitudes predict with some reliability the extent of turnover, absenteeism, and union activity. Job satisfaction apparently does not exert much influence on conventional measures of performance. However, there is reason to believe that characteristic moods such as "active satisfaction" do influence a number of "citizenship behaviors" valued by organizational officials.

CONCEPTS TO REMEMBER

"spillover" hypothesis
"segmentalist" hypothesis
Gallup surveys of job
  satisfaction

job alienation thesis
Lawler-Porter model of
  satisfaction and performance
citizenship behaviors

QUESTIONS FOR DISCUSSION

1. What could be done by employers to prevent the "trough" in job satisfaction that seems to characterize younger workers? What could be done by schools and colleges?

2. If member job satisfaction is a criterion for evaluating organizations, should the satisfaction of subordinates also be a criterion for evaluating supervisors and managers? Defend your position.

3. What might cause a person to be actively rather than passively satisfied with a job? Actively versus passively dissatisfied?

4. Why do so many people believe "satisfaction causes performance"?

5. Is it fair to stockholders for profit-seeking organizations to try to increase member satisfaction *beyond* the point of demonstrable savings to the firm?

6. Identify from your own experience or observations a work situation where morale was very poor and one where it was very good. What seemed to be the major causes in each case?

CASE

Refer back to the case following Chapter 2. What light does the present chapter on job satisfaction shed on the arguments voiced by Max and Jack?

312

REFERENCES

Adams, J. S.   Inequity in social exchange. In L. Berkowitz (Ed.), *Advances in experimental social psychology* (Vol. 2). New York: Academic Press, 1965.

Austin, W., & Walster, E.   Equity with the world: Transrelational effects of equity and inequity. *Sociometry*, 1975, *38*, 474–496.

Bateman, T.   A longitudinal investigation of role overload and its relationships with work behaviors and job satisfaction. Unpublished doctoral dissertation, Indiana University Press, 1980.

Blau, P.   *Exchange and power in social life*. New York: John Wiley & Sons, 1964.

Brayfield, A. H., & Crockett, W. H.   Employee attitudes and employee performance. *Psychological Bulletin*, 1955, *52*, 396–424.

Bullock, R. P.   *Social factors related to job satisfaction*. Columbus: Bureau of Business Research, Ohio State University, 1952.

Gallup, G. H.   *The Gallup Poll*. New York: Random House, 1972.

Gallup, G. H.   *The Gallup Poll, 1972–77 (V. 1)*. Wilmington, Del.: Scholarly Resources, 1978.

Gannon, M. J., & Noon, J. P.   Management's critical deficiency. *Business Horizons*, 1971, *14*, 49–56.

Gellerman, S. W.   *Motivation and productivity*. New York: American Management Association, 1963.

Gooding, J.   *The job revolution*. New York: Walker, 1972.

Hamner, W. C., & Smith, F. J.   Work attitudes as predictors of unionization activity. *Journal of Applied Psychology*, 1978, *63*, 415–421.

Herzberg, F.   *Work and the nature of man*. Cleveland: World, 1966.

Herzberg, F., Mausner, B., Peterson, R., & Capwell, D.   *Job attitudes: Review of research and opinion*. Pittsburgh: Psychological Service of Pittsburgh, 1955.

Isen, A. M., Clark, M., & Schwartz, M. F.   Duration of the effect of good mood on helping: Footprints on the sands of time. *Journal of Personality and Social Psychology*, 1976, *34*, 385–393.

Jurgensen, C. E.   Job preferences (what makes a job good or bad?). *Journal of Applied Psychology*, 1978, *63*, 267–276.

Kabanoff, B.   Work and nonwork: A review of models, methods, and findings. *Psychological Bulletin*, 1980, *88*, 60–77.

Kahn, R. L.   Productivity and job satisfaction. *Personnel Psychology*, 1960, *13*, 275–287.

Katz, D., & Kahn, R. L.   *The social psychology of organizations*. New York: John Wiley & Sons, 1966.

Landy, F. J.   An opponent process theory of job satisfaction. *Journal of Applied Psychology*, 1978, *63*, 533–547.

Lawler, E. E., III, & Porter, L. W.   The effect of performance on job satisfaction. *Industrial Relations*, 1967, *7*, 20–28.

Levin, P. F., & Isen, A. M.   Further studies on the effect of feeling good on helping. *Sociometry*, 1975, *38*, 141–147.

Metzner, H., & Mann, F.   Employee attitudes and absences. *Personnel Psychology*, 1953, *6*, 467–485.

Organ, D. W.   A reappraisal and reinterpretation of the satisfaction-causes-performance hypothesis. *Academy of Management Review*, 1977, *2*, 46–53.

Palmore, E.   Predicting longevity: A follow-up controlling for age. *Gerontology*, Winter, 1969; pp. 103–108.

Roethlisberger, F. J., & Dickson, W. J.   *Management and the worker*. New York: Wiley Science Editions, 1964.

Rosenhan, D. L., Underwood, B., & Moore, B.   Affect moderates self-gratification and altruism. *Journal of Personality and Social Psychology*, 1974, *30*, 546–552.

Schriesheim, C.   Job satisfaction, attitudes toward unions, and voting in a union representation election. *Journal of Applied Psychology*, 1978, *63*, 548–552.

Scott, W. E., Jr.   The development of semantic differential scales as measures of "morale" *Personnel Psychology*, 1967, *20*, 179–198.

Seashore, S.   Group cohesiveness in the industrial work group. Ann Arbor: University of Michigan, Institute for Social Research, Survey Research Center, 1954.

Sheppard, H. L., & Herrick, N. Q.   *Where have all the robots gone?* New York: Free Press, 1972.

Smith, F., Roberts, K. H., & Hulin, C.   Ten year job satisfaction trends in a stable organization. *Academy of Management Journal*, 1976, *19*, 462–469.

Smith, F., Scott, K. D., & Hulin, C.   Trends in job-related attitudes of managerial and professional employees. *Academy of Management Journal*, 1977, *20*, 454–460.

Vroom, V. H.   *Work and motivation*. New York: John Wiley & Sons, 1964.

Walker, C. R., & Guest, R. H.   *The man on the assembly line*. Cambridge, Mass.: Harvard University Press, 1952.

Work in America.   Report of a Special Task Force to the Secretary of Health, Education, and Welfare. Cambridge, Mass.: MIT Press, 1973.

12

Group Formation and Development

Why and how do individuals become integrated into psychological groups?

What are the antecedents and the consequences of group cohesiveness?

How do groups differ in structure, and what are the effects of such differences?

In the previous chapters, a great deal of attention has been given to the individual within the organization. As you may recall, we often referred to the importance of the co-workers' and the supervisor's influence on the individual's performance or satisfaction level. That is, we know that the other people with whom a person interacts can greatly affect how that person thinks, feels, and acts. In this chapter we will examine individual-group relationships in organizations in order to better understand the importance of the group's impact on the individual's contribution to the organization.

GROUP MEMBERSHIP

Under the assumption that people join groups voluntarily, we need to ask, Why do people join groups? Of course, there are some task activities (for example, assembly line production) that can only be accomplished by groups. However, we often form groups when the task does not dictate group performance (for example, a study group or a travel group). A number of social and organizational psychologists have proposed theories of *interpersonal attraction* to explain the attractiveness or lack of attractiveness of others with whom we interact.

Thibaut and Kelley (1959) proposed the *exchange theory of attraction*. This theory explains group interaction in terms of the rewards and costs incurred by the participants in the interaction. A reward is any satisfaction gained from the relationship. Costs include the punishments resulting from the relationship, such as fatigue, boredom, anxiety, and fear of embarrassment.

According to the exchange theory of attraction, a person evaluates the outcomes from a relationship (current or prospective) by two standards. One of these standards is the *comparison level* (CL). The CL represents a level of outcomes which the person has become accustomed to receiving in many previous relationships. Someone who has been accorded high status and deference in various other groups will experience little satisfaction in a new group if not given the same status. On the other hand, someone accustomed to being "low man on the totem pole" in previous groups will be quite satisfied even to be a "member in good standing" in a new group. Whether the outcomes from a relationship exceed or fail to match the CL will largely determine the satisfaction with that relationship.

The *comparison level for alternatives* (CLalt) is the best level of outcomes a person could derive from presently available alternative relationships. No matter how good the outcomes from lunching with a particular group, if a person thinks they could be even better with a different group, then he will gravitate toward that other group. On the other hand, even if present outcomes are below the CL—and thus not satisfying—a person would stay with the present group if outcomes from other relationships would be even worse.

The relative magnitudes of present outcomes compared with CL and CLalt present several possible solutions:

1. If outcomes exceed *both* the CL and CLalt, a person will experience satisfaction with the relationship and remain in the relationship.
2. If outcomes exceed the CLalt but not the CL, a person will remain in the relationship but not be highly satisfied with it.
3. If outcomes exceed the CL but not the CLalt, a person will be satisfied but not particularly committed to the relationship.
4. If outcomes fall below both the CL and CLalt, the person will feel frustrated in the relationship and uncommitted to it.

Newcomb (1961) proposed a different theory of attractiveness. Drawing on the aphorism "Birds of a feather flock together," Newcomb argued that people with similar *attitudes* become attracted to one another. He postulates a "strain toward symmetry" in interpersonal relationships: individuals who have similar attitudes toward important issues are attracted to one another. This is illustrated by two studies conducted by Newcomb. In the first of these (1943), the effects of three years' attendance at Bennington College (a liberal arts college) were studied. The students whose values became more liberal, in accordance with the dominant campus climate, identified with others who were liberal. The students who did not depart from their initial conservative attitudes identified more closely with their predominantly conservative families.

Newcomb's later study (1961) examined the "acquaintance process" in a group of 17 students at the University of Michigan. These 17 students, who were initially strangers to one another, shared common living quarters for several months. Newcomb found that perceived similarity of attitudes was the most significant determinant of interpersonal attraction.

Newcomb's theory does not contradict Thibaut and Kelley's exchange theory. Rather, it suggests that attitudinal agreement and support are very important outcomes to people in a relationship.

Winch (1958) argues that attraction is explained by the *principle of complementarity* rather than by the principle of similarity. Under this theory, the adage "Opposites attract" refers to the fact that people with complementary needs and/or abilities are attracted to one another. This theory is really in harmony with the exchange theory offered by Newcomb. That is to say, social psychologists predict that people who have *similar attitudes but complementary needs and abilities* are more likely to find one another mutually rewarding than are people who do not possess these characteristics.

Festinger's (1954) *social comparison* theory argues that membership in a group is necessary because we all have a drive for self-evaluation, which is the need "to know that one's opinions are correct and to know precisely what one is and is not capable of doing" (p. 217). The individuals in the group "test" themselves against other members as a way of determining whether or not their opinions, ideas, and judgments correspond to social reality.

Finally, a *reinforcement model* of attraction (Byrne and Clore, 1970; Lott and Lott, 1960) argues that attraction to another person derives, in a general fashion, from experiencing reinforcement associated with that person. The reinforcement model is compatible with the other viewpoints described above; for example, to hear one's attitudes endorsed by another person represents a reinforcement from that person. Furthermore, liking someone who has a complementary skill or trait can also be interpreted in terms of reinforcement. If you have no interest in carburetors, fuel pumps, and other esoterica of automotive mechanics, you nonetheless will like someone who has those interests if that person helps you get your car started.

The reinforcement model, however, goes beyond the other theories by proposing that we like persons who simply are *associated* with reinforcing stimuli. Byrne (1971) notes that our affective response (recall from Chapter 6 that the affective or emotional response is one of the components of an attitude) to any object, including a person, can be conditioned by its temporal and spatial proximity to any other object which already elicits an affective response (see Figure 12–1). You can doubtless think of persons toward whom you have especially warm feelings because they were present as you watched your favorite team win a national championship on television, who were with you when you saw your final grade of A in accounting posted, or present when you found your expensive Rolex watch that you thought had been irretrievably lost. In such instances, the other person or persons did not administer or cause the reinforcement, but the affective

Figure 12–1
Liking for Another Person as a Function of Reinforcing Stimuli Associated with the Person

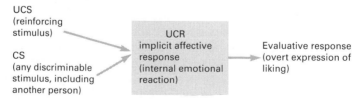

Note. CS, conditioned stimulus; UCS, unconditioned stimulus; UCR, unconditioned response.
Adapted from *The Attraction Paradigm* by D. Byrne (New York: Academic Press, 1971), p. 269.

Figure 12–2

According to a reinforcement model of attraction, liking for others is enhanced by experiencing any reinforcement (e.g., winning) in their presence.

response elicited by the reinforcement generalized to the surrounding stimuli. As Byrne (1971) concluded, "if a person is rewarded in the presence of others, he will develop positive attitudes toward them" (p. 291).

WHAT IS A GROUP?

From the above discussion on group membership, it may seem that all interaction with other people represents group behavior. However, it is useful to delimit somewhat our conception of a psychological group. When you ride on a bus, go to the movies, buy groceries, and so forth, you are probably not engaging in *psychological* group behavior as we conceive it. As Schein (1970) says, *"A psychological group is any number of people who (1) interact with one another, (2) are psychologically aware of one another, and (3) perceive themselves to be a group"* (p. 69). We would add a fourth criterion: *(4) A psychological group works toward a common goal.* The key words in the above definition are *interaction, awareness,* and *goal accomplishment.*

Collective action can involve as few as two people. In some respects everyone on earth is dependent upon everyone else, though such interdependencies often go unrecognized. Within a society, for example, people rely upon one another for military security, protection from disease, and economic stability. However, awareness of such mutual relationships is likely to be intense only when wars, epidemics, or depressions are a possibility. On other occasions, people scarcely realize that they are participating in a nationwide network of cooperative activity. Examples of nationwide groups of which we are probably aware include political groups, church memberships, business organizations, and social fraternities. Such awareness forces us to recognize the need to find a collective solution (for example, electing a particular person president) to the group's problems. We are probably more aware of and more active in smaller units, such as families, work groups, and friendship cliques, in which people generally employ face-to-face communication to coordinate their individual efforts. We refer to the larger groups as *secondary* groups and to the smaller groups or subgroups as *primary* groups.

In the work organization there are two types of primary groups. First, there are *formal* groups—that is, the groups to which a member is assigned as a part of the work role. Second, there are *informal* groups—that is, friendship groups, which develop on the basis of mutual attraction. It is important that a manager understand the psychology of the interaction in both types of groups, since both types influence member behavior.

The importance of the impact of informal groups on work behavior can be seen in Roy's (1961) descriptive studies of the culture and interaction patterns of work groups. In one of his studies, "Banana Time," Roy describes a small group of men engaged in exceedingly simple manual work operating a punch press. The entire task could be learned in about 15 minutes. While working in this small group, he noticed that several of the men had formed an informal group in order to reduce the boredom of the task. The men engaged in bantering and kidding, which Roy described as follows:

> What I saw at first, before I began to observe, was occasional flurries of horseplay so simple and unvarying in pattern and so childish in quality that they made no strong bid for attention. For example, Ike would regularly switch off the power at Sammy's machine whenever Sammy made a trip to the lavatory or the drinking fountain. Sammy invariably fell victim to the plot by making an attempt to operate his clicking hammer after returning to the shop. And, as the simple pattern went, this blind stumbling into the trap was always followed by indignation and reproach from Sammy, smirking satisfaction from Ike, and mild paternal scolding from George. My interest in this procedure was at first confined to wondering when Ike would weary of his tedious joke or when Sammy would learn to check his power switch before trying the hammer.

But, as I began to pay closer attention, as I began to develop familiarity with the communication system, the disconnected became connected, the nonsense made sense, the obscure became clear, and the silly actually funny. And as the content of the interaction took on more and more meaning, the interaction began to reveal structure [p. 161].

Group formation does not stop with the affiliation of members. Instead, groups develop over a moderately long period of time and probably never reach a completely stable structure. Tuckman (1965) identified four stages of group development. In the realm of group structure, the first stage is that of *testing and dependence (forming)*. The term *testing* refers to an attempt by group members to discover from the reactions of other group members what interpersonal behaviors are acceptable in the group. This is a period of establishing the "ground rules" both for task requirements (How much am I expected to do? Which rules are not enforced?) and for interpersonal relationships (Who has the real power? What behavior is OK?).

The second stage in the development of group structure is labeled *intragroup conflict (storming)*. Group members become hostile toward one another and/or toward the leader as a means of expressing their individuality and of resisting the formation of a group structure. During this stage, goals set by the leader may be ignored and resistance to task requirements is common.

The third stage described by Tuckman is a stage in which in-group feelings and close-knit relationships develop, new standards evolve, and new roles are adopted. In the task realm, intimate, personal opinions are expressed. This stage is commonly referred to as the *norming* stage of group development.

Finally, the group attains the fourth and final stage, in which interpersonal structure becomes the tool of task activities. Roles become flexible and functional, and group energy is channeled into the task. Structural issues have been resolved, and structure can now become supportive of task performance. This stage is labeled the *"performing"* stage of group development. The sequence of group development can be seen in Figure 12–3.

According to this model of group development, then, groups can be in any one of these four stages of development at any time. But the farther a group is from the performing stage, the longer it takes to become an effective work unit. Those of you who follow professional

Figure 12–3
Stages of Group Development

| Forming (selection) | Storming (power gathering) | Norming (rule making) | Performing | Goal accomplishment |

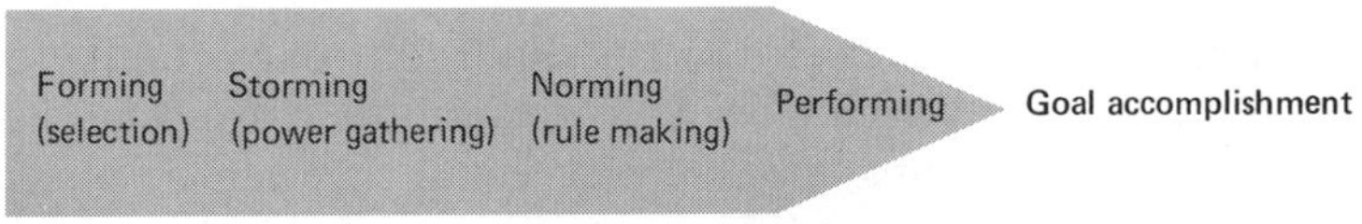

sports can see your favorite teams go through these four phases each season. First, new players are selected and old favorites are cut or traded. Then personality power plays and position power plays (for example, starting position versus reserve position) occur. Also, with each new season a fresh testing of the rules (for example, the rules governing dress, outside interests, and curfews) generally takes place. It is hoped that these first three stages will end prior to the start of the official season. If not, we generally find that the collective performance of the group is lower than expected.

PROPERTIES OF GROUPS

Every group has a unique "personality." This is due in part to the uniqueness of each member of the group, but it is also due to the *structure* of the group. When individuals join together for the first time and interact with one another, differences will develop among the members of the new group. Some persons exert more influence than others. Some have more prestige, some more influence, and some more knowledge. *Group structure* can be defined as the relatively stable pattern of relationships among members within a group. There are numerous dimensions of group structure along which the group becomes differentiated. Among the known dimensions of group structure, perhaps the most significant ones for group functioning are size, cohesiveness, communication, norms, and role assignments.

Size

The number of individuals in a group can determine the activity levels of individuals within the group. As you can imagine, the larger the number of people in a group, the less intimate the relationships. Sheer volume of interactions tends to make any concerted effort more difficult. The group leader is much more crucial in larger groups than in smaller groups.

The appropriate size of a group depends on the group's situation and purpose. Sargent and Williams (reported in Kolasa, 1969) found that a fact-finding group is probably most effective when it is composed of about 14 members. An executive or action-taking group functions best at a size of approximately seven members. According to Kolasa (1969), the validity of these figures is reinforced by information from many legislative bodies which indicates that the number of members in these two types of groups hovers close to the figures given.

Berelson and Steiner (1964) conclude that even-numbered groups show more disagreement than do odd-numbered groups because in even-numbered groups subgroups of equal size can be pitted against each other. Berelson and Steiner also conclude that the "perfect" group size is five because if subgroups develop in a group of five, a minority group of two is large enough to permit participation and individual development in support of a position, and a majority of three is strong enough to prevail, yet is not completely overwhelming.

Thelen (1949) proposed that groups achieve maximum *productivity* when they contain only as many members as are needed to supply the necessary task and interaction skills. Steiner (1972) has drawn a series of charts depicting relationships among group size and the potential and actual productivity of individual group members. These charts are shown in Figure 12–4.

Figure 12–4
Illustrative Curves Depicting Relationships among Group Size and Potential Productivity, Process Losses, Total Actual Productivity, and Mean Actual Productivity per Member.

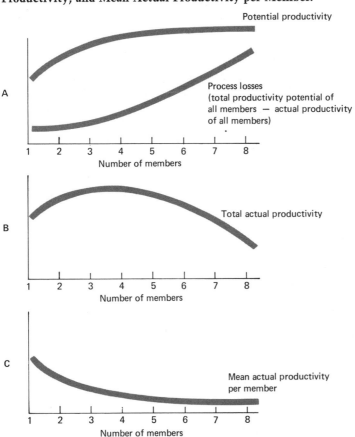

Source: From I. D. Steiner, *Group Processes and Productivity* (New York: Academic Press, 1972), p. 96.

The curves in Figure 12–4 show how group size might affect productivity. Although the curves are not intended to depict universal trends, they do indicate relationships that are postulated to prevail in many situations. As group size increases, potential productivity rises at a decelerating rate, whereas process losses (potential productivity minus actual productivity) increase at an accelerating rate. Given the relationships described in Figure 12–4B, actual productivity reaches its maximum when the group contains four or five members. Average productivity per member is greatest when an individual works alone on the task, and it declines as more people are added (Figure 12–4C). The most desirable group size depends upon whether one wishes to maximize total productivity or productivity per member.

Hellriegel and Slocum (1976) summarize the effects of size on group behavior, as shown in Table 12–1. Again we see that as the size of the group increases, the "personality" and the performance of the group shift.

Table 12–1
Some Possible Effects of Size on Groups

Dimensions	Group Size		
	2–7 Members	8–12 Members	13–16 Members
Leadership			
1. Demand on leader	Low	Moderate	High
2. Differences between leaders and members	Low	Low to moderate	Moderate to high
3. Direction of leader	Low	Low to moderate	Moderate to high
Members			
4. Tolerance of direction from leader	Low to high	Moderate high	high
5. Domination of group interaction by a few members	Low	Moderate to high	High
6. Inhibition in participation by ordinary members	Low	Moderate	High
Group processes			
7. Formalization of rules and procedures	Low	Low to moderate	Moderate to high
8. Time required for rendering decisions	Low to moderate	Moderate	Moderate to high
9. Tendency for subgroup to form	Low	Moderate to high	High

Source: From D. Hellriegel and J. W. Slocum, *Organizational Behavior: Contingency Views* (St. Paul: West Publishing, 1976), p. 166.

Cohesiveness

The cohesiveness of a group refers to the degree to which its members are attracted to the group, are motivated to remain in the group, and mutually influence one another. According to Shaw (1971), members of highly cohesive groups are more energetic in group activities, are less likely to be absent from group meetings, and are happy when the group succeeds and sad when it fails, whereas members of less cohesive groups are less concerned about the group's activities.

There is substantial evidence that both the quality and the quantity of group interactions are related to the cohesiveness of the group. Lott and Lott (1961) studied groups of from 6 to 10 friends from college student organizations representing religious, academic, athletic, and social activities, and compared them to groups of strangers who were taking classes together. As one would expect, the more cohesive groups had greater amounts of communication when they met to discuss a preassigned topic than did the "stranger" groups who were assigned the same topic, even though the opportunity for interaction was the same in both types of groups.

Studies have also shown that members of highly cohesive groups are more likely to conform to group pressures than are members of groups with little cohesiveness. Festinger, Schacter, and Back (1950), for example, found that members of cohesive groups in university housing units held uniform opinions and usually acted in conformity with group standards. They also found that pressures toward uniformity increased with increasing group cohesiveness.

Whether or not high cohesiveness affects productivity in a positive way depends to a great extent on the *goals* of the group. High cohesiveness in a work group may actually be associated with low productivity if the goals of the group are contrary to organizational and/or managerial goals. Roy (reported in Whyte, Dalton, Roy, Sayles, Collins, Miller, Strauss, Fuerstenberg, & Bavelas, 1955) described the pressures against deviance from the point of view of a person who had been the object of such group pressures. Roy's job was paid on a piece-rate basis; the more he produced, the more he earned. He reported:

> From my first to my last day at the plant I was subject to warnings and predictions concerning price cuts. Pressure was the heaviest from Joe Mucha, . . . who shared my job repertoire and kept a close eye on my production. On November 14, the day after my first attained quota, Joe Mucha advised: "Don't let it go over $1.25 an hour, or the time-study man will be right here! And they don't waste time, either! They watch the records like a hawk! I got ahead, so I took it easy for a couple of hours."
>
> Joe told me that he had made $10.01 yesterday and warned me not to go over $1.25 an hour. . . .
>
> Jack Starkey spoke to me after Joe left. "What's the matter? Are you

trying to upset the applecart?" Jack explained in a friendly manner that $10.50 was too much to turn in, even on an old job. "The turret-lathe men can turn in $1.35," said Jack, "but their rate is 90 cents, and our rate is 85 cents."

Jack warned me that the Methods Department could lower their prices on any job, old or new, by changing the fixture slightly or changing the size of the drill. According to Jack, a couple of operators . . . got to competing with each other to see how much they could turn out. They got up to $1.65 an hour, and the price was cut in half. And from then on, they had to run that job themselves, as none of the other operators would accept the job.

According to Jack, it would be all right for us to turn in $1.28 or $1.29 an hour, when it figured out that way, but it could not be all right to turn in $1.30 per hour.

Well, now I know the maximum is—$1.29 an hour.

Seashore (1954), in a study of 228 small work groups in a plant manufacturing heavy machinery, found that:

1. Productivity among workers was more uniform in highly cohesive groups than in groups with lower cohesion, suggesting that cohesion had a conformity effect (that is, reduced *within-group* variance).
2. Productivity differences among work groups were greater in high-cohesion groups than in low-cohesion groups (maximizing between-group variance).
3. High cohesiveness was associated with either high or low productivity, depending upon the degree to which members felt that management was supportive or threatening to them.

The cohesiveness of the group has an impact not only on the group's performance level but also on the group's level of satisfaction. Members of cohesive groups are generally better satisfied with the group than are members of noncohesive groups. Seashore found that workers in cohesive groups felt less tension and anxiety and were better able to cope with the pressures of work.

Other Consequences of Cohesion. The more cohesive a group, the greater the extent to which its members will differentiate insiders from outsiders (Dion, 1973). In other words, cohesiveness generates a collective feeling of "we-ness" as opposed to "they-ness." This condition, in turn, may lead to bias and hostility toward outsiders, especially other groups, and lead to active conflict between groups. Cohesive work groups are more likely to perceive other groups as inferior in some sense and are more likely to interpret the actions of outsiders in conspiratorial terms. Thus, to cohesive groups, seemingly insignificant management decisions or apparently trivial gestures by outsiders become invested with profound symbolism and are regarded as threats, disparagements, or inequity. The group's unified response may trigger a succession of moves and countermoves that escalate into psychological combat.

In addition, the more cohesive a work group is, the more likely are its members to resist changes that affect the structure, membership, or activities of the group. It has been documented that well-intentioned attempts by management to improve job motivation and satisfaction by redesigning jobs have backfired because job redesign broke up the group. Work group cohesion constitutes a strong conservative force in favor of the status quo.

Highly cohesive groups identify more strongly and immediately with their own product or function than the larger goal or purpose of the organization to which they belong. This creates a tendency toward *suboptimization:* the attempt to optimize at a lower level of a social system. Thus, a very cohesive product-development group will care much more about their success in designing and promoting that product—regardless of costs—than about the profit the product generates for the firm, a close-knit group in the credit department of a company may take such pride in its ability to minimize uncollectible receivables that it closes the door to potentially profitable accounts.

Obviously, then, a manager is well advised to consider the cohesion of a group before making important decisions that affect it. If the group is strongly cohesive, it is imperative that the manager try to anticipate the group's interpretation of, and response to, the contemplated action. Some degree of participation on the part of the group—ranging from informal consultation with informal leaders of the group to possibly full discussion with the assembled group—may be advisable. To paraphrase Congreve, hell hath no fury like that of a scorned cohesive work group.

Antecedents of Group Cohesion

Size. Smaller groups, other things being equal, have a greater likelihood of developing a cohesive structure. No magic number or formula can be offered, but the number seven, plus or minus two, often represents the cutoff point between members' conceptions of a single social entity and a larger conglomeration of distinct subgroups. Small size provides ease of interaction between all possible pairs of members and enables some participation by even the least assertive members. Beyond a certain number of persons, interaction stabilizes into cliques and interest groups, and participation in group activities becomes more disproportionately accounted for by a smaller number of group members.

External Threat. If there is one unifying force stronger than mutual affection, it is a commonly shared hatred or fear. Fraternities have a long tradition of bringing pledge class members closer together by capitalizing on their collective wrath toward the pledge trainer; it is rumored that drill sergeants utilize the same principle in basic training to weld a cohesive military group. Work groups are known to close ranks, not always for the most constructive purposes, in resistance to a disliked supervisor or in protest against a management perceived as arrogant and inequitable.

Homogeneity. In line with Newcomb's theory of interpersonal attraction, similarity of group members on certain psychological dimensions promotes cohesiveness. Not all dimensions of similarity, however, are equally important. Commonly held *values* seem to represent the most critical factor. For example, *ethnicity* frequently has served as a basis for work group cohesion; workers conscious of their Italian, Polish, Jewish or transplanted Appalachian heritage coalesce around shared values concerning religion, the family, the meaning of work, and tradition. Shared values, ideologies, and world views promote agreement on criteria for behavior in the group and purposes of group activities. On the other hand, homogeneity of sex, age, or educational attainments does not seem to be as critical for group cohesion (Seashore, 1954).

Isolation. The greater the extent to which a group is physically removed from others, the more cohesive it is likely to become. There are two explanations for this. First, the sheer cost of interacting with outsiders becomes prohibitive, in many instances, so that almost all communicative activities are directed internally. The recurrent interactions internal to the group establish a stable constellation of agreed-upon rules for behavior. Secondly, physical isolation promotes the psychological sense of distinction between outsiders and the members of the group *as a group.* Group members can more easily distort and stereotype their conceptions of outsiders as "different from us." The cohesion of mining crews is legendary, in large part due to their chronic isolation from others.

Patterns of Dependence. Groups are most likely to develop cohesion when the members are *reciprocally interdependent* upon each other for important outcomes. In other words, when each member has to count upon the contribution of the others for achieving personal ends and the individuals' outcomes are positively correlated, there is a strong impetus toward unifying interpersonal bonds.

Dependence patterns in work groups arise from two sources: (1) the reward system, and (2) the technology that shapes the work flow. *Independence,* at least in a relative sense, occurs when each member is rewarded only for individual efforts and productivity and when these efforts do not depend on others in any significant way. This attribute characterizes most classes in school and college; to a large extent it is true also of sales positions. Independence neither promotes nor retards cohesion.

Deutsch (1954) uses the term *contrient interdependence* to characterize groups in which any member's efforts to achieve personal outcomes interferes with or inhibits the efforts of others. Competitive reward systems, in which members receive rewards for doing better than others in the group, create such interdependence. Also, when group members each depend upon a fixed pool of scarce resources for doing their respective jobs, such interdependence arises. The more any one member draws upon that resource—an important power tool, an overloaded typist, a copying machine, or expensive raw material— the more difficult it becomes for other members to perform their tasks. Not suprisingly, contrient interdependence tends to inhibit cohesion in a work group.

Another pattern that militates against cohesion is *serial dependence,* a situation that exists when each group member is dependent upon the prior efforts of another member in the work flow, but not vice versa (see Figure 12–5. This pattern characterizes assembly line work: each worker "inherits" what another worker has performed and passed along, then performs new operations and passes the job along to the next worker. The obstacle this presents to cohesion is that it causes various forms of displaced aggression to ripple through the chain of task relationships. An operator who receives a sample of work botched by the previous worker has a more difficult job to do, and with no means of preventing this. Instead, the operator typically vents frustration by compounding the errors in the work sample and

Figure 12–5
Patterns of Dependence in Groups

A. Independence

B. Contrient interdependence

C. Serial dependence

D. Reciprocal interdependence

E Pooled interdependence

passing it along in the sequence to the next operator—who, of course, now has the same problem and may react in the same fashion. Each operator becomes a scapegoat for the next in line, with no system of checks and balances that would exist if workers were reciprocally dependent on each other.

The more the reward system and technology create a condition of reciprocal interdependence of members for task accomplishment and valued outcomes, the more likely that *promotive* acts will be socially reinforced and unifying relationships established.

Groups are characterized by *pooled interdependence* when each member can work largely independently of the others, but the rewards derived from their total efforts are positively correlated for the individual members. For example, each member of a bowling team contributes independently of the others; individual bowling is not directly influenced by how well or how poorly the others bowl. But each bowler's performance contributes to the team's total score, and the better each person bowls, the more likely is the team to share in winning the match. Pooled interdependence, like reciprocal interdependence, generally promotes cohesion.

Success. Whether or not cohesion makes a team a winner, winning usually leads to greater cohesion among team members (the 1970–72 Oakland Athletics and the 1977–78 New York Yankees representing apparent exceptions to the rule). Remember that reinforcement in the presence of others creates a conditioned response of liking those others. Groups that experience success—as defined by increased status, prestige, growth, victory, survival against the odds, or solving an important problem—experience an enhanced warmth toward each other. Success becomes a psychological prism which filters the interpersonal perceptions the members have of one another. By the same token, the aftermath of defeat or failure often features dissension within the group.

Communication Patterns

From the previous discussion, it is obvious that size and cohesiveness affect the possible communication patterns or "networks" that take place in groups. A *communication network* is defined as the flow of verbal and nonverbal messages exchanged between two or more group members. The volume, capacity, and distribution of communication networks all affect group functioning, especially in solving problems, distributing information, and organizing for work. Groups differ in the degree to which members are free to communicate with one another. For example, in a company it is necessary for a management trainee to go through proper channels in order to communicate with the company president.

In 1948, Bavelas suggested a procedure by which the complex structures found in large and rather formal organizations might be reduced to manageable size and studied in a simulated (laboratory) setting. Each of five persons could be given one fifth of the information needed to solve a problem, and the freedom of those individuals to communicate with one another could be restricted, messages flowing along only specified channels. Figure 12–6 shows several possible communication networks, each providing a different combination of open channels of communication. For example, in the *circle*, adjacent persons can talk directly with one another, but persons who are not adjacent to each other can establish contact only by having their messages relayed by one or more intermediaries.

Several interesting findings have been made in studies using these communication networks (Leavitt, 1951; Guetzkow, 1960). In general, a person who occupies a centralized position (for example, person A in the *wheel*) is more satisfied than are persons who occupy peripheral positions with limited communication facilities. Overall group satisfaction is greater in decentralized networks (for example,

Figure 12–6
Five-Person Communication Networks

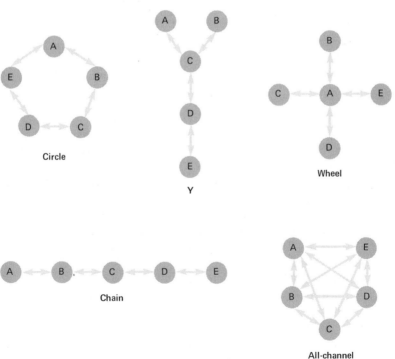

Note: Arrows depict direction messages flow. Lines denote target and sender of message.

the *all-channel) than in centralized networks (for example, the chain)* The study by Leavitt (1951) showed that centralized networks were most efficient for solving simple problems. The circle network was least efficient in terms of time required for solution, number of errors, and number of messages, whereas the Y, the wheel, and the chain were most efficient by these criteria.

Although these results may seem to lack "real-world" importance, many uses have been made of them. Sommer (1967), for example, has studied the restrictions which the environment can place on group interaction. He found that different seating patterns in groups were associated with different types of group atmosphere. In studies with students, different sections of the same class were experimentally scheduled for rooms with quite different physical layouts. It was found that students participated more in the discussions if a circular layout of chairs was used. They participated least in a setting with a series of parallel benches. These results suggest that the wheel and the Y are better for simple tasks and that the all-channel network is better for complex decision-making tasks.

These findings have enormous practical implications. They show that decisions customarily made by architects and interior designers have a marked effect on the social structures which emerge. Herman Miller, Inc., maker of expensive, high-quality office furniture, has used these findings in designing office layouts. After studying the existing communication flow in an office, Herman Miller designs both furniture and office layouts in such a way that the flow of communication is enhanced and the efficiency of the office is improved.

Norms and Goals

It is difficult to separate a group's activities from its goals, and most individuals are attracted to a group because they enjoy the group's activities and value its goals and purposes. The role of group goals in the foundation stage of group development has been well established. Sherif and Sherif (1953), for example, investigated group relations and found that, even after the experiments established intergroup hostility and tension, the members of the groups attempted to reestablish harmony and integration. In the initial stages of this study, members of a boys' summer camp were formed into five groups on the basis of selected activities. For approximately five days, situations were arranged in which it seemed that one group interfered with or frustrated another group. For example, following an athletic victory by the Bulldogs (Camp 1) over the Red Devils (Camp 2), both groups were invited to attend a party in the mess hall with the stated purpose of reducing intergroup conflict. However, it was arranged to have the Red Devils get to the mess hall first. There they found that half of the refreshments were battered and broken, whereas the other half was in good condition. The Red Devils were told to serve themselves and to leave the Bulldogs their share. Without comment, they chose the good half and carried it to their table. The reaction of the Bulldogs to this treatment was predictable. They called the Red Devils "pigs" and "bums" and generally lambasted them. When the intergroup conflict created by procedures of this sort had been firmly established, Sherif and Sherif attempted to reduce the conflict and to rearrange group boundaries by introducing common "supraordinate" goals. The most effective of these was a campwide softball game in which a team of best players from both groups was elected by the boys from the entire camp to compete with a team from a neighboring camp. Although the supraordinate goal approach did not completely eliminate the hostilities produced by the earlier manipulations, there was a significant reduction in the amount of hostility and tension and some realignment of group boundaries.

Thus we see that in the early stages of group development, conflict between groups leads to increased intragroup cohesiveness. One element of this cohesiveness is the "common enemy" phenomenon. However, Sherif and Sherif demonstrated that a common group goal can produce new group memberships and reduce hostilities.

Whereas group goals are the specification of desired objectives to be reached by a group, *group norms* are "shared ways of looking at the world,"—that is, the attitudes, values, and rules for member behavior. These norms result in agreed-upon standards of members and group behavior that are anticipated and expected by the members of the group. Once a standard or norm is established, there is pressure to adhere to it. McGrath (1964) says that group norms include: *(a)* a frame of reference for viewing relevant objects; *(b)* prescribed "right" attitudes or behavior toward those objects; *(c)* affective feelings about the rightness of these attitudes and about tolerance of norm violations; and *(d)* positive and negative sanctions by which proper behavior is rewarded and improper behavior is punished.

Festinger (1950) states that two factors are responsible for the emergence of group norms. First, groups provide individuals with a frame of reference for understanding their world, which they might lack alone. Second, some degree of uniformity of action is necessary if the group is to survive and move toward its goal. Control and coordination of norms regulating the conduct of members promote the continuity and success of the group.

Hackman (1976) specifies five major characteristics of group norms, which have been disclosed by studies in organizational settings.

1. *Norms are structural characteristics of groups which summarize and simplify group influence processes.* Thus, norms represent a

means of "shortcutting" the need to use specific stimuli (for example, the presence of a manager) on a continuous basis to control the behavior of individual group members. In this way, group norms obviate the need for power plays. Norms become an impersonal means for resolving differences.

2. *Norms apply only to behavior—not to private thoughts and feelings.* Although the origin of norms may be emotionally or attitudinally based, organizations can really only control behavioral compliance. *Private acceptance* of norms by individuals is an unnecessary requirement and can be detrimental to the survival of the group if it is imposed too rigidly.

3. *Norms are generally developed only for behaviors which are viewed as important by most group members.* Norms generally develop only for continuously required behavioral patterns which otherwise would have to be controlled by direct and continuous social influence.

4. *Norms usually develop gradually, but the process can be shortcutted if members so desire.* If, for some reason, group members decide that a particular norm is now desired, they may simply agree to institute such a norm suddenly by declaring that "from now on" the norm exists.

5. *Not all norms apply to everyone.* High-status members often have more freedom to deviate from the letter of a norm than do other people. This is why more employees with more seniority and more rank seemingly have more freedom to break rules, whereas other employees are forced to follow the letter of the law.

We would add this observation: *Norms may become dysfunctional* for group goals. One of the reasons why norms develop is to specify and coordinate behavior of group members in a way that contributes to achieving the group's goals. Norms, however, can become ends in themselves because of tradition and their symbolic nature, which imparts a sort of uniqueness to the group character. Long after the conditions which made specific norms useful have changed, the norms may endure—even to the point that they become counterproductive. A work group, for example, may protect itself from a hostile supervisor by insisting that members refrain from casual socializing during breaks or lunch hour with any "white-collar people." This dictum may continue in force when a new, more supportive, boss succeeds the old one. The new supervisor, in turn, may thus be alienated and prevented from demonstrating the support and consideration that would otherwise be offered. Even when group members wonder about the usefulness of a long-standing norm, they may be afraid to take the chance of violating it. Usually it is up to the leader to adjust the group's norms to new conditions.

Roles, Leaders, and Status

One of the general characteristics of all systems, including social systems, is that they develop from an undifferentiated state to one of increasing internal differentiation (Miller, 1965). Small groups in their formative stages show little differentiation: members perform in roughly similar fashions and share roughly equal status. Emergent norms apply to all in an across-the-board fashion. With the passage of time, it becomes apparent that some members can contribute more than others to group goals, that some are more psychologically committed to those goals, and that each member has a *comparative advantage* in carrying out some function for the group. As this occurs, *roles* develop. A role is a set of norms for the behavior of one or more but not all persons in the group. Roles consist of the norms that differentiate the behavioral expectations of members from one another.

In most groups, the first role to emerge is that of the *task specialist* or task leader (Bales, 1949). Whether the group be an intramural basketball team, a case study group, or a work group, it soon becomes clear that one person has the edge over the others in some skill or trait most relevant to the group's objective. That person is then looked to for advice, instructions, and decision making. Whether or not this selection is formalized by a title (e.g., captain or chairman) it is expected that the task leader will behave differently from the others. Furthermore, the leader is accorded an elevated *status* in the group because of his or her contributions. He or she will be accorded a deference not shown toward others and rightfully expected to receive a disproportionate share in the outcomes (honor, prestige, perquisites) realized by the group.

Sooner or later, the task specialist—despite the higher status—will "wear down" the morale of group members by continually exerting task pressure on people. Members may chafe at the restrictions and chores, especially if the rewards for group activity are only dimly seen in the distant future. In the meantime, the task leader imposes only costs. At this point a different kind of leader, the *human relations* or *maintenance specialist* emerges (Bales, 1949). The maintenance specialist bolsters morale—by smoothing over ruffled feathers, injecting a note of humor, taking a personal interest in members' feelings. Only rarely do the task and maintenance specialist roles coincide in the same person, since serving either role tends to conflict with the others. It is very difficult to play disciplinarian and humorist simultaneously. Those who have served as residence hall counselors are familiar with this dilemma: they are expected to serve as confidante and father confessor to troubled undergraduates, yet are also looked upon to impose law and order on residence hall life.

Depending upon the size and goals of the group, additional roles may crystallize. Often an *administrator role* is played, by someone other than the task leader, for the purpose of attending to routine "housekeeping" chores; one or more *emissary roles*, for representing or interlocking the group with outside groups, may emerge. With each role is associated a specialized set of behavioral prescriptions.

The status of a group member is determined, in part, by the importance of the role performed and his or her effectiveness in performing it. Also contributing to status in the group is the extent to which a person's behavior lives up to the general norms and values of the group. Even a "regular," who plays no special role, may earn the status of "member in good standing" by carefully observing the rules set by the group and serving in good spirit. At the bottom of the status hierarchy are two types: (1) those who lack the ability or resources to contribute in any significant way (e.g., the softball player who makes six errors per game and always pops up to the infield) and (2) those who continually violate group norms. The latter frequently are *marginal members* of the group; they might prefer to belong to a different group, from which they are for some reason excluded, and they look to this other *reference group* as a guide for beliefs and behavior. Strict adherence to the rules of the group to which they now belong would increase their costs above the comparison level for alternative courses of action (including "going it alone"); on the other hand, increased status in this present group, as a reward for following group norms, means relatively little to them.

Sociologists have found that, in the larger society, the middle classes hold most tenaciously to accepted conventions of social behavior. In small groups, the middle-status members are also the least likely to deviate from group norms. The "regulars" have more to lose (in lost status) from deviance and stand to gain more by compliance. The lower-status members, as we have argued, have the least to gain by compliance. On the other hand, high-status members—including the accepted leaders—may have what Hollander (1964) termed "idiosyncrasy credits." Their contributions to the group and "credits" for generally conforming to important group norms give them the latitude for occasionally departing from group norms, especially if they do so in a fashion that actually may benefit the group. In any case, they have the "political capital," as it were, for taking the risks of controversial actions. Political theorists in 1972 explained that President Nixon, precisely because of his unquestioned credits among conservative voters, could take the bold step of seeking a diplomatic breakthrough with the People's Republic of China. Similarly, leaders with ample credits are the only group members who can flout a group tradition that has become dysfunctional for group goals but still exerts a symbolic hold on members' behaviors.

SOCIALIZATION OF THE NEW GROUP MEMBER

In our discussion on the properties of groups, we referred to the need of groups to establish and abide by norms in order to maintain the high degree of group cohesion needed to accomplish group goals. Mann (1969) says that through the process of socialization the individual becomes a member of a group, endowed with the social attitudes and role behaviors appropriate to the particular group and the member's place in it. The individual adjusts to the group by learning behavior which meets with group approval. Socialization occurs throughout life, especially at transitional phases, such as entering school, taking a job, and getting married. Mann states:

> The aim of socialization is to induce the individual to conform willingly to the ways of society and the groups to which he belongs. On the surface it may appear that socialization and conformity are synonymous, that a person must be slavishly conventional in his behaviors and attitudes if he is to be an accepted member of the social group. This is true to some extent in childhood, but in adulthood, after the person learns what the social group expects of him, greater variation in behavior is not only permissible, but desirable. The rigid conformist is not regarded as an ideal product of socialization because he is unable to adjust to changing circumstances [p. 6].

Schein (1970) agrees. He says that the organizational group and the individual mutually attempt to influence each other in the early stages of interaction (when the socialization process occurs) for the purpose of establishing a workable "psychological contract." The process of socialization is a method by which a group establishes psychological contracts with its new members. Schein states:

> For example *organizational socialization* is one such concept [by which people establish psychological contracts], referring to the fact that organizations have goals, norms, values, preferred ways of doing things which are usually taught systematically, though not necessarily overtly, to all new members. Some of the norms can be thought of as *pivotal*, in the sense that adherence to them is a requirement of continued membership in the organization. For a manager it is required that he believe in the validity of the free enterprise system; for a professor, that he accept the canons of research and scholarship. Other organizational norms are *peripheral* in the sense that it is desirable for members to possess them but not essential. For example, for a manager it may be desirable from the point of view of the organization that he be a man, have certain political views, wear the right kind of clothes. . . . In thinking, about the adjustments of the individual to the organization, we can identify three types of possible adjustments, based on which sets of norms are adhered to. Acceptance of *neither* pivotal nor peripheral norms can be thought of as *"active rebellion"* and is likely to lead to voluntary or involuntary loss of membership. Acceptance of *both* pivotal and peripheral norms can be thought of as

"conformity" and is likely to lead to the loyal but uncreative *"organization man"* or *"bureaucrat."* Acceptance of pivotal norms but rejection of peripheral norms can be thought of as *"creative individualism"* [p. 79].

Schein's comments underscore the perennial dilemma of the individual versus the group. On the one hand, the individual needs and values the support which only a collective order can provide, and such orders can endure only by sacrificing some measure of individual autonomy. On the other hand, a group which enforces rigid uniformity and unthinking capitulation denies itself the full contribution of its members. The optimum resolution of this dilemma, as Schein argues, is to create conditions which make it possible for members to be creative individualists rather than conformists or rebels.

SUMMARY

Organizations of necessity create groups of interacting individuals. The attraction of the individual to the formal or informal group can be explained in terms of exchange concepts, attitudinal similarity, complementarity, social comparison processes, and conditioned reinforcement. Work groups vary in cohesiveness, or the extent to which members identify with the group and exert mutual influence on each other. Variables that influence cohesion are size, extent of isolation, external threat, the nature of dependence relationships among members, and the success of the group. Cohesive groups develop norms for behavior and distinct roles, including those of leadership, for members. The effect of cohesion on productivity depends on whether group norms support organizational and management goals. Cohesive groups are more prone to conflict with outsiders, more likely to resist change, and tend to identify more with the group's own success than with contribution to more general organizational goals. However, cohesion also adds substantially to members' job satisfaction and ability to copy with job stress.

CONCEPTS TO REMEMBER

comparison level	
comparison level for alternatives	Y
principle of complementarity	chain
reinforcement model of attraction	all channel
psychological group	supraordinate goal
primary groups	group norms
secondary groups	task specialist
forming	maintenance specialist
storming	marginal member
norming	reference group
performing	pivotal norms
group structure	peripheral norms
cohesiveness	active rebellion
dependence patterns	conformity
circle	creative individualism
wheel	idiosyncracy credits

QUESTIONS FOR DISCUSSION

1. What are the advantages to the *employing organization* of cohesive groups? disadvantages?

2. If a manager wanted to make a group more cohesive, what could the manager do to accomplish this?

3. What type of person is most likely to resist pressures by a group to conform?

4. Given what was discussed in the chapter, what predictions would you make about the relative cohesion of: basketball versus football teams; coal miners versus auto-assembly workers; textile workers in a small town versus home-office insurance workers in a metropolitan area; a submarine crew versus a naval shipyard maintenance unit?

REFERENCES

Bales, R. F.   *Interaction process analysis: A method for the study of small groups.* Reading, Mass.: Addison-Wesley, 1949.

Bavelas, A.   A mathematical model for group structure. *Applied Anthropology,* 1948, 7, 16–30.

340

Berelson, B., & Steiner, G. *Human behavior.* New York: Harcourt Brace Jovanovich, 1964.

Byrne, D. *The attraction paradigm.* New York: Academic Press, 1971.

Byrne, D., & Clore, G. L. A reinforcement model of evaluative responses. *Personality: An International Journal,* 1970, *1,* 103–128.

Deutsch, M. A theory of cooperation and competition. *Human Relations,* 1954, *7,* 114–140.

Dion, K. L. Cohesiveness as a determinant of ingroup-outgroup bias. *Journal of Personality and Social Psychology,* 1973, *28,* 163–171.

Festinger, L. Informal social communication. *Psychological Review,* 1950, *57,* 271–282.

Festinger, L. A theory of social comparison processes. *Human Relations,* 1954, *7,* 114–140.

Festinger, L., Schacter S., & Back, K. *Social pressures in informal groups.* New York: Harper & Row, 1950.

Guetzkow, H. Differentiation of roles in task-oriented groups. In D. Cartwright & A. Zander (Eds.), *Group dynamics: Research and theory.* Evanston, Ill.: Row-Peterson, 1960.

Hackman, J. R. Group influence on individuals. In M. P. Dunnette, *Handbook of industrial and organizational psychology.* Chicago: Rand McNally, 1976.

Hellriegel, D., & Slocum, J. W. *Organizational behavior: Contingency views.* St. Paul: West Publishing, 1976.

Hollander, E. P. *Leaders, groups, and influence.* New York: Oxford University Press, 1964.

Homans, G. C. *Social behavior: Its elementary forms.* New York: Harcourt Brace Jovanovich, 1961.

Kolasa, B. J. *Introduction to behavioral science for business.* New York: John Wiley & Sons, 1969.

Leavitt, H. J. Some effects of certain communication patterns on group performance. *Journal of Abnormal and Social Psychology,* 1951, *46,* 38–50.

Lott, A. J., & Lott, B. E. Group cohesiveness, communication level, and conformity. *Journal of Abnormal and Social Psychology,* 1961, *62,* 408–412.

Lott, B. E., & Lott, A. J. The formation of positive attitudes toward group members. *Journal of Abnormal and Social Psychology,* 1960, *61,* 297–300.

Mann, L. *Social psychology.* New York: John Wiley & Sons, 1969.

McGrath, J. E. *Social psychology: A brief introduction.* New York: Holt, Rinehart & Winston, 1964.

Miller, J. G. Living systems. *Behavioral Science,* 1965, *10,* 193–237.

Newcomb, T. *Personality and social change: Attitude formation in a student community.* New York: Holt, Rinehart & Winston, 1943.

Newcomb, T. *The acquaintance process.* New York: Holt, Rinehart & Winston, 1961.

Roy, D. Efficiency and "the fix": Informal intergroup relations in a piece-work machine shop. In S. M. Lipset and N. J. Smelser (Eds.), *The progress of a decade.* Englewood Cliffs, N.J.: Prentice-Hall, 1961.

Schein, E. *Organizational psychology* (2d ed.). © 1970. Reprinted by permission of Prentice-Hall, Inc., Englewood Cliffs, New Jersey.

Seashore, S. E. *Group cohesiveness in the industrial work group.* Ann Arbor: University of Michigan Press, 1954.

Shaw, M. E. *Group dynamics.* New York: McGraw-Hill, 1971.

Sherif, M., & Sherif, C. W. *Groups in harmony and tension.* New York: Harper & Row. 1953.

Sommer, R. Small group ecology. *Psychological Bulletin,* 1967, *67,* 145–152.

Steiner, I. D. *Group processes and productivity.* New York: Academic Press, 1972.

Thelen, H. A. Group dynamics in instruction: Principles of least group size. *School Review,* 1949, *57,* 139–148.

Thibaut, J. W., & Kelley, H. H. *The social psychology of groups.* New York: John Wiley & Sons, 1959.

Tuckman, B. W. Developmental sequence in small groups. *Psychological Bulletin,* 1965, *63,* 384–399.

Whyte, W. F., Dalton, M., Roy, D., Sayles, L., Collins, O., Miller, F., Strauss, G., Fuerstenberg, F., & Bavelas, A. *Money and motivation: An analysis of incentives in industry.* New York: Harper & Row, 1955.

Winch, R. F. Mate-selection: A study of complementary needs. New York: Harper & Row, 1958.

13

Groups at Work

How does the presence of others affect individual performance?

How do the problem solving and the decision making of groups differ from the problem solving and the decision making of individuals?

How does group structure affect group performance?

The study of the importance of group properties for individual performance was begun in the United States in the late 1920s. A series of studies which first gave an indication of how groups affect individual performance and satisfaction was conducted at the Hawthorne works of the Western Electric Company (Roethlisberger & Dickson, 1939). In the first study, conducted in the relay assembly test room of the plant, various changes were made in the working conditions of a group of five women. It was discovered that, regardless of the change introduced (increased lighting, decreased lighting, break time allocation, hours of work), productivity increased. This was true even after the 14th change, which eliminated all the benefits previously introduced and restored the status quo. The investigators concluded that the changes in productivity were due to the fact that, at each stage, the experimenters had sought the women's advice and that the women had been allowed to coalesce as a group. Thus, by expressing interest in the women, the experimenters had modified the situation in an unintended manner.

In a second study, a group of 14 men wired telephone banks for nine months while under constant observation. No changes were deliberately introduced. The level of work of the group was maintained at a very steady, less than maximum rate. Roethlisberger and Dickson concluded that this modest level of performance was maintained by a variety of social influences within the work group. The norm of 6,600 connections per day, though unstated, was understood by all. Members of the group who exceeded or failed to reach the group norms were ostracized by the other group members. When group norms supported high productivity (as in the relay assembly test room), productivity was generally higher than when the group norms discouraged high productivity (as in the bank-wiring room).

After the Hawthorne studies were published, behavioral scientists became very interested in how the group environment affected an individual's performance and satisfaction in a work setting. Managers and behavioral scientists have discovered two important phenomena related to the group's impact on the individual. First, there are apparently *psychological effects* of participating in group activities. Second, the *structure* of the group affects the level of output of individual members.

THE PSYCHOLOGICAL EFFECTS OF PARTICIPATION IN GROUPS: BEHAVIOR IN THE PRESENCE OF OTHERS

Several theories have been introduced to explain why and how the presence of other people affects our behavioral patterns.

Social Facilitation

One of the first studies in psychology (Triplett, 1897) investigated the manner in which an individual's performance is enhanced by the presence of others. Social facilitation deals with how an individual's task performance is affected by working in the presence of other individuals, but independently of them. Allport (1924) called this a coacting group situation and predicted that the presence of others has an energizing effect on ,the individual, causing him or her to work with greater intensity but to lose accuracy. Thus the conclusion was that the presence of other people increases motivation but reduces the quality of performance. How could this be?

Zajonc (1965), a psychologist at the University of Michigan, found the solution to this seemingly inconsistent statement. He postulated social facilitation theory as we know it today. *The presence of other people, either in a setting in which they act together or in front of an audience, impairs the learning of new responses but facilitates the performance of those previously learned.* This is true because the presence of other people has drive-producing properties which raise our awareness, arousal, or activation level. In a well-learned task this energizing effect enhances performances (for example, a new actor in a play), but in a poorly learned task the individual is "overenergized." That is, the new task (learning one's lines) has drive-producing properties, as does the presence of other people. Thus one tends to be "overaroused," and performance quality is therefore impaired. This is illustrated in Figure 13–1.

As the figure shows, a person's level of performance (*y*-axis) increases as external sources of stimulation are presented. For example, if you are driving on a long trip and start to get sleepy (fatigued), then the task has lost drive-arousal properties and fatigue is detrimental to performance. But if you turn on the radio or talk on the Citizen's Band radio, then the interaction with other people raises your arousal level, and highly productive performance (cue-attentive behavior) returns. In heavy traffic, driving in a new city, or driving for the first

Figure 13–1
The Effect of One's Level of Arousal on Performance

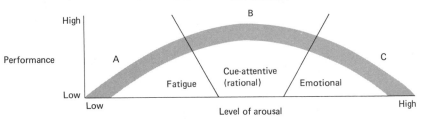

Figure 13–2

According to Zajonc's theory of social facilitation, the presence of coacting others will enhance performance on simple, structured, or well-learned tasks.

time, you are already highly aroused. The presence of several passengers or the noise of a radio may introduce additional arousal that causes a person to be nervous (emotional), and performance efficiency is reduced.

Based on social facilitation theory, Zajonc (1965) concludes that practical advice for students can be offered. "These results would lead us to discourage study groups and other togetherness aids in learning, while they would simultaneously lead us to encourage taking exams in large groups and preferably in the presence of large audiences. This latter advice applies only when the student has learned the material rather well. An audience during exams will otherwise have disastrous effects" (p. 27).

Social Comparison

The theory of social comparison (Festinger, 1954) postulates that we each have a drive to evaluate our opinions, abilities, and performance appropriateness. If we have a choice, we prefer to compare our responses against an objective standard (for example, in a footrace, a four-minute mile). Often, however, objective standards are not available, and under such circumstances we compare our responses to those of other people who are similar to ourselves. This theory, then, would predict that we are always comparing ourselves to others in our peer group to "see where we stand." The theory has great importance for performance feedback and reward administration.

Adams (1961) uses social comparison theory to explain how individuals compare their work efforts and work rewards to the work efforts and work rewards of an other. If this ratio, as depicted in Figure 13–3, is unequal, then dissatisfaction is likely to result.

Figure 13–3
Equity Relationship and Satisfaction

A. $$\frac{\text{Work rewards of person A}}{\text{Work input of person A}} = \frac{\text{Work rewards of person B}}{\text{Work input of person B}} =$$ A is satisfied with the treatment he is receiving from supervisor

B. $$\frac{\text{Work rewards of person A}}{\text{Work input of person A}} > \frac{\text{Work rewards of person B}}{\text{Work input of person B}} =$$ A is overpaid and will either increase input or rationalize overpayment

C. $$\frac{\text{Work rewards of person A}}{\text{Work input of person A}} < \frac{\text{Work rewards of person B}}{\text{Work input of person B}} =$$ A feels deprived and will leave, reduce inputs, change comparison, sabotage the work of B

We see from Figure 13–3 that perceived inequity (13–3B and 13–3C) can have a detrimental effect on performance and on the satisfaction of individual members in a group and thus on group productivity and morale. Obviously, the most problematic form of inequity for managers is some form of perceived underpayment or relative deprivation among some of his or her group members. Unfortunately, this type of inequity is also most prevalent. As Brickman and Campbell (1971) have noted, it may be virtually impossible to remove the perception of deprivation for all members of a given group. Yet, it may be possible to manage the consequences of perceived deprivation more effectively.

Some practical recommendations can be made from equity theory. First, it would seem that the entire process of performance evaluation must be made an explicit, public process, perhaps even with provision for some form of adjudication or appeal. At the very least, it would seem essential that managers make explicit exactly what inputs are valued for members of their group. Similarly, outcomes (rewards) within work groups should be overtly tied to work inputs.

DECISION-MAKING GROUPS

Problem Solving and Decision Making: Groups versus Individuals

An enormous amount of research has been addressed to the question of whether interacting groups make better decisions, generate more creativity, or solve problems better than an equivalent number of individuals working alone. The comparison has been made using various tasks that require logic, factual data, subjective judgments, and novel insights. The closest thing to a general conclusion one can offer is that groups as a whole *usually* perform better than the *average* of the individuals working alone, but seldom as well as the *best* individual effort of those working privately. Even this conclusion has to allow for a number of exceptions, and its validity depends somewhat on the nature of the task. The overriding impression from the research literature is the inconclusiveness of the comparison.

Maier (1973) argues that groups present both assets and liabilities for individuals engaged in problem solving. Among the assets are, first of all, a *greater pool of information* potentially available to each member. Furthermore, there is a *richer stimulus context* for triggering nonobvious associations. One person may offer an observation that is not in itself very compelling, but some peculiar choice of words or gestures may "ring a bell" in someone else's thinking that otherwise would have remained silent. Also, an interacting group is capable of bringing to light a *greater number of approaches* to an issue, which is especially valuable when the task is unstructured or ill defined. Individuals working alone often "get in a rut," working through the same sterile approach over and over again. Individuals in a group discussion are more apt to practice *covert rehearsal and critique* of their ideas than they would if working alone. Finally, members are more likely to feel *committed* to a solution or decision thrashed through in open forum. Everyone understands the trade-offs made, why certain approaches had to be rejected, and what the competing criteria were. Therefore, the conclusion is not so likely to be regarded as arbitrary as if the same decision were simply announced by an individual decision maker working alone.

On the other hand, not all of these assets may be realized, because other group processes act as liabilities. A few members—because of dominant personalities, aggressiveness, or status—may monopolize the discussion so that potential contributions of other members are not shared. Some members who have much to contribute may experience *evaluation apprehension* in a group setting; afraid of possible criticism or ridicule, they do not voice their ideas. A *win-lose psychology* may develop as members or subgroups become ego-involved with a particular alternative and thus care more about saving face and pushing their pet projects than arriving at a good solution. Finally, a group setting presents the chance that purely *social motives* will take precedence over a hardheaded task orientation. Much time may be spent in activities irrelevant to the task.

What we would like, obviously, is some means of capturing the assets of groups while minimizing their liabilities. Fortunately, recent work has identified two techniques for accomplishing this: they are the *nominal group technique* (Van de Ven & Delbecq, 1974) and the *delphi technique* (Dalkey, 1969).

The *nominal group technique* is a meeting in which a structured format is utilized for decision making among individuals seated around a table. This structured format proceeds as follows: *(a)* Individual members first silently and independently generate their ideas on a problem or a task in writing. *(b)* This period of silent writing is followed by a recorded round-robin procedure in which each group member (one at a time, in turn, around the table) presents one idea to the group without discussion. The ideas are summarized and written on a blackboard or a sheet of paper on the wall. *(c)* After all the individuals have presented their ideas, the recorded ideas are discussed for the purposes of clarification and evaluation. *(d)* The meeting concludes with a silent, independent vote on priorities through a rank ordering procedure or a rating procedure, depending upon the group's decision rule. The *group decision* is the pooled outcome of individual votes.

Unlike the interacting or nominal group technique processes, participants in the *delphi technique* are physically dispersed and do not meet face-to-face for group decision making. Although considerable variance exists in administering the delphi process, the basic approach is as follows: Only two iterations of questionnaires and feedback reports are used. First, a questionnaire designed to obtain information on a topic or problem is distributed by mail to a group of respondents who are anonymous to one another. The respondents independently generate their ideas in answering the questionnaire, which is then returned. The responses are then summarized into a feedback report and sent back to the respondent group along with a second questionnaire which is designed to probe more deeply into the ideas generated in response to the first questionnaire. After receiving the feedback report, the respondents independently evaluate it and answer the second set of questions. Typically, respondents are requested to vote independently on priority ideas included in the feedback report and to return their second replies, again by mail. Generally, a final summary and feedback report are then developed and mailed to the respondent group.

The comparisons between interacting groups, nominal groups, and the delphi method are shown in Table 13–1.

Table 13–1
Comparison of Qualitative Differences between Three Decision Processes Based upon Evaluations of Leaders and Group Participants

Dimension	Interacting Groups	Nominal Groups	Delphi Technique
Overall methodology	Unstructured face-to-face group meeting High flexibility High variability in behavior of groups	Structured face-to-face group meeting Low flexibility Low-variability in behavior of groups	Structured series of questionnaires and feedback reports Low-variability respondent behavior
Role orientation of groups	Socioemotional Group maintenance focus	Balanced focus on social maintenance and task role	Task-instrumental focus
Relative quantity of ideas	Low; focused "rut" effect	Higher; independent writing and hitchhiking round robin	High; isolated writing of ideas
Search behavior	Reactive search Short problem focus Task-avoidance tendency New social knowledge	Proactive search Extended problem focus High task centeredness New social and task knowledge	Proactive search Controlled problem focus High task centeredness New task knowledge
Normative behavior	Conformity pressures inherent in face-to-face discussions	Tolerance for non-conformity through independent search and choice activity	Freedom not to conform through isolated anonymity
Equality of participation	Member dominance in search, evaluation, and choice phases	Member equality in search and choice phases	Respondent equality in pooling of independent judgments
Method of problem solving	Person centered Smoothing over and withdrawal	Problem centered Confrontation and problem solving	Problem centered Majority rule of pooled independent judgments
Closure decision process	High lack of closure Low felt accomplishment	Low lack of closure High felt accomplishment	Low lack of closure Medium felt accomplishment
Resources utilized	Low administrative time and cost High participant time and cost	Medium administrative time, cost, preparation High participant time and cost	High administrative time, cost, preparation
Time to obtain group ideas	1½ hours	1½ hours	Five calendar months

Source: From "The Effectiveness of Nominal and Delphi Techniques in Interacting Group Decision Making Processes" by A. H. Van de Ven and A. L. Delbecq, *Academy of Management Journal*, 1974, 17, 618.

"Groupthink"

Irving Janis (1972) has pointed out that cohesiveness, while often a desirable attribute of groups, can nonetheless contribute to disastrous results when groups make decisions under pressure. If a decision-making group has developed a close-knit, clubby feeling of "we-ness," the group may become so preoccupied with *seeking consensus* on a course of action that critical thinking is suppressed. This constitutes the malady which he has labelled "groupthink." Its symptoms are:

1. *The illusion of invulnerability.* Members overemphasize the strengths of the group (and the organization to which it belongs) and gloss over possible weaknesses. Even to admit of weakness or liability is taboo because doing so would puncture the cozy consensus sought by the group. This bias leads the group to approve of risky actions about which each member acting along might have had serious reservations.

2. *Stereotypes.* The group distorts and oversimplifies its conceptions of competing or opposing groups, viewing them as weak, unprincipled, or ridiculous. The stated aims of outside groups or anticipated reactions of outsiders to the group's decision are dismissed as not worth considering.

3. *Assumption of morality.* The group assumes that its own ends and purposes are of such unquestioned morality that any means adopted to pursue those ends is justified. Thus, members feel no need to debate ethical issues.

4. *Rationalization.* Members attempt to explain away any negative feedback about the group's previous decisions or any information that does not square neatly with its emerging consensus. Unlike the rationalization employed by individuals in private thought as a defense mechanism to reduce dissonance, this is a shared and collectively structured form of rationalization that inhibits the group from looking critically at the pros and cons of a course of action.

5. *Self-censorship.* Because the group is cohesive and the members want to provide psychological support to each other, each person suppresses any doubts or disagreements with the enveloping consensus.

6. *Illusion of unanimity.* Because each member censors any privately held misgivings, each person mistakenly thinks he or she is the *only* one with doubts. Thus, no one wants to challenge what is erroneously considered to be a unanimous agreement.

7. *Mindguarding.* Much like a bodyguard who physically protects a leader, Janis observes that some members take it upon themselves to prevent negative feedback (e.g., from outside experts) from reaching the influential members of the group.

8. *Direct pressure.* In the rare instance that some member timidly injects a note of caution into the deliberations, the other members quickly respond in a manner that puts pressure on the deviant to step into line with the group's thinking.

The consequences of "groupthink" are that the group fails to examine the full set of options available, does not make use of expert knowledge that might be contributed by outsiders who are immune to the clubby "we-feeling," does not formulate contingency or backup plans, and generally suspends critical, hardheaded thinking. The decision then reached may result in disaster. Indeed, Janis has studied a number of decisions made by government policy groups that resulted in colossal blunders (such as the ill-fated Bay of Pigs invasion of Cuba, 1961), and in every instance he found an elaborate, documented pattern of "groupthink" leading up to such decisions. Thus, before the Bay of Pigs invasion, President John F. Kennedy assembled his cabinet and members of his White House staff to plan a strategy for dealing with Cuba. White House adviser Schlesinger noted:

> Had one senior advisor opposed the adventure [the invasion of Cuba], I believe Kennedy would have canceled it. No one spoke against it. . . . Our meetings took place in a curious atmosphere of assumed consensus. . . .
>
> In the months after the Bay of Pigs I bitterly reproached myself for having kept so silent during those crucial discussions in the Cabinet Room, though my feelings of guilt were tempered by the knowledge that a course of objection would have accomplished little save *to gain me a name as a nuisance.* I can only explain my failure to do no more than raise a few timid questions by reporting that one's impulse to blow the whistle on this nonsense was simply undone by the *circumstances of the discussion* [quoted in Janis, 1972, pp. 39–40].

Janis does not regard groupthink as an inevitable consequence of cohesion. From a careful study of policy-deliberating groups that avoided the dangers of unrestrained concurrence seeking, he recommends several measures for preventing groupthink. Groups should invite *outside experts*—individuals not susceptible to the "we-feeling" of insiders—to present their views. At each session, the group should appoint one or more of its members to play the role of *devil's advocate* and challenge the assumptions voiced by the others. The leader of the group should studiously refrain from disclosing his or her own views and, ideally, not attend some of the critical sessions to further remove inhibitions against expressing misgivings. Finally, after a decision has been reached, a *"last-chance" meeting* should be held for anyone to express any residual doubts or uncertainties.

Groups Shifts

Imagine that you are one of a five-person committee that meets on a monthly basis to decide expenditures on product development. One of the decisions to be reached at the next meeting concerns whether to invest $300,000 in bringing a radically new product to market. The product is so different in design and concept from existing products (either yours or competitors') that it is almost certain either to be a fantastic success—paying back its investment in under three years and achieving at least a 30 percent return on invested funds—or a total flop, resulting in an almost total waste of the money. Alternatively, the money can be spent on minor improvements of the existing product line, with a return on investment of at least 5 percent virtually certain, but no more than a 10 percent return. What probability of success for the new product, from 1 in 10 to 9 in 10, would you require before allocating the funds to that option?

Research (as reviewed by Myers & Lamm, 1976) has amply demonstrated that *after* discussion there will be a significant shift in the positions of the group members toward a more *extreme* position in the direction toward which they were already leaning. Suppose your own position before the discussion is that you would go with the new product if it presented a .4 chance of success. You really do not yet know the minimum acceptable odds demanded by the others, but they happen to be .6, .5, .4, and .3. The group as a whole, then, leans slightly to the risky side of the neutral point, prepared to invest in the new product if the chances of success are between .4 and .5. It can be predicted with near certainty that *after* group discussion, the following will result:

1. The group as a whole will accept greater risk with the new product than the prediscussion average would suggest; it will probably be willing to accept a probability of between .3 and .4.
2. Each individual member is likely to accept more risk after the decision than he or she would have beforehand, although the largest shift will occur among the initially more cautious members.

Why does this occur? One answer could be that group decision making produces a *diffusion of responsibility.* No one single person can be held accountable for any fiasco that might result. Blame can be shared with others; indeed, it may even be plausible to shift the blame entirely from oneself to the others. Research (e.g., Mynott & Sherman, 1975) does support the argument that collective decision making diminishes the individual's sense of accountability for negative outcomes.

But if diffusion of responsibility were the entire explanation, groups would *invariably* make riskier decisions than individuals, and this is not the case. If, as happens in a minority of the research instances, the prediscussion profile of the group members tilts toward *caution,* discussion leads to the group's becoming *more cautious.* The general principle that seems to hold is that on almost any *attitudinal dimension,* group discussion produces a shift toward greater extremity in the direction in which the members already lean. If the tilt is toward conservatism, group discussion results in a conservative shift.

Myers and Lamm (1976), who call this phenomenon *group polarization,* have attempted to account for the processes in group discussion which cause the shift. First of all, the prediscussion leaning of individual members creates a bias toward the kinds of information and arguments that will be generated in the discussion. If the modal tendency is toward risk, the preponderance of arguments voiced will be in support of risk. Moreover, not all of these arguments will have been initially available to all members. In effect, each person who leaned toward risk to begin with, and had some rationale for that leaning, hears new reasons in support of risk. Second, in the group discussion, *social comparison* processes are at work. If risk is a general cultural value in the context of the issue discussed, those who *thought* that they stood favorably on this cultural value realize that others stand even more favorably—i.e., are even more in favor of risk. The motivation to present oneself favorably in comparison to others induces a shift in opinion and attitude by those who were less extreme in the attitude. The model provided by the more extreme members (or those perceived as such) "releases" the less extreme members from some of their countervailing sentiments. Finally, the process of publicly verbalizing one's arguments on an attitudinal issue has a dissonance-producing effect. The more one finds oneself verbally supporting a position, the more one must believe that *is* one's true, strongly held position. The more people talk, the more they believe what they say. And this, according to Doris Kearns (1976), is the reason why Lyndon Johnson, as Senate majority leader, preferred *not* to deal with important policy issues in no-holds-barred open debates. He reasoned, intuitively but soundly, that such discussion leads to rigidity and polarization of attitudes within different groups.

The group shift phenomenon fits nicely with some of the observed instances of "groupthink," although group shift in its general sense is not necessarily either a desirable or an undesirable occurrence. If, however, group leaders wish to guard against its effects, one means of so doing is to require members to write down in advance both pro and con considerations on the issue and share all of these with each other. Also, as Myers and Lamm suggest, the "group leader might profitably suppress mention of initial preferences while eliciting relevant arguments."

THE IMPACT OF GROUP STRUCTURE ON INDIVIDUAL PERFOR-MANCE AND SATISFACTION

As we reported earlier in this chapter, not only does behavior in the presence of others have a psychological effect on task perfor-mance, but the *structure* of the group also tends to influence the sat-isfaction and performance of individual members. We now need to examine how several structural properties of groups can affect these variables. We have already discussed in Chapter 12, for example, how group size and communication patterns can affect productivity and satisfaction. Let us now look at other structural variables.

Unorganized versus Organized Group Structures

In 1941, French compared the behavior of individuals in unorga-nized and organized groups. The unorganized groups were college un-dergraduates assembled for the purpose of solving problems. The or-ganized groups were college athletic teams and community clubs. The groups were given problems to solve, some requiring intellectual ability and others requiring motor coordination. The problems in most cases were difficult or insolvable, even though they looked easy initially. One of the insolvable problems required group members to fill in rows and columns of numbers that would add across and down to a certain sum. One of the difficult problems required each member of a group to take one handle of a large cone-shaped apparatus and then, in unison with the other members, to roll a small ball up a path from the base to the top. French was interested in determining how the differently structured groups would respond to the frustration these tasks generated.

Once the previously unorganized groups failed to meet with initial success, they lost interest in the problems fairly rapidly and either worked in subgroups or talked about unrelated matters. The orga-nized groups had the greatest number of disruptions, however. They appeared more deeply frustrated, directed more aggression toward one another, and felt freer to express their feelings. Apparently, their com-mon interest in doing well as a team kept them focused on the prob-lem. French argued that the members of the organized groups were motivated not only by the demands of the experiment, but also by a group-shared desire to do well as a team.

Lambert and Lambert (1973) interpreted these and similar studies as showing both the advantages and the disadvantages of group orga-nization. The mutual attraction of group members sustains motiva-tion to succeed and keeps members functioning as a team. These characteristics can be of great advantage in many circumstances. But groups that are too well organized might suffer from a lack of flexi-bility in adjusting to frustration or danger. For example, in another part of French's experiments (1944), he put organized and unorganized groups to work on various tasks in separate rooms of an old building. After a short time, smoke began to fill the rooms, fire engine bells rang, and the rooms appeared to be on fire. When the students tried to get out, they found the doors locked. The organized groups were less effective at resolving this crisis dilemma, and fear and panic appeared to spread more rapidly among the organized groups.

Homogeneity-Heterogeneity of Group Membership

Most people would agree that, for many group activities, a variety of skills and knowledge is required. Therefore, the more heterogeneous a group, the more likely it is that the necessary abilities and information will be available and the more effective the group is likely to be. Triandis, Hall, and Ewen (1965) conducted experiments to investigate the relationship between the heterogeneity of group members and creativity. In one experiment, subjects were given 18 opinion questionnaires concerning such issues as war, socialized medicine, and immortality. Groups were then formed on the basis of responses to these scales, in such a way that they were either high, medium, or low on cognitive similarity. Experienced heterogeneous groups performed better than experienced homogeneous groups. Other studies (for example, Hoffman & Maier, 1961) have substantiated these findings.

Shaw (1971) summarizes our knowledge about the composition of groups along the homogeneity-heterogeneity dimension. He says that when a group is heterogeneous in terms of personality, opinions, abilities, skills, and perspectives, the probability is increased that the group as a whole will possess the characteristics necessary for efficient group performance. These findings about the advantages of a heterogeneous group have a direct relevance for managers. In the selection process, particular attention should be paid to the ability of the new member to complement the existing talents of the group. Unfortunately, we often tend to rate people who are like ourselves higher than we rate those who are unlike us. This tendency may be detrimental to the overall success of the group.

Competitively and Cooperatively Structured Groups

Deutsch (1949) created cooperative and competitive classroom atmospheres by varying the information students received about the class makeup and the grading system. The competitive classes were told that students would be ranked from the best to the worst in terms of skill in analysis and discussion, and that each student's final grade would be based on the average of his or her daily ratings. The cooperative classes were told that the major part of individual course grades would depend on the quality of discussion shown by the group as a whole. The results showed that the cooperative groups developed into psychological groups, whereas the competitive groups did not. The cooperative groups were rated as superior on ideas generated, communication among their members, interpretation of ideas, friendliness, and satisfaction of the members with the group performance.

On the basis of these and other findings, many management theorists believe that competition *among* groups is healthy but that competition *within* groups is not. However, because each of us is brought up differently and because competition plays a major part in our development, we find that learning to work together is sometimes difficult. One purpose of the socialization process, as you recall from our discussion in Chapter 12, is to develop group cohesiveness and cooperation.

Whereas most organizations do not demand total cooperation, or attempt to get it through coercion, cooperation within groups is often structured into the task and the compensation system. Many firms, such as Donnelly Mirror, Herman Miller, and Kaiser Aluminum, base their salary increases on group and organizationwide performance. Under this method, known as the Scanlon plan, a representative committee within the organization participates in determining how much of the quarterly profit or the profit from some other period to allocate to a bonus pool. Each individual's percentage of the bonus pool is based on his or her salary as a percentage of all the salaries paid by the company. For example, if an employee earned $10,000 a year and all the salaries paid by the company totaled $1,000,000, the employee would receive 1 percent of the bonus pool. Under this system, cooperation is encouraged and competition is discouraged.

Task Structure

As discussed in Chapter 8, task characteristics can have positive or negative motivational impacts on individuals. Research has shown that task assignments have the same impacts on groups. Moderately difficult group tasks are more stimulating and produce better-quality performance than do easier group tasks (Hackman, 1968). Changing the task structure to make it easier, and at the same time changing the interaction patterns of the individual members to make them less dependent on one another, has been shown to reduce morale. For example, Trist, Higgins, Pollock, and Murray (1963) investigated changes in group structures in the coal-mining industry. The coal-mining industry developed a more mechanized system of coal extraction which reduced overall cost, even though the labor cost per individual continually increased. In a study of the Durham coal mine,

Trist et al. described the replacement of the "room-and-pillar" method of coal extraction by the "longwall advance" method of coal extraction. In the room-and-pillar system, a small group of men worked autonomously, sharing all the requisite tasks among themselves and bargaining for the piece rate directly. The newly introduced system of longwall advance divided the component tasks into a number of specified roles. The coal-mining process became a three-phase cycle, whereby each successive shift was given different tasks to perform.

The small-group system was, in effect, replaced by a factory production line system. The work team became a unit of 30 to 40 men, but these men were not all in the mine or pit at the same time. Although the changes increased productivity per man, they drastically reduced the morale of the workers. A great deal of conflict developed among the shifts. The preceding shift was invariably accused of leaving work for the next shift.

Changes were made in the work-group assignments in order to reduce the negative effects created by the new task structure. The rigid system of fixed roles was abandoned, and a rule of "composite" working was introduced. Under composite working, each miner worked on whatever needed to be done next and the *team* took responsibility for the task as a whole. Morale was thus restored, and fighting among the teams was drastically reduced.

Participation in Group Decision Making

Participation in group decision making has been shown to be an effective way to increase the productivity and morale of work groups. Participation increases the accuracy of the information workers have about work practices and the group contingencies associated with those practices. Hackman and Lawler (1971) found that groups of workers who participated in the design of a new pay plan aimed at reducing absenteeism responded more quickly and more positively to the new plan than did other groups which had the same pay plan imposed on them by the company. One of the reasons the Scanlon plan has been successful is that it too is based on the principle of participation (see, for example, Frost, Wakeley, & Ruh, 1974).

The Hackman and Lawler (1971) study also pointed out a second advantage of participation. Participation was found to increase the degree to which members feel that they "own" their work practices and therefore to increase the likelihood that the group will develop a norm of support for those practices. Such norms provide a striking contrast to the "restrictive" output norm which often emerges when control is perceived to be exclusively under the control of management.

Hackman (1976) says that participative techniques can facilitate group effectiveness under three conditions:

1. The participation is relevant to the work itself. Participation in planning the company picnic, for example, will probably have little effect on work productivity.

2. The objective task and environmental contingencies in the work setting are actually supportive of more-effective performance. If participation causes the group members to discover that hard work leads only to more hard work, then productivity may decrease after participation.

3. The task structure and task activities are such that increased effort or a better work strategy can lead to higher work effectiveness. If the worker has little control over the amount of work which arrives at his or her station (for example, the assembly line phenomenon), then participation is not likely to change output significantly. (This issue is discussed further in our treatment of the "participation controversy" in Chapter 15.)

Integration of the Group with Other Groups in the Organization

In organizations, competition for scarce resources often causes conflict among groups. Likert (1961) has proposed a method for reducing such conflict by ensuring that groups are integrated into the organization (a larger group). Likert argues that the overlapping group memberships of a large organization constitute the major channel of influence within the organization. A group leader's role, in Likert's view, is to act as a "linking pin" among the various groups to which he or she belongs. The manager will have high power (as the supervisor) in some of these groups, will be a peer in other groups, and will be a subordinate in still other groups. These relationships are shown in Figure 13–4.

The goal of the linking pin agent is to ensure that the demands of the various groups are communicated and decided upon. The ease or difficulty of doing this will depend in part on the nature of the task and the norms of the groups with which the leader interacts.

As Smith (1973) argues, unacceptable pressure from above may easily produce a hierarchical system of integrated coalitions rather than Likert's model of linking pins extending both vertically and horizontally throughout the organization. Lawrence and Lorsch (1967) paid considerable attention to the process of organizational integration in the plastics industry. They found that integrative procedures in more-successful firms differed greatly from those used by less-successful firms. The plastics firms had a considerable need of integration since their structures were strongly differentiated in response to their var-

Figure 13–4
Likert's Linking Pin Model of an Organization

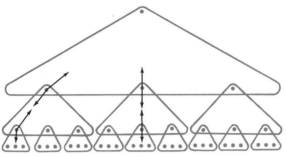

The arrows indicate the linking pin function.
Source: Taken from *New Patterns of Management* by R. Likert
(New York: McGraw-Hill, 1961), p. 369.

ied and changing environments. In addition to using the integrating procedures found in most organizations, such as hierarchy to resolve disputes and standardized reporting procedures, the firms also had one or more cross-functional liaison teams act as a separate department whose prime function was to achieve integration among the different groups in the organization.

The more-successful firms were found to differ from the less-successful ones in six ways. First, the integrating department contained individuals from the departments whose efforts it sought to integrate. In the less-successful organizations, the integrating department tended to be more similar to one or another of those departments and was therefore seen as partisan in disputes. Second, the integrator's power was seen as being based on technical expertise rather than on the integrator's position in the organization. Third, the integrator groups in the more successful firms felt that their own rewards were contingent on achieving integration, whereas such groups in the less-successful firms did not. Fourth, the managers in the more-successful firms felt that they had more influence in general than did the managers in the less-successful firms. Fifth, in the more-successful firms there was a close match between the levels at which information was available and the levels at which relevant disputes were involved. Finally, in the more-successful firms there was a greater tendency for conflicts to be resolved through constructive confrontation of differences, rather than through smoothing things over.

SUMMARY

The celebrated Hawthorne studies sensitized managers and behavioral scientists to the psychological effects of groups on individual task performance and to the effects of structure on performance of the groups as a whole. Studies of the phenomenon known as social facilitation suggest that the mere presence of others increases the arousal level of individuals working at a task; increased arousal may, in turn, have either a positive or a negative effect on performance. The presence of coacting others also leads to social comparisons by members concerning equity of treatment. Groups possess certain assets as well as liabilities for decision making and problem solving when compared to individuals working alone. When the liabilities outweigh the assets, the result can be "groupthink" or undesired shifts toward the extreme poles of attitudinal dimensions, especially attitudes about risk. The nominal group and delphi techniques have been proposed as formats for capitalizing on group assets while minimizing the effects of liabilities. Group performance is affected by the extent of structure of its organization, heterogeneity of membership, competitive versus cooperative reward orientation, and extent of participation in decision making. An important function of supervision is the vertical and horizontal linking of groups in a fashion that coordinates their activities and goals toward a common purpose.

CONCEPTS TO REMEMBER

Hawthorne studies	linking pin role of leader
social facilitation	assets and liabilities of group problem solving
social comparison	lem solving
groupthink	nominal group technique
group shift	delphi group technique

QUESTIONS FOR DISCUSSION

1. Use Zajonc's theory of social facilitation to formulate a possible explanation for *(a)* groupthink and *(b)* group shifts.
2. A few corporations in this country have experimented with the concept of "Office of the President," in which three persons share the role of chief executive officer. What do you anticipate would be the advantages and disadvantages of such a system?
3. Groups in organizations are of essentially two kinds: ongoing work groups and decision-making groups (such as committees and management teams). Discuss the implications of this distinction for *(a)* the desired level of cohesion, *(b)* the handling of conflict within the group, and *(c)* the role of the leader.

REFERENCES

Adams, J. S.   Wages in a clerical task. Unpublished study, General Electric Company, New York, 1961.

Allport, F. H.   *Social psychology.* Boston: Houghton Mifflin, 1924.

Brickman, P., & Campbell, D. T.   Hedonic relativism and planning the good society. In M. H. Appley (Ed.), *Adaptation-level theory: A symposium.* New York: Academic Press, 1971.

Dalkey, N. C.   *The delphi method: An experimental study of group opinions.* Santa Monica, Calif.: Rand Corporation, 1969.

Davis, J.   *Group performance.* Reading, Mass.: Addison-Wesley, 1969.

Deutsch, M.   A theory of cooperation and competition. *Human Relations,* 1949, *2,* 129–152.

Festinger, L.   A theory of social comparison processes. *Human Relations,* 1954, *7,* 114–140.

French, J. R. P.   The disruption and cohesion of groups. *Journal of Abnormal and Social Psychology,* 1941, *36,* 361–377.

French, J. R. P.   Organized and unorganized groups under fear and frustration. *University of Iowa Studies in Child Welfare,* 1944, *20,* 229–308.

Frost, C. F., Wakeley, J. H., & Ruh, R. A.   *The Scanlon Plan for organizational development.* East Lansing: Michigan State University Press, 1974.

Hackman, J. R.   Effects of task characteristics on group products. *Journal of Experimental Social Psychology,* 1968, *4,* 162–187.

Hackman, J. R.   Group influence on individuals. In M. D. Dunnette (Ed.), *Handbook of industrial and organizational psychology.* Chicago: Rand McNally, 1976.

Hackman, J. R., & Lawler, E. E.   Employee reactions to job characteristics. *Journal of Applied Psychology Monographs,* 1971, *55,* 259–286.

Hoffman, L. R. & Maier, N. R. F.   Quality and acceptance of problem solutions by members of homogeneous and heterogeneous groups. *Journal of Abnormal and Social Psychology,* 1961, *62,* 401–407.

Janis, I. L.   *Victims of groupthink.* Boston: Houghton Mifflin, 1972.

Kearns, D.   *Lyndon Johnson and the American dream.* New York: Signet, 1976.

Kriesberg, M.   Executives evaluate administrative conferences. *Advanced Management,* 1950, *15,* 15–17.

Lambert, W. W. & Lambert, W. E.   *Social psychology* (2d ed.). Englewood Cliffs, N.J.: Prentice-Hall, 1973.

Lawrence, P. R., & Lorsh, J. W.   Organizations and environment: Managing differentiation and integration. Cambridge, Mass.: Division of Research, Graduate School of Business, Harvard University, 1967.

Likert, R.   *New patterns of management.* New York: McGraw-Hill, 1961.

Maier, N. R. F.   *Psychology in industrial organizations* (4th ed.). Boston: Houghton Mifflin, 1973.

Myers, D. G., & Lamm, H.   The group polarization phenomenon. *Psychological Bulletin*, 1976, *83*, 602–627.

Mynatt, C., & Sherman, S. J.   Responsibility attribution in groups and individuals: A direct test of the diffusion of responsibility hypothesis. *Journal of Personality and Social Psychology*, 1975, *32*, 1111–1118.

Roethlisberger, F. J. & Dickson, W. J.   *Management and the worker*. Cambridge, Mass.: Harvard University Press, 1939.

Shaw, M. E.   *Group dynamics*. New York: McGraw-Hill, 1971.

Smith, P. B.   *Groups within organizations*. New York: Harper & Row, 1973.

Triandis, H. C., Hall, E. R., & Ewen, R. B.   Member heterogeneity and dyadic creativity. *Human Relations*, 1965, *18*, 33–55.

Triplett, N.   The dynamogenic factors in pacemaking and competition. *American Journal of Psychology*, 1897, *9*, 507–533.

Trist, E. L., Higgins, G., Pollock, H. E., & Murray, H. A.   *Organizational choice*. London: Tavistock, 1963.

Van de Ven, A. H., & Delbecq, A. L.   The effectiveness of nominal and delphi techniques in interacting group decision making processes. *Academy of Management Journal*, 1974, *17*, 605–621.

Zajonc, R. B.   Social facilitation. *Science*, 1965, *149*, 269–274.

14

Social Influence, Power, and Control in Organizations

What are the common misconceptions about control and influence in organizations?

What is the social exchange context of reciprocal influence patterns?

How and why do political processes operate in organizations?

What are the different bases for influence in organizations, and how do their dynamics vary from one another?

It is probably impossible for two or more people to interact without having each member of the group influence, and be influenced by, the others. This is not to say that anyone necessarily aims at influencing, or that the cumulative effect of everyone's influence accomplishes any constructive ends. The point is that a person's behavior is not merely a set of responses; the behavior also represents stimuli to which others respond. These may be discriminative stimuli (cues which signal the occasion for the responses of others) or reinforcing stimuli (cues which reinforce or punish the behavior of others).

Influence—the process by which one person affects the behavior of another person—is therefore not unique to formal organizations. Nor is *power*, which we define as the potential or the ability to influence. What sets organizations apart from informal interaction seems to be a higher degree of *control*—the influence of behavior to a predetermined range of responses. If I see you coming down the street and, knowing that I owe you $25, I duck into an alley, you have influenced my behavior, but you have not controlled it. If you arrange to dine with me at an expensive restaurant and leave your wallet at home, thus forcing me to pick up the tab, you have controlled my behavior. The exercise of control serves the function of limiting the variability of behavior.

MISCONCEPTIONS ABOUT CONTROL IN ORGANIZATION

Although everyone recognizes the fact of and the need for control in organizations, many people cling to oversimplified assumptions about the nature of control (and the related concepts *influence* and *power*). For example, many people seem to have the notion that power and control are concentrated in some physical location. Student activists in the late 1960s seemed to believe that they could capture control by seizing some office or quarantining some university official. That is, power and control were thought to be "located" or "hidden" somewhere. Even their more law-abiding comrades, who petitioned college presidents and deans, held the notion that control was personalized. Although the activists may have had a flair for the dramatic and certainly received their share of publicity, they did not find the control they were looking for, because control is diffused throughout an organization. This is not meant to imply that universities or any other organizations are inherently democratic, since democracy is defined by the distribution of formal authority, and formal authority is only one of the influence bases which contribute to control. Control is diffused because of the complex web of interdependence among parts of the system.

What about business corporations? Surely these efficient engines of enterprise must be tightly controlled by a handful of tough-minded titans at the top. Here again, however, we are misled by such symbols as organization charts, titles, and written descriptions of formal authority. Galbraith (1967) argues that control is broadly distributed throughout the middle layers of the business organization in what he calls the *technostructure*, the phalanx of engineers, scientists, accountants, and other professionals whose combined efforts shape the activity of the firm. As Galbraith notes, "Thus decision in the modern business enterprise is the product not of individuals but of groups. The groups are numerous, as often informal as formal, and subject to constant change in composition. . . . Effective participation is not closely related to rank in the formal hierarchy of the organization. This takes an effort of mind to grasp" (pp. 65–66).

The widely diffused nature of control in organizations has two consequences: (1) Organizations do not change or adapt easily or quickly. No one is more impressed with this fact than are university presidents and corporate chief executives, who are often amused at the amount of power attributed to them by casual observers. (2) On the other hand, organizations have a certain degree of protection against turbulence in the environment or the insanities of any one participant, however lofty the rank. Although we may sometimes moan, as frustrated participants, about the inertia and the hidebound resistance to change of the sprawling bureaucratic organization, we should also recognize that these characteristics afford us a measure of stability and predictability.

A second widespread misconception is that, for any organization, there is a fixed amount of control. One consequence of this assumption is the belief that, if some groups exert an increased degree of control, there must be a corresponding decrease in the amount of control exerted by other groups. Thus, if workers or staff gain more control, then managers sacrifice control. This erroneous belief has given rise to pointless controversies about the proper way to divide up the "influence pie."

However, the research conducted by Arnold Tannenbaum and his colleagues at the Survey Research Institute of the University of Michigan has shown that the *total amount of influence* in an organization can increase, and that what differentiates effective from ineffective plants, unions, and voluntary organizations is *not the distribution* of the influence pie, but the *total amount* of control exerted by all groups, officers and members alike. In fact, Tannenbaum's research demonstrated that the correlation between the control exerted by rank-and-file groups and the control exerted at the management levels is not negative, as we are accustomed to thinking, but positive: when lower-ranking groups exert more influence, the management and administrative echelons also exert more influence.[1]

---

[1] The reader should note that the Tannenbaum studies were correlational in nature. Thus, the effectiveness of the organization may have led to greater total and mutual influence, rather than the other way around.

Finally, there is the mistaken idea that influence and control are one-way processes. Campbell, Dunnette, Lawler, and Weick (1970) have called attention to the implicit assumption in discussions of management style that the "initiating behavior" of managers is unidirectional: "That is, managers are viewed as persons who initiate actions for others and whose interactions end once these directives are issued. . . .

"The basic factor that is missing from these unilateral views is that persons who interact undoubtedly behave as if relationships were reciprocal rather than unilateral" (p. 422).

The manager's action and words are indeed stimuli to which others respond. When an administrator makes a request, issues a directive, specifies a procedure, or clarifies a situation, subordinates typically respond in some manner. But that by no means ends the influence episode. The responses made by subordinates are also stimuli—stimuli which the manager cannot ignore. If the subordinates comply in good spirit, they strengthen the behavior of the manager; furthermore, they earn credits with the manager, credits that they may draw upon if they later seek favors, privileges, or special consideration. If regular compliance generates expected credits that are later "presented for payment," the manager is likely to feel an obligation to reciprocate. If subordinates show reluctance to comply, the manager is likely to amend his directive and/or to seek modification of procedures from his or her own superiors. The point, then, is that the manager can hardly hope to exert influence without displaying a willingness to be influenced in turn.

An experiment conducted by Lowin and Craig (1968) provides further proof of the reciprocal flow of influence and control. Applicants for a temporary office manager's job were asked to supervise the work of a Job Corps typist named Charlie while the recruiter stepped out, supposedly to attend a short meeting. Actually, Charlie was a stooge who played a predesigned role. For some applicants, Charlie worked conscientiously and competently; for other applicants, he deliberately appeared to be incompetent, casual, and frivolous about his work responsibilities. Charlie's behavior had an overwhelming impact on the applicant's leadership style. The "good" Charlie received special breaks, was allowed to make his own decisions about handling the typing work, and elicited friendly social reactions from the prospective supervisor. The "loser" Charlie got no privileges, was ordered to follow a rigid routine in his work, and got a cold shoulder when he tried to approach the applicant on a social basis.

David Mechanic (1962) has pointed out that lower-ranking participants in organizations often exert considerable influence by their control of access to information, persons, and resources. In addition, the members of the "lowerarchy," by making decisions which their superiors delegate because of lack of interest, often exert leverage over the implementation of organizational policies. Lower-ranking participants then actually *make* policy, and they have the power to sabotage the entire system if they perceive their rights to be in jeopardy.

THE SOCIAL EXCHANGE BASIS OF INFLUENCE

Influence and control in organizations occur in the context of a *social exchange* process. Gouldner (1960), Homans (1961), Blau (1964), and Adams (1965) have been the leading architects of theoretical frameworks of social exchange.

Gouldner (1960) proposed the *norm of reciprocity* as one which appears to apply in all cultures. According to this norm, when a person does something for you, you are obligated to return the favor in some way.

Homans (1961) contributed the concept of *distributive justice* as a rule governing social exchange. According to this rule, a person expects *profits* or outcomes in the exchange relation with another person to be proportionate to the *investments* made. Such investments can take the form of time, effort, foregone opportunities, deprivations, and the value placed by the person on any special skills or expertise that he or she provides. A person who receives less than distributive justice is likely to demonstrate emotional behavior, take aggressive action to restore justice, or if possible, withdraw from the relationship. In organizations withdrawal may take the form, not of physical withdrawal or resignation, but rather of an unwillingness to enter into informal exchanges not specifically required by the job definition. Such unwillingness can threaten the existence of an organization, since organizational survival hinges upon many informal, spontaneous social exchanges to meet exigencies (great or small) that can never be foreseen and provided for in organizational blueprints (Katz, 1964).

Blau (1964) developed the conceptual framework of social exchange theory. Blau defines social exchange as "voluntary actions of individuals that are motivated by the returns they are expected to bring and typically do in fact bring from others" (p. 91). Unlike the exchange of physical or economic goods and services, social exchange entails unspecified obligations—when one person does a good turn for another, "there is a general expectation of some future return [but] its exact nature is definitely *not* stipulated in advance" (p. 93). In other words, there always exists some ambiguity concerning the nature, value, and timing of the reciprocal obligations incurred in social exchange.

Antagonistic forces govern the timing of reciprocated favors. On the one hand, we generally feel uncomfortable about prolonged indebtedness to others. This may arise in part from guilt. In addition, indebtedness in social exchange narrows our flexibility and freedom. As long as we are indebted to a person, we are hard put to decline any reasonable service requested by that person, and the greater our indebtedness, the more difficult it is to refuse the request, regardless of the cost or inconvenience to us. Thus, we prefer to "even the account" as soon as possible, and to return favors sooner rather than later. However, Blau (1964) notes that "posthaste reciprocation of favors, which implies a refusal to stay indebted for a while and hence an insistence on a more businesslike relationship, is condemned as improper . . . social bonds are fortified by remaining obligated to others as well as by trusting them to discharge their obligations for considerable periods" (p. 99).

Due to special abilities, resources, or knowledge, some persons are in a position to do frequent good turns for other persons who are hard pressed to find ways to suitably repay them. It's not unlike the familiar dilemma of "what kind of Christmas gift do you get for someone who has everything." Yet the obligation to repay is real and remains. Therefore, those who have received generous benefactions may be able to reciprocate only by a generalized "willingness to comply" or by according their benefactor superior status in the group. "Willingness to comply with another's demands is a generic social reward, since the power it gives him is a generalized means, parallel to money, which can be used to attain a variety of ends. The power to command compliance is equivalent to credit, which a man can draw on in the future to obtain various benefits at the disposal of those obligated to him. . . . Exchange processes, then give rise to differentiation of power" (Blau, 1964, p. 22).

Adams (1965) added precision to social exchange concepts with his notion of equity. This notion resembles Homans's rule of distributive justice, except that it takes more factors into account, is more precise, and specifies various means of restoring equity to an inequitable relationship. Adams argues that whether or not we feel that we have been treated equitably (for example, whether we feel that we have been equitably compensated for our job efforts) does not depend solely on the absolute magnitude of our rewards or outcomes (such as wages, privileges, benefits, or status). We also take into account what we believe to be our relevant inputs: effort, training, seniority, productivity, or deprivations. But there is yet another factor that we take into account, namely the outcomes and inputs of one or more "comparison persons," such as colleagues, co-workers, friends, or some imaginary person whom we see as "justly treated" as defined by a standard ratio of outcomes to inputs. As we have noted in previous chapters, we implicitly compare the outcomes to oneself divided by one's inputs versus the outcomes and inputs of the comparison person:

$$\frac{Os}{Is} \text{ versus } \frac{Ocp}{Icp}$$

If the ratios are judged to be equal, we feel equitably treated. If the first ratio is greater than the second, we experience inequitable overpayment. We may restore equity by reducing our outcomes, increasing our inputs (so that we feel justified in receiving the outcomes), or seeing that the comparison person receives greater outcomes or is required to furnish fewer inputs. Or we can simply rationalize by altering our perceptions of one of the numerators or denominators. For example, we may decide that our original appraisal of our inputs was too modest: we really gave up more, or worked harder, or contributed things of greater value than we had assumed earlier. Adams suggests that when inequity in the form of overreward is experienced, we may be more likely to change our perceptions of various factors than to alter the actual outcomes we receive, especially if the inequity is not great.

If we experience inequity in the form of underpayment, we feel anger and resentment, as Homans predicted, and we try to increase the outcomes we receive, to decrease our inputs (for example, by reducing our work efforts or by keeping our resources to ourselves), to get others to increase their inputs, or to reduce the outcomes of others. Again, we may change our perceptions (for example, upgrade the estimate we place on certain benefits), but we will probably be more reluctant to change our perceptions of inequitable underreward than of inequitable overreward. Finally, we may terminate the relationship.

Adams's equity theory has stimulated considerable research, most of which has been applied to the study of work performance under conditions of inequitable overpayment or underpayment of wages. Clearly, the concepts involved have a broader range of applicability in social exchange, and they fit well with Blau's treatment of power and influence in the exchange process. For example, a superior who gives special rewards or privileges to subordinates probably generates feelings of inequitable overreward. One way in which the subordinates can restore equity is by manifesting an increased willingness to comply with the superior's requests, including those which go beyond the contractual requirements of the job or the official job description. The reverse is also true. When subordinates go "beyond the call of duty," for example, by willingly enduring unusual deprivation or by helping the boss out in a pinch, they can place the boss in a condition of inequitable overpayment. The boss can then restore equity by granting special breaks, increasing his or her own efforts, or agreeing to a lower level of future inputs by workers.

The fact that reciprocity and equity in social exchange involve *un-*

specified, imprecise obligations raises a number of issues. First of all, the parties in the social exchange relationship often differ in their subjective perceptions of the nature and the degree of the obligations incurred. Suppose that the boss gives the crew an unscheduled break. He or she might believe that this obligates the crew to work through lunch if the need should arise on that day or the next. The workers, however, might not see it that way. They might feel that the break only evened up the score because they had already been working up a head of steam. Or they might view the break as neutral in social exchange value, since past practice had made occasional unscheduled breaks something of a tradition—as Homans observes, "Precedents become rights"; or as Blau puts it, "Regular rewards create expectations that redefine the baseline in terms of which positive sanctions are distinguished from negative ones" (p. 117). In either case, the workers obviously feel no obligation to accede to the boss's request. Moreover, even if the workers do recognize the break as a social gift and are willing reciprocate in some fashion, they might regard the request as disproportionate to their debt. So they refuse to comply with the boss's request. Now the boss regards himself as inequitably treated, responds in anger and resentment (for example, enforcing rules to the hilt), and the crew now regard *themselves* as inequitably put upon; they attempt to restore equity by dragging their feet through the next morning's work ("reducing inputs"). This vicious circle would end only when one party stoically endured what it might regard as inequity simply in order to start the social exchange process anew on a more auspicious footing.

A study by Martin Patchen (1974) nicely illustrates the working of social exchange influence processes. Patchen, who was interested in identifying the relative importance of various factors in organizational decision making, conducted in-depth interviews in 11 firms with people who had been involved in 33 major purchase decisions. Patchen found that the most frequently mentioned characteristics of those judged to be most influential concerned the *extent to which a person would be affected* by the decision. In other words, organizational officials tended to defer to the party who had to "live with the consequences." This proved to be more important in determining influence than did such characteristics as expertise, official responsibility for making the decision, authority, or the capacity to reward and punish.

Patchen (1974) poses the question, Why should being affected by, and thus having a stake in a decision, give one strong influence on the outcomes? The answer, he suggests, basically boils down to the norm of reciprocity. Those who defer to the wishes of the party most affected by a decision can expect that on other decisions the latter will similarly defer to the parties most affected; "those who are affected by a decision usually have resources (their cooperation at least) which are relevant to the needs of others." Thus influence works by a quid pro quo process of accommodation. Patchen cites a passage by Raymond Bauer (1968) which underscores the importance of reciprocity:

> In any ongoing institution, the ability to get important things done is dependent upon maintaining a reservoir of goodwill. The person who fights every issue as though it were vital exhausts his resources including, most especially, the patience and goodwill of those on whom he has to depend to get things done. Therefore, it should be considered neither surprising nor immoral that, when an issue is of low salience, the sensible individual may use it to build goodwill for the future, or pay off past obligations, by going along with some individual for whom the issue is of high salience [Bauer, 1968, p. 17].

ORGANIZATIONAL POLITICS: THE PURSUIT AND USE OF POWER

Traditionally, the word *politics* has had an unsavory connotation among managers. Political explanations are invoked only when things do not go our way or when a fiasco results. We are prone to request that certain issues be "above politics." "Political appointments" implicitly refer to instances when undeserving people are promoted.

Yet politics is virtually inevitable in organizations, given what Pfeffer (1977) has aptly described as the *limits of rationality*. Rational decision making is limited by the extent to which an organization has operational goals, a consensus of preference orderings among members concerning those goals, and a consensus of opinion as to the means for achieving those goals. In fact, the publicly espoused goals of organizations seldom provide a basis for making operational decisions. A university may be said to exist in order to "disseminate knowledge, train tomorrow's leaders, and search for truth," but these laudable aims do not tell us whether to emphasize the humanities or professional schools or where the new student union building should be located. A private firm supposedly has as its goal to maximize return on stockholder investment, but in the here and now, no one can say which of an infinite array of options for uses of funds would really accomplish that end. Publicly stated abstract goals serve only to mask the reality that organizations serve a plurality of interests which are almost never totally consonant with each other (Yuchtman & Seashore, 1967). A corporation may well seek a favorable rate of return on investment, but simultaneously it may seek growth, prestige in the industry, leadership in development of new products, high morale among its work force, good relations with the community, maintenance of the corporate tradition, contributions to social goals, and so on. Perhaps each of these enterprises, in some distant future, may indirectly lead to a high rate of return, but they cannot all do so simultaneously, since in the short run emphasis on any one of those ends conflicts with one or more of the others. Pfeffer cites a study by Friedlander and Pickle (1968) which found negative or small correlations among measures of organizational effectiveness on seven different dimensions of goals or interests.

The major function of organizational politics, then, is to fill the void of vague, inoperable goals with goals that are specific and that can be translated into commitments. The greater the dissensus of preferences and interests, the greater the need for political process to effect a working agreement of commitments to action.

Furthermore, Pfeffer (1977) argues persuasively that the extent of the political process will also be determined by the degree of concentration of authority in the organization. If one person or a very small group can dictate a course of action regardless of the sentiments of others, there is no point in politics. On the other hand, the greater the interdependence and counterpower of various interest groups with respect to each other—i.e., the greater the extent to which different groups can impede or limit the actions of each other—the greater will be the role of organizational politics in the decision-making process.

To summarize, politics exists in organizations because of nonoperational goals, dissensus over concrete goals, and interdependence among interest groups in the organization.

Organizational Politics and the Individual

We have described the functions that politics serves for the organization as a system, but we should note the importance of the political process for the interests of the individual participant as well.

If groups in organizations are dependent upon each other, then even more so is any given individual dependent upon others. At the practical level, this means that the individual can accomplish virtually nothing of any importance without depending on the efforts of other people. To some extent, one can rely upon well-established working rules and procedures for ensuring this support, but only for the most routine and trivial operations. Inevitably, as one goes beyond this level of routine, one needs cooperative actions of a kind or degree not mandated by established policies. The only recourse then is to informal bases of influence that arise from negotiation, the implicit appeal to reciprocity for past favors, or a tacit acknowledgement of how each party stands to gain from a cooperative relationship. *The fundamental motive basis for the individual to participate in the political process is the management of dependency relationships* (Kotter, 1977).

Individuals also need a political base for self-defense. Decisions in organizations never affect everyone equally; quite often, they benefit some persons very much while severely damaging the interests and welfare of others. The implications of a decision may result in diminished resources, lower status, more onerous constraints, harder work, or even loss of job for some individuals. When decisions have to cut in such a fashion, the ones with little or no clout will be the ones sacrificed. Those who have some power will have a better chance of defending themselves.

Finally, the political process offers to some individuals an intrinsic appeal. We noted in Chapter 9 that some people have a strong need for power. The ability to exert influence on the social environment can satisfy the deeper underlying motive of experiencing a sense of competence. Schein (1978) believes that those people who eventually gravitate in their careers toward managerial roles are those who discover that they actually enjoy the wheeling and dealing, the working out of compromises, the horse-trading, the bluffing and calling of bluffs, and the coalition building that are required in order to be effective in such roles. Maccoby (1976) contends that the leaders of corporations in high-technology, dynamic industries are individuals who are, at heart, "gamesmen," motivated by the desire to win the game defined by the political process which leads to policy decisions.

The Political Process

Tushman and Nadler (1980) have provided an overview of the process by which politics contributes to organizational decision making. First of all, they view organizations as *networks* of individuals who interact with one another on a stable basis. A network may evolve simply because the flow of work requires a distinct patterning of interaction, or it may develop because of shared values, interests, attitudes, or reciprocal interpersonal attraction. For example, an attorney in the legal department of an insurance company may belong to a network of four colleagues in his department but also be a member of a network with half a dozen young managers in other departments who share his conservative political views; simultaneously, he may belong to a network that includes some older and higher-level executives who, like himself, would prefer to see a more growth-oriented posture in the company. An individual may belong to any number of networks, but individuals will vary greatly in the number of networks in which they are involved. Furthermore, within any one network, individuals vary in terms of the frequency with which others initiate interaction with them—some people are "stars" frequently sought out by the others. Tushman and Nadler call these overlapping networks *cliques* and consider them the "basic building blocks of political organizations, much as the formal work group or subunit is seen as the major building block of formal organizations" (p. 182).

A clique, by itself, is usually too small to exert much control over major issues concerning the organization. Instead, cliques come together in *coalitions* to influence the outcome of major decisions. Coalitions are not as stable as cliques; they develop around specific issues that arise. Once the issue has been decided, the coalition may dissolve; the cliques may realign themselves in a different fashion when a totally different issue comes to the fore. However, some cliques may constitute an *axis* because they recurrently form coalitions that are capable of determining organizational policy, commitments, and plans.

The purpose of the coalition is to pursue a cooperative strategy so as to resolve an issue to the advantage of the affected cliques. However, the constituent cliques will not have perfectly correlated preferences for outcomes, nor will all cliques stand to gain equally from an outcome. The clique most affected will have to offer some inducements to others in order to form a coalition. Obviously, then, that clique will seek the smallest possible coalition that is sufficiently strong to dictate the outcome—too many cliques in a coalition will result in diluting the gains or an excessively costly set of compensating "debts." Equally obviously, then, a clique will prefer powerful or influential cliques to form coalitions, since the more powerful the partners, the fewer are needed. However, a powerful ally will be in a position to extract a high price for cooperation.

The analysis of political power seems to turn inward upon itself. A clique that is best able to dictate policy is one that is an attractive ally in coalitions and able to extract concessions from those seeking such alliances. But in order to accomplish this, the clique must be powerful to begin with. How do we account for such power at the clique level?

The Strategic Contingencies Model of Power

Crozier (1964), a student of bureaucratic organizations in France, came upon an apparent anomaly in one French factory. The maintenance engineers, although characterized by modest formal rank and authority, exerted considerable influence in the organization. Analysis revealed that the only critical area of uncertainty and unpredictability facing plant personnel was the periodic breakdown of machinery. The maintenance engineers were the only members who could cope with this uncertainty; consequently they possessed power vastly disproportionate to their hierarchical station.

Hickson, Hinings, Lee, Schneck, and Pennings (1971) have proposed a general theory to account for Crozier's example. They suggest that power in an organization accrues to those groups who have the ability or expertise to cope with *strategic contingencies* that pose uncertainty. For example, if the volume of business of a contracting firm depends heavily on government orders, those who have important contacts with officials in the relevant government departments will have considerable power in the firm. If an organization is highly vulnerable to lawsuits (as an insurance company or publisher of periodicals might be), legal officers' sentiments will carry weight. If a college or university depends to a great extent on external funding, then both fund raisers and faculty adept at bringing in grants will have more power than others.

Groups that can reduce uncertainty for others, then, become natural candidates for alliances. Dominant coalitions tend to include those networks that are capable of handling the pressing problems of the day. On the other hand, groups that handle only routine operations or work in areas outside the mainstream of the critical problems facing an organization will have a much less decisive voice on major policies and decisions.

Individual Clout

Our analysis has viewed the political process from the perspective of networks or cliques and coalitions. Yet, in the ultimate sense, individuals do the sensing, calculating, and communicating which maintain this process. And even the casual observer of organizations knows that individuals differ in informal power to an extent not accounted for by rank. What accounts for such differences?

The strategic contingencies hypothesis suggests, first, that individuals who are members of units that are highly visible, in the mainstream of the organization's strategic operations, will be in a better position than others to wield influence. Second, those individuals who belong to several overlapping networks of strategic groups will exert more influence than those who belong to only one. Recall that our definition of a network or clique is not at all synonymous with a formally designated work unit. A person's patterned interactions may include, not only the department in which he or she is housed, but others outside, above, and below the group. Power accrues to those individuals who have easy access to various networks, because those persons will typically play an important catalytic role in forming coalitions between these cliques. These persons, by dint of their ability to "plug" into several intersecting grapevines, will be sensitive to areas of mutual concern and interest to various groups. Thus, a manager—in order to "bring home the bacon" for the group—must cultivate entrée into networks outside the department and be more sensitive to external power than internal formal authority.

Rosabeth Kanter's (1977) sociological study of a large multinational company found that executives there equated *credibility* with "competence plus power."

> People with credibility were listened to, their phone calls were answered first, because they were assumed to have something important to say. People with credibility had room to make more mistakes and could take greater risks because it was believed that they would produce. . . . They could back up their words with actions [p. 169].

Kanter also detected a common syndrome among managers who lacked such credibility, that is, lacked external clout. Such officials, as if to compensate for having no real power, overemphasized their authority over subordinates. They kept a restrictive rein over their departments, allowing little latitude for independent action and exercising close supervision. Also, such managers exhibited "rules-mindedness" in the extreme. Fearing the ambiguity or flexibility which would give the advantage to those with informal clout, powerless managers sought protection in overcomformity to written rules and rituals. This posture was associated with a cautious, conservative, play-it-safe attitude; the status quo was preferred over change, because change usually redounds to the advantage of those with power. Finally, cloutless managers bordered on the paranoid with their jealous and obsessive concern for "territoriality," or defending their own little bailiwick of operations against encroachments of other people and departments. This led to a narrowly specialized focus that "was enough to kill a proposal with which other units would have to cooperate if the idea originated in one that was temporarily more powerful" (p. 195).

As you can doubtless surmise, a junior staff officer or professional assigned to a powerless manager would face a severe obstacle to career advancement. There would be little chance for taking on interesting assignments, for exercising one's abilities to the full, or getting the resources from other departments for doing any but the most routine projects. Thus, powerless managers either lose or waste their most promising subordinates.

Kanter concluded that powerlessness begets more powerlessness. The defensive mechanisms used to cope with the fact of little clout tend to alienate potential allies and undercut the effectiveness of those who work for powerless managers. Only rare and major upheavals, perhaps brought on by revolutionary changes in the organization's external environment, seem capable of interrupting this spiral.

AUTHORITY, EXPERTISE, AND FRIENDSHIP AS BASES OF INFLUENCE

Authority

Katz and Kahn (1966) define authority as "simply legitimate power, power which is vested in a particular person or position, which is recognized as so vested, and which is accepted as appropriate not only by the wielder of power but by those over whom it is wielded and by the other members of the system" (p. 203). In other words, authority is the ability to influence specified others in accordance with the definition of certain organizational role relationships. Authority in contemporary formal organizations represents a highly rationalistic-legalistic basis of influence, in comparison to the influence bases of *traditional status* and *charismatic power* so dominant in preindustrial revolution times or even today in some non-Western cultures (Weber, 1947). Authority inheres in the office occupied by an individual; all persons holding a given office possess the same degree of authority. Some, of course, may be more influential than others due to their ability to draw upon other bases of influence (such as expertise or friendships).

The social exchange character of influence by authority is represented by something like an "informal contract" entered into by the individual and the organization. The individual, in exchange for material benefits of the type Katz calls instrumental system rewards (accruing to all who hold membership) or the attainment of some valued goal (achievable only by organizational action), endorses the authority structure of the organization—implicitly agreeing to comply with any request by a superior which the authority structure legitimates. Failure to comply with such requests constitutes ground for disciplinary measures (since formal authority is typically bolstered by some degree of coercive power) or expulsion. Discipline and expulsion, however, represent exceptional cases, since deference to authority figures arises from a more generalized respect for legitimated authority which is inculcated by socializing influences in the larger cultural context.

Barnard (1938) believed that the range of authority—the extent of a subordinate's behavior to which authority applies—correlates with the *zone of indifference* in each person, within which orders are acceptable without conscious questioning. The zone of indifference refers to those orders toward which a person is relatively indifferent; "such an order lies within the range that in a general way was anticipated at the time of undertaking the connection with the organization." Furthermore, "the zone of indifference will be wider or narrower depending upon the degree to which the inducements exceed the burdens and sacrifices. . . . it follows that the range of orders that will be accepted will be very limited among those who are barely induced to contribute to the system" (p. 169).

What functions does authority serve? First of all, it constitutes a force toward the "reduction of human variability" (Katz & Kahn, 1966). The natural variability and alternation inherent in human action (among and within persons) must be constrained if organizations are to survive; individuals must operate reliably within the range of behaviors specified by their roles. Since organizational roles are usually imperfectly defined by such documents as formal job definitions—which can never completely anticipate all the contingencies created by a changing environment and unforeseen operational problems—authority is the means by which the roles of subordinates are "pieced out" by superiors in order to respond to task demands and to reduce behavioral variability.

Second, authority helps in coping with the time lag between subordinates' inputs and ultimate outcomes. It would be awkward if subordinates had to be tangibly reinforced for every role-relevant response; furthermore, organizational participants must often endure prolonged periods of deprivations and impositions *en route* to the attainment of goals. Authority helps overcome the extinction in task behavior that would otherwise occur during such periods when rewards are not at hand or their future receipt is not highly salient.

Third, authority—since it is an organizational creation—outlives the specific individuals who use it. This guarantees that from the outset replacements will possess some minimum degree of power by which to influence subordinates. Lacking authority, they would require an inordinate amount of time to establish other bases of influence by means of informal social exchange processes.

Finally, authority gives the administrator "chips to bargain with" (Gouldner, 1954). The manager often has the power to enforce a great many housekeeping rules (such as no smoking, no early breaks, no extended breaks, no early punch-out, and no gambling on the premises). If he or she chooses to enforce these rules to the letter, subordinates may defer to authority but concede nothing beyond the absolute minimum. On the other hand, the boss may wink if members of the crew match coins to see who buys the Cokes, smoke occasionally, or take a few minutes extra lunchtime during the World Series, *in exchange for which* the crew may do some things (say, work extra hard to clear up a production bottleneck) which the boss could not demand by pure authority. Ironically, the boss may gain power by occasionally giving up some power—by not exercising authority to the hilt. "By not using some of his power, he invests it in social obligations. . . . The advantages subordinates derive from his pattern of supervision obligate them to reciprocate by complying with his directives and requests" (Blau, 1964, p. 206).

Limitations of Authority.   Authority would hardly suffice as the sole basis of influence in organizations. This is because of the limiting conditions under which authority is appropriate or feasible and because of certain side effects generated by its use.

Barnard (1938) noted that "if a person is unable to comply with an order, obviously it must be disobeyed, or better, disregarded." Since authority, like the law, must apply equally to all subordinates, it must therefore be geared toward the lowest common denominator among those to whom it applies. As Leavitt (1972) puts it, authority "is an important and efficient tool because it has the advantages of the shotgun over the rifle." By the same token, "emphasis on the legalities of organizational control tends in practice to mean that the minimal acceptable standard for quantity and quality of performance becomes the maximal standard" (Katz & Kahn, 1966). Once a person has complied with the minimum standard, authority alone can hardly influence him to do more. Otherwise, authority would become so subjective in varying demands from one person to another that eventually the consensus which legitimates authority would break down.

The official authority inherent in an organizational position applies only to those subordinates who report directly to the occupant of that office. Most responsible organizational officials, however, must also exercise *lateral* (and occasionally, *upward*) influence. A production line supervisor depends upon people outside the unit for materials, maintenance, information, and various other services. The purchasing officer depends upon parties totally outside the organization—for example, vendors or suppliers. The sales or marketing manager must influence the people in the plant to schedule production; the financial manager needs the services of experts in the data-processing department. All of these cases illustrate situations in which a manager must influence people who, by definition, are not under the "jurisdiction" of his authority. At these times, the manager simply has to operate with other bases of influence, such as friendship or exchanges of favors. The manager who becomes so accustomed to influencing subordinates by authority that he makes requests in lateral job contacts in an "authoritative tone" may find himself dealing with uncooperative colleagues. The latter will be only too quick to remind him, in words or in manner, that "I don't work for you" or "You're not my boss!"

The exclusive use of influence processes that strongly emphasize authority often generates unwelcome side effects. Most people have ambivalent feelings toward authority figures. On the one hand, they respect authority (provided, of course, that it is not abused to their disadvantage). On the other hand, they incline toward a generalized *avoidance* response to authority figures. Differences in authority imply such differences as superior-inferior, more valuable–less valuable, more mature–less mature; and people generally do not like to be confronted in such a way that they are on the shorter end of these dimensions. Furthermore, authority figures are associated with the threat of punishment, which means that people generally prefer not to be around such persons. Kids on the playground at recess time become uneasy when the principal is nearby, even though they are behaving themselves; drivers start to squirm when they see a police car close behind in the rearview mirror, even when they know that they haven't been committing any traffic violations. This generalized avoidance tendency works at cross-purposes with the superior's aims to coach, teach, and nurture. The point here is not that authority per se is undesirable, but rather that influence based solely on authority has costs associated with it.

Expertise

Physicians, attorneys, and tax accountants have no formal authority over their clients. Yet they often exert influence. They influence others who attribute a degree of *expert power* to them (French & Raven, 1959) and who need that expertise in order to solve a problem or get something done. Galbraith (1967) believes that, in today's large corporations, it is increasingly expert power which runs the operations.

What conditions must exist in order for me to influence another person by this means? First of all, someone else must admit ignorance on a subject and become aware of a need for another's expertise. A financial analyst can influence a client's investments only to the extent that the client realizes he or she lacks the expertise for selecting stocks and bonds.

Second, the other person must recognize that I have the requisite information, expertise, or judgment. This condition may be fulfilled by my official credentials, the testimonials of others whom I've helped, or by my assertions about my knowledge. It is most likely to be guaranteed, however, by my demonstrated ability to solve certain kinds of problems. Furthermore, my credibility is apt to be preserved by my refraining from making prescriptions about things in which I have no expertise and by my open-mindedness on topics that aren't an exact science—showing that I know the limits to my knowledge.

Third, I must be careful not to punish—however unintentionally—the other person's admission of ignorance and request for help. Otherwise, he or she will not soon ask for help again, and I will be prevented from influencing the person further. If a student asks in class, "What is a correlation?" and I respond with "Didn't you study the assignment?" or "Just where did you go to school?" I will extinguish such inquisitiveness. Along the same lines, the manager should reinforce (or in any case, not punish) admissions of ignorance.

Fourth, people find it easier to seek knowledge from others if they can also occasionally give knowledge to those same others. Repeated requests for information, no matter how genuine or urgent, do something to the status of requesters by making them feel obligated and in a sense inferior; such obligations are easier to bear if requesters can count on repaying the obligation by sharing some of their own expertise. A superior, therefore, should feel no hesitancy about seeking the expertise of subordinates, for that makes it easier for the subordinates to approach the superior with questions. Thus, expertise works best as a two-way street of influence. Unfortunately, some managers are afraid that they will lose respect if they admit ignorance; if they then try to bluff it, they probably *do* lose respect. Most of us, of course, are more inclined to respect the superior who is mature enough to admit to areas of ignorance.

Of course, a superior may draw upon expertise in the exercise of authority. The boss's engineering knowledge may be the basis for ordering a subordinate to use certain procedures. But now the dynamics of the social exchange process are different. "Indeed, giving advice and issuing orders have opposite consequences; advising another creates obligations, while ordering him to do something uses them up, as it were, by enabling him to discharge his obligations through his compliance" (Blau, 1964, p. 131).

Ordering people to do something in a specified manner is a credit to their account and a debit in yours. Giving helpful, solicited advice to people to help them accomplish an end they're committed to is a credit for you, a debit for them.

Friendship

Some people influence others simply on the basis of a relationship of mutual liking. When two persons enjoy an association built over a period of time marked by mutually rewarding interactions, reciprocated esteem, and interpersonal attraction, they generally wish to continue and reinforce that association. Each of these persons wants to continue to be well thought of by the other. Therefore, when one of them makes a request of the other, the latter must either grant the request (if it is reasonable and can be granted without excessive cost) or else place a sudden strain on the relationship. To the degree that such a strain is an unpleasant consideration because it threatens to cut off the rewards from the association, the friend will comply with the request.

In this case, influence is based on the intrinsic gratifications of a relationship. Here, as Blau (1964) notes, "it is not so much a specific kind of social reward as the fusion of a variety of rewards in a given association that makes these fused rewards inseparable" from the individual who is their source (p. 38). The basis of the social exchange, then, is compliance in return for continuation or enhancement of a personal relationship.

Undoubtedly a substantial amount of influence in organizations rests on the compelling power of friendships. The impact of cohesive groups over their members attests to the force of friendship power. And even aside from ongoing work groups, the influence of friendship power is felt. For example, a sales manager who gets along with the credit officer may finagle an extended credit line for important clients.

The recognized force of friendship power has led some observers to suggest that a manager should go easy on exercising authority and try instead to build personal relationships with subordinates. The assumption is that they will then carry out their roles conscientiously because they want to (that is, because they like the boss) rather than because they have to; and that they will be willing to do a number of things that they could not legitimately be ordered to do. This argument, however, should not overlook some subtle aspects of influence based on friendship.

Friendship must be genuine if it is to endure. A facade built on contrived attempts at *ingratiation* (Jones, 1964) soon wears out and may even backfire. A superior who only wants to appear friendly in order to cash in on the relationship for ulterior motives will be put to the test when subordinates come back with personal requests of their own. If it begins to look as if the favors run on a one-street, even the most obtuse underlings will get the message and see the relationship for what it is—a calculated manipulative tactic in the form of ingratiation. Of course, once someone acquires the reputation of being manipulative, others are likely to limit social exchange transactions to only formal interactions.

INFLUENCE: CONCLUDING NOTES

This chapter does not in any sense represent an exhaustive treatment of influence. One could argue that this entire book, and indeed the bulk of the published literature of the social sciences, bears in one way or another on the subject. Certainly the shaping of behavior by reinforcement and punishment, attitude change, and group dynamics, to cite a few examples, carry immediate implications for power, influence, and control. It would seem that practically all behavior in organizations represents either attempts to influence or the results of influence attempts. (Much organizational behavior is, of course, influenced by impersonal mechanisms, such as technology, job design, and other physical components of the organizational ecology. Cartwright and Zander, 1967, discuss some nonobvious aspects of ecological control.)

The social exchange flavor of the discussion in this chapter underscores the bidirectionality of interpersonal influence. From his studies of influence patterns in effective plants, unions, and voluntary organizations, Tannenbaum (1962) concludes that the inevitable price of influencing is to leave oneself susceptible to influence.

SUMMARY

Organizational control is the exercise of power, influence, and authority toward specific ends. Misconceptions about the nature of control in organizations include the belief that it is localized, the assumption that the total amount of control is fixed, and the notion that control is a one-way process. Control in organizations works through a social exchange process, in which the norms of reciprocity, distributive justice, and equity govern participants' behavior. The effect of these norms is illustrated in Patchen's (1974) study of decision making.

Organizational politics inevitably arises from the conditions of inoperable goals, dissensus, uncertainty, and interdependence. The political process is founded upon overlapping networks or cliques of recurrently interacting persons. These cliques form coalitions in order to determine the outcomes of significant issues. Groups that are capable of resolving critical areas of uncertainty for the organization have the advantage in forming decisive coalitions. Individuals who belong to many overlapping networks and thus initiate dominant coalitions are those with significant power bases. Managers lacking such external influence often exhibit a self-defeating syndrome of restrictive supervision, conservatism, rules-mindedness, and territoriality.

Authority, expertise, and friendship represent three important bases of influence in organizations. The differing character of the social exchange dynamics operative within these bases has also been discussed.

> ## CONCEPTS TO REMEMBER
>
> | | |
> |---|---|
> | technostructure | coalitions |
> | norm of reciprocity | axis |
> | distributive justice | strategic contingencies |
> | equity | powerlessness syndrome |
> | comparison persons | zone of indifference |
> | limits of rationality | expert power |
> | network | ingratiation |
> | cliques | |

QUESTIONS FOR DISCUSSION

1. Lyndon Johnson, as Senate majority leader in the 1950s, defined politics as "the art of the possible." Explain.

2. What are the implications of the Lowin and Craig "Charlie" study for evaluating different styles of supervision?

3. What are the implications of the fact that equity is ultimately subjective? What other criteria of "fairness" or "justice" are there besides equity (as defined in Adams's theory)?

4. The fact that organizational decisions are often made through the type of reciprocity described by Patchen does not mean that such decisions are always optimal. What are the pros and cons of reaching decisions in such a manner?

5. Some observers believe that authority is becoming less and less viable as a basis for influencing people in organizations. In his book *Nice Guys Finish Last*, Leo Durocher has a chapter entitled "Whatever Happened to Sit Down, Shut Up, and Listen?" What developments do you suppose account for this observation?

6. In some organizations there exists a traditional, though subtle, proscription against off-the-job, informal social interaction among people of different ranks. What considerations give rise to such a proscription? What are the pros and cons with respect to it?

CASE[2]

Shortly before 1960 the assets of the Falls City Savings and Loan Association were acquired by a small group of investors headed by

[2]Reprinted with permission from Edgar G. Williams, *People Problems* (Bureau of Business Research, Indiana University Graduate School of Business, Bloomington, Ind.), 1962.

Taylor Rapp, a local construction magnate. The rapidly increasing economic prosperity of the community coupled with Rapp's initiative and drive caused the association to expand rapidly. He was both brilliant and energetic; but, he ran a "one-man show"—as he always had in his many successful enterprises. Delegating authority to someone else did not come easily for him.

As the association grew, it became necessary to increase the appraisal staff to handle the increased flow of work. Rapp brought in his nephew, Eldon Brant, to be trained as an appraiser. Brant was in his late 40s, had little formal education, and had no previous savings and loan or real estate experience.

His age and inexperience tended to work against him. He had trouble adjusting to the demands of the appraisal work, but eventually he learned to do a creditable job and then his uncle permitted him to make real estate and construction appraisals on his own.

Rapp believed that normal inflation or appreciation would cure most of the mistakes an inexperienced appraiser might make. Then, too, the association confined itself to making conservative loans on residential properties. Because of these facts, Rapp was not overly concerned with the inadequacies of his nephew although he certainly was aware of them.

Brant worked as an appraiser for three years and finally was able to do an adequate and satisfactory job—at least according to his uncle's standards.

Rapp, ever alert to new business opportunities and perhaps a little bored, decided to form a mortgage company. He installed Dick Fisher, who had been chief appraiser for the Falls City Savings and Loan Association, as the manager. Brant was promoted to chief appraiser even though it was the consensus among his associates that he was the least well qualified of the four appraisers on the staff. At no time did he make an effort to improve his knowledge through outside study. Even at this time he possessed only a rudimentary understanding of the fundamentals of appraising. He did work hard, however, and was completely loyal to Rapp and the association. It was much to his credit that he had acquired fairly good judgment of real estate values in the area.

While there was some resentment from the other appraisers, it wasn't too overt or serious. As individuals, they were, for the most part, competent; but none was very anxious to assume additional authority and responsibility.

Surprisingly, Brant did not encounter a lot of difficulty in his new position. His staff was competent and good loans were easy to arrange. Before long his uncle had him appointed to the loan committee and named to a vice presidency.

Two years after Brant was made chief appraiser, Bill Davis was hired as an appraiser. He was very capable and ambitious for advancement. The tough assignments soon gravitated toward him and he handled them with ease. No one was surprised when after a year he became Brant's chief assistant.

A short time later Rapp sold his interest in the association. He did not want to continue as the managing officer, but he did consent to remain on the board of directors. A. J. Hockwalt, a very capable man, was brought in as his replacement.

It didn't take Hockwalt very long to learn about Brant's weaknesses as chief appraiser. He knew that the increased lending volume of the association made it absolutely necessary that its chief appraiser be well qualified administratively as well as technically. He was certain that Brant was weak in both of these areas. He knew, too, that Davis, who was well qualified to assume the duties of the chief appraiser, would not be satisfied to remain indefinitely as Brant's assistant. Davis was aware, as were all of the other employees, that Brant was the obstacle that stood between him and another immediate promotion—that of chief appraiser.

Hockwalt decided on a solution to the problem, but carrying it out was an entirely different matter. Rapp was still a power on the board of directors with whom to reckon, and he was not an easy man to reason with. The manager was certain that Rapp would not take kindly to the demotion or dismissal of Brant. In addition he needed the former owner's support on the board in order to carry out some of his plans for the future expansion of the association.

Questions

What are the influence bases of *(a)* Rapp, *(b)* Brant, and *(c)* Hockwalt? Suggest an approach by which Hockwalt might manage the dilemma he faces.

REFERENCES

Adams, J. S. Inequity in social exchange. In L. Berkowitz (Ed.), *Advances in experimental social psychology* (Vol. 2). New York: Academic Press, 1965.

Barnard, C. I. *The functions of the executive.* Cambridge, Mass.: Harvard University Press, 1938.

Bauer, R. The study of policy formation: An introduction. In R. Bauer & K. Gergen (Eds.), *The study of policy formation.* New York: Free Press, 1968.

Blau, P. *Exchange and power in social life.* New York: John Wiley & Sons, 1964.

Campbell, J. P., Dunnette, M. D., Lawler, E. E., III, & Weick, K. E., Jr. *Managerial behavior, performance, and effectiveness.* New York: McGraw-Hill, 1970.

Cartwright, D., & Zander, A. Power and influence in groups: Introduction. In D. Cartwright & A. Zander (Eds.), *Group dynamics: Research and theory.* New York: Harper & Row, 1968.

Crozier, M. *The bureaucratic phenomenon.* Chicago: University of Chicago Press, 1964.

French, J. R. P., Jr., & Raven, B. The bases of social power. In D. Cartwright (Eds.), *Studies in social power.* Ann Arbor, Mich.: Institute for Social Research, 1959.

Friedlander, F., & Pickle, H. Components of effectiveness in small organizations. *Administrative Science Quarterly,* 1968, *13,* 289–304.

Galbraith, J. K. *The new industrial state.* Boston: Houghton Mifflin, 1967.

Gouldner, A. *Patterns of industrial bureaucracy.* Glencoe, Ill.: Free Press, 1954.

Gouldner, A. The norm of reciprocity. *American Sociological Review,* 1960, *25,* 161–178.

Hickson, D. J., Hinings, C. R., Lee, C. A., Schneck, R. E., & Pennings, J. M. A strategic contingencies theory of intraorganizational power. *Administrative Science Quarterly,* 1971, *19,* 22–44.

Homans, G. C. *Social behavior: Its elementary forms.* New York: Harcourt Brace Jovanovich, 1961.

Jones, E. E. *Ingratiation.* New York: John Wiley & Sons, 1964.

Kanter, R. M. *Men and women of the corporation.* New York: Basic Books, 1977.

Katz, D. The motivational basis of organizational behavior. *Behavioral Science,* 1964, 131–146.

Katz, D., & Kahn, R. L. *The social psychology of organizations.* New York: John Wiley & Sons, 1966.

Kotter, J. P. Power, dependence, and effective management. *Harvard Business Review,* July-August 1977.

Leavitt, H. *Managerial psychology,* 3d ed. Chicago: University of Chicago Press, 1972.

Lowin, A., & Craig, J. R. The influence of level of performance on managerial style: An experimental object-lesson in the ambiguity of correlational data. *Organizational Behavior and Human Performance,* 1968, *3,* 440–458.

Maccoby, M. *The gamesman.* New York: Simon & Schuster, 1976.

Mechanic, D. Sources of power of lower participants in complex organizations. *Administrative Science Quarterly,* 1962, *7,* 349–364.

Patchen, M. The locus and basis of influence on organizational decisions. *Organizational Behavior and Human Performance,* 1974, *11,* 195–221.

Pfeffer, J. Power and resource allocation in organizations. In B. M. Staw and G. R. Salancik (Eds.), *New directions in organizational behavior.* Chicago: St. Clair Press, 1977.

Schein, E. *Career dynamics: Matching individual and organizational needs.* Reading, Mass.: Addison-Wesley, 1978.

Tannenbaum, A. S.   Control in organizations: Individual adjustment and organizational performance. *Administrative Science Quarterly*, 1962, 7, 236–257.

Tushman, M. L., & Nadler, D. A.   Implications of political models of organization. In Miles, R. H. (Eds.), *Resourcebook in macro organizational behavior*. Santa Monica, Calif.: Goodyear Publishing, 1980.

Weber, M.   *The theory of social and economic organization*. Glencoe, Ill.: Free Press, 1947.

Yuchtman, E., & Seashore, S. E.   A system resource approach to organizational effectiveness. *American Sociological Review*, 1967, 32, 891–903.

15
Leadership

How important are personal attributes of the leader?

What are the dimensions of leader behavior?

How does leader behavior affect subordinate satisfaction and performance?

How important is participative decision making in leadership?

Is leader behavior a cause or an effect of subordinate performance?

Is leadership a myth?

Depending on how broadly one uses the word *leadership,* it can be argued that this entire book—not just this one chapter—is about leadership. If leadership is simply a shorthand term for the multifaceted process by which people's behavior is influenced, then conditioning, motivation, group dynamics, and recognition of personality differences, to mention only a few areas, are part and parcel of leadership. There is, moreover, an increasingly verbalized acknowledgment that leadership is best viewed in this broad sense, referring to the aggregate patterns of reciprocal influence by all members of a group or organization.

In practice, however, as well as in the tradition of most studies of the subject, leadership is viewed as a *role,* and the term refers to either the attributes or the behavior of the person executing that role. The role need not be formal or official. Both laboratory and field studies have found that individuals carry out leadership functions not formally defined within their job description or responsibilities. In this sense, leadership, like gold, "is where you find it." For the most part, however, students of organizational behavior are interested in leadership primarily as it pertains to persons who are expected—by virtue of their official roles or their assigned responsibilities—to be leaders. In other words, we want to draw from leadership studies the implications for supervisors, managers, administrators, officers, and others who are organizationally responsible for the performance and behavior of subordinates.

LEVELS AND FORMS OF LEADERSHIP

Even within this somewhat delimited context of looking at leadership as a formal role responsibility, we should recognize that the leadership function can take many different forms. Leadership at the first level of supervision, for example, may involve primarily rule enforcement and communicating the technical knowledge needed for task completion (Katz & Kahn, 1966). At middle-management levels, leadership may require more sophistication and subtlety in dealing with people, modifying or adapting existing rules and the existing structure, and unprogrammed decision making. At upper levels of an organization, leadership takes the form of long-range planning, dealing with parties outside the organization, and developing conceptual models for relating the organization's identity and missions to the broader societal matrix in which it exists. Alfred Sloan, who as chief executive officer brought General Motors to a position of dominance in its industry and the economy, attributed his success to the fact that very early in his career he had formulated a "concept of the industry." He had developed a model of the kind of organization structure needed to combine flexibility and decentralized decision making with centralized control of resource allocation (Sloan, 1965).

Krech, Crutchfield, and Ballachey (1962) have developed a catalog of leadership functions, which probably vary in importance with the organizational level of leadership responsibility. Among these functions are the following: coordinating the activities of subordinates; acting as a father figure; formulating ideology; settling internal disputes; dispensing rewards; representing the group to outsiders; serving as the scapegoat for group failure; providing a model of behavior for group members to emulate; and negotiating for resources for the group. The reader can probably add to this list.

The complexity and multidimensional character of leadership should keep us from jumping prematurely to prescriptions and generalizations from leadership research. Not all of the leadership functions have received equal emphasis from researchers. There has been, for example, a surprisingly narrow preoccupation (some would say obsession) with the style of the leader's interpersonal relationships with subordinates. The great bulk of leadership studies have been directed at this single issue. It is undoubtedly an important issue, but it is far from being the only issue, and in many cases it may not be the crucial issue for leadership effectiveness, particularly at levels of institutional leadership in the upper echelons of the formal organization. In the years to come, we would hope that the study of leadership will become more balanced, with studies about how the leader copes with organizational dependence on outside agencies, derives a "concept of the industry," negotiates, and administers justice. These are not idle questions.

THE PARADIGM OF LEADERSHIP THEORY AND RESEARCH

Traditionally, leadership studies have taken as their *independent variable* (that is, the cause or antecedent) either an *attribute* of the leader (such as a skill or a personality trait) or a *dimension of leader behavior* (such as the style of supervision or interaction with subordinates).

Dependent variables (effects or results of the independent variables) have been *satisfaction* of subordinates and *performance* (productivity, effectiveness, efficiency, or adaptation to the environment) of the group or organization. Some theories have gone further and speculated about *intervening variables,* those that link or transmit the independent leader variables to ultimate dependent variables. Examples of intervening variables include the motivations, attitudes, or expectancies of subordinates.

It should be noted that the ways in which the criteria of leader success are measured and weighted, as well as their *time* of measurement, are ultimately arbitrary—the more so, the higher the level of leadership to which we direct our attention. At the level of first-line supervision, it seems quite appropriate to evaluate leadership effectiveness by the productivity or efficiency of the group. However, there are complications involved. First of all, productivity and performance are themselves usually multidimensional. Quantity of production may be attained at a cost of reduced quality, and vice versa. Either or both may be maximized in the short run, yet in such a way that long-term problems arise (perhaps for the leader's successor after he or she has been promoted) if subordinates gradually lose interest, commitment, and motivation, ultimately leaving the organization for alternative employment. The reverse may also be true—a leader can invest heavily in the development of subordinate skills at a cost to short-run performance measures (due, possibly, to experimentation in the learning process) but bearing fruit in the long run. Sports fans are intimately acquainted with the contrast between the professional coach or manager who endures losing seasons with raw personnel before becoming a winner, versus the one who sacrifices draft picks of new talent for seasoned veterans who win for a couple of years before retiring. Thus, whether a leader is "effective" depends on which criteria are used and when they are measured.

Before reviewing the development and progress of leadership research, we should introduce a note of caution about the effect of leadership on productivity. Whatever the effect is, leadership is certainly not the sole determinant of level of productivity. Technology and subordinate skills must surely be considered. In fact, if we look at productivity, we must agree with Dubin (1965) that the crucial determinants of employee productivity over time have been improvements in methods, machinery, and power sources. These factors are not always totally independent of leadership variables, of course; leaders, supervisors, and managers sometimes produce improvements in work methods through the cooperation or motivation they induce in subordinates, and the adoption of new methods by a group may depend on how its leader introduces them. Furthermore, leader behavior represents a potential determinant of some modest increment in level of performance beyond that attributable to technology. Nevertheless, we would be unrealistic if we assumed that leadership overcomes all obstacles.

The reader should also beware of the tautological statements sometimes uttered about leadership. Often, when a company or an athletic team experiences a dramatic turnaround from failure to success, and no other obvious explanations suggest themselves, by a process of elimination we conclude that leadership is the answer. This is then offered as proof that leadership is the crucial ingredient in organizational effectiveness. Such circular reasoning does not improve our understanding of organizational performance. At worst, it misleads us into thinking that we have explained something and that further investigation is unnecessary.

LEADER ATTRIBUTES

The oldest tradition in the study of leadership—and one that continues in various forms—has been the search for a cluster of traits, attributes, or other types of individual differences which set leaders apart from their followers or which discriminate effective from ineffective leaders. This search, though it has failed to unearth a pure prototype of the leader personality, has not been unfruitful.

R. M. Stogdill (1948), in an article which stands as a benchmark in the leadership literature, reviewed 124 empirical studies of personal factors associated with leadership. These studies ranged chronologically from 1904 to 1946; included such diverse samples as children's play groups, high school peer groups, athletic teams, business executives, and biographies of famous persons; and employed such varied methodological techniques as questionnaires, observer ratings, personality tests, and controlled laboratory studies.

Stogdill found 27 attributes which had been studied by three or more investigators. The results suggest some dimensions of individual differences along which leaders, with considerable consistency, stand apart from their groups. One is height—leaders tend to be taller than the average height of group members. Another is intelligence; this dimension includes not only IQ or overall measures of intelligence, but also some identifiable components of such measures, including verbal fluency, knowledge, insight, and originality. The relationship between intelligence and leadership, however, seems to hold true only up to a point: extreme differences in intelligence between one person and the rest of a group seem to make it difficult for that person to attain leadership status. Such differences might make it more difficult for the group to identify with or relate to the person as a leader, might make it harder for them to stay "on the same wavelength," or might cause the person to be too openly critical of and impatient with the others.

The other dimension discriminating between leaders and subordinates does not easily lend itself to a one-word label, because it represents a core or commonality among various overlapping "traits" studied by a number of different people. If one were to choose a short label, it might be something like *energy* or *activity*. Initiative, persistence, ambition, and application are among the traits that connote this dimension and that were found to be associated with leadership.

Attributes which proved unreliable in predicting leadership status included emotional stability (11 studies found leaders to be more stable, 5 found them to be less stable, and 3 found no differences between leaders and others); and extraversion (5 studies indicated that leaders were more extraverted, 2 revealed them to be introverts, and 4 found no differences between leaders and others).

One important pattern of evidence unearthed by Stogdill—one which, more than any other, made his 1948 review a watershed in the transition of leadership studies to the pursuit of fresh questions— was his citation of 19 studies which found the profile of leadership traits to vary with the situation. Differences in group tasks and group composition, in particular, seemed to require leaders with different types of attributes. As Stogdill concludes, "The total weight of evidence presented in this group of studies suggests that if there are general traits which characterize leaders, the patterns of such traits are likely to vary with the leadership requirements of different situations."

Stogdill's review raised, but did not answer, the question, Is leadership transferable? Does the person who emerges as leader in one situation have a better-than-even chance of rising to the fore in a different situation? Or is leadership specific to the immediate task and group characteristics? Carter (1953) and Gibb (1949) conclude that leadership is far from situation-specific; it seems, rather, to be general over some range of related tasks and some cluster of situational components. Just how broad the range and how dense the cluster (or, indeed, what task factors or situational dimensions are the crucial ones) are still open questions.

Two points deserve mention. First, most of the studies reviewed by Stogdill attempted to find correlates of *leadership status, not correlates of leader effectiveness* within the leadership role. In other words, the issue was whether certain attributes (such as intelligence) reliably predict who will be appointed, elected, or deferred to as leader. In effect, this may be equivalent to asking, What attributes do people seek in their leaders? or What attributes do people *believe* to be important for leadership? People just might have a naive, stereotyped conception of what makes an effective leader, and thus they may screen out potential leaders who deviate markedly from this stereotype.

Second, as Krech, Crutchfield, and Ballachey (1962) suggest, "It is of interest to speculate that the personality traits which have been found to characterize leaders may, in part, *develop* in individuals as they act as leaders." People respond to the expectations of others concerning what is viewed as appropriate role behavior, and continued reinforcement of such behavior presumably affects personality.

Since 1950, the study of leadership has, for the most part, de-emphasized the importance of personal attributes. The loss of interest in leader traits may stem from a fairly widespread belief that measures of personality have not demonstrated the precision or power needed to advance our understanding of behavior. Furthermore, reviews by Guion and Gottier (1965), Hedlund (1965), and Campbell, Dunnette, Lawler, and Weick (1970) found little evidence that personality measures could reliably predict effectiveness in the specific leadership role of the manager.

LEADER BEHAVIOR

Since 1950, the study of leadership has turned to looking more closely at what the leader does as opposed to the traits of the leader. Paving the way in this direction were the pioneering Ohio State Leadership Studies, carried out at that institution in the late 1940s and early 1950s under the direction of Carroll Shartle, Ralph Stogdill, John Hemphill, Edwin A. Fleishman, A. W. Halpin, and B. J. Winer.

These studies identified two relatively independent dimensions of behavior along which leaders differ. One of these, *consideration*, involves the extent to which the leader establishes mutual trust, rapport, and communication with subordinates. A high consideration score indicates psychological closeness between leader and subordinate; a low consideration score indicates a more psychologically distant and impersonal posture on the part of the leader.

The second factor, *initiating structure*, pertains to leader acts of organizing, defining relationships, setting goals, emphasizing deadlines, giving directions—in short, concern for the task or getting the work done.

The two factors uncovered by the Ohio State studies resemble the two types of leaders Bales (1953) found to emerge in laboratory discussion groups: the task leader or specialist and the human relations specialist. However, whereas Bales concluded that these roles conflict somewhat and are usually split between two persons, the Ohio State studies suggested that the roles were independent (that is, not necessarily correlated or conflicting) dimensions of leader behavior. A leader could be high on both consideration and initiating structure, low on both, or high on one and low on the other. Leadership style, then, could be defined by the combination of relative standings on these two dimensions of behavior.

A comprehensive review of empirical studies investigating the relationships between consideration and initiating structure, on the one hand, and various criteria of leader effectiveness, on the other, would be inappropriate here. However, reviews by Korman (1966) and Fleishman (1973) provide some perspective on the cumulative evidence. Leader consideration appears to be a consistent, reliable predictor of subordinate satisfaction and the behavioral consequences of job satisfaction-dissatisfaction. In a study conducted in the factories of a farm equipment manufacturer, the rates of subordinate turnover and officially processed grievances accelerated as the consideration scores of the leader declined. Grievances and turnover changed very little as the level of initiating structure moved from low to moderate, but at

Figure 15–1
Leader Behavior and Subordinate
Responses

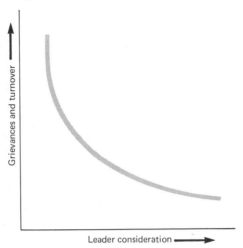

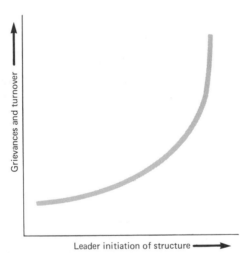

Source: From E. A. Fleishman, "Twenty Years of Consideration and Structure," in E. A. Fleishman and J. G. Hunt (Eds.), *Current Developments in the Study of Leadership* (Carbondale: Southern Illinois University Press, 1973).

very high degrees of initiating structure, grievances and turnover again accelerated markedly. While high consideration seemed to offset the otherwise negative effect of high initiating structure, the reverse was not true: low consideration, even when coupled with low initiating structure, led to dissatisfaction and low morale.[1] However, while consideration generally correlates positively with subordinate job satisfaction, the magnitude of the relationship does vary from situation to situation according to the level of the job, the nature of the task, and the characteristics of subordinates.

The relationship between these two dimensions of leader behavior and subordinate performance or productivity cannot be summed up so easily. In fact, Korman (1966) found no accurate way to predict group performance from measures of leader consideration and initiating structure. The extent to which these leader behaviors affect subordinate performance is either *(a)* negligible or *(b)* very much dependent on the situation (a statement which, in itself, tells us little). Korman issued a call for more explicit categorization of situations in order to determine when consideration or initiating structure, or both, become important determinants of group functioning.

Source: Copyright King Features Syndicate Inc., 1976.

Intuitively, one would regard the high consideration–high structure combination as the optimal blend of leader behavior. After all, both task effectiveness and human relations (or participant satisfaction) represent desirable end products of group activities; presumably, initiating structure facilitates task accomplishment and consideration promotes group maintenance and involvement by affecting participant attitudes.

These assumptions formed the basis of the *Managerial Grid*, a management development program that Robert Blake and Jane Mouton (1968) have used in numerous corporations. Blake and Mouton conceptualize "concern for production" and "concern for people" as two independent but essential factors for managerial effectiveness. Concern for each factor can be represented as varying from 1 (very low) to 9 (very high). A 9,1 manager places high emphasis on produc-

---

[1]These results are not necessarily generalizeable to nonindustrial or nonfactory settings.

Leader's Initiating Structure and Subordinate Response

Source: G. B. Trudeau, *The President Is a Lot Smarter Than You Think* (New York: Popular Library, 1973).

tion and little on people; a 1,9 leader invests all of his emotional reserves in attention to the feelings and satisfactions of subordinates. A 5,5 leader compromises by placing moderate emphasis on both production and people. All three of these combinations apparently reflect an individual's assumption that concern for production and concern for people conflict with each other rather than being reconcilable. The Managerial Grid program uses diagnostic tools to help the manager realize his or her current blend of these concerns and then embarks on a training regimen to bring each manager to a 9,9 philosophy—maximal emphasis on both task and relationships, without making a trade-off between the two.

We would do well, however, to reexamine our instinctive beliefs that what the leader does is either necessary or sufficient to achieve high task effectiveness or high participant satisfaction. To take an extreme case, the 1,1 leader style (low concern for production and people) might well be associated with high group performance and

Figure 15–2
The Managerial Grid®

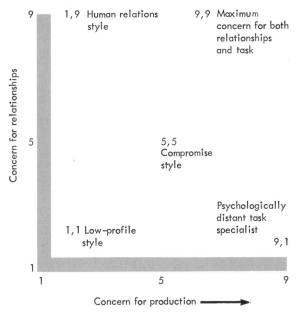

Source: R. R. Blake and J. S. Mouton, *Corporate Excellence through Grid Organizational Development* (Houston: Gulf Publishing, 1968).

satisfaction provided that the members of the group were "mature" (for example, experienced and competent, achievement oriented, deriving intrinsic gratification from interesting jobs). Hersey and Blanchard's life cycle theory of leadership (1972) suggests that, with such a group, the low-profile leadership style is the appropriate one. The point we wish to underscore here is that leader behavior is only one variable among many that determine subordinate behavior and attitudes. The evidence from empirical studies investigating initiating structure and consideration lend little support to the notion that the 9,9 blend represents the ultimate leadership style for which every manager should strive.

HOUSE'S PATH-GOAL THEORY

Taking note of the varying magnitudes of the relationships between leader behavior dimensions and group effectiveness criteria, Robert J. House has formulated a Path-Goal theory of leadership in order to identify the situations in which the leader's consideration or initiating structure become important determinants of performance or satisfaction. House's theory is derived from an expectancy model of motivation. The model identifies five crucial components of subordinate motivation: (1) the intrinsic rewards of work-related activities; (2) the intrinsic rewards of task accomplishment or work achievement; (3) the extrinsic rewards which depend upon achievement; (4) the clarity of the "path" or "plan" by which work behavior culminates in achievement; and (5) the subjective probability that extrinsic rewards do follow from achievement. All of these motivational components, House (1971) argues, depend in part on what the leader does: "the behavior of the leader is clearly relevant to all of the independent variables in this formulation" (p. 322). The leader, in part, determines how extrinsic rewards depend on achievement and the degree to which subordinates perceive this to be the case. The leader may, by instructions, clarify the path or plan of work activities that lead to achievement. The leader may affect the intrinsic gratification derived by subordinates from work activities by allowing them choice or discretion in such activities, or by cultivating interpersonal relationships which establish a pleasant climate.

House's theory predicts that the consideration displayed by the leader is most important when the work itself is uninteresting, tedious, or irksome: "If you've got a lousy job, you don't want a lousy boss also." When the work provides intrinsic satisfaction by its challenges, stimulation, or use of important skills, consideration is less important.

House believes that initiating structure contributes most to group effectiveness and subordinate satisfaction when the task is unstructured, when subordinates experience a high degree of ambiguity about their work roles, or when crisis threatens the group. On the other hand, when the work is already highly structured, a high level of initiating structure by the leader becomes an unnecessary added irritant; subordinates perceive it as unwarranted close supervision.

Tests of House's theory have yielded mixed results. The most consistent evidence in his support reaffirms the importance of leader consideration when the work itself provides no immediate reinforcement or, by itself, would only be aversive. However, most of the studies testing House's propositions have taken the form of cross-sectional surveys. These are weak tests of any theory and allow numerous extraneous or uncontrolled variables to contaminate the results. House's theory will undoubtedly be refined and modified in the future to take into account unpredicted findings from more precise tests. In any case, it represents a significant step forward from previous theorizing about leadership, one which defines explicitly the conditions under which dimensions of leader behavior have decisive impact on group performance and sentiments.

SUBSTITUTES FOR LEADERSHIP

It can be argued that, in order for a group to perform effectively, two things are needed. First, the people must know what they are supposed to do and how to do it. Second, they must have a reason for doing it—they must, in some sense, imagine themselves better off for doing the task than if they did not do it. Much of leader behavior, then, is a mixture of defining the task and providing instructions or role assignments, on the one hand, and on the other hand giving people a stake in the outcomes of work—directly or indirectly, by positive incentives or the use of threat. Thus, leaders initiate structure in order to clarify roles and expectations, and sometimes as a punitive consequence for unacceptable job behavior. Leaders may use consideration in various forms to reinforce desired behavior, or withhold consideration when performance is below par.

Kerr and Jermier (1978) have argued, however, that certain attributes of the subordinate, of the task, and of the organization may serve as *substitutes for leadership* in providing the functions otherwise served by leader-initiated structure or consideration. For example, substitutes for the leader's initiating structure, in clarifying the "what" and "how" of task activities, may include the professional training of the subordinates, a highly mechanized and unvarying task design, or detailed rules and procedures specified by the organization. Substitutes for leader consideration could include any intrinsic appeal of the task itself, a supportive and very cohesive work group, or the esteem of professional colleagues (see Table 15–1).

The greater the extent to which substitutes for leadership exist in the work setting, the less influence leader behavior will have upon subordinate attitudes and performance. Alternatively, one may draw the conclusion that appropriate leader behavior is that which *complements* existing sources of structure and performance-related rewards. For example, a work setting may contain such abundant sources of structure that virtually any degree of additional structure provided by the leader is redundant; but the same work setting may not offer alternative sources of reinforcement. In that case, supervision which emphasized supportiveness would be appropriate. Thus, the concept of "substitutes for leadership" leads toward many of the same predictions as does the Path-Goal theory concerning the situational requirements of effective leadership.

Kerr and Jermier (1978) also note the significance of "neutralizers" which simply blunt or negate the influence of leader behavior. For example, if subordinates have strong needs for independence, are indifferent to the rewards which the leader can provide, or work at considerable spatial distance from the superior, the leader's behavior is essentially nullified insofar as its psychological impact on subordinates is concerned. Unlike substitutes, neutralizers do not in themselves provide any function otherwise contributed by leadership; they simply suppress the effect of leadership. To the· extent that several strong neutralizing variables exist in the work situation, no leadership orientation is likely to be much better than

Table 15–1
Substitutes for Leadership

		Will Tend to Neutralize	
Characteristic		Relationship-Oriented Supportive, People-Centered Leadership: Consideration, Support, and Interaction Facilitation	Task-Oriented, Instrumental, Job-Centered Leadership: Initiating Structure, Goal Emphasis, and Work Facilitation
Of the subordinate			
1.	Ability, experience, training, knowledge		X
2.	Need for independence	X	X
3.	"Professional" orientation	X	X
4.	Indifference toward organizational rewards	X	X
Of the task			
5.	Unambiguous and routine		X
6.	Methodologically invariant		X
7.	Provides its own feedback concerning accomplishment		X
8.	Intrinsically satisfying	X	
Of the organization			
9.	Formalization (explicit plans, goals, and areas of responsibility)		X
10.	Inflexibility (rigid, unbending rules and procedures)		X
11.	Highly specified and active advisory and staff functions		X
12.	Closely knit, cohesive work groups	X	X
13.	Organizational rewards not within the leader's control	X	X
14.	Spatial distance between superior and subordinates	X	X

Source: From "Substitutes for Leadership", by S. Kerr and J.M. Jermier, *Organizational Behavior and Human Performance*, 1978, 22, 378.

any other, because none will have enough impact to be very good or very bad.

As Kerr and Jermier note, "few organizations would be expected to have leadership substitutes so strong as to totally overwhelm the leader. . ." (p. 400). In others, leader roles are necessary. The point is that, while structure and rewards are needed, it is seldom the case that leadership must carry the entire burden of providing them. The varying degree to which other sources provide structure and incentives, combined with the varying degree to which factors neutralize leader behavior, rule out any universally valid prescriptions about a particular leader style.

THE PARTICIPATION CONTROVERSY

Should leaders exercise influence in an autocratic or a democratic fashion? This emotionally charged issue continues to reverberate in the leadership literature as well as in informal discussions about managerial behavior. Unfortunately, the labels *autocratic* and *democratic* contain explosive value connotations which have made it difficult to investigate this issue in a detached, dispassionate mood. The labels suggest analogies with dictatorial versus democratic regimes, and such analogies are not necessarily appropriate when viewing leader behavior in the context of groups striving to achieve task goals. More-recent discussion of this issue has employed the terms *participation* and *decision centralization* (Yukl, 1971), which are not as value laden.

We can define the dimension of participation in terms of such leader behavior as the following: the degree to which the leader unilaterally makes decisions (especially the important ones); the extent of consultation by the leader with subordinates; the amount of communication flowing between leader and subordinates in comparison to that which takes place in interaction among subordinates; and the degree of input by subordinates in setting goals. A highly participative leader consults frequently with subordinates concerning both the group's goals and means for pursuing those goals, and encourages subordinates to work out numerous problems among themselves. The directive, more nonparticipative leader makes decisions based on his own convictions and expertise, and exercises greater surveillance over group members' activities. He or she leans toward the formal authority of the role as the dominant mode of influence, whereas the participative counterpart prefers collaborative, reciprocity-based influence modes. Of course, the directive-participative dimension is a continuum, and as Tannenbaum and Schmidt (1958) suggest, a variety of styles exist between the extremes.

A question that sometimes arises is whether participation = consideration and nonparticipation = initiating structure. Intuitively, we might expect a leader who emphasizes consideration to be participative and a leader high in initiating structure to be directive. Conceptually, however, these are separate issues. Remember that consideration and initiating structure emerged as independent (not polar opposite) dimensions of leader behavior, whereas the participation continuum represents a single dimension anchored by opposite styles. Furthermore, one could imagine a highly directive, nonparticipative

Figure 15–3

Professionalization may function as a substitute for leadership.

manager who nevertheless exhibits considerable concern over the welfare and feelings of subordinates (the "benevolent autocrat"). Similarly, a manager might view a highly participative style as mandated solely by task considerations, not to be rationalized by any socioemotional results that might or might not coincidentally correlate with such a style.

The argument for directive leadership rests implicitly on a number of assumptions about human nature and about the manager's job: that most people have strong needs for security and for clarity in what is expected of them; that people hold more respect for the leader who acts decisively; that groups find it vexing to try to achieve consensus; and that the "buck stops" with the manager.

The case for participative leadership follows from two identifiably separate sets of premises, first noticed by Miles (1965). One rationale, which he dubs the *human relations* argument, says that if subordinates have the opportunity to contribute to the definition of group goals and strategies, they satisfy higher-order needs for self-esteem and achievement. This need satisfaction leaves them more pliable and amenable to organizational influence, more committed to resultant group goals, and more motivated to perform in a fashion that will achieve those goals. In other words, participation leads to greater satisfaction, which in turn leads to greater effort, efficiency, and effectiveness. Miles suggests that this is the rationale managers use when justifying the use of a participative style with subordinates, but that they often "fudge" by simply going through the ritual of participation in order to sell their own decisions by making them seem like group decisions.

The *human resources* rationale for participative management rests on the assumptions that knowledge and expertise are widely distributed throughout work groups and that decisions are best made by those closest to, or most conversant with, the particular problem addressed. Participation, then, because it represents decentralized decision making, leads to higher-quality and more informed decisions, which lead to better group performance, which may result in greater satisfaction (to the extent that rewards hinge on performance criteria). This, Miles conjectures, is the argument managers pursue for urging a participative style on the part of their bosses.

So much for the argument. What does the empirical research literature have to say? Again, space does not permit a detailed review of the evidence bearing on this question, but we will look briefly at some of the more celebrated studies that have investigated this issue.[2]

Beginning in the late 1930s, Lippitt and White (1958) carried out a series of experimental studies regarding the effects of adult supervisory styles on the behavior of groups of 11-year-old boys. The adults had been trained to supervise the recreational activities of these boys in either a democratic, an autocratic, or a laissez-faire fashion. When the leader was present, the groups under autocratic leaders spent more time at work than did the groups under democratic leaders, but the reverse was true when the leader left the room. No overall objective measures of productivity were reported, so the studies failed to provide an answer to the question of which leadership style leads to greater productivity. The investigators did find that the autocratic groups expressed more hostility to the leader and to each other, and that they seemed to exhibit less spontaneous interest in work activities than did the democratic groups. Moreover, the democratic groups experienced no dropouts, whereas the autocratic groups did.

---

[2]For a more comprehensive review, see P. Blumberg, *Industrial Democracy: The Sociology of Participation* (New York: Schocken Books, 1974), especially chapters 5 and 6; or S. M. Sales, "Supervisory Style and Productivity: Review and Theory," *Personnel Psychology*, 1966, *19*, 275–286.

McCurdy and Eber (1953) and Shaw (1955) compared laboratory groups working under autocratic or democratic leaders on problem-solving tasks. McCurdy and Eber found no differences in productivity, whereas Shaw found that autocratic groups took less time to solve problems and made fewer errors.

Coch and French (1948), in a classic field experiment, studied the effects of participation on worker resistance to changes in methods of production. The Harwood Company, where the study took place, had historically encountered stiff resistance by the work force whenever it had introduced more sophisticated work processes. Such resistance took the form of higher turnover, hostility toward management, grievances, and output restriction. Coch and French seized on the occasion of a work-methods change to compare the subsequent behavior of groups allowed to participate in the change versus those not allowed to participate. One group, the no-participation group, was simply called together and told about the changes that would be effected. A second group was allowed to elect representatives, who discussed with management and the engineering staff the best ways of implementing the change. Two other groups were given a "total participation" treatment—all members of those groups participated in planning the job modifications. In the no-participation group, 17 percent of the workers quit in the first 40 days after the change, and a number of those who stayed processed grievances about the new production standards. Furthermore, production dropped and stayed low long after the passage of the time needed to master the changes in work methods. No turnover occurred in either the representative-participation or the total participation groups, and productivity in both types of groups climbed to record highs after a temporary drop. The total participation groups experienced the highest rates of productivity increases.

Two confounding variables in the Harwood experiment complicate the interpretations of the results. First, all three of the participation groups were given a demonstration of two pieces of material produced in the factory, one of which had cost twice as much to produce as the other. The workers were asked to identify the cheaper cloth, but could see no difference between them. This demonstration, which vividly illustrated the economic and competitive rationale for production methods changes, was not given to the nonparticipation group.

Second, the two total participation groups were smaller than the two other groups. Group size often correlates inversely with cohesiveness, satisfaction, and productivity per person, and affects the structure and interaction of the group (Thomas & Fink, 1963).

To what extent these confounding differences—by themselves and apart from differences in participation—might have accounted for subsequent differences in turnover and productivity is unknown.

Given the very dramatic attitudinal and performance differences between the nonparticipation and participation groups, one could argue
plausibly that the demonstration and group-size effects probably do
not account for the full effects attributed to participation. A subsequent development at Harwood adds weight to this view. The workers who had originally been in the no-participation group and had
stayed with the company were given the participation treatment on
other assignments several months later. No additional turnover followed, and productivity among these workers showed the same recovery and increase that had characterized the earlier participation
groups. Of course, it is possible that the most discontented workers
had already left and that the remaining workers therefore constituted
a rather select group.

Coch and French attempted a repeat of this study at a Norwegian
shoe factory. In general, the participation groups expressed greater
satisfaction with the company and displayed better morale on a number of indices. Unlike the Harwood study, however, the Norwegian
experiment found no differences in productivity between participation and nonparticipation groups. The authors suggest that the Nor-
wegians might not have regarded participation in managerial decisions as culturally legitimate (but if so, why were the participating
groups more satisfied?). In addition, the procedures by which the investigators implemented worker participation in the Norwegian experiment varied somewhat from those used in the Harwood study.

Morse and Reimer (1956), in an 18-month study conducted in the
offices of a large insurance company, varied the level of decision making for 500 clerical workers in four divisions. Decision making was
made more centralized in two divisions and more decentralized in the
other two. Both groups showed increases in productivity over the
$1^1/2$-year span, with the centralized (autocratic) divisions registering a
slightly greater increase than the decentralized divisions. Morse and
Reimer suggest that this difference in productivity increases was attributable to the fact that the centralized groups experienced greater
turnover, leaving fewer women to accomplish a roughly constant
flow of work and therefore yielding higher production per individual
employee. With regard to job attitudes, the centralized groups showed
a *statistically* significant drop in job satisfaction and the decentralized groups a *statistically* significant increase. The actual changes,
however, were quite small. On a five-point scale, the mean decrease
for hierarchically controlled sections was $-.13$ (2.37 to 2.24) and the
increase for the autonomous sections was $+.14$ (2.43 to 2.57).

Vroom (1960) investigated the extent to which differences in personality might determine people's responses to autocratic versus participative management. His study, which focused on supervisors in a
delivery service company, found that supervisors who scored high in

need for independence or low in authoritarianism preferred a participative boss. Those low in need for independence or high in authoritarianism were indifferent to the degree of participation they were allowed. Tosi (1970) found a positive relationship between participation and satisfaction, but—unlike Vroom—did not find need for independence or authoritarianism to affect this relationship.

Numerous other studies, varying in methodology and the types of populations used, have addressed the participation issue, but those cited above will suffice to illustrate the mixed nature of the empirical results accumulated. Generally speaking, we find that participative leadership is associated with greater satisfaction on the part of subordinates than is nonparticipative leadership; or, at worst, that participation does not lower satisfaction. We cannot summarize so easily the findings with respect to productivity. Some studies find participative groups to be more productive; some find nonparticipaive groups to be more effective; and quite a few studies show no appreciable differences in productivity between autocratically versus democratically managed work groups.

One might conclude from the numerous technological, ability, and work-flow variables which determine level of productivity that leadership style has a greater effect on subordinate satisfaction than on subordinate productivity. To rest on this conclusion—of course, many of us would prefer not to—does *not* represent a denial of the importance of leadership. Subordinate satisfaction, after all, often does predict absenteeism, turnover, loyalty, spontaneous cooperation, and other desirable behaviors. Absenteeism and turnover represent potentially significant labor costs.

The other, more persevering, reaction to the mixed findings relating participation and productivity emerges as a search for *situational factors* which determine whether participative leadership affects productivity positively or negatively. The cohesiveness of the group, the nature of the task, the maturity of subordinates, time pressures, the vested interests of members in the outcome of the decision, and a host of other situational variables could conceivably moderate the effects of leadership style on the performance of the group. No one so far has formulated a theory of leadership which takes account of all these variables, but Fiedler (1964) has offered a model which tries to incorporate three pivotal components of the situation in order to predict the effects of leadership style on group performance.

FIEDLER'S CONTINGENCY MODEL OF LEADERSHIP EFFECTIVENESS

Fiedler's work on leadership actually began over 25 years ago when he found that psychotherapists with reputations of clinical effectiveness tended to see their clients as more similar to themselves than did therapists not regarded as effective. This suggested that a counselor or helping agent who sees similarity between himself and others tends to feel psychologically closer to them and to be more supportive and less judgmental. The analogy between a counselor and a group leader immediately suggested itself, since a leader's responsibilities include—but are not limited to—the nurturance, coaching, and developmental growth of subordinates.

In order to extend this inquiry to the study of leadership in applied settings, Fiedler developed an instrument which purports to measure the leader's "Esteem for Least Preferred Co-worker" (LPC). Fiedler asks the leader to think about the person he least prefers to work with, and to rate that person in terms of a number of adjectives that imply personal evaluation ("pleasant-unpleasant," "friendly-unfriendly," and so forth). The higher the LPC score, the more the leader can distinguish between the person as a worker (not wanted) and the person as an individual (who may have a number of good qualities, despite his deficiencies as a co-worker). The lower the LPC score, the more the leader rejects his least-preferred co-worker out of hand—not only as a worker, but as a person. Fiedler assumed that the leader who scores high on the LPC measure tends to operate in a nondirective, relationships-oriented manner toward group members, whereas the leader with a low LPC score acts in a more controlling, task-oriented, even punitive manner.

Impressed by the results he had obtained in the psychotherapy study, Fiedler anticipated that high-LPC leaders would generally show greater group effectiveness than their low-LPC counterparts. However, his early leadership studies—carried out with high school basketball teams and student surveying parties—suggested just the opposite. Contrary to expectation, leader LPC score correlated negatively with group performance. These results cast doubt on the utility of viewing the leader as one who must play primarily the role of therapist, and raised the possibility that in task-oriented groups the leader must be able to reject poor performers. Presumably, a psychologically distant leader does this best.

Further studies with other types of work groups muddied the waters even more, for sometimes the low-LPC leaders proved more effective and at other times the high-LPC leaders were associated with better team performance. After a decade of seemingly inconsistent, erratic findings, Fiedler attempted to sort out the crucial situational factors that determined which leadership style would predict effectiveness. Fiedler (1964) identified three situational parameters which, in combination, helped account for the inconsistent findings: leader-group relations, task structure, and position power.

The *leader-group relations* parameter refers to the tone or climate of the personal relationships between the formal leader and his or her subordinates, especially key subordinates. The more positive and pleasant the tone of these relationships, the more the leader feels accepted by the group.

Task structure concerns the clarity or ambiguity of the task confronting the group. Tasks can vary from the highly programmed (such as assembling an appliance or planting pine seedlings) to the vague and amorphous (developing a policy for corporate social responsibility or formulating a program to decrease employee absenteeism). Task structure is defined by the degree to which the final decision can be verified as correct or incorrect, the ease with which procedures for accomplishing the task can be specified, the number of ways to approach the problem, and the number of solutions that are equally correct or good.

Position power is defined by the formal authority that inheres in the leader's organizational role and the leverage he or she has over the rewards and punishments meted out to group members.

Leader-member relations, task structure, and position power—in that order of importance—interact, according to Fiedler, to determine the ease or difficulty with which the leader can influence group members. Put another way, these factors make the situation more or less favorable for the leader, as shown in Figure 13–4. The extreme left combination—good leader-member relations, highly structured task, and high position power—represents a very favorable situation for the leader, one in which it should be easy to influence subordinates. The opposite extreme (relatively poor relationships with subordinates, unstructured task, low power) is a leader's nightmare.

Fiedler found that psychologically distant (low-LPC) leaders were more effective—in terms of objective performance criteria—than psychologically close leaders when the situation was either very favorable or very unfavorable for the leader, whereas high-LPC leaders were more effective in situations of intermediate favorableness.

> In very favorable conditions, where the leader has power, informal backing, and a relatively well-structured task, the group is ready to be directed on how to go about its task. Under a very unfavorable condition, however, the group will fall apart unless the leader's active intervention and control can keep the members on the job. In moderately favorable conditions. . . a relationship-oriented, nondirective, permissive attitude may reduce member anxiety or intra-group conflict, and this enables the group to operate more effectively [Fiedler, 1964, p. 165].

Fiedler has assumed that the LPC measure taps a dimension of the leader's personality which predisposes the leader toward a certain interpersonal style vis-à-vis subordinates. He therefore argues that leaders cannot easily change their behavioral styles since, in the mature adult, personality does not change easily within reasonably short pe-

Figure 15–4
Fiedler's Analysis of Situations in Which the High- or the Low-LPC Leader is the More Effective

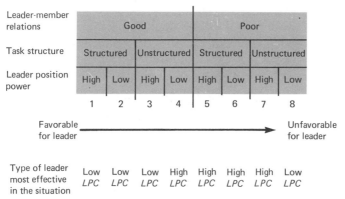

riods. Therefore, in order to maximize managerial or administrative leadership effectiveness, we must try to make the situation fit the leader's style—or, as Fiedler puts it, "engineer the job to fit the manager." We can do this by altering the position power of the leader, changing the task structure, or improving the interpersonal climate between the leader and subordinates.

Fiedler's model, which at one time gave promise of making a major breakthrough in the use of the situational approach to leadership, has been the focus of considerable controversy in the past few years. Critics of the model contend that the LPC measure remains something of a mystery. Little evidence exists that it accurately reflects a person's predisposition toward any particular leadership style, either in terms of participativeness or of initiating structure and consideration levels. Critics charge that Fiedler used inappropriate statistical analysis to support his propositions and that laboratory studies designed to test the theory provide little or no support for the validity of the model. Fiedler's critics have also raised the question of whether Esteem for Least Preferred Co-worker is independent of the three major situational dimensions proposed by Fiedler, especially relations between the leader and group members.

Fiedler readily concedes that the personality factor tapped by the LPC instrument needs clarification. Recently, he suggested that it reflects a leader's behavioral inclinations only under stress. Low-LPC leaders may display a relationships-oriented style in a climate of security, but when threatened by the possibility of group failure on a task they change to a task orientation and maintain psychological distance toward subordinates. Fiedler dismisses the evidence from laboratory studies of ad hoc groups as irrelevant to his model, which he regards as an attempt to understand and predict leader effectiveness in ongoing organizations where there are important stakes in the outcomes of group efforts.

Although the status of Fiedler's model remains in doubt, his theory shares with other contemporary approaches a concern for task dimensions that moderate the effects of leader behavior on group effectiveness. While a considerable amount of effort has gone into the analysis of task characteristics, we still do not have consensus on what the most important aspects of the task are (aside, perhaps, from task ambiguity), nor do we have as reliable or valid measures of task dimensions as we would like. Indeed, a workable theory of task requirements as they affect behavior and a set of improved measurement tools appear to be the bottlenecks we must work through before we can add significantly to our knowledge of leadership.

THE VROOM-YETTON NORMATIVE MODEL

Vroom and Yetton (1973), like Fiedler, take a situational approach to the issue of participation. Unlike Fiedler, however, they envisage a continuum in which there are at least five possible levels of participation by subordinates in decision making. At one extreme, the leader makes the decision based on his or her information at the time. A second strategy would involve making the decision after collecting relevant information from subordinates. A third technique would be to discuss the problem on a one-on-one basis with individual subordinates, soliciting their individual thoughts but then unilaterally making the decision, regardless of whether the decision actually reflected subordinates' views. A fourth approach would be for the leader to share the problem with the *group as a whole*, but once again preserve the prerogative of rendering a final judgment. Finally, the leader might involve the group in the decision from beginning to end, acting as a broker for the exchange of information and as a representative of the group's consensual decision.

The desirability—indeed the *feasibility*, in Vroom and Yetton's model—of any one of the above strategies depends on certain characteristics of the decision problem. Particularly crucial attributes are the immediate availability of information to the leader versus the amount of additional information possessed by subordinates, the importance of group acceptance of the final solution, and the extent to which the group is willing to accept the leader's decision. The more important group acceptance is in determining the implementation of the decision, the greater the degree of input required of the group.

The Vroom-Yetton model is actually embodied in a decision tree with branch points representing sequential questions concerning the attributes of the decision problem, thus generating 14 types of problems. Vroom and Yetton specify which levels of participation are acceptable for each type of problem. (The interested reader may consult Vroom and Yetton, 1973, chapter 3, for a more detailed exposition of the logic of this model.)

Vroom and Yetton present evidence, based on how managers indicated they would deal with a number of hypothetical problems, which suggests that many managers intuitively practice what the model prescribes. At present, however, there is limited evidence documenting the validity of the model for maximizing leadership effectiveness in decision making.

THE RECIPROCAL CAUSALITY QUESTION

Studies about leadership style or leader behavior have typically proceeded on the assumption that leader behavior affects subordinate behavior. Particularly in correlational field studies, any correlation between leader behavior and subordinate performance has been interpreted as measuring the impact of the leader's actions on group responses.

Lowin and Craig (1968), in a study referred to in the previous chapter, raised the question of whether correlations between leader style and subordinate behavior might not also be reflecting a reverse causal sequence: the effect of subordinate behavior on what the leader does. To answer this question, they conducted a study in which they had a stooge typist named Charlie deliberately play the role either of conscientious-competent worker or of unconscientious-incompetent subordinate. The subjects, who were actually applicants for a temporary supervisory job, were exposed to one of these two subordinate work styles enacted by Charlie. The results showed quite clearly that when Charlie performed competently, the supervisor displayed more consideration, initiated less structure, and allowed more participation by Charlie in decision making.

Greene (1975) conducted a field study of reciprocal causality between leader and subordinate behavior. His study took place in ongoing organizations, but his method of research represented something of a departure from the usual field studies of leadership. He obtained measures of subordinate performance and satisfaction, along with descriptions of supervisors' leadership styles (in terms of consideration and initiating structure) at three different points in time, each separated by one-month intervals. His analysis took the form of cross-lagged correlations. If, for example, leader consideration exerts a positive effect on subordinate performance, then we would expect to find a reasonably high positive correlation between leader consideration at time 1 and subordinate performance at time 2. On the other hand, if leader consideration is a *result of* (or response to) subordinate performance, then we would expect the correlation between subordinate performance at time 1 and leader consideration at time 2 to emerge as high and positive.

Greene did find, in support of previous thinking, that leader consideration directly affected subordinate job satisfaction. However, his evidence suggested that the causal relationship between leader style and subordinate performance ran in the reverse direction. When subordinates' performance was unsatisfactory, supervisors responded by increasing the emphasis on task and structure; when subordinates' performance was satisfactory or better, supervisors reacted by decreasing the emphasis on structure and increasing the emphasis on consideration toward subordinates. In other words, whether knowingly or unconsciously, supervisors appeared to be using consideration as a contingent reinforcer for performance and initiating structure as a punisher for unacceptable quality of work.

THE VERTICAL DYAD LINKAGE MODEL

If leader behavior toward a subordinate is at least partly a function of the subordinate's performance, and if subordinates vary considerably in the quantity and quality of their performance, then leaders will probably experience different types of relationships with different subordinates. Dansereau, Graen, and Haga (1975) have taken this conclusion as the starting point for the development of their Vertical Dyad Linkage (VDL) model. They argue that it is misleading to think of a leader's "style," in a general or average sense, with respect to the group as a whole—unless the group is rather homogeneous in terms of work attitudes, skills, and performance. More typically, subordinates vary widely on such dimensions. Given such diversity, it is more fruitful to look at the dyad, the relationship between the leader and a particular subordinate, rather than the relationship between the leader and the group.

Some members of the group will have neither the ability nor the inclination to exceed the minimum performance required of them by the formal job definition. Such persons will accept the authority of the leader insofar as that authority is legitimated by the implicit contract between the member and the organization. They will do what they *have* to do and little beyond that. In return, the leader will provide the support, consideration, and assistance likewise mandated by his or her own role duties but will not go beyond such limits. In effect, the leader is practicing a *contractual exchange* (Kim & Organ, 1979) with such members. Dansereau et al. refer to these members as "hired hands," who are being influenced by *supervision* rather than *leadership.*

But quite often the leader's responsibilities are such that they cannot be carried out merely by holding subordinates to minimal role obligations. The leader's own time and energy may be insufficient to attend to all of the critical functions performed by the group.

> Fortunately, a subset of his members usually can perform the majority of the critical functions of the unit. Therefore, the superior invests a disproportionate amount of his time and energy in developing a select subset of his members. Once these members shoulder their share of the burden of the unit, the superior maintains his disproportionate attention to these members and their critical tasks... [Dansereau et al., p. 72].

In short, the leader will come to count on contributions by some members beyond their contractual obligations. However, in order to obtain such contributions, the leader must allow those members some latitude in their roles—in effect, the leader and key subordinates *negotiate* (perhaps *renegotiate*) the latter's responsibilities in a *noncontractual exchange relationship.*

> The superior for his part can offer the outcomes of job latitude, influence in decision-making, open and honest communications, support of the member's actions, and confidence in the consideration for the member, among others. The member can reciprocate with greater than required expenditures of time and energy, the assumption of greater responsibility, and commitment to the success of the entire unit or organization, among others. The larger the extent of this vertical exchange, the more the superior must be ready to negotiate... [Dansereau et al., p. 49–50].

Those with whom the leader negotiates become "cadres," or "ins" (as contrasted to the "outs," who are merely supervised in conformity with contractual obligations).

The VDL approach suggests that effectiveness in a leadership role is a function of the following: *(a)* the ability to identify those subordinates who can provide critical contributions beyond their formal role obligations and *(b)* the ability to obtain and maintain these contributions by offering inducements beyond those guaranteed by the contractual relationship. The latter may, in turn, depend upon the external power of the leader—the ability to obtain resources from superiors, other work units, or parties external to the organization.

IS LEADERSHIP A MYTH?

Is leadership, in fact, causally related to organizational performance? Instinctively we respond, either as an article of faith or as a self-evident truism, "Obviously it is." But Pfeffer (1978) has presented some arguments, supported by empirical findings, which would appear to challenge this assumption.

Pfeffer offers three reasons why we are unlikely to find unambiguous evidence showing significant effects of leaders on organizational success or failure. To begin with, organizations tend to limit the range of attributes or behavioral styles permitted in leadership roles. We have already noted the apparent existence of a broadly accepted "lay theory" of leadership holding that only persons with certain characteristics are likely to have an opportunity to demonstrate leadership. Beyond this conception of what leaders "in general" should be like, specific organizations superimpose their own norms and traditions concerning what is acceptable or ideal in a candidate for a leader role (for example, according to Wright, 1979, General Motors does not want a flashy, individualistic sort of executive for its top management positions). The result is that, in a given organization, one can observe little variation among those who succeed each other as leaders. Therefore, any variation over time in an organization's functioning cannot logically be explained by variation in leadership.

Second, the leader is contrained by the expectations of others in the organization. Even should a maverick slip through the gate, his or her behavior will be restricted by prevailing norms and role pressures exerted by others—such as peers, subordinates, and the general "climate" or "personality" of the larger organization.

Finally—and, for Pfeffer, the most important consideration—the organization's success is predominantly determined by external forces over which the leader has no control:

> Consider, for example, the executive in a construction firm. Costs are largely determined by the operation of commodities and labor markets over which the executive has little, if any, control. Demand is largely affected by interest rates and the availability of mortgage money. These, in turn, are affected by governmental policies over which the executive has little influence.
>
> . . . School superintendents have little influence on birth rates and community economic development, both of which profoundly affect school system budgets.
>
> . . . Organizations have capacities—strengths and weaknesses that are relatively enduring [Pfeffer, 1978, p. 21].

Pfeffer concludes that the importance we attach to leadership stems from a profound need to believe that we can control our fate. To think that we are totally at the mercy of distant, vague, uncontrollable, and inexorable forces is frightening and therefore to be repressed. If we believe that leaders cause success or failure, however, we can retain a sense of self-control, since we can select and remove leaders. Thus, we attribute organizational outcomes to leader characteristics, leader strategies, leader behavior. A widely shared consensus on this attribution maintains the legend of leadership. Also, since some leaders have enough insight to anticipate a turn in fortunes for good or bad, they may calculatedly take steps that will lead observers to associate the leaders personally with the success and disassociate them from failure.

> For instance, if a manager knows that business in his division is about to improve because of the economic cycle, he may...undertake actions...that are highly visible and that will tend to identify him and his behavior closely with the division. If [he] perceives failure or a decrement in performance coming, he will attempt to associate the division and its policies and decisions with others... [Pfeffer, 1978, p. 30].

Pfeffer's point is not literally that leaders make no difference whatever. Rather, he suggests that we have vastly exaggerated the difference they do make. This sobering analysis need not suggest a moratorium on leadership theory and research, but it should temper our expectations as to what we hope to find.

LEADERSHIP: CONCLUDING NOTE

Clearly, we are a long way from being able to offer leaders prescriptions about how to behave. The effect of several decades of leadership research has been largely to cast doubt on the meager fund of knowledge we thought we had acquired from naturalistic observation. House's Path-Goal theory offers promise for predicting when and how leader consideration and initiating structure will affect subordinate attitudes, but we have little to go on if we want to predict what the leader's behavior will do to productivity.

Again, as noted in the opening pages of this chapter, we may be looking in the wrong places for the causes of productivity. Technology and work methods surely account for much of the variance in worker productivity. To the extent that anything about the leader fits in here, it is the leader's intelligence, training, experience, or skills—not interpersonal "style"—that come to the fore. Other determinants of productivity include, of course, the cognitive and/or motor skills of subordinates and perhaps their deeply ingrained work habits developed through previous histories of reinforcement. For example, Merrens and Garrett (1975) found that subjects who strongly endorsed the Protestant work ethic (presumably a residual of early reinforcement contingencies) spent more time and produced more on a boring, repetitive task than did subjects who tended to reject the Protestant work ethic. Finally, the larger organizational environment, as a complex system of many variables, exerts behavioral effects on both the leader and the group. Even such mundane and unglamorous factors as noise level, heat, humidity, lighting, and space can, in some cases, account for a considerable proportion of differences in productivity.

Perhaps we need to look more at the possible effects of leader behavior on criteria other than productivity—for example, its possible effects on *variability* in productivity (from one subordinate to another or from one time to another), on subordinates' informal modes of cooperation with or accommodation to organizational requests, or on the informal contributions which subordinates make to departments other than their own. Such criteria may not directly or immediately affect overall organizational effectiveness, but they nevertheless represent behavioral dimensions that are of concern to practically all organization members.

SUMMARY

The study of leadership has traditionally taken as its independent variables the attributes of the leader, dimensions of leader behavior, or leadership styles; dependent variables have included measures of performance and satisfaction. Stogdill (1948) found certain attributes to be somewhat consistently related to attainment of the leadership role, but little evidence that any single trait or cluster of traits predicted the effectiveness of persons in leadership positions. The Ohio State Leadership Studies identified initiating structure and consideration as two dimensions of leader behavior. Empirical work has shown leader consideration to be consistently related to subordinate satisfaction and correlated subordinate behaviors, such as turnover and grievance processing. However, relationships between initiating structure and satisfaction, or between productivity and either consideration or initiating structure, have varied in size and direction from study to study. House's path-goal theory of leadership attempts to identify situational factors that would explain such variations. Participative styles of leadership generally produce greater subordinate satisfaction than do directive styles, but again the relationship with performance varies. Fiedler's Contingency Model of Leadership Effectiveness has demonstrated some explanatory power in resolving inconsistencies in the effects of participation on group performance; but the logic and research underlying Fiedler's theory have been subjects of considerable controversy. Recent evidence strongly suggests that leader behavior is itself determined by level of group performance—as much as or more than it determines group behavior. Further advances in our understanding of leadership effectiveness will probably hinge on a viable taxonomy of tasks and a suitable reconceptualization of causes and effects of the leader's behavior.

CONCEPTS TO REMEMBER

Ohio State Leadership Studies
consideration
initiating structure
Managerial Grid®
Path-Goal theory of leadership
Substitutes for leadership
participation controversy
human relations rationale for participation

human resources rationale for participation
Contingency Model of Leadership Effectiveness
Esteem for Least Preferred Co-worker (LPC) scale
reciprocal causality
Vertical Dyad Linkage (VDL) model

QUESTIONS FOR DISCUSSION

1. How do you explain Fleishman's finding that leaders high in consideration could also generate high levels of initiating structure without increasing turnover and grievances?

2. Under what job conditions, or in what types of work environments, would a leader profile high in both consideration and initiating structure probably *not* be appropriate?

3. What are the risks inherent in holding a "human relations" rationale for participative supervision?

4. What background, motivational, or personality factors do you think would make a leader high LPC or low LPC?

5. Why have leadership theorists and researchers only recently addressed the reciprocal causality question?

6. Suppose that we are eventually forced to conclude from accumulated empirical research findings that differences in leader behavior or leader style have a negligible effect on group or unit productivity. Should we then discontinue the study of leadership? Why or why not?

CASE[3]

The ABC Company is a medium-sized corporation which manufactures automotive parts. Recently, the company president attended a leadership seminar and came away deeply impressed with the effect

---

[3]W. D. Heier, "Which Style is Best?" Reprinted from J. E. Dittrich and R.A. Zawacki (Eds.), *People and Organizations* (Plano, Tex.: Business Publications, 1981). ©1981 by Business Publications, Inc.

various leadership styles could have on the output and morale of the organization.

In mulling over how he might proceed, the president decided to utilize the services of Paul Patterson, a management consultant, who was currently reviewing the goals and objectives of the company. The president told Paul about the leadership seminar and how impressed he had been and that a leadership survey of the company was desired.

It was determined that the division headed by Donald Drake should be the test case and that Paul would report to the president upon completion of that survey. Some of the notes made by Paul in his interviews with the key managers in Drake's division follow.

Ancil Able

Ancil is very proud of the output of his section. He has always stressed the necessity for good control procedures and efficiency and is very insistent that project instructions be fully understood by his subordinates and that follow-up communications be rapid, complete, and accurate. Ancil serves as the clearinghouse for all incoming and outgoing work. He gives small problems to one individual to complete, but if the problem is large he calls in several key people. Usually, his employees are briefed on what the policy is to be, what part of the report each subordinate is to complete, and the completion date. Ancil considers this as the only way to get full coordination without lost motion or an overlap of work.

Ancil considers it best for a boss to remain aloof from his subordinates, and believes that being "buddy-buddy" tends to hamper discipline. He does his "chewing out" in private and his praising, too. He believes that people in his section really know where they stand.

According to Ancil, the biggest problem in business today is that subordinates just will not accept responsibility. He states that his people have lots of opportunities to show what they can do but not many really try too hard.

One comment Ancil made was that he does not understand how his subordinates got along with the previous section head who ran a very "loose shop." Ancil stated his boss is quite happy with the way things go in his section.

Bob Black

Bob believes that every employee has a right to be treated as an individual and espouses the theory that it is a boss's responsibility and duty to cater to the employee's needs. He noted that he is constantly doing little things for his subordinates and gave as an example his presentation of two tickets to an art show to be held at the City

Gallery next month. He stated that the tickets cost $5 each but that it will be both educational and enjoyable for the employee and his wife. This was done to express his appreciation for a good job the man had done a few months back.

Bob says he always makes a point of walking through his section area at least once each day, stopping to speak to at least 25 percent of the employees on each trip.

Bob does not like to "knock" anyone, but he noted that Ancil Able ran one of those "taut ships" you hear about. He stated that Ancil's employees are probably not too happy but there isn't much they can do but wait for Ancil to move.

Bob said he had noticed a little bit of bypassing going on in the company but that most of it is just due to the press of business. His idea is to run a friendly, low-keyed operation with a happy group of subordinates. Although he confesses that they might not be as efficient in terms of speedy outputs as other units, he considers he has far greater subordinate loyalty and higher morale and that his subordinates work well as an expression of their appreciation of his (Bob's) enlightened leadership.

Charles Carr

Charlie says his principal problem is the shifting of responsibilities between his section and others in the division. He considers his section the "fire drill" area that gets all the rush, hot items, whether or not they belong in his section. He seems to think this is caused by his immediate superior not being too sure who should handle what jobs in the division.

Charlie admits he hasn't tried to stop this practice. He stated (with a grin) that it makes the other section heads jealous but they are afraid to complain. They seem to think Charlie is a personal friend of the division manager, but Charlie says this is not true.

Charlie said he used to be embarrassed in meetings when it was obvious he was doing jobs out of his area but he has gotten used to it by now, and apparently the other section heads have also.

Charlie's approach to discipline is just keep everybody busy and "you won't have those kinds of problems." He stated that a good boss doesn't have time to hold anybody's hand, like Bob Black does, and tell the guy what a great job he's doing. Charlie believes that if you promise people you will keep an eye on their work for raises and promotion purposes, most of the problems take care of themselves.

Charlie stated that he believes in giving a guy a job to do and then letting him do it without too much checking on his work. He believes most of his subordinates know the score and do their jobs reasonably well without too much griping.

If he has a problem, it is probably the fact that the role and scope of his section has become a little blurred by current practices. Charlie did state that he thinks he should resist a recent tendency for "company people above my division manager's level" to call him up to their offices to hear his ideas on certain programs. However, Charlie is not too sure that this can be stopped without creating a ruckus of some kind. He says he is studying the problem.

Donald Drake

As division manager, Don thinks things are going pretty well since he has not had any real complaints from his superiors in the company, beyond the "small problem" type of thing. He thinks his division is at about the same level of efficiency as the other divisions in the organization.

His management philosophy is to let the section managers find their own level, organizational niche, and form of operation and then check to see if the total output of the division is satisfactory. He stated that he has done this with his present section heads. This was the policy being used when he (Don) was a section head and it has worked fine for him.

Don considers his function as that of a clearinghouse for division inputs and outputs, and sees his job basically as a coordinating one, coupled with the requirement for him to "front" for the division. He believes that you should let a man expand his job activities as much as he is able to do so. Don noted that Charlie Carr had expanded greatly as a manager since he (Don) had arrived. Says he frequently takes Charlie with him to high-level meetings in the company, since Charlie knows more about the division's operations than anyone else in it.

Don noted that both Ancil and Bob seem to do a creditable job in their sections. He has very little contact with Ancil's employees but occasionally has to see one of Bob Black's boys about something the employee has fouled up. This results from the fact that Bob considers such a face-to-face confrontation between the division manager and a lower-level section employee a good lesson to impress upon the subordinate that he has let down his boss. Don Drake said he is not too keen on this procedure but that Bob considers it a most valuable training device to teach the employee to do a good job every time, so Don goes along with it.

Questions

How is the Vertical Dyad Linkage model illustrated in this case? How can both Ancil and Bob "seem to do a creditable job in their sections" with such contrasting approaches?

REFERENCES

Bales, R. F.   The equilibrium problem in small groups. In T. Parsons, R.F. Bales, & E. A. Shils, *Working papers in the theory of action.* Glencoe, Ill.: Free Press, 1953.

Barrow, J. C.   Worker performance and task complexity as causal determinants of leader behavior style and flexibility. *Journal of Applied Psychology,* 1976, *61,* 433–440.

Blake, R. R., & Mouton, J. S.   *Corporate excellence through grid organizational development.* Houston: Gulf Publishing, 1968.

Blumberg, P.   *Industrial democracy: The sociology of participation.* New York: Schocken Books, 1974.

Campbell, J. P., Dunnette, M. D., Lawler, E. E., III, & Weick, K. E., Jr.   *Managerial behavior, performance, and effectiveness.* New York: McGraw-Hill, 1970.

Carter, L. F.   Leadership and small group behavior. In M. Sherif & M. O. Wilson, *Group relations at the crossroads.* New York: Harper & Row, 1953.

Coch, L., & French, J. P.   Overcoming resistance to change. *Human Relations,* 1948, *1,* 512–532.

Dansereau, F. D., Jr., Graen, G., & Haga, W. J.   A vertical dyad linkage approach to leadership within formal organizations: A longitudinal investigation of the role-making process. *Organizational Behavior and Human Performance,* 1975, *13,* 46–78.

Dubin, R.   Supervision and productivity: Empirical findings and theoretical considerations. In R. Dubin, G. C. Homans, F. C. Mann, & D. C. Miller, *Leadership and productivity.* San Francisco: Chandler, 1965.

Fiedler, F. E.   A contingency model of leadership effectiveness. In L. Berkowitz (Ed.), *Advances in experimental social psychology* (Vol.1). New York: Academic Press, 1964.

Fleishman, E. A.   Twenty years of consideration and structure. In E. A. Fleishman & J. C. Hunt (Eds.), *Current developments in the study of leadership.* Carbondale: Southern Illinois University Press, 1973.

French, J. P., Jr., Israel, J., & Äs, D.   An experiment on participation in a Norwegian factory. *Human Relations,* 1960, *13,* 3–19.

Gibb, C. A.   The emergence of leadership in small temporary groups of men. Unpublished doctoral dissertation, University of Illinois, 1949. Cited in C. A. Gibb, Leadership. In G. Lindzey (Ed.), *Handbook of social psychology* (Vol. 2). Reading, Mass.: Addison-Wesley, 1954.

Greene, C. N.   The reciprocal nature of influence between leader and subordinate. *Journal of Applied Psychology,* 1975, *60,* 187–193.

Guion, R. M., & Gottier, R. F.   Validity of personality measures in personnel selection. *Personnel Psychology,* 1965, *18,* 135–164.

Hedlund, D. E.   A review of the MMPI in industry. *Psychological Reports,* 1965, *17,* 874–889.

Hersey, P., & Blanchard, K. H.   *Management of organizational behavior* (2d ed.). Englewood Cliffs, N.J.: Prentice-Hall, 1972.

House, R. J.   A path-goal theory of leader effectiveness. *Administrative Science Quarterly*, 1971, *16*, 321–338.

Katz, D., & Kahn, R. L.   *The social psychology of organizations.* New York: John Wiley & Sons, 1966.

Kerr, S., & Jermier, J. M.   Substitutes for leadership: Their meaning and measurement. *Organizational Behavior and Human Performance*, 1978, *22*, 375–403.

Kim, K., & Organ, D.   Predicting leader exchange behavior: Effects of subordinate compentence, task stress, and leader LPC. Paper presented at 1979 Academy of Management meetings, Atlanta, Ga.

Korman, A. K.   "Consideration," "Initiating structure," and organizational criteria—a review. *Personnel Psychology*, 1966, *19*, 349–361.

Krech, D., Crutchfield, R. S., & Ballachey, E. L.   *Individual in society.* New York: McGraw-Hill, 1962.

Lippitt, R., & White, R. K.   An experimental study of leadership and group life. In E. E. Maccoby, T. M. Newcomb, & E. L. Hartley (Eds.), *Readings in social psychology* (3d ed.). New York: Holt, Rinehart & Winston 1958.

Lowin, A., & Craig, J. R.   The influence of level of performance on managerial style: An experimental object-lesson in the ambiguity of correlational data. *Organizational Behavior and Human Performance*, 1968, *3*, 440–458.

McCurdy, H. G., & Eber, H. W..   Democratic versus authoritarian: A further investigation of group problem-solving. *Journal of Personality*, 1953, *22*, 258–269.

Merrens, M. R., & Garrett, J. B.   The Protestant ethic scale as a predictor of repetitive work performance. *Journal of Applied Psychology*, 1975, *60*, 125–127.

Miles, R. E.   Human relations or human resources? *Harvard Business Review*, July–August, 1965, 148–163.

Morse, N., & Reimer, E.   The experimental change of a major organizational variable. *Journal of Abnormal and Social Psychology*, 1956, *52*, 120–129.

Pfeffer, J.   The ambiguity of leadership. In M. W. McCall, Jr., and M. M. Lombardo (Eds.), *Leadership: Where else can we go?* Durham, N.C.: Duke University Press, 1978.

Sales, S. M.   Supervisory style and productivity: Review and theory. *Personnel Psychology*, 1966, *19*, 275–286.

Shaw, M. E.   A comparison of two types of leadership in various communication nets. *Journal of Abnormal and Social Psychology*, 1955, *50*, 127–134.

Sloan, A. P., Jr.   *My years with General Motors.* New York: MacFadden Books, Doubleday, 1965.

Stogdill, R. M.   Personal factors associated with leadership: A survey of the literature. *Journal of Psychology*, 1948, *25*, 35–71.

Tannenbaum, R., & Schmidt, W. H.   How to choose a leadership pattern. *Harvard Business Review*, March–April 1958, pp. 95–102.

Thomas, E. J., & Fink, C. F. Effects of group size. *Psychological Bulletin,* 1963, *60,* 371–384.

Tosi, H. A. A reexamination of personality as a determinant of the effect of participation. *Personnel Psychology,* 1970, *23,* 91–99.

Vroom, V. *Some personality determinants of the effects of participation.* Englewood Cliffs, N. J.: Prentice-Hall, 1960.

Vroom, V. H., & Yetton, P. W. *Leadership and decision-making.* Pittsburgh, University of Pittsburgh Press, 1973.

Wright, J. P. *On a clear day you can see General Motors.* New York: Avon Books, 1979.

Yukl, G. Toward a behavioral theory of leadership. *Organizational Behavior and Human Performance,* 1971, *6,* 414–440.

16

Organizations:
Internal Structure

What is organizational structure?

What are the functions of structure?

What are the classical principles of structure?

How does technology affect structure?

How does structure affect professionals?

Until well into the 19th century, most of the industrial production in England was carried out in a process known as the cottage industry or "putting out" system. In the making of cloth—which until the 19th century was England's most important industry—a wealthy merchant would buy the wool and distribute small amounts to individual families in their respective cottage homes. Wife and children, working with simple tools, would card the wool and spin the yarn, and the weaver would weave the whole cloth. The merchant would dispatch wagons to collect the finished product and transport it to warehouses in urban settings for sale or shipment abroad.

Such a system was simple and required no special genius for organization or management. The financial resources and business acumen of the capitalist merchants were the major requirements of success. Since work was done in small amounts by many independent individuals and families, using their own skills and basic implements, organizational requirements were minimal.

The Industrial Revolution changed all this. The overseas expansion of English territories opened vast new markets for finished goods; this incentive for increased production stimulated the invention of machinery and its application to manufacturing processes. With the new machinery, manufacturers could increase their output tremendously. However, the cost of the machines put them beyond the reach of almost all yeomen craftsmen; the merchant became, not only the procurer of raw materials and distributor of finished goods, but also the owner of the equipment for production. Furthermore, many of the new machines, in order to realize their potential for increased output, required a greater critical mass of personnel than could be obtained in the family cottage. Finally, the machines depended on a source of energy (such as water or steam power), which in turn meant that machinery had to be concentrated in a central location, such as next to a waterfall or near a plentiful supply of coal. The end result was the rise of the factory system: bringing large numbers of workers to a common location, assigning them to work the respective components of the larger and more complex machines, and paying a wage.

The factory system, unlike cottage industry, created a high order of *interdependence* among the individual participants. It meant that owners had to devise systems of organization not heretofore required. In short, the new methods of production created a need for the design of organizational *structure*.

STRUCTURE DEFINED

One dictionary tells us that structure is the "arrangement or interrelation of all the parts of a whole." Organization structure, then, is the formal, systematic arrangement of the operations and activities that constitute an organization and the interrelationships of these operations to one another. Miles (1980) captures this essential notion and makes it more precise by characterizing structure as the systematic patterns of *differentiation* and *integration* of organized activities. *Differentiation* refers to the process of breaking down the total system into parts that perform different, specialized functions. *Integration* refers to the process of relating the different parts to each other. To design a structure is, first of all, to divide the organization into various parts according to some criterion. Second, to design a structure is to provide some means of coordinating the functions of these parts, to link them in a coherent fashion so that various functions complement and support each other.

FUNCTIONS OF STRUCTURE

The meaning of the word *structure* tells us at once, on a general level, the functions provided by a structure: to differentiate the elements of an organization and simultaneously to integrate them. Pursuant to accomplishing these ultimate aims, however, structure fulfills certain attendant functions.

First, structure *defines the division of labor*. It does this on two levels: it determines what operations the individual participants will execute, and it specifies how the individual operations will be grouped together (e.g., at unit, department, or division level). For example, if you form an organization for washing and waxing cars, your structure will determine whether people will specialize according to process (such as hosing down, applying soap, washing, drying, applying wax, polishing) or according to job (such as having each individual do all the functions for a specific part of the car—the roof, front end, and so on). Structure would further specify whether people would work together in teams of complementary functions—a hoser, soaper, and so on making up a team—or would be treated according to common function (with hosers grouped together, polishers likewise grouped together, and so forth).

Second, structure provides the basis for *coordinating* the specialized roles and units. Whereas division of labor is accomplished by *horizontal* differentiation, coordination typically requires some degree of *vertical* differentiation. Certain roles are carved out and given a "higher" status than others; persons who enact these roles are endowed with some means of influence (official authority, charisma, expertise, reward or coercive power) for adjusting individual and group behavior. These adjustments ensure that various activities "mesh" according to some preconceived objective—e.g., that a full-sized car be completely washed and polished within some time and resource constraints.

Third, structure specifies a system of *controls,* a mechanism by which individual and group activities can be measured, evaluated, and modified at appropriate stages. As the organization becomes larger and more complex in its differentiation, this means that additional roles evolve for the purpose of monitoring the operations. For example, in your car wash 'n' wax organization, you would need some means of ensuring that the finished job met some minimal criterion (even if it were subjective), that waxers were not left idled because dryers and polishers were too far behind, that excessive amounts of water and wax were not being used. There are various methods of creating such controls; the structure will specify just which method or combination of methods will be in force.

Fourth, the structure specifies the *flow of information and communication.* When a large number of people are assembled, you obviously cannot have each individual free to communicate with each and every other person. Structure prevents such chaos by delimiting who can communicate with whom. It creates a small number of communication channels between the horizontally and vertically differentiated units. If a polisher needs a new cloth, he does not simply "ask around" until he finds one; the structure specifies to whom he should make his requisition. If the quality control specialist sees a mud spot on the grille of an otherwise gleaming Corvette, the structure provides a basis for knowing to whom to report the defect.

To say that organization structure serves these functions is not to say that any specific structural form necessarily serves them well. A structure, for example, may specify grouping people according to common function when actually a different arrangement (e.g., teams of complementary specialists) would be more efficient. Nor is structure in any sense inevitable. To be sure, we have noted that informal groups often do spontaneously generate a structure of sorts in terms of the roles played by individual members, recurrent patterns of interactions, and status distinctions. And undoubtedly it becomes arbitrary at some point whether we call such groups organizations. The key to distinguishing between informal group structure and formal organization structure is that the latter is not only formal—i.e., explicit and deliberate—but *independent of the identity of specific individuals.* We can and do describe the structure of an organization by means of a chart without reference to persons, whereas we cannot describe the emergent structure of an informal group without indicating the particular individuals involved. A small group may "become" an organization by formalizing a structure already created by informal processes, but now the structure exists apart from any unique personalities—and, of course, has a basis for outliving such personalities. We may note, then, a final function served by organization structure: *continuity of process and function* across the generations of participants.

PRINCIPLES OF STRUCTURE

Most of us are so familiar with formally structured organizations that we take contemporary organizational structure for granted. It seems "obvious" to us how the parts of an organization should relate to each other. But the people who established the industrial organizations in the 19th century had few precedents or existing principles for designing structure. The most familiar large-scale organizations were the military, the Roman Catholic church, and the political state.[1] Somehow, by trial and error, by inspiration, by observation of which organizations prospered and which had severe problems, those who ran the factories and trading firms inched their way toward a set of principles for structure.

In the process of evolving a set of such principles, many of the industrial organizations were characterized by what Webber (1979) calls the "traditional structure." One person or family owned the enterprise. The owner placed relatives in a few positions of supervision and control over a large work force that was relatively uneducated and unskilled. The ruling elite owed their positions to family ties, not to formal training, credentials, or demonstrated competence; even the rare outsider who breached the small management group owed allegiance to the owner, much like the medieval vassals showed personal fealty to the lord or baron. The objectives of the firm, beyond that of retaining family ownership, derived from the personal feelings of the owners. These sentiments might change from day to day and be interpreted differently by the few managers who ran operations. Workers might be told one thing one day by one manager and something althogether contradictory the next day by a different manager; they might have no basis at all for knowing which manager to obey, but disobedience to either could mean lost wages or dismissal simply because of offending one of the high and mighty. A certain routine in operations might develop simply from habit and inertia, but never with the force of policy or authority. Deviations from customary practice might suddenly occur simply because of the whim of the owner or his personal lieutenants.

Over the years, organizations operating with such structures might prosper during flush times, but periodic contractions in the national economy forced them into one of three fates: they had to close doors; sell out to a new owner and thus become part of a larger enterprise; or "go public" as owners diluted their personal control by selling stock to a large number of investors. In either case, the effect was substantially the same. Ownership became more and more distant

---

[1]Actually, there were quite a few large-scale economic organizations, in Europe and elsewhere, long before 1800, and many of these were remarkably well administered. However, the basis of their structure was not made explicit and was not well known to most entrepreneurs.

from the day-to-day running of the organization. The stage was set for the emergence and growth of a new managerial class: a kind whose rewards would depend upon performance rather than family ties and who could manage without constant meddling from the owner or his relatives. By the end of the 19th century, the larger industrial organizations reflected fewer traces of the traditional structure and revealed a different type of structure: the rational bureaucracy.

The Bureaucracy

German sociologist Max Weber (1864–1930) was perhaps the first to offer a compelling description of the more rational organizational structure that had emerged in industry. Weber used the term *bureaucracy* to describe it, and it is important to note that he used the term in the most *favorable* sense. Weber described the defining characteristics of the bureaucratic structure as follows:

1. The organization is founded upon a system of authority that is legal in character. Authority inheres in an office, not in the person who holds the office. Participants consent to the influence of those whose power is legitimated by the formal rules defining the offices and their relationships one to another.
2. Activities required for organizational purposes are distributed in a fixed way as official duties.
3. Authority is distributed in a stable way and "strictly delimited by rules concerning the coercive means, physical, sacerdotal, or otherwise, which may be placed at the disposal of officials" (Gerth & Mills, 1968, p. 196).
4. There is an explicit system by which each office is made subordinate to others in authority.
5. Selection and promotion of officials is based on training and objective criteria; entrance into an office means acceptance of specific obligations, rights, and compensation. Dismissal can result only from unwillingness or inability to carry out such obligations.
6. Management follows a set of written and publicly available rules, policies, and procedures.
7. Official duties are performed according to "calculable rules," without regard to "personal, irrational, and emotional elements which escape calculation."

Of course, no organization then known to Weber or to us today would operate strictly and perfectly according to such guidelines. Weber was making use of an abstract concept, the "ideal type," toward which emergent organizations seemed to be developing. The closer an organization's structure approximated such ideals, the more it constituted his notion of a rational bureaucracy. This, he contended, would increasingly dominate modern life because of its

> . . . purely technical superiority over any other form of organization. The fully developed bureaucratic mechanism compares with other organizations exactly as does the machine with the non-mechanical modes of production.
>
> Precision, speed, unambiguity, knowledge of the files, continuity, discretion, unity, strict subordination, reduction of friction and of material and personal costs—these are raised to the optimum point in the strictly bureaucratic administration . . . [Gerth & Mills, 1968, p. 214].

PRINCIPLES OF STRUCTURE

During the first half of this century, the published works of a number of management theorists—such as Henri Fayol in France, Oliver Sheldon of Great Britain, and in the United States, James D. Mooney, Allan C. Reilly, Luther Gulick, and Lyndall Urwick—laid the foundation for what was conceived as a set of universal principles of administration within a rational bureaucracy. The individual contributors did not agree totally with each other, and in some cases were unaware of each other's work. Nonetheless, their reflection upon years of experience in public administration and private industry all seemed to converge upon a body of precepts now known as Classical Management Theory.

The Scalar Principle.   According to Massie (1965), "the heart of the classical organizational structure is the idea of hierarchy, which the classical theory calls the scalar principle" (p. 396). This principle states that authority should flow in an unbroken line from top to bottom of the organization. Starting from the bottom, every position is related by subordination to another position to which it is accountable. Everyone has a boss.

Unity of Command.   No member of an organization should be responsible to more than one superior. Violation of this principle would only result in conflicting orders, confusion, and hesitation. Some theorists recognized that perfect fidelity to this principle might in some cases be impossible and qualified it to state that no member of an organization should be accountable to more than one superior for any single function. Most of the early management writers, however, felt that any qualification whatsoever of this principle should be contemplated only with the greatest reluctance.

Span of Control.   This principle stated that the number of subordinates responsible to any one superior should be limited to a range of about three to eight. Among the classical theorists themselves there was considerable difference of opinion as to whether the optimum span was closer to three or eight, but they agreed on the rationale for limiting it: As the number of subordinates increases arithmetically (say, from 4 to 5), the number of possible *relationships* among them and with the superior increases geometrically (from 44 to 100).[2] And the classical theorists never doubted that the superior was responsible for monitoring and controlling these relationships.

In our own times, a number of popular writers have suggested that many contemporary problems in organizational functioning have arisen because of disregard of the span of control, especially at the CEO level. A management team that studied the organizational structure of a large state university found that the university president had a span of control of over 30. Classical theorists would have regarded this as an atrocious state of affairs.

Preserving a narrow span of control does, however, exact a price of its own. With a given number of total members, the narrower the span, the greater the number of levels in the hierarchy. Narrow spans lead to steep, tall structures while wider spans result in flatter organizations.

Distinction between Line and Staff. Classical theorists took account of the increasing role played by highly specialized experts in such areas as engineering, logistics, and quality control. The impressive victories of the Prussian army in the latter part of the 19th century were attributed in large measure to the availability of a technical staff to the commanding generals. That occasion also offered a solution to the problem of how to use such expertise without violating the principle of span of control. Classical writers carefully distinguished between the *line*, which performs the major functions of the organization, and *staff*, the offices which provide support, service, and advice to line officials. Formal authority follows the line; staff officials have no line authority but rather an advisory role. Only over other, junior staff specialists should staff officers exert authority.

Specialization. Classical theorists offered essentially four criteria for dividing and grouping activities: by the major purpose served (e.g., the type of product or services), by process, by type of clientele, and by location or geography. Whichever basis was chosen, it was important that the categories so defined not overlap. Also, while the basis for specialization might vary from one level to another—for example, the divisions might be separated according to type of product, while

---

[2]V.A. Graicunas is credited with deriving the formula for computing the number of possible relationships between a superior and n subordinates. The total set of possible relationships equals the number of direct relationships between the superior and each individual subordinate, n; plus the relationships between each pair of subordinates, $n(n-1)$; plus the relationships between the superior and each subset of subordinates $n\left(\dfrac{2^n}{2} - 1\right)$.

within divisions the smaller units could be defined by process—the unity-of-command principle dictated that the basis of specialization be consistent across any one level of authority. In other words, you should not have someone simultaneously responsible to both a product manager and a process manager.

The four bases of specialization each offered certain comparative advantages. The bias of classical theory tended to favor, where practicable, a scheme of departmentation according to process or function, because it encouraged refinement of technical skills and a high degree of specialization of labor.

An Overview of Classical Principles of Structure. Taken as a whole, the precepts converged upon by classical theory concern themselves primarily with the *internal control* function of structure. The classical theorists implicitly assumed that one could previsualize all necessary operations, and the relevant criterion of structure was the *efficiency* with which these operations could be carried out. The principles espoused by classical theory were proposed as providing for strict adherence to a master plan for speed and economy in operations. Essentially, these principles rested on a *closed-systems* view of organizations (Katz & Kahn, 1966), or—like Weber—a conception of organizations as machines. This was perhaps a reasonable approach to take if one could ignore the shock effects of an organization's environment.

It should be obvious that classical principles of structure rested on *formal authority* as the definitive solution to problems of control and coordination. Otherwise, they would not have given such attention to the questions of span of control, unity of command, and hierarchy. This concern made eminently good sense in a culture whose socialization processes predisposed individuals to accept and internalize symbols of authority, in a time when authority levels correlated quite well with differences in expertise and understanding of operations, and when the hierarchy within an organization accurately reflected clear-cut class distinctions in the larger society. If and when these conditions failed to exist, authority might be insufficient by itself to serve as a basis for structure.

Lest the reader conclude that we have simply been constructing some kind of historical straw man only to demolish it later, we should emphasize that the classical principles still have enormous relevance and usefulness in many quarters. The conditions giving rise to them and the implicit assumptions on which they were based have not by any means been entirely nullified by subsequent history. We suspect that a great many business and public-service organizations would operate more effectively if managed more closely in line with classical principles. However, these principles aimed at universal applicability, a claim to be challenged by subsequent empirical work.

TECHNOLOGY AND STRUCTURE

Organizations have characteristic *technologies,* mandated in part by the product or service they provide. A technology is a blend or sequence of human and mechanical activities that transforms information, materials, or people (such as clients or patients) from one state to another. Put another way, a technology is an interrelated set of operations for processing inputs into outputs. The technologies of our hyopthetical car wash 'n' wax outfit include the high-pressure hose, the application of soap, the use of sponges and chamois cloth, the application of "elbow grease" in an overlapping circular motion, and so on. More sophisticated technologies involve the use of computers, typewriters, telephones, assembly lines, pipes, and lasers.

A pioneering study conducted by British sociologist Joan Woodward in the late 1950s and early 1960s produced evidence challenging the classical principle that any one form of organization structure has universal applicability. Her findings suggested that structure is contingent upon technology.

Woodward (1965) included in her study about 100 manufacturing firms in the South Essex region of England. She found no basis for predicting effectiveness from span of control, steepness of hierarchy, type of departmental specialization, or mix between line and staff. Only when the firms were sorted out according to the dominant form of technology employed did structure predict effectiveness.

Woodward identified three distinctive types of technology: *unit* (or small-batch) *production; continuous process,* and *mass production. Unit* or small-batch companies produced made-to-order products in small lot sizes in order to meet requirements of specific customers—for example, custom-tailored suits and special-purpose tools. Technologies in the category of *mass* production manufactured standardized products in huge volumes according to fixed specifications, typically in an assembly line format. Finally, those firms that employed continuous-process technology were associated with homogeneous products—such as chemicals, pharmaceuticals, petroleum, or gases—that underwent intensive refinement, typically in highly automated processes.

Woodward found that structure tended to vary with the dominant technology employed; furthermore, the most successful firms possessed a structure generally similar to the statistical average of those firms using a particular technology. Unit and small-batch production technologies were associated with a relatively low-pitched hierarchical structure (few levels of authority), a small proportion of staff officials, a relatively low degree of formalization in terms of standardized procedures and explicit rules, and a narrow span of supervisory control. Mass production technologies were associated with the widest span of supervisory control, the sharpest distinction between line and staff functions, and the most formalized control and sanction procedures. Continuous-process technologies were characterized by steep hierarchical structures, a narrow span of control for top-level managers, and a greater ratio of managerial personnel to total work force.

Thus, Woodward's work seemed to "establish the idea of a contingency theory linking organizational effectiveness to an appropriate match between structure and technology" (Miles, 1980, p. 59). This has become known as the *technological imperative hypothesis.*

Subsequent work (e.g., Hickson, Pugh, & Pheysey, 1969) has led to findings that suggest a modification of the technological imperative. It appears that technology determines structure only for those units directly impinged upon by the production work flow. Furthermore, the smaller the organization, the greater the effect of technology upon overall organizational structure. In larger firms, technology exerts less influence on structure. Another study (Child & Mansfield, 1972), while supporting the view that technology influences structure for small organizations, also found that large organizations—regardless of technology—coverge toward similarity in overall structure: high degree of specialization, formalization, and standardization.

BUREAUCRACY AND PROFESSIONALS

We noted that classical principles of bureaucratic structure placed a heavy emphasis on the role of formal authority in controlling and coordinating operations. So long as differences in authority match differences in expertise and requisite knowledge of operations, this emphasis on authority seems appropriate. The need for highly specialized experts could be handled by putting them in staff positions, separate from the line of functional authority and operating in an advisory or supporting relationship to line managers. But what would happen if the line activities themselves became so sophisticated and complex that specialized expertise were needed at all levels of operations? What would be the result if the *authority* to make decisions were not accompanied by the *ability* or *knowledge* required to make a rational decision? How would managers use authority to control the activities of diverse, specialized personnel whose expertise exceeded that of the manager?

One result of this discrepancy between authority and expertise is the syndrome which Thompson (1961) labels *bureaupathy.* Managers are caught between the horns of a dilemma. They are accountable to a superior for results but must discharge this accountability by reliance upon subordinates whose skills they do not understand. This produces insecurity and anxiety. Managers may attempt to cope with this insecurity by using structure to reduce uncertainty and assert personal control. This coping is manifested by a compulsion for more and more rules, insistence on the rights of office, exaggerated aloofness, excessive concern for quantitative criteria as controls, and resistance to change. As Hall (1972) notes, "these reactions are organizationally and personally damaging" (p. 185). Bureaupathy is a condition in which bureaucratization has been distorted and misdirected.

Almost coincident with the development of bureaucratic structure has been the increasing professionalization of much of the work force in organizations. Both of these trends follow from the rationalization of work. Yet theorists such as Kornhauser (1962) consider these simultaneous trends to pose a dilemma. The professional "knowledge worker"—for example, the research scientist in industry—values autonomy, while bureaucratic structures constrain individual freedom of action for the purposes of control and coordination. The professional believes that any control over professional activities should rest with professional colleagues, while the bureaucracy exerts control through the hierarchy. Professionals view expertise as the appropriate base of influence, but formalized structures define authority as the proper means of influence and decision making. Finally, professionals are torn between loyalty to the employing organization and to an external professional association. Thus, in the opinion of some theorists, professionals and bureaucratic structures simply do not mix. Either the bureaucratic structure must adapt to the value system of the professional—thus evolving into some new form of organization—or the professional will experience *alienation*. In a state of alienation, professionals no longer internalize the goals of their work; they become disenchanted, estranged from the essential nature of their work, and lacking in ego involvement. Thus the potential contribution of the professional is diminished.

However, research by Hall (1968) found that the supposed irreconcilability of professional value systems and bureaucratic structures has been somewhat overstated. He developed measures of five dimensions of professional values—identification with an external professional association, belief in public service, belief in self-regulation, a sense of calling, and desire for autonomy—and administered these measures to a varied sample of professional employees that included physicians, lawyers, engineers, nurses, accountants, social workers, and teachers. He also obtained measures of six dimensions of bureaucracy in the employing organizations: the importance of hierarchical authority, the extent of division of labor, the importance of rules, the extent of specified procedures, the emphasis on impersonality, and the value placed on technical competence. While all of the bureaucracy measures except technical competence had strong negative relationships with feelings of autonomy, the general pattern was one of only a very slight negative relationship between dimensions of bureaucratic structure and professional values. Hall concluded:

> The presence of relatively rigid hierarchy may not adversely affect the work of professionals if the hierarchy is recognized as legitimate...the presence of a hierarchy may facilitate communications from the professionals to the top of the organization.

Organ and Greene (1981) found that, while structural formalization precipitated a sense of role conflict for professional scientists and engineers, it also had the positive result of reducing role ambiguity. Professionals, like everyone else, seem to need a certain amount of structure to communicate what is expected of them, help them organize their own activities, and facilitate interaction with other professionals. Therefore, it cannot be concluded that bureaucratic structures necessarily cause alienation among professionals. This can happen, but when it does it is more apt to result from the *content* of the structure than from structure *per se.*

To conclude, the classical principles or organization structure have been challenged by two points of view. The technological imperative hypothesis holds that classical principles lack general validity because technology type leads to variation in structure. The professional-alienation hypothesis argues that bureaucratic structures cannot accommodate professional value systems and therefore they adversely affect professionals' sense of job involvement. But a number of empirical studies suggest that these challenges are somewhat less than decisive. There is reason to believe that technology type has less impact on structure as organizations become larger, and there is evidence that formalized structures can have positive effects on professionals that match or exceed any adverse effects.

In the next chapter we will consider what has become a much more serious threat to the universal applicability of classical principles—the influence of the organization's environment.

SUMMARY

Organization structure is the pattern of differentiation and intergration of the parts of the organization. The rational bureaucratic structure developed in the 19th century as a device for efficiently running industrial operations on a large scale. The bureaucracy was characterized by Max Weber as a form of organization vastly superior to traditional structures. Its distinguishing features were a system of legalistic authority, the rights and obligations of office, formal rules and procedures, and impersonality. Classical management theory proposed a universally applicable set of principles for the design of bureaucratic structures: the scalar principle, unity of command, limited span of control, distinction between line and staff, and criteria for specialization. Woodward's technological imperative hypothesis challenged the validity of any notion of universally optimal form of structure by demonstrating empirically that structure followed from technology type. Later research suggested that technology affected structure only in a limited fashion and that its general effect diminished with increased size of organization. Other theorists argued that the bureaucratic structure could not accommodate the employment of professionals on a large scale, but empirical studies found that structure has favorable as well as adverse effects on professionals.

CONCEPTS TO REMEMBER

traditional structures	line-staff distinction
bureaucracy	technology
scalar principle	technological imperative hypothesis
unity of command	bureaupathy
span of control	professional alienation hypothesis

QUESTIONS FOR DISCUSSION

1. Max Weber expressed nothing but admiration for the rational bureaucratic structure. Yet in our own times we often use the word *bureaucracy* as a term with thoroughly negative connotations. Why?

2. Classical theorists put a limit of about eight on supervisory spans of control. Yet Woodward's study found many instances of successful manufacturing firms with spans of control in the teens and 20s. How would you account for this?

3. Make a list of the pros and cons of having a highly formalized structure with strict rules and standard procedures. Under what conditions would the pros outweigh the cons, and vice versa?

4. In the chapter on leadership we noted the functions that leadership performs and the possibility of substitutes for leadership. Considering the functions performed by organization structure, can you identify substitutes for structure? Under what conditions are these substitutes most likely to be practical and viable?

REFERENCES

Child, J., Mansfield, R. Technology, size, and structure. *Sociology*, 1972, 6, 369–393.

Gerth, H. H., & Mills, C. W.   *From Max Weber: Essays in sociology.* New York: Oxford University Press, 1968.

Hall, R. H.   Professionalization and bureaucratization. *American Sociological Review,* 1968, *33,* 92–104.

Hall, R. H.   *Organizations: Structure and process.* Englewood Cliffs, N.J.: Prentice-Hall, 1972.

Hickson, D. J., Pugh, D. S., & Pheysey, D. C.   Operations technology and organization structure: An empirical reappraisal. *Administrative Science Quarterly,* 1969, *14,* 378–397.

Katz, D., & Kahn, R. L.   *The social psychology of organizations.* New York: John Wiley & Sons, 1966.

Kornhauser, W.   *Scientists in industry.* Berkeley and Los Angeles: University of California Press, 1962.

Massie, J. L.   Management theory. In J. G. March (Ed.), *Handbook of organizations.* Chicago: Rand McNally, 1965.

Miles, R. H.   *Macro organizational behavior.* Santa Monica, Calif.: Goodyear Publishing, 1980.

Organ, D. W., & Greene, C. N.   The effects of formalization on involvement: A compensatory process approach. *Administrative Science Quarterly,* 1981, *26,* 237–252.

Thompson, V.   *Modern organizations.* New York: Alfred A. Knopf, 1961.

Webber, R. A.   *Management: Basic elements of managing organizations.* Homewood, Ill.: Richard D. Irwin, 1979.

Woodward, J.   *Industrial organization: Theory and practice.* London: Oxford University Press, 1965.

17

Organizations:
The External Environment

How is an organization's functioning affected by its external environment?

What are the important dimensions of organization environments—and what are the implications for organization structure?

What functions do organization boundaries serve?

What are the distinctive qualities of organization boundary roles?

What structural forms have evolved to adapt to turbulent environments?

The classical principles of bureaucratic structure rested on the assumption of a *deterministic* system. It was assumed that the necessary operations leading to goal attainment could be previsualized in an all-encompassing master plan; therefore, some fixed scheme of differentiating and integrating components of the organization could be specified for maximizing the efficiency of its operations. At each stage of analysis, rational decision making under conditions of certainty could prevail. The organization was seen as an essentially *closed system*—a microcosm unto itself, impervious to the shocks of external forces.

Modern organization theory, by contrast, conceives of organizations as *open systems* which can only be defined with respect to some larger *environment*. The organization must, both in structure and process, reach some working accommodation with this environment—otherwise, like the hapless dinosaurs who could not adapt to the Ice Age, the organization does not survive.

Modern organization theory does not in any sense erase the contributions of the classical school. Rather, it redefines classical principles, seeing them as rules that apply to a restricted range of conditions—much as Einstein's Relativity Theory redefined Newtonian principles as rules that apply to a limited range of phenomena. Beyond this, modern organization theory embraces a different criterion for evaluating organizational effectiveness: survival. Again, it would be too simplistic to state that efficiency now becomes irrelevant. Efficiency still matters, but it is a *bounded* notion of efficiency. Effective structures are those that attain an efficiency of operations subject to the proviso that they have the flexibility, or slack needed to adapt to changes in their environment.

The ultimate principle reached by the modern, open-systems approach is that of *contingency*, which states that the optimal structure of an organization is one which is suited to its environment. Classical principles of the rational bureaucracy have relevance to certain organizational environments but not all.

THE ENVIRONMENT

Churchman (1968) defines the organization's environment as comprising those variables that affect the performance of the organization, but over which the organization has no direct control. This definition has the advantage of generality but fails to specify the significant external forces that affect an organization and to which it must accommodate. Dill (1958) offers the concept of *task environment* and defines it in terms of four sectors:

1. *Sources of inputs* to the organization. These include suppliers of labor, raw materials, capital, technology, and information.

2. *Receivers of outputs* from the organization, such as customers, users, distributors, clients.
3. *Competitors* for the organization's sources of inputs and for its relationships with output receivers. This category may be broadened to include the notion of *contenders*—those other organizations which seek to usurp, annex, or transgress the organization's domain or sphere of action.
4. *Regulatory groups* such as government agencies, community action organizations, trade associations, and unions. More broadly, one could define this category as those external groups that, to some extent, are able to impose their criteria of *legitimacy* upon the organization's purpose and activities.

To an increasing extent, the environment of organizations in modern societies is composed of other organizations. Evan (1966) has offered the concept of *organization set* as a methodological tool for characterizing an organization's interaction and relationships with its environment. Figure 17–1 provides an example of a hypothetical organization set. The *focal organization* in this case is a state-supported university. The university's survival and effectiveness depend upon inputs in the form of money from the state legislature, foundations, and alumni groups. The university's raw materials—educable pupils—come predominantly from state and area high schools. Its output—educated students—flows to corporations, government, and other schools (for graduate work or to join their faculties). The legiti-

Figure 17–1
Example of the Organization Set: A Focal Organization and Its Relationships with Environmental Organizations

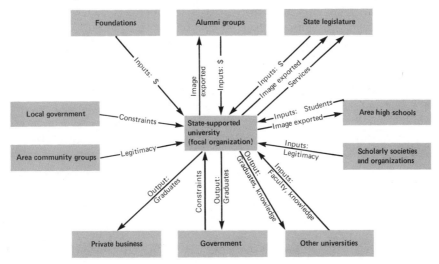

macy of the university is a function of the perceptions of scholarly societies, alumni, community groups, and other organizations which include in their purposes the evaluation of the university's service to the public. The local municipal government, state government agencies, and similar groups exert some constraints on the university's activities.

Not all of these interorganizational relationships need to be formalized, nor are they all characterized by similar frequencies of interaction episodes. One could follow the example of Hall (1972) by using darker or thicker lines to represent more frequent interaction episodes, or use dotted lines to represent unofficial or ad hoc interaction patterns.

Evan developed the idea of organization set from Merton's (1957) concept of the *role set*. The role set is composed of the roles and role relationships that an individual has by virtue of occupying a particular focal role or office. The analogy is useful, for organizations experience stresses in their relationships with other organizations similar to those that an individual experiences in his or her relationships with other individuals. Just as a person may fall prey to role conflict due to the conflicting expectations of other persons, so an organization can find itself caught in the middle among the conflicting demands of its various publics. The state university in our example may be called upon by the legislature to adopt expense-saving measures which scholarly societies or other universities regard as inimical to quality teaching and the pursuit of new knowledge. Just as an individual may experience role overload, the state university may be pressed to do so many different things that it ends up doing none of them very well. One suspects that organizations use much the same coping mechanisms that individuals employ for managing such stresses. These coping mechanisms include the following: formulating a policy by which some claims are given greater priority than others; tilting toward the agents who possess greater capacity to reward or harm; double-talk, by which verbal but not substantive concessions are made to some agents; outright repudiation of some expectations; and simple "muddling through," taking whatever steps are necessary when dealing with one public or one problem at a time. As a consequence, the operational goals of an organization seldom coincide with those expressed in its charter or publicly espoused by its leader. The goals of day-to-day organizational functioning represent a continuous evolutionary process that is shaped in part by components of the organization's environment (Thompson & McEwen, 1958).

A further observation that Figure 17–1 implies, but that should be made explicit here, is that the relationships in the organization set exert influence on the functions *inside* the focal organization. The state university represents a good case in point. From the end of World War II until the mid-1960s, universities easily disposed of their outputs, flourished in a cultural climate which readily endorsed the value of higher education and research, and went about their business in a relatively autonomous fashion. (A deviation from this trend occurred in the early 1950s—the McCarthy era—when some states exacted loyalty oaths from faculty in publicly supported schools.) Beginning around the late 1960s, many universities began to face difficulty in placing their graduates; the value of higher education became a moot point in the views of many community groups; state legislatures and alumni tightened their grip on the money faucet; and both federal government and civil rights agencies demanded that universities demonstrate affirmative action in the treatment of women and minority groups. The placement problem has increased the concern of officials over ensuring adequate curriculum options for vocational training. The reappraisal of the unquestioned value of higher education has permeated the classrooms with an atmosphere that puts the burden of proof on the scholars ("Just why is this course or this material essential to our knowledge?"), and this defensive posture complicates the design and implementation of curricula. The scarcity of input dollars tends to stimulate competition among departments for students, a development which could ideally be a healthy guard against complacency but could also compromise traditional educational values. Accountability for affirmative action corrects old wrongs but also makes more legalistic and formalistic certain processes that were previously handled in easy informality. The foregoing analysis is not to be interpreted as a lamentation, or as a chastisement of either the university or its publics. Hindsight is 20-20, and few university officials even in the 1950s, no matter how forward-looking, could have foreseen the changes in store. Moreover, the other organizations in the university's organization set (state legislature, federal government, economic organizations, and others) had *their* own environments to respond to. Our point has been to show how changes in the university's environment have, for better or for worse, made university functioning vastly different from what it was two decades ago.

DIMENSIONS OF ORGANIZATIONAL ENVIRONMENTS

Because the external environment has a significant effect on organizational functioning, modern organization theory has sought to develop a basis for describing and analyzing environments. Organization theorists have attempted to identify the important dimensions along which environments differ and which seem to have the most critical implications for an organization's strategy and structure. The most noteworthy characteristics of external environments concern their *complexity, rate of change, uncertainty,* and *beneficence.*

Complexity

Organizations vary in the number and heterogeneity of the elements in their environments. The greater the number of discrete components of the environment, the more complex the environment. A large, state-supported university, for example, tends to have a more complex environment than a small, private school because the former is dependent on more different sources of inputs for faculty, funds, accreditation, and students, and—because of its use of taxpayers' money—is subject to the political pressures of more groups.

Increasing complexity of an organization's environment threatens the ability of organization officials to make rational decisions for two reasons: (1) it increases the amount of information that must be processed, and (2) it makes it more difficult to take actions that are maximally effective with respect to all environmental elements simultaneously. Put another way, the more diverse and heterogeneous the environment, the more constraints the organization has to satisfy in its decisions and operations.

Nonetheless, organization officials are often observed to plot strategies that actually create greater complexity in their environments. Corporations seek new consumer markets, financial institutions search for more variety in their sources of money, government agencies attempt to serve a greater variety of clientele. Complexity of environment often is the natural consequence of growth. Furthermore, it may be essential in order to survive, as it tends to lower the risks otherwise entailed by dependence on a single input source.

Rate of Change

Although the environments of all organizations in modern societies change to some extent over time, environments differ both in their rates of change and in the importance of such change to the operations of specific organizations. A company in the plastics industry, for example, faces an environment in which technological innovations cause extremely short product life cycles, constant revision of customers' product specifications, and frequent restructuring of work assignments. The pharmaceutical, electronics, and aerospace industries provide some of these same environmental characteristics. On the other hand, a firm in the container industry operates in a relatively placid technological and economic environment. Because of the consumer market orientation of the packaged food industry, its rate of change is perhaps greater than that of the container industry, but it is not as great as that of the plastics industry (Lawrence & Lorsch, 1964).

Like complexity, high rates of change in organization environments constitute a threat to rational decision making. A decision which is optimal with respect to external dependencies today is likely to be suboptimal tomorrow. Again, the effect is to increase the amount of information that must be processed per unit of time, while introducing a greater number of trade-offs between alternative courses of action.

Uncertainty

Correlated with rate of change, but distinguishable from it as a dimension of organizational environments, is the uncertainty (about both the present and the future) created by complex interdependence and interaction among environmental forces. Lawrence and Lorsch (1969) identify three components of uncertainty: (1) lack of clear information about the existing state of crucial environmental variables; (2) lack of knowledge about cause-and-effect relationships among organizational actions and environmental responses; and (3) the time span of definitive feedback—the length of time that must pass before an organization can ascertain the effectiveness of its decisions.

The more uncertain the environment of the organization, the greater the premium placed on organizational flexibility and slack, and the riskier it becomes to invest all of the organization's eggs in one strategy basket. At the extreme, environmental uncertainty may render long-range planning a farcical form of soothsaying, since forecasting will probably be based on scarcely tenable assumptions. In 1963, *Dun's Review* ("Long-Range Planning and Cloudy Horizons," 1963) questioned the utility of long-range planning after surveying the track records of the planners themselves. The alternative, it seems, is simply to avoid like the plague any organizational overcommitment to a single product, market, technology, area of expertise, or philosophy. This posture (or lack of one) encourages diversity and even conflict within the organization's boundaries in order to maximize the array of options needed at any given time.

Beneficence

Environments vary considerably in the degree of generosity and leniency they grant to organizations. Of course, no organization enjoys unlimited or unqualified support from all of its publics, but some enjoy easier access to important inputs (dollars, personnel, scarce resources) or greater autonomy in functioning than do others. Some organizations are allowed to perish when not able to hack it on their own, whereas others are bailed out of recurring crises even when these crises are of their own making.

The beneficence of the environment is determined mainly by two related but separate factors: (1) the perceived contributions that the organization makes to the environment by means of its output, and (2) the perceptions of the organization's publics that its dominant goals, values, and ideals are consonant rather than dissonant with the prevailing cultural ethos. The two factors are not necessarily the same for the simple reason that the organization may dispose of its output to environmental sectors that are totally distinct from the sectors that have the potential to reward, harass, or exert constraints upon the organization. One consequence of this is that organizational leaders, quite understandably, sometimes seem to expend more effort in shaping the image of their institution than they do in actually trying to improve its product or service. The major oil companies, for example, have recently invested heavily in institutional advertising designed to combat the widespread view that their refineries and tankers are systematically despoiling nature or that they are artificially restricting the supply of gasoline in order to gouge the consumer. In the 1950s, arguments for government support of agricultural commodity prices rested, not so much on the economic contributions of small farms (which were alleged to be negligible by some economists), but rather on the assertion that the life-style of the small farm helped perpetuate some of the finest ideals and attributes of the American national character. On the other hand, major firms whose contribution to the economy of modern America is undeniable find themselves increasingly hamstrung by constraints because of allegations that they are callous, authoritarian, insensitive to the aesthetics of our physical surroundings, or use their size unfairly in competition against the "underdogs."

Ironically, it is when organizations fail to make their contributions that image problems become less troublesome. One Machiavellian strategy an organization might use is to deliberately give clients a taste of what happens when the organization is so hemmed in that it cannot cope with its primary mission effectively. Presumably, that could have the effect of making active allies out of those who depend on the organization's product or service.

Implications for Organizations

Thompson (1967), in an attempt to combine classical principles of structure with modern organization theory based on open systems, defined a sort of fallback position for classical principles. He argued that, "under norms of rationality, organizations seek to seal off their core technologies from environmental influences" (p. 19). In other words, he recognized that organizations, as open systems, must respond and adapt to their respective environments. Yet simultaneously, they wish to preserve a deterministic structure which maximizes the efficiency of their basic technologies—the operations used to transform inputs into outputs. Technologies are maximally efficient when performed in a context of certainty, predictability, and fixed rules. Therefore, organizations seek to keep their technologies amenable to classic principles of the bureaucratic structure. Thompson suggested that organizations try to accomplish this by decoupling the core technology from direct contact with environmental variables.

Organizations with complex, heterogeneous task environments try to insulate their technical core from environmental disturbance by designing an outer layer of *boundary-spanning units* or positions. Particular boundary units are created to handle particular transactions between the environment and the organization. As Thompson put it, "under norms of rationality, organizations facing heterogeneous task environments seek to identify homogeneous segments and establish structural units to deal with each" (p. 70). Thus, large universities can "leave the teaching to the instructors" by establishing boundary structures for recruiting and selecting students, raising funds, and negotiating with pressure groups. If successful, these outer structures buffer the core technology from the environment, much as shock absorbers on a car leave the driver free to focus his or her psychomotor capacities on the road ahead. Trade-offs and contradictions arising from diverse environmental pressures can be resolved at the boundary and collapsed into simpler constraints for internal structures. In effect, boundary units (e.g., purchasing, sales, credit, and personnel offices) deal with the uncertainty and disruptions arising from the environment, so that the technical core (e.g., production) can structure its operations in a climate of certainty and predictability.

Organizations with environments that have high rates of change will seek to establish structures for regulating the flow of inputs and outputs into and from the core technology. For example, in order to keep the technical core operating at a fixed rate under standardized rules, firms will stockpile materials and supplies and maintain warehouse inventories.

Organizations that face highly uncertain environments—especially if the environment is also dynamic and complex—have a more difficult task in sealing off the core technology from environmental shock. One strategy, of course, is to devote increased resources at the boundary to monitoring and researching the environment. Kelly (1974) identifies four methods used to do this:

1. The *delphi method*, which offers a means of pooling and refin-

ing the collective subjective judgments of experts by a process of successive polling and feedback.

2. The *scenario*, which represents essentially the narration of a fictitious sequence of future events in order to bring to light the repercussions of one phenomenon upon others and to identify critical branch points beyond which certain options are precluded.

3. *Computer simulation*, which starts with a simplified mathematical or statistical model of real-world relationships and processes past or current data in the model to predict the future states of critical variables.

4. *Technological forecasting*, which may combine any of the first three methods along with more intuitive or informal clinical insights in order to assess the ultimate ripple effects of technological innovations, looming resource shortages, or changing trends in resource usage. Utterback and Brown (1972) argue that there is a sound basis for technological forecasting, since technological change is "a relatively continuous process which casts shadows far ahead." As an exercise in technological forecasting, they trace the impact of a developing shortage of silver on photography (to date, photographic film has been based on silver compounds).

SUBSYSTEM ENVIRONMENTS

Although it makes some sense to think in terms of the environment of the total organization, it is also useful to consider the different sectors of the environment which affect the functioning and decision making of various subsystems of the organization. The different sectors of the environment generally will vary in the four dimensions discussed in the preceding section—complexity, rate of change, uncertainty, and beneficence. Even though the aggregate environment of the organization may tend toward placidity, the research and development subsystem may confront volatility and uncertainty in its relevant subenvironment. On the other hand, though a company may have to contend with a hostile environment on most fronts, its purchasing department may be enjoying a state of fond cordiality with the outside agents on whom it depends.

The work of Lorsch and Lawrence (1965) cogently illustrates the importance of recognizing the differential environments of organizational subsystems. Lorsch and Lawrence began their research with the study of innovation in the plastics industry. Effective innovation in an enterprise requires the collaboration of its production, sales, and research subsystems: the final product must satisfy the constraints set by production costs and scheduling; it must meet a consumer need and the other tests of marketability; and, of course, it must draw upon the latest advances in scientific knowledge. However, the production, sales, and research subsystems are attuned to vastly differing environments. Production typically deals with an environment marked by a high degree of certainty and stability and operates on a very short, almost immediate, time cycle of feedback. Sales grapples with an environment manifesting somewhat less certainty, frequent change (a function of fickle consumer preferences and aggressive competitors), and a time cycle that is measured in weeks or months as compared to the hours or days of the production time cycle. Research gazes outward to an environment which is unstructured and uncertain, sometimes changing markedly with the latest research report and sometimes requiring years before relevant cause-and-effect relationships crystallize.

The differing environments of these subsystems dictate drastic differences in the structure and internal work orientation of the three areas. Production departments tend toward a high degree of structure and formalization, managed by a rather directive and controlling leadership style. Research activities are quite unstructured, marked by collegial rather than authority-based relationships, and research people do their work in a "play-it-by-ear" style, guided by informal rules and procedures. Sales departments exhibit a level of structure and formalization intermediate between those of production and research having a somewhat permissive and casual tone of interpersonal relationships, but disciplined by a cycle of reasonably quick and unequivocal performance feedback.

All very well, and as it should be; as Lorsch and Lawrence note, "Specialized orientations and structures (appropriate for the environmental sector confronted) facilitate a unit's task performance." Furthermore, of the two plastics firms studied by Lorsch and Lawrence, the more innovative one showed the *greater* differences in the internal structure, orientation, and style of its departments. But given such differences, how does an enterprise achieve the integration and coordination necessary to make an abstract model on the drawing board into a marketable product which also satisfies the binding constraints set by production tools and efficiency considerations? Paradoxically, the company that achieved the more effective integration for product innovation was the company with greater differences in orientation among the three subsystems. Both companies had official coordinating departments, comprising representatives from the different functions. However, the less-successful firm had a coordinating department which was overconcerned with immediate market considerations, whereas its counterpart in the more innovative organization dealt with a balance of issues posed by all three orientations. Furthermore, the latter group freely encouraged open conflict and disagreement (as a natural consequence of differences in environmental perspective), but having once arrived at a consensus, the group's decisions were final and were upheld by higher management. A by-product of this give-and-take was that representatives of each subsystem acquired an understanding and appreciation of the problems faced by the other subsystems.

The research by Lawrence and Lorsch brings to light two noteworthy observations: (1) different subsystems require different structural forms, a requirement that further increases the differentiation within organizations; (2) this increased differentiation creates a need for additional integrative mechanisms.

ORGANIZATION BOUNDARIES

Organizations are differentiated from their environments by *boundaries*. The boundary includes, but is not limited to, physical barriers between internal activities and outside forces. It entails differences in lingo, norms, and intensity of interaction. Furthermore, there are degrees of "boundariness"—boundariness is not an all-or-nothing phenomenon. Although the elusive concept of organization boundary is difficult to capture in a crisp definition, the presence of such a boundary is manifested by the increased effort necessary to sustain a flow of movement, communication, or activity across it. It is easy, for example, to carry all manner of personal belongings in your car as you drive from city to city in the United States; but when you reach the Canadian border, a slight increase in effort (stopping your car and checking with a customs official) is needed. If you wish to carry those same belongings to Soviet Russia, you will require an enormous increment in effort to accommodate a much stricter search and inquiry about what you are bringing along. The boundary between the United States and the USSR is much more rigid and less permeable—in psychological, sociological, and political terms—than is the boundary between the United States and Canada. Similarly, I easily converse with my immediate friends and colleagues in the School of Business but find that I have to be more selective, deliberate, and formal when circumstances require me to call upon a faculty member in another area of the university. Furthermore, my increase in effort is greater when I communicate with someone in classics or chemistry rather than with someone in economics or social psychology, and greater still when I communicate with a city official outside the university.

Boundaries serve important functions for organizations. Boundaries *buffer* the organization's internal operations by smoothing or balancing input and output transactions. Boundaries also serve a *filtering and coding* function, by which inappropriate inputs are either screened out or, in the case of human inputs, are socialized in some fashion in order to fit organizational needs. In addition, boundaries code information so that communication systems are not choked by excessive "noise," but rather flow smoothly. Finally, boundaries *protect the integrity* of the organizational system, preventing it from being absorbed by the environment or from losing the distinctive character that distinguishes it from other systems.

To say that boundaries serve these functions is not to suggest that they serve them in any optimal or promotive fashion. Boundaries, like the organizations they surround, are not "natural" in any spontaneous or automatic sense. They are contrived, and they require deliberate human actions to ensure their maintenance and viability. An organization may lose sight of its distinctive missions by being too receptive to distracting goals urged on it by the environment. Some critics of present-day universities suggest that, in their well-intentioned efforts to help solve a broad spectrum of society's social and political problems, they have lost their systemic uniqueness as educational institutions. Organizations may admit into their fold persons with values and motives incongruent with organizational purposes and processes.

However, the most perplexing dilemma in boundary management arises from the fact that boundaries must ideally strike a balance between permeability to appropriate inputs and impenetrability to irrelevant or disturbing inputs. An organization cannot hermetically seal itself off from its surroundings; it must interact with the environment to import needed energy, information, and other inputs, to maintain legitimacy in the larger social system, and to maintain relationships with the sectors toward which its output is disposed. The more uncertain, turbulent, or hostile an organization's environment, the greater its problem of striking the appropriate balance between boundary permeability and rigidity. Consider the case of the firm that produces a homeogeneous, standardized product for a well-defined and stable target market. The purchasing personnel may confidently shoo away all vendors except those few who supply its traditional materials. The production and sales managers can restrict their business reading to a few specialized trade journals. The company president need not devote much time to outsiders, confining his attention to a few large customers and perhaps to informal or ceremonial activities involving local community leaders. In contrast, the president of the United States must take into account a heterogeneous, unstable, and highly uncertain domestic and foreign environment. On the one hand, the president must be protected from trivia that would consume the time he needs for serious thought on important policy matters; on the other hand, he must not lose touch with the publics he serves. Yet how can anyone know just what is trivial? In this instance, there are no ready-made formulas for programming boundary coding and filtering functions. Every anecdotal account of a chief executive who failed because of excessive attention to detail can probably be countered with an example of one who failed because of isolation from the events of the day.

BOUNDARY ROLES

Except in a metaphoric sense, organizations do not, of course, actually interact with the environment. People interact, and they interact with other people. Relationships among organizations ultimately reduce to relationships among people. People perform the boundary functions of the organization; they do the purchasing, selling, lobbying, "impression management," negotiating, recruiting, and dispatching; and to an increasing extent in formal organizations, they do so in officially designated *boundary roles.*

A boundary role, like the boundary itself, is not an all-or-nothing matter; roles differ in *boundary relevance* as a function of the amount of time their occupants engage in boundary-spanning interactions or as a function of the importance of such interactions for role performance. However, we may simplify the discussion by speaking of boundary roles as those which are higher than average in boundary relevance, and of *internal roles* as those which are less than average in boundary relevance.

Figure 17–2 illustrates the boundary transaction system which links one organization to another in its environment. Let us take organization A as the focal organization and organization B as a member of its organization set—organization B could be a federal regulatory agency, a supplier of essential raw materials, an important customer, or a community civic organization. The boundary role person (BRP), representing *constituents* (C) or internal colleagues, engages in interaction with a counterpart BRP who also represents a constituency.

The nature of this transaction system makes the social psychology of boundary roles quite distinctive in comparison to the psychological dynamics of internal roles. The theory elaborating the psychology of boundary role behavior is found in the work of Kahn, Wolfe, Quinn, Snoek, and Rosenthal (1964) at the University of Michigan's Institute for Social Research; in the theory of labor negotiations advanced by Walton and McKersie (1965); and in the writing of Adams (1976). These authors clearly document, first of all, the fact that people in boundary roles experience *a high degree of role conflict.* The BRP must take into account, not only the expectations and influence pressures of constituents, but also the demands of his or her counterpart BRP. The BRP, then, must grapple with two different—sometimes contradictory—sets of goals, values, and beliefs.

The BRP's task is made even more difficult by the inconsistent

Figure 17–2
Boundary Transaction System

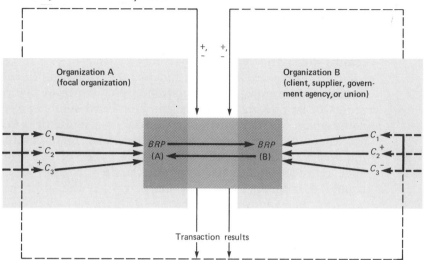

Solid arrows represent influence attempts; broken arrows represent effects of transaction results.
Source: Adapted from J. S. Adams, "The Structure and Dynamics of Behavior in Organization Boundary Roles," in M. Dunnette (Ed.), *Handbook of Industrial and Organizational Psychology* (Chicago: Rand McNally, 1976), p. 1180.

prescriptions of his or her own constituents. The latter tend to have biased conceptions of the BRP's job. For example, Strauss (1962) found in his study of purchasing agents that different departments (engineering, manufacturing, production scheduling, quality control) tried to impose their own criteria on the purchasing agent's evaluation of suppliers and parts. When specialized departments have their own narrowly defined goals or are evaluated by one-dimensional performance measures, they will exert pressure on the BRP to secure agreements with outsiders favorable to their particular interests.

Because the BRP's interactions occur with outsiders, authority cannot be used as a basis of influence. Counterpart persons owe no allegiance to the norms and rules of the BRP's organization. Consequently, the BRP must use other methods of influence in the recurring social exchange cycle (Organ & Wall, 1974). These methods may take the form of overt bargaining or negotiation, in which the BRP tempers his or her own demands and makes the concessions necessary to effect a reasonable settlement. This bargaining process, of course, holds considerable interest for the BRP's constituents, who may pressure the BRP to "hang tough" and "drive a hard bargain." Any deviation from such an aggressive posture could cause the BRP to look weak or disloyal, and thus vulnerable to punishment from powerful constituents (Wall, 1975). To the extent that the BRP's constituents demand a competitive and aggressive bargaining stance, the BRP is compelled to maneuver within a very restricted set of options. Without a working relationship with the environment, the BRP fails altogether; yet that relationship must be maintained in a fashion that retains the confidence of constituents.

In the absence of authority, the BRP may seek to influence outsiders by using friendship or ingratiation techniques. A favorite device seems to be picking up the jargon and verbal symbols of his or her counterpart. Walton and McKersie (1965) encountered a labor union spokesman who won the favor of management representatives by using businesslike language, such as "the policy of our organization" and "the decisions of our executive board." (A BRP does this with some risk if constituents know about it, since the latter may wonder whether their representative has been "brainwashed.") The BRP may also use expertise as influence, as in the case of industrial sales representatives who apply engineering and technical know-how to servicing their clients.

Due to such exposure to the environment, the BRP often senses trends and developments which dictate changes in organizational policies and procedures. Hearing the complaints and criticisms of outsiders or recognizing new dependence relationships between the home organization and environmental sectors, the BRP tends to feel the inadequacy of present organizational arrangements more keenly than do the constituents. This knowledge makes it necessary for the BRP to become an agent of change. Advocacy of change, however, may simply fall on deaf ears or may initiate protracted conflict with constituents, who do not and cannot see the organization from the BRP's perspective. Nevertheless, the boundary role person must represent the environment to his or her organization, as well as vice versa, becoming an activist broker between the viewpoints of constituents and outsiders. Doing so means influencing the "tribe", more often by persuasion and bargaining than by unilateral decision.

An article in the April 1974 issue of *Fortune* magazine ("New Kind of Challenge for Salesmen," 1974) describes some of the BRP's dilemmas and strategies for coping with them. The article dealt with the "new kind of challenge" presented to sales personnel by temporary shortages in basic industrial materials—such as steel, aluminum, plastics, and synthetic fibers—which their companies sold to other manufacturing firms. Suddenly these salespeople faced the problem, not of acquiring new orders, but of filling old ones to traditional clients. One salesman had a fight with his own production department after it began to book orders for other accounts from inventory being held in reserve for a customer of his. Another observed that his most important task during that period was to keep customers from blaming his company for the shortage. His method of managing this task was to stay "in close touch with purchasing agents, carefully explaining the causes of the shortage, . . . and keeping informed of his customers' own production and marketing plans" so that he could foresee changes in their needs. On the other hand, he felt compelled to keep "a close watch on his customers' inventories in order to prevent hoarding." This same BRP, who sold aluminum to manufacturers and distributors, had to haggle with his own product offices because they were allotting a customer one twelfth of his annual volume of purchases each month, in disregard of the cyclical fluctuations of the customer's needs. In the end he compromised, "and we got two-thirds of what we asked for." In order to get cooperation from his production personnel, he had to reciprocate by persuading customers to help reduce costs by ordering in large lot sizes. An industrial chemicals representative found that by coming through in the pinch for deliveries to purchasing agents, he could induce them to return the favor by providing intelligence about what his competitors were up to.

Organ (1971) has suggested that the distinctive demands made by boundary roles call for a particular mix of aptitudes and personality attributes. Sensitivity to semantics looms as a critical skill, since the BRP must avoid words that alienate outsiders and must translate external viewpoints into the language of his or her constituency. The BRP must be capable of a measured degree of flexibility in opinions and attitudes, not obsessed with ideological consistency or symbolic issues devoid of substantive stakes. This flexibility, however, must not appear as "wishy-washiness" to constituents, who prefer to see rock-ribbed resistance in the BRP's commitment. The BRP must not be averse to occasionally switching between two faces: one of benign reasonableness to external agents and one of corporate zeal to constituents. The BRP who cannot achieve the latter will probably be denied the latitude and discretion essential to accomplishing the former. The effective BRP values pragmatism above aesthetics, since viable solutions to conflict may not be elegant. A political instinct is essential to the BRP in order to manage the shifting coalitions through which things get done.

THE TURBULENT ENVIRONMENT

At this point, we may note the revisions effected in classical principles by modern organization theory based on open systems. First of all, the bureaucratic structure may serve as an adequate model if the organization's environment has a relatively low level of complexity, reasonable stability, and a considerable degree of certainty. Both its technical core and its boundary structures can employ repetitive task cycles governed by hard-and-fast rules. Hierarchical structures based on authority will be sufficient to coordinate the working of these structures.

As the organizational environment becomes more complex, unstable, and uncertain, the organization will be able to preserve a deterministic, bureaucratic structure for its technical components by loosening the structure of other subsystems of the organization, particularly those which perform boundary functions. To hold on tenaciously to the bureaucratic model for its technical core, successively greater departures from that model are required for supporting structures: less emphasis on authority, less reliance on formal rules and standard procedures, less emphasis on efficiency, more tolerance for slack and redundancy and more of a premium placed on flexibility. What we then have is a hybrid structure in which bureaucratic and nonbureaucratic forms must coexist.

Emery and Trist (1965) and Adams (1975) have noted that certain types of organizational environments cannot be adequately described by simple summation of their degrees of complexity, rate of change, and uncertainty. One has to take into account the *interconnectedness*, or linkages, between the organization and its environmental components; between subcomponents of the internal organization; and between the elements of the environment itself.

Figure 17–3
The Texture of a Turbulent Environment

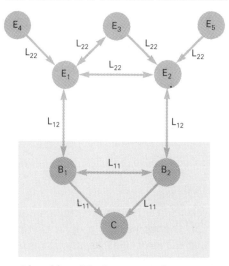

Adapted from "The Environmental Context of Negotiations between Human Systems" by J. S. Adams, paper read at the Negotiation Conference, Center for Creative Leadership, Greensboro, N.C., 1975.

Consider Figure 17–3. The organization has direct linkages (L_{12}) with environmental components E_1 and E_2; the boundary components $(B_1$ and $B_2)$ of the organization have linkages (L_{11}) with each other as well as with the technical core (C). In addition, however, E_1 and E_2 are linked to each other—as components of each other's environment—and they are linked as well to other environments $(E_3, E_4,$ and $E_5)$ not directly connected to the focal organization.

When a high degree of connectedness combines with complexity, rapid change, and uncertainty in the organization's environment, certain consequences result. First of all, a change originating in any one component of the environment tends to be amplified through the network of linkages. A change in E_3, for example, produces changes in both E_1 and E_2, thus posing the necessity for B_1 and B_2 to adapt accordingly. But since E_1 and E_2 are part of each other's environment, they have to adapt to each other as well, compounding the changes to be reckoned with by B_1 and B_2. *At some threshold, B_1 and B_2 become incapable of totally buffering C, and thus the technical core itself has to maintain flexibility of response to its own internally affiliated components.* Fixed rules of operation go by the board, the internal hierarchy becomes overloaded with information, and its coordinating function is strained.

Emery and Trist (1965) have offered the term *turbulence* to describe environments characterized by the simultaneous properties of complexity, rapid change, and interconnectedness. To the extent that an organization faces a turbulent environment, it loses the ability to insulate its technical core and preserve a static bureaucratic internal structure. Organizations must put a premium on the ability to adapt to change *throughout* their structure—even within the technical core. This requires what Burns and Stalker (1961) termed an *organic* form, which has the following attributes:

1. Continual revision of participants' role responsibilities and prerogatives, which change informally as a function of interaction with others.
2. Decentralized patterns of influence and authority, which inhere primarily in the expertise relevant to a problem rather than in office or rank.
3. A preponderance of lateral rather than vertical communication patterns, which convey expertise and advice as opposed to commands or decisions.
4. Reliance on judgment rather than detailed rules.

This may be contrasted with the *mechanistic* model of classical principles, which is manifested by:

1. A highly specialized division of labor.
2. A centralized or hierarchical basis of authority and influence.

3. A preponderance of vertical, as opposed to lateral, communication patterns.
4. Detailed policies, procedures, and rules for each participant, which are not to be deviated from.

The mechanistic form seeks to maximize the efficiency of internal processes; the organic form tolerates short-run inefficiency for the sake of flexibility. Burns and Stalker stress that neither form is innately superior to the other. Rather, each form has comparative advantages over the other for certain types of environments.

Warren Bennis (1964) has argued that time is on the side of the organic structure, which will supersede the bureaucratic organization as the dominant form of human organization. Although he credits the organizational bureaucracy for many of the achievements of modern industrial societies, he has nevertheless suggested that its long suit is the efficient execution of the routine in a stable environment. Bennis foresaw the increasing rate of change in knowledge, technology, population, and social-political constraints on the firm as mandating a new kind of organization. This new structural form—already glimpsed in the aerospace industry and the Apollo project—would consist of rapidly changing *temporary systems*, whose participants have no fixed role or office but rotate from one task force to another as their specialized expertise is needed. "Linking pin" personnel will coordinate the diverse task groups, managing not so much by authority as by their ability to translate the needs of the different groups to each other. One suspects that the activities carried out in such *organic-adaptive* organizations would appear messy, wasteful of effort, and grossly inefficient to some observers. But that might be the inevitable price for the capacity to adapt to dynamic environments.[1]

THE EVOLUTION OF NEW STRUCTURAL FORMS

Turbulent environments produce shock waves that penetrate to the technical core of the organization. The effect is to introduce enormous requirements for information processing and coordination of functions. Neither rules nor hierarchical authority are adequate to accomplish this because of the frequency of nonroutine cases. When this stage is reached, according to Galbraith (1974), organizations must modify the structure of their technical core either to (1) reduce the amount of necessary information processing by reducing coordinative requirements, or (2) increase the capacity for processing information.

---

[1]Bennis (1974) has subsequently qualified his argument to state that a precondition for the organic form of organization is a certain degree of consensus concerning basic issues or values among the constituent publics of an organization.

The major strategy for reducing coordinative requirements is to change the basis of the technical core structure from function (or process) to product (project or purpose). For example, each product group could have its own engineers, manufacturing facilities, fabricating and assembly operations, and marketing staff. Coordinative requirements are encapsulated at a relatively low level. Such an arrangement reduces the complexity of continuous reallocation of resources from a single function (e.g., engineering) to a diverse array of outputs. A change in the design of a product affects only the group or division making that product and does not require adjustment upward and across every functional line.

As Galbraith (1974) notes, the cost of a product group structure is the loss of resource specialization. No one product might justify the full-time use of an engineer in a highly specialized area of expertise, whereas that expertise could be efficiently used if allocated across different products. Thus, each product group must use personnel with more general skills, who, nonetheless, cannot do some things as well as a specialist could. The only way around the loss of specialization is duplication of human and physical resources in each product group. A consequence of duplication is that these resources are used at a rate far below capacity.

On the other hand, the technical core can retain a structure based on functional lines but increase its coordinative and information-processing abilities. The most direct way of doing this is the creation of lateral relationships which cut across functional lines of authority. Such lateral relationships include (Galbraith, 1974):

1. *Direct contact* between line officials—e.g., ad hoc conferences between electrical engineers and assembly line superintendents.
2. *Liaison roles.* A specialized role is created to handle an increased volume of communication between two functions at the operating level.
3. *Task forces.* When problems arise that involve several different line functions, a temporary task force of representatives from each function is created. Ideally, these groups resolve problems at lower operating levels without passing them on to higher levels.
4. *Teams.* Task forces may become permanent in order to handle a large volume of nonroutine problems affecting several different departments.
5. *Integrating roles.* Leadership of the teams that coordinate functional lines is formalized in a new position. This position—product manager, project manager, or program manager—is usually filled by someone with the requisite knowledge for understanding the operations and problems of the various functions coordinated.
6. *Managerial Linking Roles.* As the various functions become more

specialized and their respective requirements surpass the expertise of any one person, the integrating role is given formal authority to make coordinating decisions. Galbraith (1974) characterizes this position as "not like the integrating role because it possesses formal position power, but is different from line managerial roles in that the participants (in line functions) do not report to the linking manager" (p. 76). No one works directly for the linking manager. The influence of the office is indirect through participation in budgets and having its own budget for buying resources from specialist groups.

7. *Matrix organization.* The logical and ultimate end of the process of creating lateral relationships is to give the linking managerial roles direct authority over personnel in the functional specialties—at the same time that these personnel also report to superiors in the functional lines. At this point a dual authority structure has evolved at some level in the organization. Specialists are accountable to both a functional superior (e.g., engineering or fabrication) and yet are also accountable to a linking manager, such as a product or project manager who coordinates processes for some output.

The matrix structure appears to enable organizations to "have their cake and eat it too." On the one hand, it permits organizations to keep a functional basis of authority structure for their technical cores, thus allowing a high degree of specialization of resources and the consequent technical excellence of production. On the other hand, it provides flexibility in coordinating functions at a lower level without overloading top management.

Obviously, such an arrangement strikes at the very heart of classical principles, since it deliberately violates the precept of unity of command. At some level, functional specialists have two different superiors, presumably of equal authority. Does it work? Knight (1976) contends that there is virtually no hard evidence at all to support the supposed advantages of the matrix form, as compared to structures operating almost totally on either the product or functional basis. Moreover, as Knight emphasizes, matrix structures create problems of their own. One of these is a high level of job stress for those persons working under dual authority systems. One reason for stress is work overload—employees must spend a great deal of time in numerous meetings and other forms of communication. Stress also arises because of role conflict and role ambiguity. Furthermore, disagreements and deadlocks between functional and project managers result in a steady stream of appealed decisions passed to top-level officials for final judgment.

The consensus of organization design experts is that firms should not lightly contemplate the matrix structural form, or structural forms approximating it. It should be undertaken only by those organizations whose markets and technologies are so dynamic and volatile as to absolutely require radical departures from traditional forms in order to satisfy coordinative requirements. Even then, it should be preceded by a comprehensive program of organizational "resocialization" of norms and attitudes. The matrix-type structure does not seem to work well if married to a climate that emphasizes primarily the sanctity of legitimate authority and the clarity of individual role prescriptions. Participants must internalize values concerning the appropriateness of influence based on knowledge and the tolerance for a certain amount of conflict.

Strategies for effecting deliberate changes in organizational dynamics will receive further treatment in the succeeding, and closing, chapter.

SUMMARY

Modern organization theory views the organization as an open system, in contrast to the closed-system perspective of classical principles. The open-systems model highlights the relationships between the organization and its environment. Classical principles apply most readily to organizations with relatively simple, static, and certain environments. As environments become more complex, unstable, and uncertain, organizations attempt to preserve bureaucratic structures for their technical cores by establishing boundary positions for buffering and filtering environmental disturbances. Boundary structures must make increasingly radical departures from classical principles in order to protect the technical core. Also, boundary roles involve social-psychological processes not so characteristic of internal roles.

When the environment is characterized by a high degree of interconnectedness among its component elements, and the elements themselves are rapidly changing, the environment takes on a property of turbulence. Turbulent environments produce shocks that exceed the buffering capacity of boundary structures and penetrate to the technical core. Organic, rather than mechanistic, structures are required in the technical core in order to adapt to turbulent environments. Mechanisms for coordinating functional processes in response to the environment include liaison roles, teams, project managers, and managerial linking roles. The matrix structure attempts to preserve a technical core based on functional lines of authority but overlaid with a separate formal authority structure based on product or project lines. This practice deliberately violates the principle of unity of command and creates new problems, but it may be worth the costs in order to combine the advantages of functional specialization and the flexibility of decentralized product teams.

CONCEPTS TO REMEMBER

task environment	turbulent environment
organization set	organic form
open system	mechanistic form
closed system	temporary systems
organization boundaries	liaison roles
boundary roles	matrix organization
constituents	

QUESTIONS FOR DISCUSSION

1. Choose an organization with which you are familiar and map out its organization set. What conflicts are apparent? How does the organization cope with these conflicts?

2. Are boundary roles inherently or inevitably stressful? What circumstances may moderate the stress?

3. Do organizations always "adapt" to contingencies or changes in their environments? What other strategies are possible?

4. What developments have led to greater interconnectedness in the environments of many organizations?

REFERENCES

Adams, J. S. The environmental context of negotiations between human systems. Paper read at the Negotiation Conference, Center for Creative Leadership, Greensboro, N.C., 1975.

Adams, J. S. The structure and dynamics of behavior in organization boundary roles. In M. Dunnette (Ed.), *Handbook of industrial and organizational psychology*. Chicago: Rand-McNally, 1976.

Bennis, W. G. *Organizational developments and the fate of bureaucracy*. Invited address delivered at meetings of American Psychological Association, Washington, D.C., September 5, 1964.

Burns, T., & Stalker, G. M. *The management of innovation*. London: Tavistock, 1961. Abridged and reproduced in part in H. L. Tosi & W. C. Hamner, (Eds.), *Organizational behavior and management: A contingency approach*. Chicago: ST. Clair Press, 1974.

Churchman, C. W. *The systems approach.* New York: Dell Publishing, 1968.

Dill, W. R.   Environment as an influence on managerial autonomy. *Administrative Science Quarterly,* 1958, *2,* 409–443.

Dowling, W. F.   Conversation with Warren Bennis. *Organizational Dynamics,* v. 2, no. 3, Winter 1974, 50–66.

Emery, F. E., & Trist, E. L.   The causal texture of organizational environments. *Human Relations,* 1965, *18,* 21–32.

Evan, W. E.   The organization set: Toward a theory of interorganizational relations. In J. D. Thompson (Ed.), *Approaches to organizational design.* Pittsburgh: University of Pittsburgh Press, 1966.

Fischoff, B., & Beyth, R.   I knew it would happen: Remembered probabilities of once-future things. *Organizational Behavior and Human Performance,* 1975, *13,* 1–16.

Galbraith, J. R.   Organization design: An information processing view. *Interfaces,* 1974, *4,* 28–36.

Hall, R. H.   *Organizations: Structure and process.* Englewood Cliffs, N.J.: Prentice-Hall, 1972.

Kahn, R. L., Wolfe, D., Quinn, R., Snoek, J. D., & Rosenthal, R.   *Organizational stress.* New York: John Wiley & Sons, 1964.

Katz, D., & Kahn, R. L.   *The social psychology of organizations.* New York: John Wiley & Sons, 1966.

Kelly, J.   *Organizational behavior* (Rev. ed.). Homewood, Ill.: Richard D. Irwin, 1974.

Knight, K.   Matrix organizations: A review. *Journal of Management Studies,* 1976, *13,* 111–130.

Lawrence, P. R., & Lorsch, J. W.   *Organization and environment.* Homewood, Ill.: Richard D. Irwin, 1964.

Lawrence, P. R., & Lorsch, J. W.   *Developing organizations: Diagnosis and action.* Reading, Mass.: Addison-Wesley, 1969.

Long-range planning and cloudy horizons. *Dun's Review,* 1963, *18.*

Lorsch, J. W., & Lawrence, P. R.   Organizing for product innovation. *Harvard Business Review,* 1965, *43,* 109–120.

Merton, R. K.   *Social theory and social structure* (Rev. ed.). Glencoe, Ill.: Free Press, 1957.

A new kind of challenge for salesmen. *Fortune,* April 1974, pp. 156–166.

Organ, D. W.   Linking pins between organizations and environment. *Business Horizons,* 1971, *14,* 73–80.

Organ, D. W., & Wall, J. A.   Decision-making behavior in organization boundary exchanges. *Proceedings,* Midwest Academy of Management, Kent, Ohio, 1974.

Parsons, T.   *Structure and process in modern societies.* New York: Free Press, 1960.

Strauss, G.   Tactics of lateral relationship: The purchasing agent. *Administrative Science Quarterly,* 1962, *7,* 161–186.

Thompson, J. D. *Organizations in action.* New York: McGraw-Hill, 1967.

Thompson, J. D., & McEwen, W. J. Organization goals and environment: Goal-setting as an interaction process. *American Sociological Review,* 1958, *23,* 23–31.

Tosi, H. L., & Hamner, W. C. (Eds.). *Organizational behavior and management: A contingency approach.* Chicago: St. Clair Press, 1974.

Utterback, J. M., & Brown, J. W. Monitoring for technological opportunities. *Business Horizons,* 1972, *15,* 5–15.

Wall, J. A. Effects of constituent trust and representative bargaining orientation on intergroup bargaining. *Journal of Personality and Social Psychology,* 1975, *31,* 1004–1012.

Walton, R. E., & McKersie, R. B. *A behavioral theory of labor negotiations.* New York: McGraw-Hill, 1965

18

Organizational Change and Development

What is the difference between reactive and proactive organizational change?

What occasions prompt organizations to undertake planned change?

Why is organizational change a political process?

What are the conditions essential to successful long-run change in organizational behavior?

What alternative methods exist for changing behavior in organizations?

Organizations do change, inevitably. They are born, grow, and decline, and most of them eventually die. They gain and lose customers, clients, leaders, personnel, and products. They respond to changes in markets, governments, competitors, creditors, communities, even the weather. They struggle with adversity and celebrate the good fortunes of prosperity. No organization is the same today as it was five years ago, and organizations do not have to be taught to change. Whether for good or ill, organizations do change.

An important distinction lies, however, in whether change is passively unmanaged, or *reactive,* as opposed to active, managed, *proactive* change. The difference corresponds, by way of analogy, to that between instrumental, purposive behavior and reflexive behavior. Instrumental behavior and reflexive behavior both represent responses of the organism to its external environment. Similarly, both proactive and reactive organizational change are elicited by events (problems, crises, opportunities, pressures) in the organization's environment. Beyond this similarity, proactive and reactive organizational change differ just as profoundly as do instrumental and reflexive behavior.

Reactive change, like reflexive behavior, involves a limited part of the system, whereas proactive change and instrumental behavior coordinate the parts of the system as a whole. For example, an individual will respond reflexively to a sudden intense light by eye blinking or pupillary contraction. An instrumental response to the same stimulus would involve the coordination of the central nervous system and psychomotor capacities, as evidenced by a complex response such as devising a plan to shield or remove the light. Analagously, a firm's reactive change to lagging sales might take a more-or-less knee-jerk form: simply putting more pressure on the sales force, or increasing advertising. A proactive change would bring the efforts of other parts of the organization (production, finance, purchasing, personnel) into a coordinated response to the problem.

Also, reflexive behavior and reactive changes share the characteristic of responding to immediate symptoms, while instrumental behavior and proactive change respond to underlying forces producing the symptoms. In the case of individual behavior, instrumental responding involves the complex cognitive processes involved in processing information, solving problems, evaluating alternatives, and making decisions; in the case of organizations, proactive change involves diagnosis, scanning the environment, forecasting, model building, strategy formulation, and planning. In the example given above of declining sales, putting pressure on the sales force is a reactive response to the immediate symptom. The underlying problem, however, may be much more complex. The problem may be due to inferior product quality because of high turnover in factory workers; changes in distribution channels through which consumers buy the product; an unfavorable public image of the firm; or excessive demands on the sales force to spend time on paperwork. In other words, the decline in sales merely represents the tip of the iceberg. Proactive change is a response to the underlying variables that led up to the visible problem.

This chapter concerns *proactive* change: the deliberate attempt of organization officials to induce comprehensive, coordinated change by an organization toward some conceived purpose.

ANTECEDENTS OF CHANGE

Why do organizations embark upon a concerted effort toward redirection and transformation? What prompts officials to break away from the status quo and the accustomed order? Almost any issue of *The Wall Street Journal* or *Business Week* identifies one or more of the following occasions as the inspiration for planned change.

Barometers of Declining Effectiveness

Organizations have a number of ways of "taking their pulse" by looking at indicators from their own information systems. A business firm monitors data on sales, absenteeism, turnover, scrap rates, manufacturing costs, and numerous ratios of financial measures. Some firms also conduct regular opinion surveys of their work force, which may reveal slipping trends in employee morale, commitment, or motivation. Others have systematic methods of obtaining feedback from customers. Nonprofit organizations have varying means (often less direct or precise than business firms') of monitoring indicators of effectiveness; they might sample the opinion of clients whom they service, note trends in formally registered complaints and grievances, or more informally note the increasing percentage of time spent in nonproductive fashion.

As we pointed out above, proactive change does not respond in knee-jerk fashion to such symptoms as problems in themselves. Rather, it interprets them as "red flags": it sees them as evidence of underlying problems requiring diagnosis, discussion, and a coordinated strategy for addressing them.

Change in Corporate Strategy

An organization may undertake comprehensive change even when no indicators would suggest immediate problems in its performance. However, current and past performance may have been based on conditions that organization officials believe to be changing. Forecasts of long-run trends may prompt a decision to enter new markets, to pursue a strategy of growth, to become less dependent on government, to switch from a centralized to a decentralized structure, or to adopt new technologies. All of these strategic decisions have implications for changing the behavior of people in the organization. Nothing less than a "new order" is required to put such strategies into operational effect.

Strategy responds not only to opportunities and challenges in the external environment but also to the stage of development of the organization. Organization theorists who have studied the histories of numerous firms note that companies go through a characteristic sequence of stages of growth. The type of strategy appropriate to the entrepreneurial stage—when the firm is small, battling the odds against survival, and seeking to grasp and maintain a toehold in some niche of the market—typically becomes obsolete when the firm undergoes rapid growth via internal operations. At a later stage, still a different strategy mix becomes imperative when the firm tries to consolidate its position in a period of slower growth and stability. Effective transition from one stage to another requires a comprehensive program of organizational change.

Crisis

Not infrequently, the occasion for organizational change is an unforeseen crisis which makes continuation of the status quo unthinkable. The sudden death of a chief executive officer—especially after a long tenure during which that person had molded the organization into his or her own image—signals the end of the old regime and forces a reorientation of corporate posture. Similarly, the resignation of key members of a top management team, a strike by a critically important group of specialized workers, loss of a major client or supplier on whom the company has been dependent, a drastic cutback in budget for a bureau or university, even spontaneous civil disturbances directed against an organization may initiate a total revamping of policy, practice, and behavior. Crises create an unstable condition which is likely to become the stimulus for a thoroughgoing self-assessment and reform.

Personal Goals

Not all programs of organizational change have any necessary or logical relationship to organizational effectiveness. We have noted before (Chapter 14) that organizational goals—as operationally defined—reflect in part the preferences of those in a position to exert influence; and we shall argue below that organizational change inevitably is shaped by political forces. Leaders, interest groups, and coalitions have their own goals: to see the company become more aggressive, to shape the organization around some distinctive theme, to cast a particular corporate image, to further some ideology or philosophy. Seldom are these goals espoused in precisely those forms, at least for the record or for public consumption. More frequently they are clothed in rationalizations about their presumed effect on profits or service. Changes in informal power structures within organizations—for example, as Young Turks begin to tilt the balance against the Old Guard, when a traditionally family-owned and family-operated firm loses its hold on the levers of decision making, or when liberals gain the edge over conservatives—frequently signal the undertaking of thoroughgoing change.

RESISTANCE TO CHANGE

From its inception, the study of organizational change has noted the fact that many participants respond with dogged resistance to altering the status quo. Since the Industrial Revolution began, workers have at times sought—occasionally in extremely violent fashion—to block the introduction of new technology. As we discovered in Chapter 8, supervisors and lower-level managers have balked at large-scale projects in job redesign and job enrichment; even lower-level employees, the presumed beneficiaries of such projects, have fought such changes. Divisional managers have fought pitched battles against realignment of corporate structure. Even the proposal by a course coordinator to adopt a different textbook is capable of touching off a frenzy of defensive tactics to resist change.

Early perspectives on the phenomenon of resistance to change construed it either as an unhealthy trait or attribute of the persons demonstrating it or a deep-rooted frailty of human nature. Not infrequently, those proposing change and confronting resistance viewed it as "defensive," "irrational," or "pathological." The solution to overcoming resistance, it seemed, lay in "treating" the resistance by some therapeutic device.

We now realize that to view resistance to change as a form of sickness or irrationality is at best simplistic, if not self-serving on the part of those advocating change. The inescapable reality of organizational change is that it never redounds to the equal benefit of all parties affected, and—at least in the short run—it is usually the case that some parties realize a net loss in some form when change occurs. It is therefore instructive to regard most forms of resistance to change as eminently rational behavior acted out for the understandable purpose of self-interest.

What do people lose as a consequence of change? Sometimes they lose *security*, or at least have good reason to believe they will lose it.

The Luddites who wrecked the new textile machines in the early days of the Industrial Revolution feared they would become expendable; in more recent days, metropolitan newspapers that sought to install new technology for typesetting have had to contend with strikes for the same reason. Changes in formal structure or work flow may drastically reduce the *power* and *status* of certain administrators if their offices are bypassed in the chain of decision making; some units may survive in little more than window-dressing form. Often the end result for many people is an undesirable loss of *autonomy* in operations because of new procedures, controls, and constraints; people tend to resist any increase in dependence upon others in their sphere of action. Finally, as Kerr and Kerr (1972) note, the notion of "sunk cost" is useful in accounting for resistance to change. People lose their *investments in the status quo* if long years of learning and mastering a set of operations have to be written off as a result of change. Anyone comfortable with an established routine that has been painfully acquired and efficiently used to do the job competently will understandably shrink from the prospect of seeing this routine shattered and having to "gear up" all over again and stumble through the inevitably messy, inefficient relearning process. The "hassle factor" is not be be underestimated as a motive underlying resistance to change, even though it does not lend itself to a particularly eloquent basis of argument.

THE POLITICS OF ORGANIZATIONAL CHANGE

To conceptualize resistance to change as a rational response to the threat of losing security, status, autonomy, and investment in the status quo leads naturally to the consideration of organizational change as a political process. Individuals, interest groups, and coalitions favoring change presumably stand to gain—either because of their identification with measures that render the organization more effective, or because they derive personal gain through greater status, perquisites, prestige, automony, and the like. Since some people stand to lose, or at least believe that to be the case, they will defend the status quo. Obviously, in order for substantive change to be effected the forces for change must overcome resistance; and if the status quo is to be maintained largely intact, the opposite forces must prevail. What strategies and tactics will unfold?

Both sides will seek early on to appeal to the uncommitted—those who have no strong feelings for or against the change, either because they may be largely unaffected or because they cannot decide whether the outcomes to them are, on balance, positive or negative. Appeals to this group may take the forms of lobbying, distortion, propaganda, persuasion, cashing in credits from old favors, implied threats, appeals to loyalty and friendship, or mixtures of all of the above. The issues central to the proposed changes cause a realignment of *cliques* (Chapter 14), each of which is usually too small by itself to impose a resolution of the conflict, into larger but more loosely held *coalitions*. Both sides, in appealing to the uncommitted, will attempt to invoke the name of some revered or prestigious individual (such as the chief executive officer, the founder of the company, or an industry leader). Both sides will attempt (in the more-public appeals) to show the implications for long-run profitability, service to the public, and other abstract goals.

The forces for change will usually find that winning over the uncommitted is a *necessary* but not *sufficient* condition for actually ushering in a change program. Frequently the resisters, even if a small minority, will include in their ranks critically placed individuals or groups who, even if not able to block change, have the potential for sabotaging it when put into operation. Successfully implemented change requires some means of *coopting* these groups. This usually necessitates substantial modifications of the originally proposed program. Thus, change programs as finally adopted seldom have the characteristics of streamlined elegance and coherence. More often than not, they contain patch-up arrangements and tack-ons that preserve the core concepts of the original, yet make the necessary concessions to permit operational acceptance and implementation. The end result is somewhat less than total satisfaction by any particular interest group, but a workable arrangement for preserving goodwill.

One means of accommodating resisters is to invite their *participation* in the planning, design, and process of carrying out change programs. Thus, when IBM's plans to introduce the System/360 met resistance from its European affiliates, the IBM laboratories in Europe were included in the formulation of the design of the new models. Thereafter, the overseas grumblings subsided (Wise, 1966). A classic field experiment by Coch and French in 1948 (this study was also reviewed in Chapter 15) demonstrated that workers allowed participation in planning the installation of new production methods subsequently showed less resistance to learning and adopting the new methods.

As Miles (1965) has noted, one explanation often given for the effect of participation in dissolving resistance involves the concept of *ego involvement*. It has been argued that providing a participative forum gives the affected parties a sense of ego identification with the proposed change, thus leading to a commitment to see the change effectively implemented. But the effect of participation may also be explained in other ways. First of all, there is the straightforward explanation that *real* (as opposed to ceremonial) participation give the affected parties an opportunity to veto, modify, or subvert those elements of the change program which they consider most threatening. Thus, while broad participation may reduce resistance, it may do so at the expense of watering down the most important features of the change, in which case participation may be a questionable strategy. Second, the process of participation may provide sufficient exposure to information about the nature and consequences of the change so that the anxiety bred of uncertainty is reduced and distorted rumors are laid to rest.

THE PSYCHOLOGY OF CHANGE

Lewin (1947), in the most appealing and enduring metaphor yet conceived for understanding the requirements of successfully changing behavior, proposed a three-step model. First of all, the forces acting upon an individual to maintain current behavior must be *unfrozen*. Current behavior is supported by a web of interlocking variables that include the formal reward system, social reinforcement from the group, defense mechanisms used to protect against psychological threat, cues and "props" in the surrounding environment, and the individual's conception of what is proper role behavior. Any stimulus for change that does not alter these variables will either be resisted or, at the most, cause only temporary or cosmetic change. Second, once the unfreezing process has occurred, and only then, the individual must be presented with a very clear and attractive option representing new patterns of behavior and the rationale for this behavior. This may take the form of a new *role model* (i.e., a real person) who can demonstrate the competence and efficacy of different patterns of behavior. Alternatively, the person may be given a *cognitive map*—a conceptual model, a theory, or a rationale—so that the person may devise and experiment with a new role conception. Finally, the new patterns of behavior must undergo refreezing. The changed behavior must be supported by social cues and the formal and informal reward system if it is to endure.

Unsuccessful efforts to induce significant and lasting change in organizational behavior can generally be traced to failure in one of the three stages described above. Either they fail to alter in any significant fashion the forces maintaining old behavior; they fail to offer a clear, satisfying alternative; or they fail to "stamp in" the new behavior.

Successfully unfreezing the forces maintaining old behavior often requires something like "shock treatment." The individual may have to be taken completely out of the old familiar context and placed in one that is strange or ambiguous, in which familiar cues are absent and old ways of coping prove ineffectual. Alternatively, there must be some means of directing serious, unambiguous *disconfirming feedback* about the efficacy of current behavior; the feedback must be so direct and threatening that it pierces any perceptual defenses and overrides the effect of reinforcements for current behavior.

On the other hand, the arousal of threat needed to unfreeze behavior may inhibit new learning because it can lead to withdrawal, avoidance, and excessive caution. Thus, when organizations seek to establish new behavior patterns, they must provide the grounds for reducing somewhat the threats originally needed for unfreezing. Anxiety is not totally eliminated, but it is bounded so that individuals are not afraid of experimenting with new behavior.

The refreezing stage is perhaps the most difficult of all, because the new behavior patterns are weak and often ineffective at first and cause a heightened, awkward sense of self-consciousness. Thoroughgoing reengineering of the formal and informal context may be essential to reinforce the new behavior, to avoid punishing the new behavior, and to extinguish the residual components of old, undesired responses.

CHANGING THE SITUATION VERSUS CHANGING THE PEOPLE

Webber (1979) offered the following anecdote that embodies two partially complementary, partially conflicting approaches to change:

> During a period of severe electricity shortage, a university tried to help out in two ways: cards reading "Save a watt—turn off a switch" were placed everywhere, and janitors removed half the light bulbs from all fixtures. These are the two principal approaches to change: change the people or change the situation [p. 498].

"Change the people" usually refers to attempts to change behavior by first changing attitudes, opinions, or value systems through some reeducational or resocialization process. This may take the form of promotional campaigns; providing new information via memos, conferences, or brochures; or special training programs. "Change the situation," by contrast, is a strategy of altering the technological environment or the formal structure (e.g., reward system, hierarchical arrangements, reporting relationships) in order to change behavior directly. The premise of this strategy is that attitudes are unimportant if the desired changes in behavior occur, or that attitude change is more likely to follow in the *wake* of changed behavior instead of preceding it.

In practice, the issue really is not so much *which* of the two strategies is more effective but in *what sequence* they are used. Ultimately, either one alone is likely to be ineffective. A program aimed at changing attitudes may be successful to that extent (i.e., it may actually change attitudes), but—for reasons we noted in Chapter 6— it cannot be assumed that attitudes will predict behavior very well. On the other hand, changing the situation as a direct means of inducing change in behavior without corresponding attitude change may generate frustrations which lead to displaced aggression, particularly if the change is perceived as coercive. Closing the employees' canteen may curb excessive socializing away from the task, but the consequent irritations stemming from this deprivation may be expressed in varied forms of covert sabotage.

The optimal strategy would aim at changing *both* attitudes *and* the situation in alternating, overlapping phases. For example, the groundwork for structural change might be preceded by announcements that give the rationale for the change, a description of the change, and the expected consequences. Once early stages of implementation have been effected, attempts at persuasion can be more specific and aimed at helping people internalize the goals of subsequent stages of change in the surrounding structure.

PROGRAMS FOR CHANGING BEHAVIOR IN ORGANIZATIONS

Changing Personnel

Perhaps the simplest and most popular method of changing organizations is to change their leaders. A school of business that seeks to restructure faculty behavior toward the direction of scholarly research will recruit a new dean with a strong academic reputation, while a school that hopes to foster greater interaction with the business community will seek someone with status in a prestigious corporation. The Ford Motor Company in the 1940s brought Robert McNamara, Arjay Miller, and their associates (popularly known as the "Whiz Kids") into key positions in order to introduce management decision-making styles based on rigorous cost-benefit analysis. Business periodicals frequently report on companies that select particular candidates as CEOs in order to make the firm more aggressive in the marketplace, more cost conscious, or more socially responsive.

Change in leadership can sometimes be effective at the "unfreezing" stage because it often forces members of the organization to wonder whether old behavior will continue to be appropriate and rewarded. In the early days of a new "regime," people look (sometimes desperately) for clues as to who and what will now be rewarded, how existing cliques and coalitions might be realigned, what projects will be assigned top priority.

On the other hand, changes in leadership often have little more than ceremonial significance. If the new CEO does not actually have the influence to initiate structural changes, any experimentation by organization members with new behavior patterns is not likely to last through the "refreezing" stage. Perhaps for this reason, corporate leaders who accept jobs with new firms often try to negotiate a "package deal" so that they can install one or more of their trusted associates in strategic positions. The support of these lieutenants may be a critical factor in the balance of power determining whether structural change occurs.

Existing leadership can also attempt organizational change through personnel choices at lower levels, including the rank and file. Many managers doubt the usefulness of trying to change the personalities, attitudes, and habits of people already in residence and question whether it is worth trying to "teach old dogs new tricks." They prefer, instead, to recruit new people with background, motives, and skills that are congruent with the contemplated new order. Thus, when Leo Durocher (1975) wanted to change the New York Giants from a baseball team that won or lost by the home run to a team that used speed and strategy, his solution was to tell the owners to "back up the truck": trade the slow-of-foot power hitters for the hit-and-run types. Neither a business firm nor a public service organization could "clean house" in such wholesale fashion, of course. They would have to change the rank and file through the process of attrition or possibly through the selection of people added as the work force grows.

Unfortunately, using the recruitment and selection process to change behavior in organizations is a difficult and complex strategy to implement. Suppose, for example, you (as company president or personnel officer reporting to the president) seek to build a management and professional group that will be more "innovative and creative." First, you have to define precisely what these traits mean in behavioral terms. That, in itself, is no easy task. Second, you have to devise some basis for determining or predicting which prospective candidates would display innovativeness and creativity on the job. You would probably consider using interviews, information on the application blank, maybe even a standardized pencil-and-paper test for identifying which applicants have the qualities you desire. And very soon you would run into the problem that the evidence for predictive validity of these devices is scant. Even if you were lucky enough to fashion or discover a valid predictor of innovativeness, you would—according to the Civil Rights Act of 1964—have to either ensure that it did not have adverse effect on the hiring of members of minority groups or be able to demonstrate that innovativeness is a requirement for effective job performance. Given the difficulty of objectively measuring individual performance among managers and professional employees, you would have a hard time proving that innovativeness has a direct relationship to performance.

In sum, while we can appreciate the obstacles to generating lasting change in the behavior of existing members of an organization, equally or more formidable obstacles arise from a strategy of change through recruitment and selection. Nonetheless, abundant evidence from anecdotes and naturalistic observation suggests that it *can* be done, at least on a small scale (e.g., at a departmental level), where a few hiring decisions can make an important difference as a "leavening" or "catalytic" influence.

Survey Feedback

Organizations are increasingly using comprehensive audits of employee opinions as an approach to change. You may recall from Chapter 11 that opinion surveys evolved in industry initially from efforts of researchers to study the causes and effects of job attitudes. Subsequently, surveys became a standard practice by corporations for monitoring the state of employee morale. They have evolved still further in many instances as an integral part of corporate information systems, going beyond measures of job satisfaction to reflect members' perceptions of the "state of the organization" and to enlist their opinions and suggestions concerning what should be changed. Sears, Roebuck and Company, for example, conducts an opinion survey among every one of its units at least every three years; the surveys not only probe attitudes about pay and supervision but tap opinions about store esthetics, window displays, advertising, the corporate image in the community, and so on.

Floyd Mann (1957) described a program for making the survey an effective instrument of organizational change. Mann's approach involved group discussion of survey findings and analyses by appropriate "organization families." An organization family includes a supervisor at any given level and those employees reporting to him or her. Every supervisor is a member of two overlapping families: in one as a supervisee and in the other as a supervisor.

Once the survey data have been collected and statistically analyzed, the feedback process begins at the top. For example, the president and the major divisional vice presidents meet as a group and compare the survey findings for each of the corporation's functional areas—such as manufacturing, marketing, finance, industrial relations, and research and development. Each vice president is able to see the summary data for his or her whole division and discuss the problems unique to this division, the implications of the findings, and any themes common to several divisions. As Katz and Kahn (1966) note, "starting at the top of the structure means that the serious examination of survey results is sanctioned or legitimized by the executive system" (p. 418).

The next series of feedback discussions occurs as each vice president meets with subordinate department heads to discuss survey findings specific to each. The process continues until first-level supervisors discuss with hourly workers the issues raised in each work group by the survey.

The survey-group discussion approach to change offers several advantages. First of all, it gives an objective and factual basis to problems that might otherwise be dismissed as "ill-informed opinion" or "complaints by an insignificant disgruntled minority." Second, it includes the opinions of many participants who might otherwise feel inhibited from openly voicing criticisms of current policies and procedures. Third, the members of an organizational family are able to see data about the issues with which they are most familiar and which are most relevant to them; the group discussion allows them to dig deeper into the analysis. Fourth, the group members become the immediate agents for putting into effect any major changes. Finally, "one great advantage in this type of feedback with group discussion is its utilization of existing organizational structure" (Katz & Kahn, 1966, p. 421). As broadly defined directions of change are broken down into the more specific change requirements of smaller groups, the changes undertaken have the endorsement of official authority.

An important premise underlying the advantages of this method is that negative feedback of an objective nature can produce "unfreezing." The method assumes, for example, that a manager who sees statistical evidence of poor morale among subordinates will feel pressure toward change and dissatisfaction with current practice. In fact, the manager may not react that way at all, but in a defensive fashion. The manager may dispute the validity of the data (citing any of the shortcomings we noted in Chapter 2 with respect to self-report research methods), reject any interpretations of the data that might be perceived as implied criticisms of current supervisory practice, and discourage group discussion of the findings. Perhaps for this reason, some companies prefer to have outside consultants rather than the supervisor conduct group sessions to discuss the survey results. However, doing this nullifies one of the advantages of the overall approach, which is that it uses the existing authority structure.

Management Development Programs

Many organizations invest heavily in educational programs for their managers as a means of promoting long-run organizational development. Some companies send their most promising executive candidates to prestigious graduate programs; numerous firms encourage officers to attend seminars conducted by business schools or professional consultants; others conduct their own in-house programs or subsidize self-directed study in correspondence courses. The content of the programs is so varied as to defy any simple description here. Some programs, at least the more ambitious ones, offer a combination of breadth and depth approximating a two-year MBA program, including all of the major functional areas (e.g., finance, marketing, operations research, personnel) of business administration. One company sends a select group of managers to an Outward Bound–type program: the managers learn a gut-level dimension of trust and cooperation as together they confront the rigors of living in the wilderness and crossing mountain gorges.

When the goal of these programs is training in specific knowledge areas (such as financial planning, use of the computer, implication of changes in OSHA or EEOC regulations), there is little reason to question their effectiveness in producing cognitive and intellectual changes among the individual participants. When programs attempt to change *attitudes and values* of the people as an indirect means to changing their *behavior* (for example, their leadership styles, how they interact with others in groups, how they communicate with subordinates or co-workers), it is much less clear that such programs accomplish their objective. Such programs may succeed at the "unfreezing" stage of changing behavior, particularly if the target recipients are removed from the site of day-to-day work activities and exposed to fellow participants from diverse organizational cultures. The more formidable obstacle arises with the "refreezing" of new patterns of behavior when participants return to their old work environments. If the new behavior is not supported and reinforced by the formal reward system or informally by co-workers, superiors, and subordinates, the new behavior tends to extinguish rapidly—even if the changes in attitudes persist for some time.

For example, Fleishman (1953) conducted a training program in leadership for foremen from an agricultural equipment manufacturer. The goal of the program was to improve the foremen's skills in demonstrating a relationships-oriented style of supervision (a previous study at the company had found that foremen lacking such skills had high levels of turnover and grievances among workers). At the conclusion of the program, the foremen showed significant changes in their attitudes about the importance of warmth and supportiveness toward subordinates. A follow-up study showed, however, that the foremen actually demonstrated no increase in consideration-oriented leader behavior over pretraining levels; in fact, many of them actually *declined* in the practice of supportiveness, as measured by subordinate descriptions of the foremen's behavior. The problem was that the foremen themselves reported to higher-level supervisors who were much more oriented toward the "initiating structure" dimension of leadership—i.e., planning, scheduling, pressure for production. Therefore, the higher-level bosses were much more likely to reward those behaviors on the part of the foremen and either did not encourage or actively discouraged any emphasis on human relations. Only among the few foremen who reported to bosses more inclined to the "consideration" aspect of supervision did the training program yield any long-term change in behavior.

The Fleishman study supports the view of Katz and Kahn (1966), who maintain:

> The major error in dealing with problems of organizational change, is to . . . confuse individual change with modifications in organizational variables. It is common practice to pull foremen or officials out of their organizational roles and give them training in human relations. Then they return to . . . the same pressures from their superiors. Even if the training program has begun to produce a different orientation . . . they are likely to find little opportunity to express their new orientation in the ongoing structural situation to which they return.

Organizational Development

Students of organizational change in recent years have had to distinguish between organizational development with the little o and little d, and Organizational Development with capital O and D. "Little od" covers a broad array of strategies aimed at making organizations more effective. It would include, not only the major approaches we have already described, but changes in technology, reporting relationships, marketing and product policies, and investments in new facilities. "Capital OD" increasingly denotes a strategy aimed at changing the "climate" or "culture" of an organization. Its practitioners are usually consultants or corporate officials with advanced training in the behavioral sciences; the clientele are organizations which seek to foster an organizational climate based on trust, open and constructive handling of interpersonal and intergroup conflict, and receptivity to expertise and information as the ultimate basis of influence. Unlike forms of training and management development that emphasize cognitive changes among individual participants, OD views the work group as the elemental building block of the organization and places strong emphasis on team development through collaborative problem solving, openness in expressing emotional as well as task needs, a tolerance for conflict, and periodic self-assessment.[1]

We noted at the conclusion of the previous chapter that some or-

---

[1]Organizational Development defies any succinct summary of its conceptual underpinnings, aims, and methods. The interested reader should consult Beer (1980) or Beckhard (1969) for a more elaborate discussion of OD.

ganizations have had unfavorable experiences with using a matrix structure. Even though the matrix form seemed suited to their needs to adapt to a turbulent external environment, some organizations found that too much time was spent unproductively in settling authority disputes and passing unresolved issues to top management. The underlying problem in many of these cases was the assumption that a new structure could work with an older culture—one that had developed to fit a bureaucratic, hierarchical structure. Organizational designers have concluded that a precondition to the effective use of matrix-type structures is the development of a particular climate of norms, values, and interpersonal relationships.

OD traces its historical roots to the popularization of *sensitivity training* in the 1940s and 1950s as a form of management development. The goal of sensitivity training was to give the person more insight into his or her own behavior and how that behavior affected others. It also sought to increase a person's skill in giving feedback to others about their behavior and to enable people to receive such feedback without the distortions caused by psychological defense mechanisms. A standard procedure for sensitivity-training classes (or "T-groups") consisted of bringing together a group of people (usually strangers to each other) in an isolated retreat and, under the unobtrusive but watchful eye of a trainer, having them discuss their immediate reactions to each other. No agenda or structure was otherwise provided. The purpose of the meeting was that participants generate their own behavioral data and study it. The trainer intervened only when needed to prevent the group from straying away from the "here-and-now" focus of discussion, to make sure that participants based their feedback to each other on behavioral data, and to keep the level of psychological threat within acceptable bounds.

The consensus of expert opinion on sensitivity training was that it often proved quite effective at reaching its immediate goal, namely to make individual managers more interpersonally sensitive. On the other hand, there was scant evidence that this made them more effective at their jobs of managing. The conclusion was that sensitivity training was an effective means of individual growth and development but not necessarily effective for improving organizational performance (Campbell & Dunnette, 1968).

OD attempts to place the goals of sensitivity training—openness, trust, interpersonal awareness and sensitivity—into the task-oriented context of the organization. The focus of OD is only incidentally upon individual enrichment. Its orientation is toward the work group and relationships between groups. OD, as a rule, does not pull individual members of the organization out of their environment but attempts to incorporate organizational relationships within the training sessions.

The thrust of OD is guided by a *change agent,* usually an external consultant or corporate officer trained in the concepts and methods of the applied behavioral sciences. The change agent typically begins with a thoroughgoing effort at *diagnosis* of the current organizational climate. This stage of OD may consist of interviews with individual managers, questionnaire administration and feedback, or exploratory discussions with work groups. The major goal of this phase of OD is to provide *disconfirming feedback* to participants attesting to the limitations of the existing climate, to unfreeze the members from complacency with the existing order, and to generate a sense of commitment from top to bottom to strive for more effective methods of working together.

The second stage of OD builds upon the feedback provided from the first. Emphasis is usually placed on team development and constructive methods of handling conflict between groups. Participants may also experiment with structural changes. Subsequent stages of training aim at helping members systematically and critically evaluate the changes they have made. Assessments make use of "hard" performance criteria (such as profits, sales, scrap rates) as well as the "softer" data provided by opinion surveys and self-diagnosis. The more ambitious OD programs (which may run for several years) incorporate long-range planning and policy making into the training exercises.

OD is not intended as a one-shot injection to cure a particular illness. Many OD specialists insist that their goal is not to cure a sick organizational patient. Rather, they aim to help essentially healthy organizations become more adept at continual self-renewal by means of a climate that reduces interpersonal threat, enhances collaborative modes of solving problems, and legitimizes constructive conflict.

The evidence to date does not permit any categorical statement concerning the efficacy of OD. Any OD undertaking represents an uncontrolled field experiment, and so it is impossible to attribute the outcomes to any one variable. Many organizations, such as Texas Instruments and Donnelly Mirrors, have claimed a history of success with using OD; others have been disappointed. Some programs have been aborted in the initial stages because of turnover at top executive levels, because politically powerful officials somehow felt threatened by potential outcomes of the program, or because immediate financial crises overshadowed the urgency of long-run development. In some instances, OD consultants themselves have terminated the program because they felt they did not have the full support of top management—which is viewed as a precondition for effective OD. Furthermore, the time scope of most OD programs is so great that, given the state of assessment methodology, it is next to impossible to predict *when* the full benefits of OD will be reflected in unambiguous criteria of performance. Like the programs (OB Mod, Management by Objectives, and Job Redesign) which we surveyed in Chapter 8, OD must rest its case on a hopeful but unclear set of evidence.

Some critics of OD contend that it has too often been plagued by "evangelical hucksterism" (Strauss, 1973). No procedures for professional certification have evolved to separate competent, qualified OD consultants from the opportunistic amateurs who practice a simplistic set of gimmicks. Other detractors argue that OD glosses over the reality of organizational politics and is based on naive assumptions about the resolution of conflicts between persons and groups contending for power.

Nonetheless, OD goes well beyond previous forms of training in that it aims at something more than cognitive and attitudinal changes of individuals. OD seeks *systematic* change by treating the larger contexts of the work group, structural relationships between groups, and the task environment of the organization. Moreover, it is based on well-supported empirical findings concerning group dynamics. Perhaps more important, it has made considerable strides toward encouraging and developing the procedures needed to monitor its own effectiveness. While these methods do not permit unqualified conclusions about cause-and-effect relationships, the very insistence on a posture of data-based self-assessment is noteworthy.

SUMMARY

Organizations change in either a reactive or proactive fashion. Proactive change requires planning and the coordination of subsystems toward a well-defined target state. Inevitably, the process of change is influenced by the politics of coalition alignment and alliance building. Because significant structural or policy changes usually redound to the comparative advantages of certain parties and to the detriment of others, proponents of change must be prepared to meet resistance on the part of some of the affected groups.

Strategies of organizational change and development differ in the extent to which they emphasize changing the surrounding structure and technology versus changing attitudes and values. Successfully changing organizational behavior requires that the forces maintaining the status quo be "unfrozen" and that any changes be "refrozen" by reinforcement from the formal and informal reward systems. Methods chosen by organizations to effect comprehensive change include replacement of leaders or other top officials, systematic recruitment of rank-and-file personnel with different traits and abilities, survey feedback programs, and management training. Organizational Development (OD) attempts to use concepts and methods from the behavioral sciences to transform the climate of an organization. OD emphasizes team development, collaborative modes of problem solving, constructive approaches to managing conflict, and interpersonal relationships built on trust and openness rather than threat and coercion. OD has aroused more controversy than other methods of proactive change, in part due to the ideological overtones implicit in its aims and methods. However, OD must also be given credit for the explicit recognition of organization change as a content area of the applied behavioral sciences, with its own theoretical frameworks and methods of assessment.

CONCEPTS TO REMEMBER

reactive change	survey feedback
proactive change	organizational family
resistance to change	Organizational Development (OD)
the politics of change	sensitivity training
unfreeze-change-refreeze model	

QUESTIONS FOR DISCUSSION

1. What kinds of management development programs would probably be most effective at "unfreezing"? At "refreezing"?
2. One advantage cited for Floyd Mann's system of survey feedback by organizational families is that it uses the existing structure. Why might this also be a disadvantage in some cases?
3. Under what conditions might the undertaking of an OD program be ill advised?
4. How would you define the "climate" of an organization? How is an organization's climate manifested?

CASE[2]

The Southland Savings Association is one of the oldest financial institutions in its region. It is located in a trade area of approximately 200,000 population and has total deposits approaching $50 million. The association's management has always attempted to develop and maintain a progressive institution.

An outstanding feature of the association is that it seldom loses an

---

[2]"Southland Savings Association," reprinted with permission from E. G. Williams (Ed.), *People Problems* (Bloomington: Indiana University Graduate School of Business Bureau of Business Research, 1962).

employee to another financial institution. Checks made periodically with other institutions always indicate that its salary scale is one of the highest in the area. The association also has what the management considers to be a good program of fringe benefits, including hospitalization and life insurance, a retirement plan, paid vacations, sick leave, and lunchroom concessions. The entire cost of these benefits is borne by the association.

The association runs its operations on a decentralized basis. The top management has always maintained that decentralization is the best method of developing qualified managers and, in view of the organization's rapid growth during the last few years, the best way of solving the important problem of executive development.

The bookkeeping function has likewise been decentralized; each branch keeps its own books, and the auditor of the association periodically inspects them.

One day the auditor and the controller of the association decided that the current bookkeeping system needed to be revised. They had been giving attention to this area because the examiners had had trouble finding records. It had been suggested that the method of bookkeeping between the home office and the four branches could be improved.

With the above facts in mind, the two men held a conference with the officers of the association in an attempt to point out to them the action that needed to be taken.

After hearing the arguments posed by the auditor and the controller, the officers still felt the action was unnecessary. They said that the project would be too time-consuming and costly.

Two weeks later, however, the executive vice-president of the association talked to the controller and admitted to him that the idea of revising the system was sound and that he and the rest of the officers were authorizing him to take control and to initiate the project.

The controller started on the task of centralizing the bookkeeping operations. For the first week he didn't know where to begin. He discovered that operational controls had been allowed to run down so long that now his problem appeared to be almost insurmountable.

When the executive vice-president asked the controller about his progress, he was given a negative answer. The vice-president was disturbed with this reaction and was determined to settle the problem once and for all. He called an executive meeting that included the controller and the auditor. At the meeting, the possibility of centralizing some of the operations of the branches in order to afford better administrative control was discussed. Someone suggested the possibility of buying some National Cash Register posting machines to help solve some of the operating difficulties.

After a lengthy discussion it was decided that these machines were the key to the elimination of many of the association's reporting problems. The controller admitted that they would make it easier to control operations, and the assistant vice-president felt that their acquisition would add greatly to the customer service capacities of the association.

Three new machines were installed the following month. After closing hours each teller was instructed in the proper techniques of operating them. The management felt that they had made a sound investment, and their only worry was over the ability of the tellers to learn how to operate the new equipment. Most of the tellers were older women and seemed to be slow and reticent to learn the new process.

One month after the practice machines had been placed in the association, these shortcomings became so acute that immediate action had to be taken. The management realized that the morale of the teller staff was depressed and that the smoothness of operations at the home office had been completely disrupted. The personnel manager suggested that some type of formal training program should be developed and that the management should explain to the members of the work force their personal roles in the anticipated progress of the association.

The personnel manager has not found a method of eliminating the discontent, nor has he been able to give an adequate reason for it to the rest of the officers. Finally one officer stated in a committee meeting that he felt the work force had been "over human-relationed." He suggested that in many instances negative leadership was far superior to positive leadership. He stated in forceful language that he would inform those tellers who were complaining and failing to learn the process either to learn it quickly or be fired. Another officer felt that since some of them were employees who had been with the association for many years and whose work had always been satisfactory, some alternative must be found.

Questions

Why did the introduction of the new machines create problems? How might this change have been better managed?

REFERENCES

Beckhard, R. *Organization development: Strategies and models.* Reading, Mass.: Addison-Wesley, 1969.

Beer, M. *Organization change and development: A systems view.* Santa Monica, Calif.: Goodyear Publishing, 1980.

Campbell, J. P., & Dunnette, M. D. Effectiveness of T-group experiences in managerial training and development. *Psychological Bulletin*, 1968, *70*, 73–104.

Coch, L., & French, J. P.   Overcoming resistance to change. *Human Relations*, 1948, *1*, 512–532

Durocher, L.   *Nice Guys Finish Last.* New York: Simon & Schuster, 1975.

Fleishman, E. A.   Leadership climate, human relations training, and supervisory behavior. *Personnel Psychology*, 1953, *6*, 205–222.

Katz, D., & Kahn, R. L.   *The social psychology of organizations.* New York: John Wiley & Sons, 1966.

Kerr, S., & Kerr, E. B.   Why your employees resist perfectly "rational" changes. *Hospital Financial Management*, 1972, *26*, 4–6.

Lewin, K.   Frontiers in group dynamics. *Human Relations*, 1947, *1*, 5–41.

Mann, F. C.   Studying and creating change: A means to understanding social organization. *Research in Industrial Human Relations*, Industrial Relations Research Association, 1957 (17), 146–167.

Miles, R. E.   Human relations or human resources? *Harvard Business Review*, 1965, *43*, no. 4, 148–163.

Strauss, G.   Organizational development: Credits and debits. *Organizational Dynamics*, Winter 1973, pp. 2–18.

Webber, R. A.   *Management: Basic elements of managing organizations.* Homewood, Ill.: Richard D. Irwin, 1979.

Wise, T. A.   The rocky road to the marketplace. *Fortune*, October 1966, pp.

Author Index

493

Subject Index

500

This book has been set Linotron 202, in 10 and 9 point Trump Medieval, leaded 2 points. Chapter numbers are 60 point Serif Gothic Roman and chapter titles are 24 point Serif Gothic Roman. The size of the type page is 27 by 46½ picas.